PERSONALITY

AND THE

PURSUIT OF HAPPINESS

Guiding you towards an enjoyable,

fulfilling and useful life

Mark Howell

THE PERSONALITY REVOLUTION
Visit us at **thepersonalityrevolution.com**

Personality and the Pursuit of Happiness

First edition published in Great Britain in 2019 by
The Personality Revolution Ltd.

ISBN: 978-1-9999159-1-9

British Library Cataloguing in Publication Data:
A catalogue record for this book is available
from the British Library.

For misfits everywhere,
and those who love them

With thanks to Beth, James, Karen,
Mum, Ruth, Sonya and Sue

CONTENTS

PREFACE

Purpose and structure

The purpose of this book is to make you more effective, happier and more useful. It sets out the principles of personality and uses them to explain the causes of negative feelings and thoughts, inappropriate behaviours and drops in performance. It will challenge you to think about your experiences in a different way, giving you new insights into your ambitions and values, and empower you to break free from restraints that have been preventing you from making more of your life. Once you have read this volume, you will be able to:

- Recognise, interpret and manage your feelings, thoughts and behaviours;

- Interact more effectively with other people;

- Understand how you fit into groups of people, and the dynamics of these groups;

- Escape from, avoid or cope better with stress and low moods;

- Increase your level of motivation and strengthen your sense of purpose; and

- Improve your mental health and wellbeing.

Chapter 1 introduces you to the subjects addressed in the book and sets out the basic challenge that we need to meet if we are to emerge from this period of political, economic and environmental instability with a sustainable global society.

Chapter 2 uses a range of statistics to highlight the scale and breadth of poor mental health within modern society.

Chapter 3 explains the core principles of personality.

Chapter 4 enables you to determine your personality by reference to **The Personality Revolution's Model of Personality**. The model includes a free online personality test at **thepersonalityrevolution.com**, the results of which will allow you to relate the concepts in this book directly to your personality.

Chapter 5 explains the workings of your emotional system and how the interaction of your personality and environment give rise to positive feelings, stress and low moods.

Chapter 6 relates your emotional system to your thinking capabilities, discussing logic, opinions and consciousness.

Chapter 7 uses The Personality Revolution's Model of Personality to explain how personality influences the structure and culture of human groups. It also enables you to determine your relationship with particular sub-groups within society, and to identify you natural political affiliation.

Chapter 8 explains how your feelings, thoughts and behaviours are influenced by group dynamics, including discrimination and good and evil.

Chapter 9 relates performance and motivation to personality. It explains how you manage your feelings on a day-to-day basis, the importance of clarifying your objectives and how to improve your ability to achieve in the longer term.

Chapter 10 considers relationships and explains how personality influences their formation, purpose and longevity.

Chapter 11 focuses on self-empowerment, setting out eight steps in the development of emotional literacy skills. It also considers the purpose of happiness, issues of identity and the importance of wellbeing.

Chapter 12 sets out the basis of the second and concluding volume of this work, which will be entitled **The Personality Revolution** and is scheduled to be published in 2020. This volume will explain how the dynamics of groups operate at a societal level and how personality has influenced the political, economic and social dynamics that we have seen in recent years, including globalisation, Brexit, the rise to power of reactionary politicians like Donald Trump and the emergence of anti-establishment, socially responsible politicians like Bernie Sanders and Jeremy Corbyn. It will also explain the changes we need to make to society if the dynamics of self-interest, inequality and environmental destruction are to be reversed, and why it will only be possible to achieve this outcome if those who have a real interest in doing so work collectively to this end.

The two volumes may be read independently of each other, but if you read them both, they will give you a holistic understanding of the influence of personality on your life and empower you to make a difference in this world. With improved mental health, you will be equipped to exert a strong, positive influence within society. Once you understand group dynamics at a national and international level, your broadened consciousness will enable you to play a more active part in delivering an economically, environmentally and socially sustainable global society. You will then be poised to join The Personality Revolution.

Your reading experience

This volume aims to leave you with a holistic understanding of personality and its relationship with mental health. It contains elements of psychology, neuroscience, sociology and philosophy, but in a form that is accessible to readers with no knowledge of these subjects. The new perspectives on human personality and behaviour set out in this volume will, though, be interesting to those who work or study in these areas. This volume does contain some British and American political and societal references, but only for illustration purposes, and in the final chapter, to introduce the subject matter of the second volume. However, the general principles explained in this volume apply to all human groups irrespective of size or location.

There is a myriad of psychology and self-help books on the market. People are naturally drawn to ones that suit their particular personalities, situations and objectives. Many of these books focus on improving specific skills or embedding a philosophy on life. This volume will equip you with a framework that will enable you to improve your effectiveness and mental health, and support those around you who are struggling. It mentions some useful techniques, but primarily serves as a starting point for further investigation and skill development. It also helps to place other more abstract or specialist approaches in context.

The model and arguments set out in this volume are built up chapter by chapter so you will not get the most from this book if you dip into it or skip sections. Some readers will get to grips with the model more quickly than others. If you are one of the former, please be aware that, as a good understanding of the model is needed to follow later chapters, I have been careful not to leave people behind. As the volume progresses, it becomes more fluid and less iterative. In other words, it moves from a textbook format to a more conversational one. Although, the principles and concepts introduced are brought together in a coherent whole by the end of the volume, you may find some of them quite challenging on first acquaintance. You should not, therefore, expect to rush through this book in one sitting. You are likely to get more from it if you give yourself an opportunity to reflect between chapters. We tend not to create environments suitable for study and reflection in modern society, so I recommend you seek out a quiet and comfortable place to read.

For ease of reading, in most instances I have used male pronouns when setting out examples that are applicable to both sexes. This may annoy some female readers, but no discrimination is intended. Indeed, it will become clear as the volume progresses that one of its objectives is to empower women in general, and those who are abused or exploited in particular, so that they can exert a greater influence within wider society.

ABOUT THE AUTHOR

I have received different opinions as to whether to include an author biography at the front of this book. Some people who have read pre-publication copies have said that they like to know something about the author before they start reading. Others have commented that they would prefer their reading experience not to be compromised by any preconceptions that they may develop as a result of reading a biography. I have therefore decided to give you the choice whether you wish to read this section now, later or not at all.

I was born in 1968 and grew up in a middle-class family in the historic town of Stamford in the East Midlands about 90 minutes drive from London. I was educated at Stamford School and then at King's College London, part of the University of London, at which I studied Medieval and Modern History. When I was approaching graduation in 1991, I realised that I had no obvious pathway in terms of career other than teaching, which I had discounted. The economy was in recession so there were limited opportunities for graduates. Some friends in the year above had enrolled on a law course. At the time, this seemed like an easy option so I did the same. Although I did not enjoy studying law, nothing happened to knock me off the conveyor belt towards qualification.

I spent my late mid to late 20s working at a major London law firm, qualifying into the corporate and commercial department. I was essentially freewheeling, living for my holidays. I investigated some other career options, but none of them fired me with enthusiasm. However, a failed romance jolted me out of my torpor and instilled me with the determination to make something of my life. I had travelled extensively in the Middle East on holiday so when my law firm acquired a number of offices in that region, I jumped at the opportunity to work in its Cairo office. Working and living in a different culture was a fascinating experience, which broadened my mind and changed my attitude towards life.

I realised that I needed to get out of the London rat race so, on my return to the UK, I decided to explore my interest in photography, which had been reawakened in Cairo. After a false start, during which I realised that I had not done enough research into the photography world, I took a legal position working in-house for a multinational telecommunications company just outside London. During this period, I bought a house in Poole in Dorset on the south coast of England. About the same time, I was accepted on to an MA course in Photojournalism and Documentary Photography at the London College of Communication.

The year's course was a revelation. I uncovered creative abilities that I had never suspected I possessed. The course also allowed me to apply and extend my knowledge of current affairs. During the summer break, I took the opportunity to visit Birzeit University in the West Bank, part of the Palestinian Occupied Territories. I was shocked by the difference between the reality of the experience of ordinary Palestinians and the portrayal of the Israeli-Palestinian situation on television in the UK. That difference became the basis of my major project, which was ultimately refined and published as a book under the title *"What Did We Do to Deserve This? – Palestinian Life Under Occupation in the West Bank"* (Garnet Publishing; 2008).

After I graduated, I started to put down roots in Poole. I established a photography business and an arts networking group there. In my spare time, I played volleyball on the town's beaches and mountain-biked with friends on the wonderful Isle of Purbeck nearby. My experience in the West Bank made me realise that I was more of an active participant than a journalist. I felt a need to make a difference in society and recognised that the easiest place to have a positive effect is in your own community. I therefore decided to get involved in politics. Initially, I joined the Conservative Party, but as my political views crystallised, I realised that they were not represented within it. I left the party and was about to move off in another direction when a councillor in my ward died. I saw an opportunity to establish a party with independent values, so I created The Party for Poole People (the Poole People party) and ran for election to the Borough of Poole's council, which is a unitary authority - the next level down from national government in England. I was successful and have twice been re-elected together with other colleagues. Poole People councillors are focused on doing the best for the people of Poole, making common sense decisions that are not influenced by the ideologies of national political parties. I am currently Leader of Poole People and balance my councillor responsibilities with my other interests.

Looking back on my life, I have often found myself in unsuitable environments that have caused me to feel like an outsider and experience poor mental health. These feelings and my lack of direction in early adulthood caused me to become interested in personal development. I read a lot of self-help books in my 30s. Although I still have these books in a bookcase, I would struggle to describe their contents. However, I am sure that they have influenced the development of the model set out in this volume. As unitary authorities provide a wide range of local services, including children's services, adult social care, planning, transportation, licensing and environmental services, the role of councillor has exposed me to an enormous amount and variety of information. I represent the town centre ward, which includes a deprived estate and faces significant regeneration challenges. My councillor role has caused me to think hard about the needs of citizens in general, and to seek to address unfairness, poor performance and systems that disadvantage vulnerable members of society. I have, though, also kept abreast of national and international current affairs.

The knowledge of personality that I have acquired on my journey has enabled me to appreciate my talents and skills. I am a change-orientated person and have a particular ability to help people break shackles that are holding them back. I expose people to new ideas and help them to see the world in a different way. I also bring clarity to their thinking, enabling them to break down complex problems and identify ways forward. I think about things a great deal and experience has told me that my judgment is usually good. This has given me the confidence to develop this work and believe that it could be an agent for change, helping to move us towards a more sustainable society. The knowledge I have gained during this project and which is included in the two volumes has empowered me to fulfil my true purpose and opened the door to feelings of happiness. I hope that it will be similarly beneficial to you.

Mark Howell

Side by side at Temple's fountain
Gazing into each other's eyes
We shared our dreams and aspirations
Beneath London's fleeting Summer skies.

1

THE CHALLENGE

If you think about it, we all want to be happy. To achieve this state you need to experience positive feelings on a consistent basis. A small number of people push themselves to the limit to experience feelings of exhilaration. Some people seek a deep sense of fulfilment. Most of us sit somewhere in-between, satisfying ourselves with the less extreme feelings of enjoyment and contentment. You experience feelings of enjoyment and exhilaration when you explore the world and take risks, for example when you engage physically with other people, participate in dangerous or competitive activities, exercise creativity or act spontaneously. You experience feelings of contentment and fulfilment when you increase your level of security. You may do so by analysing threats, or by increasing coherency, promoting harmony or imposing order within your environment. Whether you are drawn towards exploratory or defensive behaviours at any moment will depend on how your personality and your environment interact. Your core personality is fixed, but your environment is constantly changing. Your feelings, thoughts and behaviours will vary in response.

Sometimes things go well and you feel good. You will have located yourself in an environment that is in tune with your personality. You will be able to use your natural talents productively, and develop skills and perform roles to which you are suited. At other times, you will experience traumatic events, such as financial losses or bereavements, or you find yourself in an unsuitable job role or dysfunctional relationship. The actions of other people may impact on your ability to achieve or prevent you from using your talents and skills to the full, or you may be forced to perform tasks to which you are unsuited. In such circumstances, you are likely to experience negative feelings. Negative feelings often manifest themselves in the form of stress or low moods.

Some people experience negative feelings frequently, and over long periods of time, resulting in poor mental health. They will often struggle to fit into workplaces, families or communities. A sense of dislocation can serve as a powerful motivating force, investing a person with determination to change his circumstances for the better. However, a person who is marginalised, misunderstood or ignored is more likely to experience emotional and physical harm, either directly from abusers or through self-harm, or indirectly as a result of low income, an unsuitable job role or a lack of positive social interaction. People who experience negative feelings intensely and repeatedly may develop obsessive or other unhelpful controlling behaviours, or act in aggressive or anti-social ways, as a means of coping with environmental stressors.

Groups shape the nature of your environment. Humans have evolved to live, work and socialise in groups. We naturally establish, or are born or drawn into, groups of people. A group may be tight-knit, like a close family, or a loose network, such as a social media group. Modern society consists of a multitude of overlapping groups. Your emotional state and behaviour will change as you move between different groups. For example, you may feel confident and respected within one group, but out of place in another.

As we all have different talents and skills, our natural roles within groups vary from person to person. In primeval times, a person would have belonged to a single extended family group and would have gravitated towards a suitable role within it. As systems were created that enabled fathers to transfer wealth and status to their sons, social mobility declined and this gravitational force was inhibited. The emergence of democracy resulted in the implementation of redistributive economic policies and establishment of universal education systems, making it easier for people to find appropriate roles within society. Modern society is, however, complicated, and there remain many barriers and restrictions that inhibit personal development, so it can be difficult for people to position themselves appropriately.

In modern society, people tend to attribute the achievements of others to their own individual effort and natural aptitude. Of course, it is very unlikely that you will achieve something remarkable in this world without putting in a lot of hard work. However, your ability to achieve will also greatly depend on the values, culture and objectives of the groups to which you belong, and the ability and inclination of their members to assist you. A group's values, culture and objectives will reflect the personalities of its members, the nature of its environment and the ambitions of its leader.

All members will be expected to contribute to the achievement of their group's objectives to some degree. You will therefore be constantly balancing the performance of obligations associated with your group role with the achievement of your personal objectives. In the second half of the twentieth century, peace, prosperity and government safety nets encouraged people in the UK and USA to focus on the latter and prompted the emergence of an individualistic culture. People spent less time maintaining the health of their families, communities and other groups than their predecessors. As a result, these structures weakened or disintegrated, leaving people lacking in protection and support and vulnerable to poor mental health.

Since the 1980s, bankers, international investors and multinationals have taken advantage of liberal economic policies and advances in technology, particularly in electronic communications, to increase their power, influence and wealth. They have encouraged individualistic behaviour around the globe and undermined the authority of nation states. Wealth is concentrating in a small, global elite while increasing numbers of people are struggling to make ends meet. Governments are less able, and politicians in general appear less inclined, to protect citizens from environmental influences that are causing them to experience abuse, exploitation or hardship. Populist forces have emerged in reaction to the behaviours of these elites. The era of individualism is coming to an end, as citizens seek more security. People with different views are clashing openly, as they seek to protect their interests or move societal culture towards their own values.

A fundamental rebalancing of society is necessary at all levels, from small communities to the emerging global super group, if we are to deliver a sustainable global society. If this is to be achieved, we must find ways to work together for common benefit. Individuals need to improve their understanding of the dynamics that have led us to conflict and inequality. Most important of all, they need to appreciate their natural roles within society, their values and objectives, and how they can work effectively in their families, communities and workplaces to change things for the better.

2

THE MENTAL HEALTH CRISIS

For most of recorded history, mental illness has been seen as something to be hidden away. Evidence of mental health problems within a family can still harm the marriage prospects of healthy family members in countries with traditional cultures. People with poor mental health are often stigmatised and denied the care and support that they need to recover. It is only in the last few years that it has been publicly acceptable to talk about mental illness, and it is still a brave employee who admits to suffering from a mental health condition to his or her employer.

Worldwide it is estimated that mental health problems affect one person in every four. Mental disorders make up 31.4% of the total 'burden of disease' in the UK compared to 16% for cancer and heart disease. Similar proportions have been reported in European countries that have a reputation for treating mental health very seriously. For example, mental disorders make up 30.8% of the total burden of disease in the Netherlands. The high rate in such countries will partly be due to the greater preparedness of people with poor mental health to self-report and the greater ability of their health services to connect with such people. The actual figures in countries where people with poor mental health are stigmatised or ignored are likely to be much higher than reported.

Poor mental health severely limits the effectiveness of individuals and reduces the productivity of nations. It is also expensive to treat. The Agency for Healthcare Research and Quality cited a cost of $57.5 billion in 2006 for mental health care in the USA, which is equivalent to the cost of cancer care. Poor mental health costs the UK economy in the region of £51.6 billion every year in the form of reduced performance and unemployment, and increased expenditure on social security. The World Economic Forum has estimated that it cost governments and health services worldwide an estimated $2,500 billion in 2010, a sum that is projected to increase to over $6,000 billion by 2030. To put these figures in context, the entire global health spending in 2009 was $5,100 billion.

Developed countries are being challenged economically by developing nations and many have ageing populations. Their governments can, therefore, no longer afford to disregard the loss of productivity and costs associated with poor mental health. The vast majority of people with poor mental health are suffering from stress and/or low moods as a result of unfavourable environmental circumstances rather than conditions caused by abnormalities within the brain. Work pressure, a lack of stimulation or purpose, bereavement, financial problems, relationship difficulties, social isolation, health concerns and illness, and problems with housing are common causes. Governments and citizens have the ability to reshape society to relieve these environmental pressures.

Some people argue that Western society is too tolerant of people with poor mental health, labelling them as "too soft" or "snowflakes". Life has many challenges so the ability to deal with circumstances that cause stress and low moods is an important life skill. However, the high number of reports shows that many people are struggling to cope and lack the means and support to return sustainably to a positive state. We all have an interest in ensuring that our fellow citizens are mentally healthy. There will be people suffering from poor mental health within your family, friendship circle, community and workplace. The quality of their lives, and yours, will be improved if we tackle the main causes of poor mental health and better equip citizens to cope with difficult circumstances and unfavourable environmental conditions.

Mental health at work

Work can provide identity, friendship and stability. The prevalence of stress, anxiety and depression in the workplace is, however, high. The UK's Health & Safety Executive (HSE) estimated the total number of cases of work related stress, depression or anxiety in 2015/16 at 488,000. These conditions caused the loss of 11.7 million working days, an average of 23.9 days per case. Up to 300,000 people in the UK leave their jobs each year due to mental health problems.

According to the HSE report, stress accounted for 37% of all work related ill health and 45% of all working days lost due to ill health. Women were statistically more prone to experience stress than men in the three-year period 2013/14 - 2015/16. The prevalence rate for work related stress in men was 1,190 cases for males and 1,820 cases for women per 100,000 workers. The age range 45 - 54 presents the greatest percentage of cases of work related mental ill health in both men and women.

The main causes of work related stress are tight deadlines, excessive work or too much pressure or responsibility. Other factors include a lack of managerial support, organisational changes at work, aggressive colleagues, and lack of clarity about job role and responsibilities. The report found that small workplaces with less than 50 employees had the lowest rates of stress with an estimated 990 cases per 100,000 people, followed by medium workplaces (50 - 249 employees) estimated with 1,410 cases per 100,000 people and large workplaces (250+ employees) with 1,710 cases per 100,000. Large companies impose more stress on employees because their work cultures are usually more competitive, demanding and ruthless than those of smaller companies. Their employees often have to travel further to work and spend more time away from their families. This increases levels of fatigue and weakens family and social connections.

The HSE has focused its attention on stress-related illnesses. It does not provide any detail as to incidence and effect of boredom, unhappiness and depression. These low moods often have a greater effect on productivity than stress because, while people often work at a high intensity when experiencing stress, people with low moods tend to be lethargic. The lack of attention paid to low moods is partly due to their less obvious nature. People who are stressed tend to display anger, aggression or hostility, but a person who feels down is more likely to blend into the background. Also, many people who are prone to low moods soldier on quietly, often resorting to anti-depressants to limit the extent of their negative feelings. However, low moods are a massive problem in modern society. 18.8 million American adults (9.5% of the adult population) suffer from a depressive illness each year. The World Health Organization predicts that within 20 years depression will be the second most common cause of ill health. The prevalence of low moods partly explains why productivity levels are falling in many developed countries

Female mental health

Cigarettes and alcohol help to reduce stress. Comparing the consumption levels of men and women should therefore give some indication of relative stress levels. In the UK between 1974 and 2007, smoking prevalence was significantly higher in men than women, but in 2014, the difference had narrowed to 3%. The difference in the proportion of adults smoking heavily (20 cigarettes per day or more) has also narrowed between the genders: 26% of men smoked heavily in 1974 compared to 13% of women, whereas in 2011 6% of men smoked heavily compared to 4% of women. The incidence of lung cancer among men has decreased from 108 new cases per 100,000 men in 1971 to 56 new cases per 100,000 men in 2011. This amounts to a 48% decrease over this time period. The reverse is true for women: Incidence rates have increased by 105% from 19 new cases per 100,000 women in 1971 to 39 new cases per 100,000 women in 2011.

Women have caught up with men in the amount of alcohol they drink according to a global study and are doing increasing amounts of damage to their health as a result. Women are more likely to drink at home, to under-report their consumption levels in surveys and are less likely to access treatment for alcohol abuse than men. Ease of access to alcohol has also encouraged women to drink when they socialise together in their homes. For example, young women often "pre-load" while getting ready together before a night out. These practices have been encouraged by the alcohol industry, which now markets products specifically to women.

The narrowing of the gap between men and women in substance abuse and diagnoses of alcohol and tobacco related conditions is partly due to reduced sexual inequality in the workplace and social arenas. Women who socialise in male orientated environments are likely to adopt male drinking habits. Also, although the presence of women and the introduction of sexual discrimination laws have reduced levels of competitiveness in traditionally male working environments, for reasons explained later, the average woman will still be more susceptible to stress than the average man. The number of women who report being stressed at work exceeds those of men by ratio of more than 3 to 2. Many female employees use alcohol to relieve stress after work. Women in management and professional jobs drink more than the average woman and drink more on weekdays. Even in workplaces that have been traditionally associated with women, target setting and other business practices have increased stress levels, as demonstrated by the fact that the occupations that report the highest rates of total cases of work-related stress are health professionals (in particular nurses), teaching and educational professionals, and those engaged in delivering care services (for example, welfare and housing association professionals).

Evidence suggests that smoking and alcohol consumption are more harmful to women than men. Women increase their risk of a heart attack by more than men when they take up smoking. A study has also suggested that female smokers are more susceptible to bowel cancer than men. Women suffer greater levels of harm than men at lower levels of drinking. Their smaller liver volumes make it harder for them to process alcohol safely and increase their vulnerability to developing alcohol-related problems, such as liver disease. Oxford University's Million Women Study of 1.3 million women across the world found that the relative risk of breast cancer, the most common cancer in women, increases by 6% for each 10 grams of alcohol (1 unit of alcohol) you typically drink a day. 4% of UK women are "higher risk" drinkers – someone who drinks more than 35 units a week.

Women are also much more likely than men to use prescription drugs to alleviate symptoms of stress, low moods or depression. This is partly because they can be taken surreptitiously and therefore enable women to medicate themselves without being subject to negative social judgments that are associated with more visible drug-taking, such as drinking and smoking, and which tend to be made more readily and harshly against women. More than a quarter of the adult female population of the USA were taking such drugs in 2010 as compared to 15 per cent of men. Similar statistics appear in Europe. For example, in the same year in France 21.4% were taking them as opposed to 13.3% of men.

In most developed countries violent crime has been decreasing in recent years although increasing social inequality and tougher economic circumstances are starting to reverse this trend. One violent crime statistic that has increased over this period, however, is crimes committed by women. Middle-aged women are also increasingly presenting as anti-social behaviour offenders. The greater stress levels that women are exposed to in modern society will certainly have contributed to these increases.

The have-it-all mentality that young women in developed countries have been encouraged to seek since the 1990's has contributed to deterioration in female mental health. Developing a career, being a mother and maintaining a social life is very difficult unless a woman has a very supportive partner or is financially well off. Mothers are under a lot of pressure to give their children the best possible start in life by providing a harmonious family home and emotional and educational support, but many are compromised by work responsibilities. Working mothers also struggle to find time to relax as they move from one stressful environment at work to another at home. The Internet has forced children into the wider world at a much earlier age than is desirable, increasing their susceptibility to mental health problems or abuse and causing their mothers to become more anxious.

Divorce and separation occur at high rates in liberal cultures as women have more freedom to dictate their own lives and mothers are usually entitled to receive support payments from their ex-partners or the state. However, a parent will find it difficult to fulfil work and family responsibilities alone. For example, it is difficult to play the roles of carer and enforcer at the same time. Single mothers are therefore particularly likely to experience stress.

The tendency in modern society for families to spread out geographically and for people to have fewer or no children means that increasing numbers of women are finding themselves isolated and lacking a supportive home environment. The resultant insecurity and loneliness can cause them to experience stress and depression. Older women are particularly vulnerable, as they often feel isolated when their children grow up and leave home. It is therefore no surprise that women are most likely to resort to drugs to relieve stress and depression when they are over 45. From 2001 to 2010 the number of women in America on an antidepressant grew 29 per cent with the most significant increase (40 per cent) among women who were 65 and older.

Male mental health

In the UK, men commit 76% of suicides, and suicide is the biggest cause of death for men under the age of 45. 12.5% of men in the UK are suffering from a common mental health disorder. Men are nearly three times more likely than women to become alcohol dependent, use illegal drugs and die from overdoses. Men are also increasingly turning to prescription drugs to deal with negative feelings.

There is considerable debate about the true level of common mental health disorders in men and whether larger numbers of men than women may be undiagnosed. In a 2016 survey by Opinion Leader for the Men's Health Forum, the majority of men said that they would take time off work to get medical help for physical symptoms, yet fewer than one in five said they would do the same for anxiety or a low mood. 73% of adults who 'go missing' are men and 87% of rough sleepers are men. Men also make up 95% of the prison population and 72% of male prisoners suffer from two or more mental disorders. Men are nearly 50% more likely than women to be detained and treated compulsorily as psychiatric inpatients. They also find it more difficult to obtain social support from friends, relatives and communities, and are significantly less likely to access psychological therapies, than women. During the first 3 quarters of 2015, the male/female ratio for those accessing psychological therapies was 36:64. Over a third of men have never disclosed a mental health problem to a friend or family member or waited more than 2 years to do so, compared to a quarter of women.

Men tend to suffer mental health problems when they are uncertain of their position and role within society. Historically, young men with creative abilities, sensitive natures or introverted personalities were particularly vulnerable because their behaviours conflicted with the conforming, competitive and adventurous behaviours that are typically found in male groups. Young men with these characteristics have, however, benefitted from the greater awareness of mental health issues amongst young people, and more tolerant culture and more diverse and flexible work environments that exist within modern society. In contrast, young men who are conforming by nature and who appreciate structure, many of whom are suited to traditional working-class jobs, now find it harder to establish stable friendship groups or find secure employment.

Technological innovation and the forces of globalisation have resulted in large numbers of middle-aged and older men losing their jobs and sense of purpose. A review by the Samaritans in 2012 (Men, Suicide and Society) emphasised that middle-aged men in lower socio-economic groups are at particularly high risk of suicide. It pointed to the interaction of factors such as unemployment and economic hardship, lack of close social and family relationships, the influence of a historical culture of masculinity, personal crises such as divorce, as well as a general 'dip' in subjective wellbeing among people in their mid-years, compared with both younger and older people.

Young people

Mental health problems affect about 1 in 10 children and young people in the UK. 70% of them do not receive appropriate support at a sufficiently early age. Risk factors include long-term physical illness, a parent with poor mental health, problems with alcohol, law breaking, bereavement, parental divorce, bullying, physical or sexual abuse, poverty, homelessness, discrimination, taking on adult responsibilities such as caring for a relative and having long-standing educational difficulties.

A study by the Prince's Trust and Macquarie has revealed the extent to which young people in the UK with poor life prospects struggle with mental health issues. While stress is more likely to be associated with the pressures of school, those not in employment, education or training (NEETs) are particularly vulnerable to low moods. 40% of jobless young people have faced symptoms of mental illness such as panic attacks, suicidal thoughts and feelings of self-loathing, as a direct result of being unemployed. 10% have been prescribed anti-depressants and 9% believe they have nothing to live for. More than 20% of young people with less than five GCSEs (the UK's qualification for 16 year olds) admit to drinking or taking drugs to get through the day.

Many young people are hiding mental health issues. Although a child will usually have no hesitation in letting you know when he is bored, poor mental health is a more insidious problem. A child is much less likely to interpret symptoms of stress and low moods as an illness than an adult. It is easy for a child to blame himself for the distress he is experiencing, to feel that he is in some way abnormal or simply become habituated to negative feelings. He may also worry that admitting to such feelings would in some way be letting down his parents or teachers. He may fear that bullies may see such disclosure as weakness and exploit it, or he may expect his concerns to be ignored. Unfortunately, for many children such fears are well founded as society and schools in general have manifestly failed to recognise, let alone address, the scale of mental health issues in children. 74% of unemployed young people in the survey stated that they would not ask for help if they were struggling to cope and 72% said they did not have anyone who they felt they could confide in.

Females tend to be more sensitive to disharmony and harmful behaviours than males and are more vulnerable to physical abuse, especially when they fall under the control of possessive or controlling males. Many girls are exposed to sexual activity or other destabilising experiences before they have developed the emotional capability to handle them. It is not surprising therefore that 33% of young women have felt suicidal as opposed to 19% of young men and 28% have self-harmed compared with 10% of young men. The Centre for Social Justice has highlighted how girls in gangs are leading "desperate lives" in which "rape is used as a weapon and carrying drugs and guns is seen as normal". An enquiry by the Office of the Children's Commissioner in England found that 2,409 youngsters were known to be victims of child sexual exploitation by gangs or groups, and a further 16,500 were at risk. It warned that the problem was "in every type of neighbourhood, rural, urban, deprived and not deprived". The Prince's Trust survey identified loneliness, isolation, boredom and the lack of positive role models as significant factors that cause young people to join gangs.

Most developed nations have laws in place that are designed to protect children from physical harm or neglect, and social services to look after the interests of vulnerable children. Even so, neglect features in 60% of serious case reviews into death or serious injury of a child in the UK and 32% of professionals feel powerless to help affected children. British law has recently been updated to recognise emotional neglect. The definition of emotional neglect includes a failure to protect a child from emotional abuse, which may take the form of isolation, humiliation or bullying. It also includes forcing a child to witness domestic violence and administering degrading punishments. Emotional abuse can be devastating and may lead to life-long mental health problems and, in some cases, suicide. Researchers have found specific changes in key regions of the brains of young adults who were maltreated or neglected in childhood that may leave victims more vulnerable to depression, addiction and post-traumatic stress disorder. It is frightening to consider that, even before emotional neglect was included within the definition of criminal neglect, 10% of children in the UK were victims according to research commissioned by the charity Action for Children.

The incidence of mental health problems amongst young people is a massive problem. It is inhibiting the development of children and placing limitations on the future happiness and productivity of populations. Childhood abuse and bullying are amongst the strongest direct predictors of mental health problems in adulthood. The lack of focus by national government, local authorities and schools on bullying and mental health issues is shocking. These are by far the most commonly raised issues in youth forums, yet politicians are too often fixated on adapting teaching methods and syllabuses to meet performance targets rather than improving the underlying mental health of schoolchildren.

Older people

Globally, approximately 15% of adults aged 60 and over suffer from a mental disorder. In the UK, depression affects around 22% of men and 28% of women aged 65 years and over, yet it is estimated that 85% of older people with this condition receive no help at all from the UK's National Health Service (NHS). This is an increasing problem because populations are ageing in most developed countries. Since 1974, the number of people in the UK population aged 65 and older has grown by over 47%, and made up nearly 18% of the total population in 2016. The number of people aged 75 and over has increased by 89% over this period and now makes up over 8% of the population. Between 2015 and 2050, the proportion of the world's population over 60 years will nearly double, from 12% to 22%.

Many older adults lose their ability to live independently because of limited mobility, chronic pain, frailty or other mental or physical problems, and require some form of long-term care. Older people are more likely to experience events such as bereavement, a drop in socioeconomic status or loss of stimulation as a result of retirement or disability. The speed of technological development and complexity of modern society have impacted greatly on older people, particularly those with limited educations or who have not been required to engage with technology through work. These factors can result in isolation, loss of independence, loneliness and psychological distress.

Older adults are also vulnerable to physical, sexual, psychological, emotional, financial and material abuse, abandonment, neglect and the loss of dignity and respect. Elder abuse can lead not only to physical injuries, but also to serious, sometimes long-lasting psychological consequences, including depression and anxiety. Evidence suggests that 1 in 10 older people experience such abuse in the UK.

Loneliness

Loneliness is a sad feeling caused by a lack, or the loss of, companionship. It can be felt at all ages, but its likelihood increases with age. Loneliness and social isolation are harmful to mental and physical health. A lack of social connections is as likely to result in early death as smoking 15 cigarettes a day, and is more of a threat to us than other well-known risk factors such as obesity and physical inactivity.

Research carried out in the UK over the last few decades has consistently shown that between 6% and 13% of older people say they often feel very lonely. Increasing numbers of middle-aged men and women are living alone as family units have disintegrated. Almost 2.5 million people between the ages of 45 and 64 have their own home but no spouse, partner or children to live with them. This is an increase of over 800,000 since the mid-1990s. In all, 7.6 million people are now living alone. It is estimated that 4 million people in the UK (over 6% of the population) spent Christmas Day in 2014 alone.

Domestic abuse

Domestic abuse is a major cause of poor mental health. It is usually defined as any behaviour within an intimate relationship that causes physical, psychological or sexual harm. This definition includes acts of physical aggression, psychological abuse, sexual coercion and controlling behaviours, such as isolation from family and friends, and deprivation of basic necessities. Domestic abuse is the leading cause of death for women of childbearing age globally, and the main contributory factor is the mental health consequences of abuse.

According to the World Health Organization (WHO), almost 30% of all women who have been in a relationship have experienced physical and/or sexual violence by an intimate partner. The prevalence estimates of intimate partner violence range from 23.2% in high-income countries and 24.6% in the WHO Western Pacific region to 37% in the WHO Eastern Mediterranean region, and 37.7% in the WHO South-East Asia region.

Men are less likely than women to be victims of domestic abuse, but they are abused in substantial numbers. For every three victims of domestic abuse, two will be female and one will be male. According to data from the Crime Survey for England and Wales, at least 4% of men aged 16 to 59 experienced domestic abuse in 2014/15. Male victims are more than twice as likely as women to keep quiet about the abuse.

Domestic abuse is likely to lead to depression, anxiety and other mental health disorders, and may result in sleep disturbances, self-harm, suicide and attempted suicide, eating disorders or substance misuse. A person who is experiencing stress or a low mood may resort to controlling or submissive behaviour in an attempt to relieve such feelings. Poor mental health can therefore make a person more vulnerable to abuse, and make a potential abuser more likely to abuse. Domestic violence also has an intergenerational effect, as children who witness abuse tend to have multiple health problems and are more likely to be abused and to abuse others in adulthood than those who were not abused as children. Around 1 in 5 children in the UK have been exposed to domestic abuse.

Attitudes in wider society

Since the founding of the NHS in 1948, treatment of physical care conditions and mental health care have largely been disconnected. Business people and right wing politicians struggle with ambiguous concepts like mental health. They prefer to focus on the physical world where targets, performance statistics and conditions are more easily set, measured and monitored. A person's state of mind is difficult to measure because professionals depend on patients self-reporting and because moods can vary radically from day-to-day. The lack of a reliable reporting mechanism also means that politicians feel less able to justify expenditure on mental health to their electorates.

Governments and health systems, encouraged by pharmaceutical companies, tend to encourage doctors to prescribe drugs rather than direct people towards activities that could improve their general wellbeing. Doctors can therefore end up treating physical conditions that are caused by poor mental health, such as obesity and substance abuse, without treating the actual cause. In such cases, patients are likely to find themselves trapped into managing such conditions, rather than solving the underlying problem.

Although mental ill health accounts for 28% of the total burden of disease, it gets just 13% of the NHS' budget. UK politicians have realised that mental health is starting to become a political issue, and the current Conservative government has committed to increasing funding. However, mental health trusts are facing increasing demand and pressure on their services and the promised money is not filtering through to them. There is increasing recognition within the medical profession that poor mental health can negatively impact on physical health, leading to an increased risk of some conditions. For example, untreated depression in an older person with heart disease can negatively affect recovery from the latter. In early 2019, the NHS announced that it would fund the creation of 1,000 social prescription link worker roles. Link workers help patients find suitable community activities to improve their health and wellbeing. There is, though, still a lack of recognition amongst decision-makers in the NHS of the extent to which poor mental health and a lack of general life skills are contributing to pressures on general practitioners and emergency services. In an effort to say within budget, the NHS is cutting mental health services even though such services are already massively underfunded and oversubscribed. This will only serve to increase the total burden on the NHS.

The failure of governments and health services to focus sufficiently on mental health means that the general public remains relatively ill informed about mental health issues. Consequently mental health charities find it more difficult to raise funds than, for example, cancer or heart-focused ones. Greater media coverage of the subject is, though, helping to build awareness, as is the increased preparedness of high profile public figures to share their experiences of poor mental health. For example, Prince William and Prince Harry, the sons of Princess Diana, publicly have shared the difficulties they encountered in dealing with the loss of their mother. Also, with their wives, Princesses Catherine and Meghan, they are spearheading the Heads Together initiative, which combines a campaign to tackle stigma and change the conversation on mental health with fundraising for a series of innovative new mental health services.

We cannot afford to neglect the causes of poor mental health any longer. Ageing populations, the prevalence of self-interested behaviours, the dominance of capitalist ideology and the actions of multinational companies are increasing demand for health and care services and reducing taxation receipts. The consequent pressure on public finances is causing governments to reduce spending on other services such as parks, roads, rubbish collection, library provision and social and cultural services. If governments are to balance their books, the working population will need to become more productive and efficient and the wider population will need to take more responsibility for their own health. Governments and companies must therefore create healthier working environments and invest in individuals, communities and organisations that can promote positive behaviours.

Episodes of stress and low moods, which account for the vast majority of incidents of poor mental health, are in many instances directly related to personality. In this volume, I explain how your personality traits and your environment interact to create these negative states. I set out a model of personality that will help you understand how to interpret and manage your feelings, and offer a pathway to improved mental health, increased effectiveness and happiness. In the second volume, I will address the wider societal issues described in the previous paragraph.

3

THE FOUNDATIONS OF PERSONALITY

Defining personality

The primary objectives of any living creature are to survive and reproduce. To do this it needs to fit into its environment and adapt to changing circumstances. Simple species adapt through chance mutations. More advanced animals do so by acquiring and applying knowledge and skills. The manual dexterity and mental abilities of modern humans have enabled them to learn more quickly and effectively than any other species. Their progress accelerated greatly once they formed stable societies that enabled them to store and transmit knowledge. The invention of writing and computers resulted in the creation of a knowledge bank, which is being continually refined and expanded.

Some species have evolved solitary behaviours with individuals engaging with each other only for the purpose of mating. However, many species operate in groups and assign different roles to members according to their abilities. Insects like ants and bees produce group members with different physical characteristics that have evolved to carry out specific tasks. Outwardly, the physiology of humans tends to vary significantly only in gender terms. Individuals differ in height, weight and muscularity, and this is most apparent in the sporting arena, but emotional make up and mental processing ability are often more important than physical attributes in determining the roles that people play in society. Physical attributes remain influential, though, in jobs that involve physical work and in the mating arena.

In this volume, I refer to the framework that manages our actions, behaviours and thinking processes as the **emotional system**. The performance of a person's emotional system is affected by variations in physiological structure. For example, messages are transmitted within our minds by chemicals (neurotransmitters), but their effect will depend both on the amount of such chemicals produced and the number of receptors that a person possesses. Although these variations largely result from genetic differences, environmental conditions in the womb or early childhood may influence the development of a person's emotional system and impact on a person's behaviour in adulthood. It is now clear that some genes can be switched on or off by exposure to environmental influences. These genetic and developmental factors combine to dictate a person's core personality, and cause people to develop particular characteristics, giving rise to individuality.

The behaviours that you display result from the interaction of your core personality with your environment. You will adapt your behaviour in response to your immediate environment and in the context of past experiences and future expectations or possibilities. I therefore use the term **environment** in a wide sense to include your job role, social background, workplace and social culture, relationship network and mental interpretation of your level of security. Where you environment is stable, you will display consistent behaviours that we refer to as **characteristics**. The behaviours and characteristics that you exhibit are, therefore, the product of nature and nurture, inheritance and experience, ability and opportunity, and hopes and fears.

Scientists, psychologists and practitioners have sought to organise behaviours and characteristics within coherent frameworks. As a result, various models of personality have been developed that serve as tools for personal development, recruitment and marketing. These models usually include a test that assigns various **personality traits** to the taker of the test. Each trait will be associated with a set of related characteristics and behaviours.

The most well-known models are the **Myers Briggs Type Indicator** (**MBTI**) and the **Five Factor Model** (also known as the **Big Five**). The MBTI is based upon the work of Carl Jung in the early 20th century. Jung developed theories through observation, arriving at many of his conclusions intuitively. Later in the 20th century, Katharine Cook Briggs and her daughter, Isabel Briggs Myers, codified Jung's theories into a testing format, which is now widely used as a basis for many commercial personality-testing products. Independently from the development of the MBTI theory, scientists specialising in personality developed the Big Five. The initial model was advanced by Ernest Tupes and Raymond Christal in 1961, but failed to reach an academic audience until the 1980s. At least four independent research groups (Tupes & Cristal, Goldberg, Cattell, and Costa & McCrae) have worked in this area for many years and their research has arrived at the same five personality spectrums. Psychologists have broken down personality traits into facets (sub-traits), and developed other similar models. This has resulted in multiple sub-theories and data sets. I see weaknesses in both the Myers Briggs and Big Five models, which I set out later for the benefit of those who have some prior knowledge of them.

As personality traits result from the interaction of multiple genes and bodily systems with a person's environment, it is difficult to determine their physiological origins. Also, assessment of personality relies heavily on survey information. How people respond to a question can vary significantly according to their background, education and current mood. This evidential uncertainty has deterred scientists from investigating personality. However, recent advances in brain scanning and genetics have reignited scientific interest in the field. Use of personality testing in the business world has increased as the commercial benefits have become more apparent. It is now an industry, and a wide range of personality-based services is now available. Most large corporations use some form of personality testing in their recruitment processes for senior employees and they are increasingly segmenting their customer base by personality for marketing purposes. There has, though, been little research into the relationship between personality and the behaviour of humans in groups, and few attempts to reconcile the principles of personality with behavioural and social psychological theories. This work addresses these gaps in understanding by linking together theories and scientific research generated within the disciplines of neuroscience and behavioural, cognitive and social psychology.

In this volume, I set out a new model of personality, which I call **The Personality Revolution's Model of Personality**. It has been developed intuitively, following research into a wide range of areas, through observation of human behaviour and drawing upon personal experience. The fields touched on in this work include personality, psychology, mental health, wellbeing, economics, religion and politics.

The model will enable you to gain a rounded understanding of your personality and the dynamics of the groups. It will explain how stress and low moods are related to personality and provide you with tools to escape these negative states. I have developed a new personality test to accompany the model, which you can take for free online at **thepersonalityrevolution.com**. Once you have read this volume and taken the test, you will be better placed to set appropriate objectives and achieve them. You will be poised to find a sense of purpose and primed to pursue feelings of happiness.

The model is underpinned by my explanation of the human emotional system. I do not explain how this system works in biological detail, nor do I set out a peer-reviewed scientific theory. Instead, I propose a hypothesis and aim to convince you of its veracity by presenting a coherent and rounded description of personality and societal dynamics that you can relate to your personal experience and knowledge of others. Although I have included a brief bibliography setting out books that have had a significant influence on my thought progression, in most cases I do not include references to scientific papers. However, further information about the psychological research and conditions referred to herein can be found in any standard university-level psychology textbook. If you like statements to be backed up more directly by evidence, you may struggle with this approach, but I ask you to suspend judgment until you have finished this volume and are able to assess the information within it as a whole.

The fast pace of modern society causes us to look for short cuts and deters us from devoting the time needed to develop skills. You may therefore be tempted to skip through this book. However, the model within it is developed logically chapter by chapter. Also, its content will prompt you to analyse your behaviour and environment, and challenge some of your assumptions and beliefs. You should therefore not expect to be able to rush through it. Try instead to read it in an environment that is conducive to study and reflection.

The learning cycle

Many people are sheltered from the world by protective and caring parents during their early years. However, it does not take long for actions, events and circumstances to start impacting on us. A child's initial challenge is to develop a basic range of practical, intellectual and social skills. To be effective and happy members of society in the long-term, you must discover your talents, develop specialist skills and employ these attributes for your benefit and the benefit of the groups to which you belong. You progress towards this goal by learning.

You can learn by mirroring the actions of other people, by memorising information, or by trial and error. The learning process takes place sub-consciously through environmental exposure and consciously where knowledge is deliberately acquired. We commit individual facts to our long-term memories for later recall and use. However, we also link pieces of information together to form ideas, interpret the world around us and guide our behaviour. We store the resultant opinions, values and knowledge as **schemas**. Schemas are mental templates that record particular patterns of information. They are created and embedded into your mind as a result of your life experiences. You may create your own or acquire them partially or fully formed, for example, where parents, schools or society impose values upon you.

The unknown is potentially dangerous, but information confers an advantage, so you will naturally explore your environment. Sometimes you will deliberately put or inadvertently find yourself in challenging situations. Assuming you survive, you will review the experience and learn from it. You may develop skills that can be applied in the same situation if it occurs again or build protective structures to prevent its reoccurrence. You will memorise the knowledge you have gained, and your mind may create a new schema or adapt an existing one. Your effectiveness and sense of security will increase as a consequence, and capacity within your brain will be released for further exploration and learning. Your emotional system will, therefore, prompt you to engage with more information.

I refer to this dynamic of exploration and consolidation as the **learning cycle**. The learning cycle is facilitated by the interaction of two cognitive systems, which I term the **Fast System** and the **Slow System**. These systems, which form part of your emotional system, work together to assess and order new information, make decisions and prompt actions and behaviours.

The Fast System uses a short neural pathway, which bypasses your long-term memory. It enables you to react quickly and intuitively to unexpected events and new circumstances. It promotes **exploratory** behaviours such as adventurousness, inventiveness, competitiveness or opportunism. It interprets information by identifying patterns within information and matching them to existing schemas. When it finds a match, your emotional system prompts behavioural responses that it has previously linked to the relevant schema. Information that is extraneous to the pattern is ignored, leaving capacity available within the brain to handle further information. Deployment of schemas therefore increases the amount of information that you can handle at any one time, enabling you to operate effectively in high information environments and increasing the speed with which you can perform tasks. However, because schemas are essentially "off the shelf" solutions, your Fast System is liable to make errors of judgment where important details within your current environment are not incorporated within the schema that it deploys.

In contrast, the Slow System uses a longer neural pathway, which engages your long-term memory. It processes information by assessing it in detail, relating it to your existing knowledge base and increasing the coherency and accuracy of the information that you hold within your mind. It also enables you to make reasoned decisions, solve problems and develop skills. You use the Slow System when you analyse, investigate, empathise or organise. When you apply these **defensive** Slow System skills to assess threats and neutralise them or repair damage to people and structures that provide you with protection and support, you increase your levels of certainty and security. The Slow System provides bespoke solutions, not ones derived from schemas. Knowledge gained through use of the Slow System may, though, be stored in a schema, or used to adapt an existing one. The Slow System takes longer to deliver results than the Fast System as the conclusions that it reaches are crafted for specific circumstances, but for the same reason those conclusions are likely to be more accurate than ones reached by the Fast System.

Your stock of schemas and stored knowledge will increase as you age, enabling you to expand your range of operation and develop skills. It will, though, become out-dated if your environment changes. You need to keep exposing yourself to new information and to continue learning so that you can update your knowledge bank and adapt schemas where they prove to be inappropriate. However, the incentive for people to do so usually decreases with age as their energy levels drop and they become more settled. Older people often fail to update their skills in response to technological developments or adapt to the cultural values of subsequent generations.

To help distinguish between the two systems and the different ways that they handle information, I use the word **filtering** to describe the pattern identification function performed by the Fast System and **processing** to describe the detailed review and assessment function carried out by the Slow System.

The learning cycle has four stages. You are in the first stage when you encounter new challenges or situations. Your Fast System will lack suitable schemas to apply to the information that it is filtering and will therefore resort to ill-fitting ones. This results in a drop in performance, making you more vulnerable to attack by other beings or injury through mistakes. I term this a **stress event**. Your emotional system will respond by causing you to experience shock. **Shock** jolts you out of your current activity, thereby forcing you to pay attention to the threat that you are facing.

A stress event will initiate the second stage of the learning cycle during which your emotional system will activate your **fight or flight mechanism**. Your emotional system may prompt you to confront the source of the threat (the **stressor**), but if it doubts your ability to overcome the stressor, it will prompt you to flee or hide from it. Because of the immediate nature of the threat, you will have no time to engage your Slow System to find a solution. Your emotional system will instead deploy schemas. It may, for example, deploy a schema that causes you to run away from the stressor. If it lacks appropriate schemas, for example where you have no obvious escape route, you are likely to be thrown into a state of panic. Alternatively, you may recognise the impossibility of your situation and adopt a submissive approach. Submissive acts are most likely when the stressor is human and may be accompanied by behaviours that encourage pity or the granting of mercy such as crying or begging.

Once the threat has been dealt with through confrontation, or the danger has passed either because you have evaded it or submitted to it, your emotional system will activate your Slow System to work out how to deal better with or avoid such a situation in the future. You will retreat to a place of safety where your mind is free to reflect upon the experience. You will use Slow System skills to assess the cause of the stress event, develop new strategies, and re-enforce the structures on which you depend for protection. This is the third stage of the learning cycle. Finally, you will complete the learning cycle by storing the newly acquired knowledge and creating or adapting schemas (the fourth stage). After a period of relaxation, you will return to exploratory behaviours and Fast System operation. The learning cycle is illustrated in Figure 1 below.

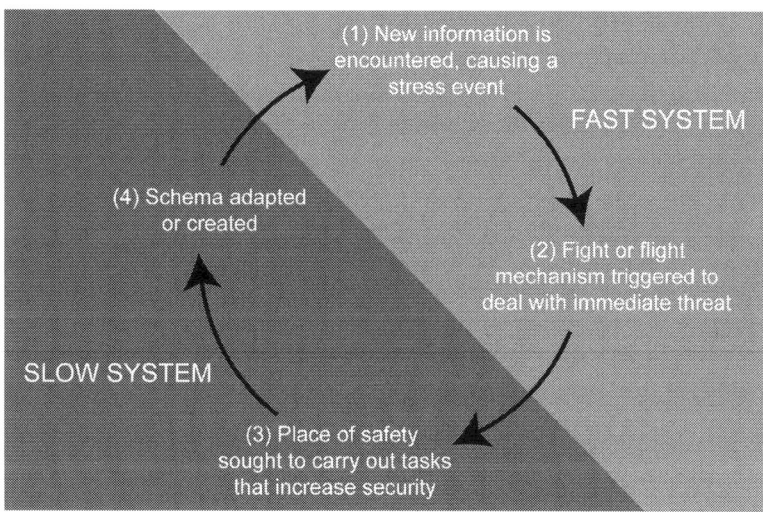

Figure 1. The learning cycle

Your behaviour will change as you move around the learning cycle. When you first engage with new information, you are likely to take small steps that do not push you out of your comfort zone. In such circumstances, you will be able to deploy schemas without experiencing stress events. You will not, however, be learning in such an environment so your emotional system will prompt you to become more exploratory. If you expose yourself to increasing amounts of information, you will eventually experience a stress event and shock. Once you have dealt with or evaded the stressor, you will find a safe space to activate your Slow System and focus on preventing or protecting against its reoccurrence. If you are successful, you will feel more secure and begin to relax. In this state, you will attend to small details, which in most cases will be inconsequential – a tidying up process. This state requires relatively little brainpower, so you will soon become restless. Restlessness is a prompt to relocate you to a more stimulating environment. It causes you to begin the learning cycle again by engaging with new information. Figure 2 below places the states described above within the learning cycle.

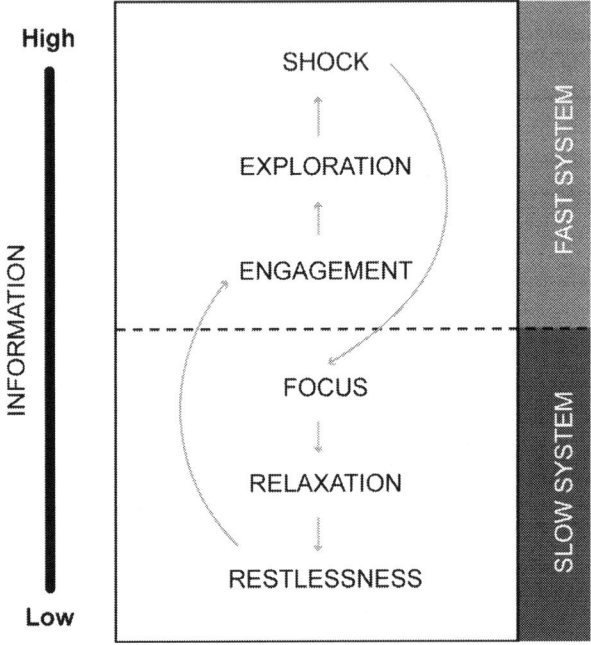

Figure 2. Activity states in the learning cycle

You are likely to experience a stress event whenever you put yourself in a situation that stretches your abilities. When you operate outside your comfort zone, your performance level drops. Your body interprets your reduced capability as a threat to your survival. The fight or flight mechanism then kicks in and you instinctively react aggressively, move away from the source of the danger or bury your head in the sand, hoping that it will pass by. When the stressor has been dealt with or has moved away, you review the stress event and take action to improve your ability to deal with the stressor in case it returns in the future.

For example, imagine that you have been allocated a task at work that you have not been trained to perform. Your emotional system is likely to recognise the danger involved in attempting the task, namely a drop in performance and a loss of reputation, and trigger a stress event. You could refuse to accept it, an act that may lead to a confrontation with your manager. Alternatively, you may take flight and pretend to be sick for a few days so that the task is re-allocated, or you may prioritise other tasks, essentially ignoring and hoping it will go away, a course of action which equates to hiding. In the absence of such options, you are likely to submit and carry out the task, putting up with the consequences. Once you have left work and returned to the safety of home, your mind will have an opportunity to review your behaviour and create or adjust schemas to prevent a repeat of the same situation. As a result, you might decide to undertake training, identify somebody more suited to perform the task or even look for a new job.

If you only need to activate your Slow System momentarily to create or adapt a schema, you will have experienced what I call a **minor stress event**. Minor stress events do not cause you to significantly change your environment or behaviour. For example, if a conversation partner says something that you find challenging, you may let him talk a bit longer to give you a few seconds of processing time. At other times, you may experience a **major stress event**, in which case you will need to relocate to a low information environment to allow your Slow System to carry out deeper or more extensive processing in safety.

I have made the distinction between minor and major stress events for ease of explanation. In reality they meld together seamlessly. Mid-level stressors require you to halt your current activity or withdraw from your current environment to perform processing tasks for just a brief period. You may, for example, struggle to undo a new kind of bottle top. In such a circumstance, you will be jolted out of your current activity and will be forced to spend a few seconds using your Slow System to work out how to achieve the task. The next time you come across the same type of bottle top, you will probably take it in your stride, as you will have created a new schema that allows you to achieve the task without dropping out of Fast System operation.

Sensitivity to information

People vary in their sensitivity to information so two people may react very differently to the same information. For example, on a rollercoaster ride, one person may experience elation whereas the person sitting next to him may feel scared. Such variations largely result from structural differences in their emotional systems, although, as we shall see later, a person's level of confidence also affects his sensitivity.

A person who has a low level of sensitivity will be suited to high information environments, such as crowds of people or brainstorming sessions, because he will be less likely to experience major stress events than an average person in such environments. When he encounters a threat, he will usually either deploy a suitable schema and remain in Fast System operation or briefly activate his Slow System to process the information associated with the threat. He will therefore be able to respond quickly to new situations and will have no need to withdraw to a safe place to engage in intense processing. Because people with a low level of sensitivity can quickly create or adapt schemas, they tend to have a large stock of them. This increases their range of options and reduces the chances of them needing to activate their Slow Systems.

In contrast, a person who is sensitive to information is more likely than an average person to experience major stress events. Such people spend much of their time either in a state of vigilance, looking out for potentially overwhelming situations or making efforts to increase their levels of security. They gravitate to low information environments, such as offices or their homes, either because they need to carry out a lot of processing or because they fear experiencing major stress events. Because they spend most of their time using their Slow Systems, sensitive people do not build up a large stock of schemas. As a result, they remain particularly susceptible to threats when they return to high information environments and are likely to experience major stress events if they are exposed to information that is only slightly different to that which he has previously experienced.

I do not use the phrase "high level of information" purely in a quantitative sense. I mean there is a lot of uncontrolled information within the environment and therefore a high degree of uncertainty as to future circumstances and considerable scope for unpredictable events to occur. When I refer to a "low level of information", I mean the information within the environment has been processed to remove potential threats and therefore has a high degree of certainty associated with it. For example, there may only be one person in the room with you, but if he is acting spontaneously, you will be uncertain as to his next move. There will be a high level of information in your environment as a consequence. In contrast, a library will have a lot of information in it, but that information will have undergone a considerable amount of processing, which will have made it more coherent and predictable. The amount of information will therefore be low unless you start to read a book that you find stimulating.

As high information environments contain varied, unpredictable and ambiguous information, they require people to be able to act quickly and flexibly. Such environments are suited to people with low levels of sensitivity because they are adept at using their Fast Systems to adapt and deploy schemas to deal with information that they encounter. This ability enables them to pursue their objectives forcefully without fear of disruption. Because a person with a low level of sensitivity will usually possess a large number of schemas and spend only brief periods processing information, he will be inclined to take a general view of a situation, see the big picture and get things done quickly. His reliance on schemas will, though, mean that he will be liable to make errors in relation to detail. Often such errors are of little consequence, but sometimes they can seriously affect the validity of a decision. For example, a person with low sensitivity who is going on holiday may renew his travel insurance policy by deploying the schema he developed the previous year. This approach is likely to have a successful outcome because most people will have no need to make claims and most policies are similar to each other. He can use the time he saves in other ways. If, however, the insurance company has introduced additional exclusions since his original purchase, he may find that it does not cover a loss that he had anticipated, such as travel expenses in the event of serious injury. Similarly, a military leader may act opportunistically to break through enemy lines when he sees a gap, but fail to consider supply chain issues and find that his army runs out of ammunition on the battlefield as a result.

Low information environments contain coherent, predictable information. They give sensitive people a sense of security and enable them to use their Slow Systems skills. Because a sensitive person spends a lot of time in Slow System operation, he will tend to focus on detail and find it difficult to take a broader view or act quickly and decisively. He is likely to get bogged down in the intricacies of a situation and lose perspective. For example, at a networking event, a sensitive person may allow himself to be drawn into a deep discussion with the first person he meets and miss out on an opportunity to extend his range of contacts. His focus on a single individual may pay dividends if he succeeds in establishing a good relationship, but in most cases it is more profitable to circulate around the room, following up on leads at a later stage. Similarly, a scientist may be able to establish that a certain foodstuff has a causal relationship with a particular disease, but is unlikely to be able to determine the level of importance that a person should give to that information in the context of the wide variety of other factors that affect general health. A sensitive person may also display naivety as a consequence of his difficulty in seeing the big picture.

How and what you learn is influenced by your sensitivity to information. A person with a low level of sensitivity will immerse himself in high information environments, linking pieces of information together intuitively. He will therefore learn quickly and develop a broad knowledge base. However, he will not be inclined to process the information in detail so he may jump to incorrect conclusions or accept statements made by others as true without testing them. In contrast, a sensitive person is likely to be wary of engaging with new information so he will prefer to locate himself in a low information environment. He will need to make sure that he has neutralised any threats within new information before proceeding to further learning. He is therefore likely to show great attention to detail, question the validity of statements made by other people and adopt a reasoned approach to learning. He will, though, learn slowly as a consequence and develop a narrower range of knowledge than a person who is low in sensitivity. People are therefore suited to different learning styles. Learning styles will be discussed in more detail in a later chapter.

Your sensitivity to information affects your ability to function effectively in any given environment. You may find yourself in an environment and role that allows you to perform well or one that restricts your ability to function. People who are low in sensitivity are drawn to high information environments because they provide them with opportunities to explore. They are likely to adopt roles that are generalist in nature such as that of leader, entertainer or jack-of-all-trades. Sensitive people are drawn to low information environments where they can exercise skills that increase their security. They will therefore be suited to roles that involve controlling information, such as analyst, engineer, mediator or organiser. The preoccupation of sensitive people with matters of detail inclines them to become specialists as they seek to extend their depth of understanding rather than the breadth of their knowledge. For example, a researcher in a scientific laboratory may search for a new piece of evidence to support a theory that he has developed.

In my explanation of sensitivity above, I have not distinguished between different types of information. People tend to think of information in a narrow, language-based sense. We encounter this type of information in documents, newspapers, on television and the Internet, and in conversations with other people. However, our senses are constantly receiving information from the things we touch, see, hear, smell and taste. Information exists in physical objects, odours, sounds, vibrations and electronic data. We also store information in the form of facts, ideas, opinions, ambitions and memories.

Any environment in which you locate yourself will contain a variety of information types. For example, when you walk into a new room, you may come across new information in a physical form such as people or furniture or you may hear somebody making a statement. You will sense whether objects and individuals are organised or chaotic. You may experience information that is novel, such as a modern artwork, or traditional, such as a person in a suit. Your senses may also pick up whether the atmosphere in the room is welcoming or hostile. The levels of each type of information will vary from one environment to another.

You will be sensitive to certain types of information and less sensitive to others, and each person will have his particular settings. The environments that you are suited to operating within and the roles you are suited to playing will be dictated to a great extent by your sensitivity to particular types of information. Your personality traits are an expression of your levels of sensitivity. A personality trait is essentially a set of characteristics and behaviours that a person is predisposed to displaying in environments with average levels of information. If your Fast System is particularly good at filtering a particular type of information, you will possess a personality trait associated with exploring that type of information. In contrast, if you struggle to filter a particular type of information and frequently resort to Slow System processing, you will possess a personality trait associated with improving your sense of security and establishing certainty. Your personality traits will therefore orientate you towards the acquisition of certain kinds of knowledge, the performance of particular roles and the achievement of certain objectives. Personality traits will be explained in more detail in the next chapter.

Your perspective on, and experience of, life will be determined to a great degree by your sensitivity settings. A wide range of personalities exists within a typical human group or population. As a consequence, there will be many different viewpoints, and importantly, nobody will see the whole picture. However, most people have close to average levels of sensitivity and locate themselves in environments with average levels of information. As a consequence, they will not have a strong bias towards the use of the Fast System or Slow System. In most circumstances, they will be able to switch between the two systems easily and will exhibit normal behaviour.

Time and workload also affect whether a person with an average level of sensitivity uses his Fast System and Slow System to complete a task. If you need to complete multiple tasks in a short time, you will need to use your Fast System to apply appropriate schemas otherwise you will be overwhelmed. If you have plenty of time, you will be under less pressure and be able to use your Slow System skills. For example, if a person is running late and knows his departure time and platform, he is likely to deploy a schema in order to catch the train. This approach will usually get him where he wants to be, but he may on occasion be caught out by a platform change. If, however, he is early, he will have time to use his Slow System to check the platform has not changed.

Some people have more extreme levels of sensitivity that cause them to adopt intensely exploratory or highly defensive behaviours or both. They may possess rare talents or develop exceptional skills as a result. However, they will have limited ability to use their Fast or Slow System in certain information environments. As a result, they are likely to display unusual or challenging behaviour, may struggle to fit in social or working groups and will be susceptible to poor mental health.

A person who has a low level of sensitivity may behave in ways that are perceived by the majority as reckless, divisive, uncaring or careless. A low level of sensitivity can, however, be useful. For example, a warrior needs to be ruthless so it is helpful for him to have a low level of sensitivity in relation to harm that he causes to others. The concerns of people who are particularly sensitive to information are often ignored because they seem inconsequential to most other people. However, when they are placed in suitable roles, such people serve a useful purpose because they are capable of alerting the wider population to potential dangers and will have the focus needed to attend to important details. For example, a counsellor may recognise when a child is being abused, and an engineer may discover a weakness in a bridge.

Most of the objectives we set require the exercise of a wide range of talents and skills. We therefore need help from other people with different personalities. Humans are usually most effective when they work together. Teams of people containing different personality traits have the flexibility to adapt to change, enable team members to develop specialisms and apply a range of skills to complex tasks. If you do not operate within a team and instead choose to associate with like minds or pursue an individualistic agenda, you will lack support and protection and your performance will be compromised. You, therefore, need to establish or join appropriate groups and help to maintain their effectiveness if you are to be successful and happy.

The following chapters will enable you to understand your personality and how it influences your ability to learn and your behaviour. They will explain why at times you experience strong emotions, misbehave or struggle to fit in. They will also explain how your personality orientates you to perform particular roles within groups, and how it relates to different cultures. Once you are armed with this knowledge, you will be able to increase your effectiveness, be more useful to the groups to which you belong, and experience positive feelings on a more sustainable basis.

4

PERSONALITY TRAITS

The eight personality traits

The Personality Revolution's Model of Personality divides the information environment into four types of information. These information types are labelled extraversion, openness, indifference and opportunism, reflecting the characteristics and behaviours associated with them.

- **Extraversion** relates to your ability to handle physical information;

- **Openness** relates to your ability to cope with novelty;

- **Indifference** relates to your ability to handle harmful information; and

- **Opportunism** relates to your ability to deal with changeable information.

Each category of behaviour is sub-divided into two, to distinguish between those behaviours relating to the Fast System from those related to the Slow System. This results in four opposing sets of personality traits (eight personality traits in total). I refer to the four personality traits associated with use of the Fast System as **high traits** because they are associated with behaviours that are suited to high information environments, and the four traits associated with use of the Slow System as **low traits** because they are associated with behaviours that are suited to low information environments. The eight personality traits are illustrated in Figure 3 overleaf.

I will now describe the behaviours associated with each personality trait.

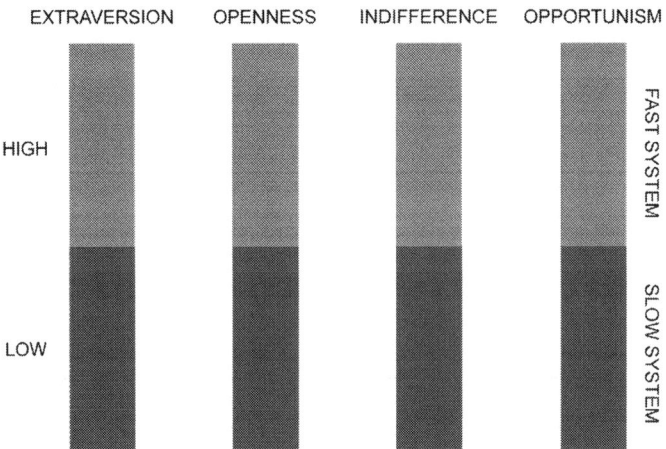

Figure 3. The eight personality traits

Extraversion

The spectrum of extraversion relates to a person's ability to interpret and deal with information associated with his physical environment.

People who are high in extraversion are by nature "hands on" and **adventurous**. They pursue intensely physical activities that give them feelings of enjoyment and exhilaration, such as adventure sports, partying and sexual intercourse. The energy they gain from such experiences compels them to intensify their effort. They tend to experience boredom or a low mood if they are forced to spend time in environments with low levels of physical information. Their lifestyles therefore tend to be frenetic, and they consume resources at a fast rate. As a consequence, they are attracted to money, inclined to be **greedy** and usually have high carbon footprints.

As the amount of physical information increases in your environment when you are in the presence of other people, people who are high in extraversion usually enjoy interacting in groups. The amount of physical information in your environment is increased if people are looking at or engaging with you. People who are high in extraversion therefore usually like to be the centre of attention. They attempt to increase the amount of information within their environment by, for example, initiating conversations with strangers. They seek positions of status because such positions attract attention and are often accompanied by financial rewards. For the same reasons, they take great care of their appearance, maximise their physical attractiveness and acquire material goods that serve as status symbols.

The desire of people who are high in extraversion for physical contact and energised environments can make them appear warm and friendly, but they will simply be acting in their own interests by manufacturing situations that allow them to express their outgoing natures and experience feelings of enjoyment. For example, when people who are high in extraversion gather in large crowds to mourn the passing of a famous figure or protest, they will derive some enjoyment from extravagantly displaying grief or anger. However, once the moment has passed, they will quickly move on and look for some other opportunity to engage in energised activity. This is because when the amount of physical energy in their environment drops, people who are high in extraversion are likely to get bored or feel low. We shall see later that it is the trait of low indifference not high extraversion that relates to empathy and caring. People who are high in extraversion can become reliant on particular individuals who excite strong positive feelings within them and this may cause them to display possessive behaviour or favouritism. They are vulnerable to corruption by people who can offer them enhanced status, wealth or sex.

In contrast, people who are low in extraversion are very sensitive to physical stimulation, such as noise or touch, and are likely to perceive it as potentially threatening when they encounter it unexpectedly or in an uncontrolled way. They are likely to experience anxiety or stress on a regular basis when engaging with the physical world and will usually be **cautious** when engaging with it. They tend to measure their actions, statements and expenditure of energy in order to minimise their exposure to danger and keep energy in reserve in case they need to take evasive action. They are orientated around their thoughts and gravitate towards quiet places where they have space to employ the Slow System skill of **analysis**. As a consequence, they tend not to be materialistic and to have a low carbon footprint.

People who are low in extraversion find interactions with other people innately stressful. They tend to keep a distance from them so that they can use their observational and listening skills to detect potential threats to their security. The fact that people who are low in extraversion gravitate to the margins of groups and are alert to physical dangers means that they naturally serve as lookouts. If such a person is approached by a stranger, even one who is being outwardly friendly, he is likely to experience a stress event and behave in a reserved way until he has satisfied that no threat is presented. Therefore, he may not give a welcoming smile and may appear arrogant or aloof. People who are low in extraversion are likely to experience stress when they are the centre of attention, even amongst friends. They tend to dress in an understated fashion to avoid attracting attention. They also prefer one-to-one conversations, as opposed to group ones, because such conversations allow them to focus their attention on a single individual without feeling a need to assess threats presented by other people in their environment. Their reserved nature means that it can take a long time for people who are low in extraversion to develop relationships.

Their sense of detachment enables people who are low in extraversion to use their analytical skills and endows them with the ability to make objective judgments. This objectivity and even-handedness make them particularly committed to the principle of **fairness**. When a person with a low level of extraversion promotes fairness and measured decision-making, his sense of security will be enhanced, and he is likely to experience feelings of contentment. However, the reluctance of people who are low in extraversion to engage in physical contact or display emotion may make them appear cold or unfeeling.

People who are high in extraversion use their Fast Systems to employ schemas when in conversation. This enables them to respond quickly, use catchphrases and tell stories. They enjoy living in the moment and are action orientated, so they rarely spend time thinking things through in advance. As a result, they tend to react instinctively to the statement made by the previous speaker. They enjoy using expressive language and gestures and feel exhilarated when they receive positive feedback from their audience. However, they have a tendency not to listen very well to conversation partners as they are easily distracted by the positive feelings that they get from the physicality of group socialisation and being the centre of attention.

In contrast, people who are low in extraversion tend to engage their Slow Systems when they speak. This allows them to choose their words with care, analyse the responses of others and think ahead. This processing slows them down. As a result, they often give delayed or ponderous responses. This can be interpreted incorrectly by those who are high in extraversion as a lack of confidence. It also means that their conversation tends to lack animation and be focused on factual information. Because people who are low in extraversion spend a lot of time thinking, they tend to develop ideas internally and release them into conversation partially or fully formed. This means that they will often find themselves out of step in a group conversation, making it difficult for other people to follow their train of thought. A person who is low in extraversion will often find that a statement that he makes within a group conversation is ignored and then repeated shortly afterwards by another member of the group who is capable of expressing it in a way and at a time that allows other members of the group to take it on board. People who are low in extraversion tend to be good listeners because their insecurity makes them alert to potential threats. They tend, however, to be less good at interpreting facial expressions and physical gestures because they are rich in information. This means they can fail to recognise cues from other people to start speaking and often struggle to enter group conversations.

A person who is low in extraversion may struggle to engage in "small talk" in social situations, feeling that he has nothing to say or that the conversation of other people is superficial. If so, he is likely to be under the misapprehension that the content of the conversation is important. It may be, however, that his conversation partners are higher in extraversion and are using conversation as a means of creating a lively environment or attracting attention to themselves. They may therefore subconsciously be energising the room with their voices and gestures, without any intention of conveying any meaningful verbal information. They will probably be expecting a similarly energised response in return, but a person who is low in extraversion is unlikely to reciprocate. People who are high in extraversion are therefore likely to feel deflated or bored in the company of people who are low in extraversion and may exclude them from groups as a consequence. In contrast, a person who is low in extraversion is likely to feel stressed when a person who is high in extraversion talks enthusiastically to him or suggests taking part in exhibitionist activities like dancing. He may avoid starting conversations or calling friends to avoid the awkwardness involved in manufacturing appropriate conversation. This may lead to him becoming isolated. In summary, a person who is high in extraversion is likely to consider a person who is low in extraversion to be dull or too serious, whereas someone who is low in extraversion is likely to view a person who is high in extraversion as shallow and indulgent.

The analytical nature of people who are low in extraversion causes them to look for meaning in events and other people's actions whereas people who are high in extraversion operate on a more superficial level. Because people who are low in extraversion assess pros and cons before acting, they tend to expect people to follow through with their commitments. In contrast, as people who are high in extraversion tend to live in the moment, seeking out enjoyable experiences, they tend to get carried away with enthusiasm and make commitments that they later decide not to honour.

People who are low in extraversion gravitate towards activities that allow them space to exercise their analytical skills or which require a measured expenditure of energy, such as individual and endurance sports. People who are high in extraversion prefer the more energised environment that working in a close-knit team delivers, and sports that involve short, intense bursts of effort. Take the sport of cycling. People who are high in extraversion will naturally be drawn to downhill mountain biking and sprinting whereas those who are low in extraversion are more suited to cross-country and time trial events.

It has been suggested that body shape is linked to personality. This seems most likely in respect of the trait of extraversion. People who are high in extraversion tend to be thick set and muscular whereas people who are low in extraversion tend to be thinner and have longer limbs. This would make sense from a practical point of view as muscle helps people who are high in extraversion acquire the resources they crave. People who are low in extraversion direct their energy into thinking rather than physical activity and tend to run rather than fight, so longer, leaner bodies suit their needs.

It appears that that the traits of high and low extraversion are associated with genes that determine the emotional system's sensitivity to the chemical dopamine. People who are high in extraversion are very responsive to dopamine, and it is the feelings of elation that this chemical induces that compels them to engage with the physical world. People who are low in extraversion have a shorter version of this gene, which means they are much less responsive to dopamine. When a person who is high in extraversion finishes a particular exercise activity, he will feel energised due to the dopamine high that he is experiencing and will usually be keen to repeat the experience immediately. Those who are low in extraversion are more likely to feel tired because they will experience stress when exercising. They will, therefore, need to relax afterwards.

People who are low in extraversion need to locate themselves away from physically stimulating environments if they are to exercise their analytical skills effectively. They will experience stress if they adopt behaviours associated with the trait of high extraversion. However, television and social media companies continuously transmit images of people exhibiting behaviours associated with a high extraversion into our living rooms and to our phones. Also, there is pressure on young people to be accepted by and socialise within groups and to be invited to parties. A young person who is low in extraversion may therefore feel under pressure to adopt behaviours that feel unnatural and cause him to experience stress.

Finally, I should point out the difference between someone who is low in extraversion and a shy person because there is often confusion between the two. Shyness occurs when a person who lacks confidence in a particular environment becomes very self-conscious. It is associated with high anxiety and related coping mechanisms, such as a reluctance to engage in eye contact,. People who are low in extraversion are more likely to be shy as they are more observant by nature and do not like to be the centre of attention. However, just because a person is displaying characteristics of low extraversion, it does not mean he or she is being shy. It may be just that he needs time and space to think. It is important for parents who are concerned about their child's ability to socialise to understand the difference. While it is a good thing for children who are low in extraversion to be encouraged to push their boundaries in the social arena to some degree, such an approach is very different from the more specific interventions that are needed to increase the confidence levels of a shy child.

Openness

The spectrum of openness relates to a person's ability to cope with difference and novelty.

People who are high in openness seek enjoyment by engaging with new ideas or activities. In other words, they display **novelty-seeking** behaviour. They enjoy engaging with ambiguous concepts and differences in opinion because they find the uncertainty associated with them interesting. They tend to be good at interpreting metaphors and symbolic representations and often enjoy the creative arts. Their enjoyment of difference gives them the ability to see other perspectives and inclines them to be tolerant and open-minded. In the absence of new information, they are likely to feel bored or experience a low mood.

People who are high in openness use their Fast Systems to link pieces of information together to create new ideas, concepts and activities. They therefore have the ability to be innovative and visionary. However, they are easily distracted by new information that enters their environment. They find it difficult to focus on an objective for a sustained period or present a consistent impression to others. As they are drawn to difference and are excited by novelty, they constantly revise their approaches, aims and values. They are drawn towards strangers who they find interesting and can appear disloyal or **fickle** to friends and colleagues as a result. They may, therefore, struggle to complete projects or operate within teams.

People who are high in openness tend to be idealistic and usually struggle to make the compromises that are needed to realise their dreams. They tend not to spend much time verifying or consolidating information that they encounter. As a result, their statements and actions can lack coherency or accuracy, and they may neglect minor details that undermine or invalidate their ideas and creations. They are likely to adopt new technology early before it has been proven to be reliable or efficient. They can also find it hard to make decisions because they see multiple perspectives and options, and can see the limitations of simpler approaches.

In contrast, people who are low in openness find novelty disconcerting or alarming. They interpret information that is different as potentially threatening. To feel comfortable, they need to assess new information in detail so that they can integrate it with their existing knowledge and beliefs, thereby increasing the **coherency** of their environment. They do this by using their Slow Systems to apply **methodical** and **investigative** skills, which enable them to identify small differences, abnormalities and faults within new information and move forward without compromising the integrity of their design or project. These skills enable them to understand how machines work and to establish efficient processes and systems. As a result, when they are well educated, people who are low in openness are suited to performing specialist roles, such as that of doctor or engineer.

People who are low in openness are naturally conservative and tend to locate themselves in traditional environments. They prefer to look back to the past rather than forward to the future because the past offers more certainty. Their fear of novelty and inclination to stick to what they know causes many people who are low in openness to fall behind in educational environments and be slow to adopt new ways of working. People who are low in openness tend to rely on existing skills and knowledge, rather than taking risks with new ideas and technology. Their commitment to existing technology means that their systems and processes are likely to be reliable in the short-term, but become obsolete in the longer term due to innovation by competitors.

People who are low in openness find environments that they know well comforting because of their lack of challenging information. Often these will be places with strong attachment to customs and traditions, but people who are low in openness may also be attracted to modern, minimalist environments because of their spartan nature. In contrast, some people who are high in openness enjoy living in historic buildings and with period furniture because they find architectural and carved detail more interesting than the generic accommodation that is the norm today. A similar reversal has occurred in the UK in relation to beer. Historically, working class males would have drunk brown ales from their local brewery. However, members of the middle classes now more commonly consume traditional ales and craft beers because they tend to be higher in openness and therefore enjoy having a wide variety of beers to choose from. Meanwhile, members of the working class, who are characterised by a low level of openness, now tend to drink lager produced by major corporations because of the uniformity and predictability it offers.

People who are low in openness often struggle to understand new concepts and are likely to experience stress when encountering them. If they do not feel that they have a safe space to assess their coherency or the intellectual ability to do so, they are likely to reject the information outright. They tend to adopt black and white opinions because this approach makes it easier for them to deal with ambiguous or novel situations. They are comforted by strong and stable values. As they tend to arrive at decisions by reference to their existing knowledge base and by ignoring or discounting outside influences, they can appear more decisive than people who are high in openness. However, such decisions will often be flawed due to their failure to consider new factors that have emerged and difficulty in envisioning a different future. This is especially the case where technological innovation and changes in social attitudes and behaviours are occurring at a fast pace.

In conversation, people who are high in openness tend to use a wide vocabulary and are likely to make intuitive leaps from one subject to another that people who are low in openness struggle to follow. Their tendency to avoid getting into detail may cause them to appear vague. They enjoy using words and phrases in a non-literal sense to make their conversation more interesting, but this may cause people who are low in openness to experience stress. In contrast, people who are low in openness use more limited vocabularies and describe things literally and prosaically. Their methodical nature inclines them to talk in detail and coherently about particular subjects. Such conversation is likely to bore people who are high in openness due to its lack of variety.

Personality traits do not vary significantly through a person's lifetime and neuro-scientific experiments suggest that people with high levels of openness have a brain structure that allows them to access information from a wider range of areas within the brain than people with low levels of openness. There is, though, a high positive correlation between years of schooling and high openness. This can be explained by two environmental factors. Authoritarian regimes and traditional communities restrict the ability of people who are high in openness to engage with new ideas by controlling or undermining educational systems and enforcing religious doctrines, thereby preventing them from discovering their talents. When information is freely available within a society, levels of openness increase. Members of the working class have historically lacked access to broad and high quality education and been constrained within traditional environments. In prosperous developed countries with progressive taxation policies, the size of the working class has decreased significantly as people with higher levels of openness have been allowed and encouraged to undertake further education and embrace technology. Also, when people are well educated, they tend to feel more capable and confident. This reduces their fear of new experiences and encourages them to take an interest in the wider world. There is, therefore, a symbiotic relationship between higher levels of openness and democracy.

Studies have shown that levels of openness decrease slightly with age. However, this research dates from a period when ageing was accompanied by a "settling down" process and a consequent reduction in new experiences. We have now moved from the analogue to the digital age where information is abundant. This has greatly benefitted those who are high in openness as it allows continued exposure to new ideas. Therefore, provided we can maintain educational standards in schools and improve adult learning environments, we can reasonably expect to see an increase in levels of openness in society in general and as people age. This statement is, however, subject to the proviso that developed countries remain peaceful and prosperous, and that governments commit to maintaining broad curriculums, high-quality universal education, and a free and pluralistic media. This is by no means certain in the current reactionary political climate.

The trait of high openness has been associated with intelligence by some researchers into personality. Certainly, an essential part of critical thinking is the ability to think around an issue and consider a range of factors, and those who are high in openness are more likely to do so than people who are low in openness. The word "intelligence", though, is better used in a much broader sense to describe the ability to acquire and apply knowledge and skills. It should not be considered to relate to any personality trait in particular.

I will discuss group behaviours in detail in a later chapter, but people who are low in openness help to strengthen groups and organisations by promoting conformity. They are likely to be disconcerted by people holding beliefs and exhibiting behaviours that are contrary to their preferences or values. As a result, they are inclined to show loyalty to members of their group and they are attracted to organisations and cultures that promote coherency. They often find comfort in religion because the concept of God gives them certainty as to their purpose and ultimate destination and their future and religious rituals provide them opportunities to engage in conforming practices and use their methodical skills. Alternatively or additionally, people who are low in openness may increase their sense of security by emphasising their national, ethnic or racial identity. A low level of openness and a narrow or limited education therefore predisposes a person to the adoption of religious fundamentalist beliefs or nationalist attitudes and the display of discriminatory or intolerant behaviours. These are most likely to emerge in times of economic or political insecurity.

Liberal attitudes and behaviours in modern society have undermined the traditions and customs that have historically bound people together. If a society becomes too incoherent, it will start to disintegrate and prompt a backlash from those who seek more stability. In developed countries, reduced job security, the disintegration of communities and large-scale immigration have increased levels of insecurity, particularly within the working class. Consequently, there has been an upsurge of nationalist sentiment and discriminatory behaviour and reactionary politicians have emerged to, at least outwardly, represent the interests of people with low levels of openness.

Indifference

Indifference relates to a person's capacity to handle situations that cause people to experience pain or discomfort.

People who are high in indifference are **competitive** and enjoy establishing dominance over others. They find tense atmospheres stimulating as they awaken their competitive instincts. They concentrate their efforts on acquiring and exerting power. They are inclined to act without regard for any harm that they may cause to their competitors or those whom they dominate because they lack natural empathy, which is the ability to share the emotional pain of another person. In other words, they are **ruthless** by nature.

People who are high in indifference thrive in highly confrontational environments such as war zones, the business world and the dating arena. Historically, they were valued for their ability to perform well in battle. Technology has, however, reduced the need for hand-to-hand fighting. Modern warfare relies more on the application of systems and processes for success than the competitive ability of individual servicemen. Also, liberal democratic countries tend to place a relatively low value on their armed forces. As a consequence, people who are high in indifference in such countries have tended to gravitate towards the business world. Their ruthlessness allows them to act in their own interests. They can drive hard bargains because they can push competitors to the limit without feeling sympathy for any hardship that they may cause them. They therefore tend to adopt a winner-takes-all or zero-sum game approach to negotiations.

In contrast, people who are low in indifference tend to be compassionate and peace loving. Their high levels of empathy cause them to experience stress or emotional pain when they see others in distress or where they anticipate such circumstances. They use the Slow System skill of **caring** to support such people. They tend to pursue careers that involve caring so they gravitate towards educational, health and welfare services. People who are low in indifference dislike competition because of the tension it creates within an environment and the harm it can cause to those who are outcompeted. They therefore seek to prevent the emergence of potentially damaging competitive forces. They promote **harmony** within society because they find it comforting. People who are low in indifference try to build a consensus before making a decision, are collaborative by nature, seek win-win solutions and try to resolve disputes by brokering compromises. When they use these skills successfully, they are likely to experience a sense of contentment.

Their need for harmony inclines people who are low in indifference to be helpful. However, their fear of hurting other people's feelings can leave people who are low in indifference unable to act for fear of creating tensions within their social and work environments or result in them behaving submissively. The consensus-building process that they need to go through slows down their decision-making processes. They are also vulnerable to attack, capture or manipulation by people who are prepared to act more ruthlessly in their own interests (i.e. those who are high in indifference).

The presence of people who are high in indifference makes it difficult to maintain harmony within a group or society. They are likely to feel bored or experience a low mood in friendly or collaborative environments, so they are inclined to provoke conflict. However, people who are high in indifference also have the ability to protect members of their group from competing individuals and groups and therefore group leaders often possess this trait. As they do not tend to factor the feelings or welfare of others into their calculations, they can make decisions that may be beneficial for a group as a whole even though they may cause distress to some individuals within the group.

Their lack of empathy means that people who are high in indifference are unlikely to put themselves out to help others. They often fail to recognise when their actions are causing emotional harm to people within their family, social or working groups. As a consequence, they may damage relationships that are important to them. They may also threaten or physically harm people who are important to them to maintain control over them. People who are high in indifference therefore have the ability to protect and abuse.

Although people who are high in indifference lack empathy, they can learn to recognise when another person is distressed and may pretend to share their pain or be sympathetic towards their situation. Such a person may adopt such behaviour to avoid causing distress to other people or he may use this knowledge or ability to exploit or manipulate them. He will be naturally inclined to do the latter, but may be persuaded to do the former by the culture of his workplace or society. People who are high in indifference may deliberately harm others for enjoyment, which they derive from exerting dominance. Sociopaths and psychopaths are therefore usually high in indifference.

People who are high in indifference do not experience discomfort when they harm other creatures or natural environments. As a result, they present a serious problem in terms of moving to a more peaceful and sustainable world. In contrast, people who are low in indifference feel distressed when species and habitats that they can relate to are being threatened. They tend to be protective of animals and the natural environments, and are more likely to be vegetarians or vegan.

Low indifference is a useful asset for an employee working in the lower levels of a company where the ability to promote camaraderie is usually valued. However, people who are low in indifference rarely reach the upper echelons of a corporate structure because they are not usually prepared to engage in the competitive, self-interested behaviours that lead to promotion, put up with the tension and hostility that people who are competing for position create or take tough decisions that cause harm to employees, communities or the natural environment. People with low levels of indifference are therefore rarely found in senior roles in corporations and politics. High indifference is not, however, positively or negatively correlated with career success in general as the ruthless behaviour that people who are high in indifference display causes many people with this trait to create enemies and lose popularity. People who are high in indifference can therefore find themselves excluded from groups and be pushed to the margins of society.

There is no significant difference between the average personality profile of a man and a woman in respect of extraversion, openness and opportunism, but the average man is significantly more likely to be high in indifference than the average woman. This can be explained by the fact that a person's level of indifference is partly related to his ability to produce testosterone and the receptivity of his body to this hormone. Testosterone is produced within males and females, but in much larger quantities within males.

Testosterone promotes competition for mates at an individual and group level by reducing a person's capacity for empathy, thereby reducing his concern for the feelings of rivals and his potential mate. Testosterone in a man's body is raised by a factor of four when he is close to a woman in her fertile period. In ape species, males work with other males to defend the females in their group and gain control over females from other groups. When they meet males from rival groups, their testosterone levels rise and they become more aggressive. The lives of modern humans are much more complex than those of our ancestors and there are many more things for which they compete. Testosterone now drives competition in the business world and is a key reason why men are on average more ambitious in terms of seeking promotion than women.

Biologically, females do not need to be as competitive as men. This is because dominant males and males within groups have evolved to protect and provide for multiple women and their children. It makes sense for most women to be low in indifference because the caring instincts of people with this trait and the harmonious environments that they create aid the development of children. A female's level of testosterone does, however, rise when she is in her fertile period, enabling her to cope better in the competitive mating arena.

Substantial numbers of people deviate from the gender norm in terms of indifference. This makes sense given the natural division of responsibility between the genders between hunting and protection on the one hand and childcare and domestic tasks on the other. If all women were low in indifference, female groups would find it very difficult to make decisions for fear of upsetting other group members, and they would lack the ability to confront abusive males. It is therefore useful for female groups to have some members with higher levels of indifference who are less concerned about the consequences of their actions on others. Likewise, it makes sense for some men to be peacemakers to help resolve conflict within male groups. Few women, however, have very high levels of indifference. Consequently, men are responsible for the vast majority of violent criminal acts.

Opportunism

The spectrum of opportunism relates to a person's capacity to deal with changing circumstances.

People who are high in opportunism are flexible and impulsive. These characteristics enable them to take advantage of sudden changes in their environment. In other words, they are **opportunistic** by nature. They like to keep their options open so they can react quickly to events, but they may be disorganised or untidy as a result, and will have a tendency to be late for appointments. As their talents lie in their flexibility, they resist the adoption of routines and imposition of structure because it could tie them down. For example, they prefer loose clothing because it allows greater freedom of action. They feel oppressed in highly organised environments and are likely to experience low moods within them. They therefore tend to act in ways that promote change, **destabilising** existing systems and structures.

People who are high in opportunism tend to drift around while they wait for an opportunity to materialise. They prefer to keep their diaries relatively free to maximise the opportunity for spontaneity. They find it difficult to maintain a steady pace of work and need deadlines to motivate them. In other words, they only become motivated when a situation moves from one requiring the implementation of routines to one requiring immediate action and the danger of non-fulfilment of the task in hand causes them to focus more intently on it. People who are high in opportunism feel a physical force repelling them from carrying out tasks like tidying up that others can mistake for laziness. In fact, their bodies are resisting the adoption of routines that might compromise their ability to act spontaneously. If they have not been strongly influenced by a positive value system in childhood, they are likely to be slovenly and to have poor hygiene standards.

If the impulsivity associated with high opportunism is channelled usefully, it can deliver intense bursts of effort. People who are high in opportunism are by nature project people as they can generate the energy and enthusiasm needed to get projects off the ground. If a project results in the creation of a permanent organisation, however, they will usually become demotivated by the routine and structure that is an inevitable consequence of such a transition. It is then time for them to move on so they can find a new opportunity.

In contrast, people who are low in opportunism get things done in a regular and planned way. They experience stress in changing circumstances so they tend to locate themselves in highly regulated environments. They try to restrict the potential for change by imposing **structure** within their environment, using the Slow System skill of **organisation** to control other people, events or circumstances. They feel comfortable when performing routines, as they do not involve change. They tend to be neat and tidy, to dress in an organised fashion and be on time.

People who are low in opportunism tend to set more goals than those who are high in opportunism and be more successful in achieving them. Their organisational skills enable them to maintain relationships, plan in detail and manage their finances. Their commitment to routine means that they are not usually tempted by new opportunities. Once they embark on a path, they are likely to continue down it without being distracted. They therefore tend to be successful in life by conventional measures and are suited to operating within systems and structures like corporations. A person's level of opportunism is related to his ability to resist temptation or defer gratification. There is evidence from a very early age that children who find it difficult to defer gratification turn out to be much less successful in life than those who find it easy. This is why the trait of low opportunism is the only one of the eight traits to be positively correlated with career advancement.

Societies establish moral codes and legal systems that require certain behaviours to be adopted. However, people who are high in opportunism will try to avoid adopting behaviours that constrain their freedom to act. They are also likely to break rules where they see an opportunity to advance their interests. Rule breaking is an important element of creativity so highly creative people usually possess a high level of opportunism. The weakening of societal values in modern society has, though, given people who are high in opportunism more freedom to litter, swear and behave in other antisocial ways. They are also more likely to overindulge. The wide availability of drugs and sugary foods offers them a shortcut to feelings of enjoyment and exhilaration. People with very high levels of opportunism tend to lead chaotic lives, have poor diets, suffer from alcohol dependency and other addictions, and may be unemployed or homeless as a consequence.

People in higher social brackets who have high levels of opportunism usually succeed in holding down jobs and managing their finances. This is because their parents and schooling have embedded basic routines and expectations within their psychological make-up. Once a person who is high in opportunism has adopted such routines, he may be able to use the flexibility that this trait endows to his advantage in his chosen career. Some of the greatest figures in history were, however, high in opportunism – Winston Churchill, Albert Einstein and Alexander Fleming to name just a few. Their high levels of opportunism gave them the ability to show flexibility in times of crisis or challenge established structures, beliefs or ways of doing things.

The effort involved in living up to the standards imposed by those who are low in opportunism can be very draining. The structured nature of society has historically resulted in many people who are high in opportunism battling at work and home against frustration and low moods. People who are high in opportunism like the flexibility of self-employment, but can find it difficult to work autonomously because they struggle to establish and maintain the routines that are needed to run a successful business. On the other hand, they are likely to resent being forced to work regular hours for somebody else, but the additional structure imposed is likely to force them to get things done. It is not surprising therefore that many people with this trait struggle to find a job that is both financially rewarding and motivating.

People are, though, generally less organised than in previous generations. As with all skills, if a person is to become good at organising he will need to practise. However, many people in modern society depend on other people or technology to organise them and have underdeveloped organisational skills as a result. Also, agility is the current buzzword in business circles as companies have recognised the benefits of being able to adapt quickly to technological change. They are therefore attributing less value to organisational skills than has historically been the case. People in general are therefore now more likely to faff when given time to complete a task or to panic when required to complete it quickly. In such circumstances, a person who is high in opportunism may step in and take advantage.

Driving it home

To show you how personality traits affect your daily life, and how you can use them to interpret wider society, I will now apply the principles of personality to driving. How do personality traits influence a person's choice of car and his behaviour when he drives it?

People who are high in extraversion are by nature thrill seekers and therefore usually enjoy driving fast. They also enjoy basking in the attention of others and acquire objects as status symbols as a consequence. As they are inclined to be adventurous, they usually enjoy ranging widely in their vehicles. They also like to have space to transport their adventure sports equipment. People who are high in extraversion are therefore attracted to fast, expensive cars, 4x4s and recreational vans. In contrast, people who are low in extraversion tend to prefer more understated vehicles that do not attract attention. They are more cautious by nature so they will be inclined to drive sensibly and be wary of other road users. As a person who is low in extraversion will tend to see his home as a refuge from the intensity of the wider physical environment, his journeys are likely to be restricted to his locality. However, his car may serve as a temporary retreat from the intensity of the physical environment.

People who are high in openness are novelty seeking by nature. As they are naturally open to new ideas, they are likely to be early adopters of electric cars. They are, though, likely to be frustrated by the homogeneity of modern cars, and may be completely uninterested in them, perceiving them as old technology. They will enjoy the freedom a vehicle gives them to play their music, as members of their family and friends will often not share their eclectic tastes. In contrast, a person who is low in openness is likely to buy a car that is similar to those of his core group of friends or work colleagues because he will be comforted by uniformity. He may feel a need to get to grips with the mechanics of the vehicle. People who are low in openness often feel comforted by classic cars because of their simple mechanics and tradition, but people who are high in openness may also be attracted to them because they present an opportunity for them to distinguish themselves from other motorists.

People who are high in indifference are naturally competitive and therefore enjoy driving sports cars. They will often be seen driving 4x4s because of the dominance they give their drivers on the roads. They are likely to drive inconsiderately because they lack empathy, have no interest in the welfare of other road users and enjoy exerting dominance over them. They will be unconcerned about the negative effects that polluting vehicles have on other people and the natural environment. In contrast, those who are low in indifference are likely to respect the interests of other road users, waiting for pedestrians to cross and allowing drivers out of side roads. They tend to drive slowly for fear of causing harm to others. Electric cars are likely to appeal to them because they cause less damage to public health and the environment. People who are low in indifference are more likely to personalise their cars by, for example, giving them names. In general, however, they are likely to have little interest in cars and prefer to focus their attention on people.

Finally, people who are high in opportunism are likely to select adaptable vehicles that can cater for their natural spontaneity. They will act impulsively on the roads and become frustrated when other motorists get in their way. The condition of their vehicles is likely to deteriorate due to their tendency not to carry out routine maintenance. In contrast, those who are low in opportunism will usually keep their cars in good condition because they will follow inspection and maintenance routines and feel a need to get to places on time. They are likely to abide by driving regulations because they value the structure of a regulated environment.

The analytical process applied above can be applied to any scenario that involves humans. For example, the genres of music that you listen to will be influenced by your personality traits. People who are high in extraversion like high tempo music that they can dance to whereas people who are low in extraversion tend to like to listen to songs with meaningful lyrics. People who are high in openness will like a wide variety of artists and will explore music from other cultures whereas people who are low in openness are more likely to listen to folk or other traditional music or to music that they have grown up with and know well. People who are high in indifference are attracted to aggressive, confrontational music like heavy metal whereas people who are low in indifference will prefer love songs and music that is harmonious. Finally, people who are high in opportunism will like music that is anarchic like punk, whereas people who are low in opportunism will like very organised music as played by classical orchestras or bands like Radiohead. Of course, most people sit somewhere in-between and choose to listen to middle of the road artists like Coldplay or Ed Sheeran.

People also give clues as to their personality through their language patterns, energy levels, conversational preferences and dress. In fact, every time you interact with your environment your behaviour allows an observer to learn more about you. Companies, in particular, are becoming increasingly adept at harvesting such data through online personality surveys and other questionnaires, many of which are disguised as entertaining games to play and share on social media. They use the information that they gather to adapt their marketing approaches to suit individual customers and determine personal risk profiles for the purposes of lending and insurance. Political parties also use specialists in personality to categorise voters so they can appeal directly to their core values.

The four personality spectrums

For ease of explanation, the description of the eight personality traits earlier in this chapter made a clear distinction between high and low traits. However, as people vary in their sensitivity to information, the columns in Figure 3 on page 64 are best viewed as spectrums. Your position on a spectrum represents your ability to filter or process a particular type of information. The further up or down a spectrum you are located, the more biased you will be towards behaviours associated with the relevant personality trait and the less likely you will be to exhibit behaviours associated with the opposing trait in that spectrum. A person who is centrally located is likely to display behaviours associated with each personality trait in that spectrum in equal measure. To illustrate this spectrum-based approach, I have marked the positions of a random individual on Figure 4 below.

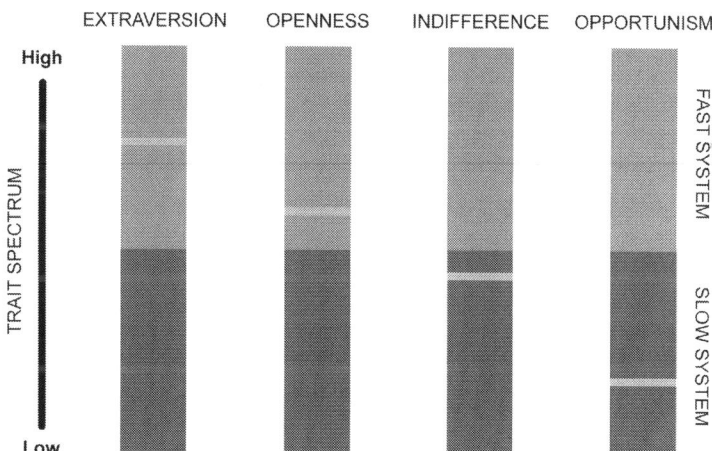

Figure 4. Scores from a PRTI test

In this example, the profile holder is located quite close to the dividing line between the two systems in respect of the traits of openness and indifference, and will, therefore, be quite balanced in his use of the two systems when encountering information related to those spectrums. He is therefore not likely to be biased towards the display of behaviours associated with one trait in that spectrum or the other. However, he scores highly in respect of the extraversion spectrum and lowly in respect of the opportunism spectrum. He will therefore predominantly display behaviours associated with the traits of high extraversion and low opportunism.

In respect of any spectrum, most people within a typical population will be located towards the centre of that spectrum. Such a population will, therefore, produce a bell-shaped curve when plotted along a personality spectrum, as shown in Figure 5 below.

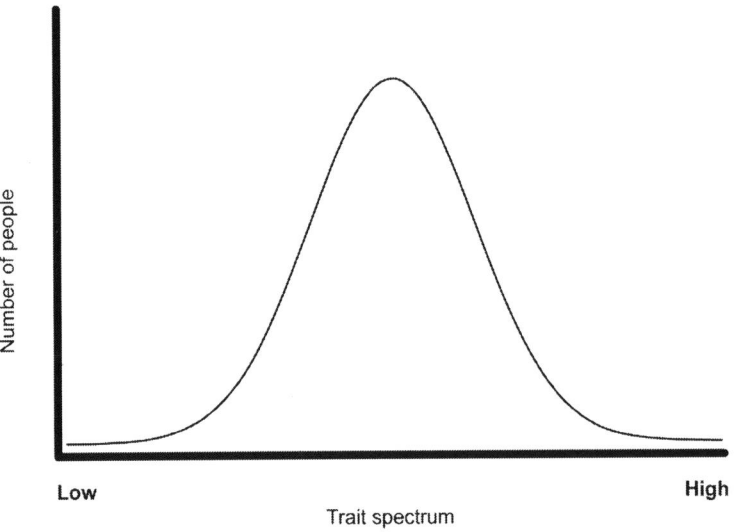

Figure 5. A bell shaped curve indicating the distribution of a typical human population on a trait spectrum

This distribution makes sense in evolutionary terms because people with **middling traits** will be better able to function in an average environment than people with extreme traits. For example, a reporter will need to seek out news stories of interest to readers or viewers (an exploratory act associated with the trait of high openness), but will need to check the accuracy of his statements methodically before publishing (a processing task associated with the trait of low openness). Where a person possesses a high or low trait, it is likely to cause him to adopt behaviours that differentiate himself from most other people. These characteristics will orientate him to particular job roles. For example, a person who is low in extraversion is likely to be suited, others things being equal, to being a lawyer because this trait is associated with analysis and measured decision-making. A small section of any population will possess multiple high and/or low traits. They are likely to struggle to fit into society and may exhibit very challenging behaviours.

Test results from some personality models suggest that, in respect of some spectrums, the bell curve shifts slightly towards the high or low end of the spectrums. This would suggest that a greater number of people in a population possess certain traits than their opposing traits. In the MBTI model the greatest shift is perceived to take place in respect of traits that roughly equate to high and low openness. It suggests that there are approximately three people who are low in openness for every person who is high in openness. This makes sense in the context of traditional society where the emphasis is on uniformity rather than creativity and large numbers of people were engaged in labouring and the performance of other methodical tasks. It makes less sense in modern society where many of those tasks are carried out by machines. Evolution may have created a bias towards the trait of low openness, but it could be that environmental conditions caused a greater number of people with middling traits to favour behaviours associated with that trait. Both explanations are probably true to some extent. It would, however, be very difficult to establish the extent to which any shift has a genetic cause. In reality, the fact that most people possess middling traits means that any shift is likely to be relatively small. The model set out in this volume therefore assumes that there are no significant shifts on any trait spectrum. Having said that, because of the gender differences in the indifference spectrum, there would be significant shifts in that spectrum if the genders were plotted separately.

The eight personality traits give rise to 16 basic combinations. However, the fact that you could be represented on any part of any spectrum means that in reality there are an infinitesimal number of combinations. This should not be surprising because you rarely come across two people whom you feel have identical personalities. Throughout this volume, I will explain the differences between opposing personality traits by contrasting behaviours associated with them. I will also identify behaviours associated with particular combinations of personality traits. For example, I may describe the characteristics of a person who is high in extraversion and low in opportunism. It is important, though, to remember that I use such dichotomies and distinctions to make the model of personality set out in this volume easier to understand. When you begin to apply this model to your life and in interpreting society, you need to take account of the subtleties introduced in the paragraphs above.

Beginning your journey of discovery

When considering another person's personality, you must be careful not to jump to conclusions based on his behaviour. Any behaviour exhibited can normally be explained by at least two different combinations of personality traits. For example, a person may be exhibiting submissive behaviour in a business team meeting because he is:

- Low in indifference and therefore avoiding conflict;

- Low in opportunism and fears that his position within the structure of his company will be weakened by the display of challenging behaviour;

- Low in openness and is therefore not generating alternative ideas; or

- Low in extraversion and feels uncomfortable participating in group conversations.

Alternatively, his behaviour may be influenced by a past experience, a specific environmental factor or an idiosyncrasy within his emotional and cognitive system. It is therefore difficult for you to determine the personality of another person without detailed knowledge of his life history and personal feelings. It is, however, much easier for you to make inroads into understanding your personality. In respect of the example above regarding submissiveness, it is likely that you will instinctively know which of these explanations would be most applicable to you.

You can improve your understanding of your core personality by noting the feelings that you experience and the behaviours that you exhibit within particular environments. You can then use this knowledge to identify your personality traits by reference to the personality model explained in this volume. You should, though, keep in mind that most people possess middling personality traits and will display characteristics of opposing traits at different times depending on the circumstances.

Most people find it easy to draw a sharp distinction between the physical world and their thoughts. Also, because we can see, hear and feel the physical world, we find it relatively easy to identify people who are adventurous or cautious within it. As a consequence, writings and research into personality tend to be weighted towards the spectrum of extraversion. However, you could use any of the other spectrums as a starting point for assessing your personality. For example, you could begin by identifying the extent to which you are held back by a fear of the harmful consequences of competition, which is associated with the spectrum of indifference.

Once you have gained an understanding of your personality, you will be better placed to identify the roles in life that you are suited to playing. You will be able to locate yourself in more favourable environments and increase your effectiveness and level of happiness as a result. You may have to make some difficult accommodations. For example, you may realise that certain long-held ambitions are not within your grasp given your personality traits and circumstances. Ultimately, however, if you develop a rounded understanding of your personality traits, you will feel more secure and be empowered to achieve.

A wide range of personality tests exists to help people identify their traits. A free test - **The Personality Revolution's Trait Indicator** (the **PRTI**) – has been designed to accompany this volume and is available at **thepersonalityrevolution.com**. It will give you an indication of where you sit on the four spectrums described in this chapter and display your results on the Circle of Power (to be discussed later). I encourage you to take the test now. There is no requirement to provide any of your personal details. Alternatively, you can make your own assessment of where you stand on the four spectrums by determining which of the characteristics and behaviours set out in the table in the next section of this chapter are most applicable to you.

Personality testing is not an exact science. Results give an indication of an individual's basic personality. Your responses to the questions may change as you become more familiar with the principles of personality, as your environment changes or as you develop your talents, skills and knowledge. Completing a personality test should therefore just be the start of a journey of exploration of your personality.

Personality Traits Table

To get the most out of this book, you will need to remember the basic characteristics associated with the eight traits. I will frequently refer to scenarios where a person is, for example, high in extraversion or low in openness. If you have not got to grips with these key principles, you are likely to miss out on much of the benefit to be gained from reading this book

I have listed behaviours and characteristics associated with the eight traits in the table overleaf. I have made a distinction between positive/neutral and negative descriptions, as trait-based behaviours may be perceived differently depending on the personality traits of the viewer and the culture of the group or society in which they are displayed. If you are aware of negative behaviours that your traits pre-dispose you to displaying, you can consciously work to counter or moderate them, when appropriate.

High extraversion		Low extraversion	
Positive/Neutral	Negative	Positive/Neutral	Negative
Physically adventurous	Foolhardy	Reserved	Aloof
Outgoing	Show off	Thoughtful	Hesitant
Talkative	Self-absorbed	Cautious	Killjoy
Possessive	Greedy	Unassuming	Wallflower
Acquires resources	Materialistic	Likes his own company	Loner
Socialises in groups	Runs with the crowd	Observer	Withdrawn
Status seeking	Social climber	Objective	Blunt

High openness		Low openness	
Positive/Neutral	Negative	Positive/Neutral	Negative
Imaginative	Incoherent	Traditional	Old-fashioned
Likes new experiences	Fickle	Rejects new ideas	Ignorant
Visionary	Dreamer	Methodical	Plodding
Full of ideas	Scatterbrain	Conservative	Mundane
Inquisitive	Easily distracted	Conformist	Yes man
Tolerant	Irresponsible	Fixed values	Intolerant
Non-conformist	Divisive	Loyal	Discriminatory

High indifference		Low indifference	
Positive/Neutral	Negative	Positive/Neutral	Negative
Uncompromising	Ruthless	Compassionate	Bleeding heart
Competitive	Win at all costs	Consensus-seeking	Weak
Dominating	Abuser	Accommodating	Submissive
Lacks empathy	Heartless	Helps others	Do-gooder
Hard-nosed	Callous	Tender-minded	Sentimental
Bargains hard	Exploits others	Caring	Soft touch

High opportunism		Low opportunism	
Positive/Neutral	Negative	Positive/Neutral	Negative
Flexible	Disorganised	Organised	Resists change
Project orientated	Rejects routine	Has staying power	Routine-bound
Values freedom	Rebellious	Follows rules	Uncreative
Spontaneous	Impulsive	Plans ahead	Inflexible
Likes change	Anarchic	Obeys orders	Servile
Challenges rules	Ill-disciplined	Understands systems	Manipulative

5

THE EMOTIONAL SYSTEM

Your emotional system manages the learning cycle. It interprets the information that you receive from your senses and prompts a change in your behaviour when it recognises your performance level can be increased or your security is threatened. This chapter explains how your emotional system influences your behaviour and emotional state. The biological workings of the emotional system are not fully understood by scientists so this explanation has been developed to some degree intuitively.

We are all exploring the world to a greater or lesser degree and acquiring knowledge as a result. Your emotional system manages this learning process by generating emotions and feelings, which encourage you to adapt your environment in a way that enables activation of the appropriate stage of the learning cycle. When you are prevented from acting on such prompts, you experience stress or low moods.

Once you understand how your emotional system works, you will be better able to recognise the boundaries within which you and other people operate, and to appreciate why people are exhibiting particular emotions or behaviours. You will therefore be able to avoid potential personality clashes and manage your relationships more effectively. There cannot be a more useful skill in life.

Emotional responses

Emotions, feelings and moods

Your emotional system helps you to survive and reproduce. Any mammal faces the following key challenges: the sourcing of food, water and shelter, the passing on of its genes through mating, and the protection and rearing of its young. A core set of emotions – anger, fear, happiness, sadness and disgust - has been identified which help you to achieve these objectives. **Anger** promotes aggression, which helps you to overcome obstacles and deal with threats. **Fear** causes you to take action to protect yourself. **Sadness** is a reaction to loss, most powerfully felt when a member of your family is killed or dies. It prompts consolidation and restructuring of your support structure. **Disgust** is associated with repulsion and has evolved to prevent you from consuming dangerous foodstuffs. Finally, you experience **happiness** when you are operating effectively within an environment that is suited to your particular attributes. You also experience other emotions, such as contempt, but they arise when two or more of the core emotions occur at the same time and have a combined effect.

It is useful to make a distinction between emotions, feelings and moods. An **emotion** is a physical response to particular circumstances, stimuli or stressors. Emotions are action-orientated and propel the body into physical activity of one type or another, for example, running away, crying or smiling. They are caused by the release of chemicals within our bodies that prompt muscle contractions, sweating, diversion of blood flow and other bodily changes including the display of specific facial expressions. A **feeling** is the conscious manifestation of an emotion. It is a sensation resulting from physical and chemical changes within the body caused by the emotion. It is important to make the distinction between an emotion and a feeling because there is a tendency in medicine to attempt to improve mental health by adjusting a patient's feelings rather than addressing the environmental circumstances that are causing the underlying emotion. In other words, medical practitioners often treat the symptoms rather than the cause. In the absence of strong emotions, you may experience a **mood**, which is a less intense, more complicated and longer lasting emotional state than an emotion. Moods are influenced by your wider environment and thoughts, including your reflections on the past and expectations of the future, and are therefore more difficult to attribute to particular circumstances than pure emotions. They will give rise to feelings, but you may experience a mood without being consciously aware of it. In this volume, the term **emotional response** is used as a general term to cover emotions, moods and feelings.

Evidence suggests the ability of people to differentiate between different feelings is quite limited, with many of us unable to be more specific than describing them as pleasant or unpleasant. People can label feelings more specifically when they link them to a particular context. For example, if you are aware that you are feeling low when thinking about a loss, then you will interpret such feelings as sadness. Most people are capable of reporting their feelings at the time of experience on two scales which psychologists have termed **arousal** and **positive/negative affect**. Arousal is a measure of intensity that is related to your heart rate. It is essentially a representation of the threat level within your environment as perceived by your emotional system. Positive/negative affect is simply a measure of whether you experience a feeling as positive or negative. In this volume, I use the terms **positive feelings** and **negative feelings** instead as they are more easily understandable

Your emotional system uses feelings as a means of alerting you to information within your environment that holds out the prospect of reward or presents a threat. Positive feelings encourage you to stay within your current environment and to continue with your current activities or pursue them more intently. Negative feelings encourage you to change your circumstances or behaviour in response to danger or a lack of stimulation. Whether your emotional system interprets your immediate environment positively or negatively will be determined by your sensitivity to the types of information within that environment, your mental and physical capabilities and the amount of appropriate protection and support you have from other people.

Self-awareness

You will usually not be aware of your current emotional state. You will be too busy concentrating on the task in hand. Sometimes, however, you become aware of how you are feeling or behaving. You will naturally drift in and out of states of awareness. For example, you may suddenly become aware that you are feeling happy or relaxed, or are experiencing feelings of sadness or regret. Usually these states of self-awareness last for only a few seconds, and without realising it, your attention quickly returns to your daily tasks. Scientists term the state of being aware of one's thoughts, feelings and behaviours **metacognition**, but I will use the term **self-awareness** in this book because it is a more user-friendly term.

You can consciously deploy your self-awareness capability to assess your happiness, confidence and skill levels, and analyse your thinking and decision-making processes. Your ability to do so improves with practice and age. Young people often find it more difficult to put their feelings into context because they tend to experience stronger emotions and have less experience of life. Self-awareness is associated with use of the Slow System because it involves the processing of information. When you are in Fast System operation, you will be deploying schemas so you will essentially be operating on autopilot.

You can become trapped in a state of self-awareness that prevents you from taking positive action. For example, where a person ruminates excessively over the causes of a relationship breakdown. Psychologists have tended to focus on such negative aspects of self-awareness. However, self-awareness is the key to understanding your emotional system and increasing your effectiveness and level of happiness. You can use your powers of self-awareness to monitor your feelings and behaviour in the context of your environment and personal experiences. Refined self-awareness skills enable you to analyse your emotional state, identify stressors and the causes of low moods, and take remedial action. You can also use them to compare your abilities and behaviours with those of other people, and to assess to what degree they conform to societal expectations or your own internal ideals.

You can also use your self-awareness skills to avoid actions that might have unfortunate consequences. You may, therefore, decide to step back from a potential argument because you have thought ahead to the relationship damage that may be caused. Similarly, an employee who is high in openness who is asked to undertake a methodical task may recognise that it is likely to cause him to experience negative feelings and ask for it to be re-assigned to someone more suitable. Of course, sometimes you have to make a stand, engaging in an argument or forcing a confrontation, or put up with an undesirable situation. You may, for example, wish to challenge somebody who has breached an important societal value, or realise that keeping quiet may put you in a better position to achieve your longer-term objectives. If you successfully maintain access to your self-awareness skills in such circumstances, you will be better placed to achieve a beneficial outcome. You may use them to avoid becoming highly stressed and losing control, or prevent a descent into a debilitating low mood. The key to doing so is to maintain control of your arousal level.

Arousal

Your emotional system uses your arousal level to determine the threat level within your environment and whether to activate the Fast System or Slow System. Changes in your arousal level therefore prompt movement around the learning cycle. Your arousal level increases as you are exposed to greater amounts of information. Your pulse quickens, and you become more expressive and active. At a moderate to high level of arousal, you feel energised and experience enjoyment. You will be using your Fast System, adapting and deploying schemas with ease. As your arousal level increases further, your Fast System will be forced to work harder and you feel exhilarated. At some point, though, as your arousal level increases even further, you will experience a stress event as your fight or flight mechanism kicks in. You may become aggressive, freeze or panic, as your emotional system prompts you to confront the source of stress, or hide or escape from it.

Once you have avoided, escaped from or dealt with the source of stress, your pulse will slow, and you will become less agitated. Your arousal level will drop, and when it reaches a low enough level, your emotional system will conclude that you are in the place of safety and activate your Slow System to assess the cause of the stress event and take remedial action. Initially, you will be in a very focused state as your Slow System works intently on the task in hand. As you feel more secure, your arousal level will drop further, and you are likely to experience feelings of contentment and then fulfilment as you near completion of the resolution process. Once you have completed the process, created a new schema and relaxed, you will be prompted to return to Fast System operation by feelings of restlessness.

The arousal level of a person with a high trait will rise slowly where the amount of information related to that trait within his environment is increasing because he will be capable of handling a large amount of such information. In other words, he will have a high level of elasticity at the upper end of his optimal range. However, at the lower end, his arousal level will drop quickly and he will have a low level of elasticity so he will soon get bored in low information environments. In contrast, the arousal level of a person with a low trait will rise quickly where the information level is increasing, leaving him vulnerable to major stress events. However, it will reduce slowly in low information environments because of his capacity to involve himself in detail. He will, therefore, have an elastic lower end of his optimal range, and an inelastic upper end.

Most people do not consciously monitor their arousal level because it is an advanced self-awareness skill. You are most likely to notice your state of arousal when you are in a highly stressful situation; for example, immediately before you have to give a presentation. Unless you are high in extraversion and indifference, presenting to a group of strangers is intimidating, especially if they are male. This is because, in primeval times, an individual would have been very vulnerable if he came face to face with males from another group. Your fight or flight mechanism is therefore likely to be triggered. You may experience butterflies in your stomach, or start to sweat or shake as your arousal level rises.

Take a moment to check your arousal level. It will probably be low as you are reading a book. However, when you come across a new idea that you find challenging or interesting within it, your arousal level will rise. You are likely to experience a quickening of the heartbeat and an increased sense of alertness. You may experience a minor stress event and be able to process the idea in real time while you continue reading. This is most likely to be the case if you are high in openness or have existing knowledge of personality. If you are low in openness or new to the subject, you may experience a major stress event in which case you are likely to stop reading to give your Slow System time to focus on processing the new information. You may stare into space to enable your arousal level to drop to the appropriate level. However, if you are in a noisy room, your arousal level is likely to remain too high to engage in effective processing. This is why academic study is best suited to quiet places.

Optimal functioning and flow

We have seen that the learning cycle involves transitions between different states - engagement, exploration, focus and relaxation – when it is working well. The positive feelings that are associated with these states are exhilaration, enjoyment, contentment and fulfilment. They are illustrated in Figure 6 below. This diagram is a reworking of Figure 2 on page 56, which set out the different states associated with the learning cycle.

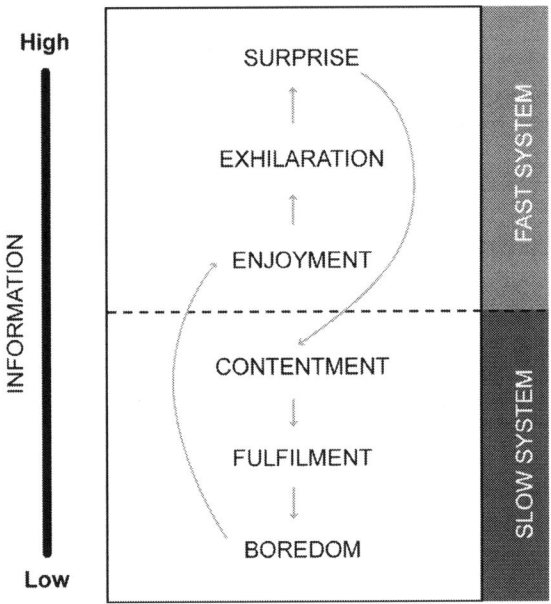

Figure 6. Emotional states in the learning cycle

When you encounter new information that you can filter easily, you will experience a feeling of enjoyment that will encourage you to continue with exploratory activity. As you engage with a greater amount of information, your arousal level will increase, and you are likely to move to a state of exhilaration. At this point, you will be pushing the limits of your filtering ability. If you keep exposing yourself to greater amounts of information, you will experience a stress event. Your arousal level will spike, and you will be jolted out of your current activity by shock, which may be accompanied by the feeling of surprise. Once the stressor has been dealt with or evaded, you will seek out a safe place to carry out a resolution process. Your arousal level will drop and you will activate your Slow System. During this stage, you will be focusing intently on exercising Slow System skills. You will experience a sense of contentment as you make progress. As the processing tasks that your emotional system is undertaking near completion you will experience a sense of fulfilment. Once the remedial action is completed and your security has been restored, you will relax briefly before being prompted to seek out feelings of enjoyment and exhilaration by restlessness, which may be accompanied by the feeling of boredom. **Boredom** brings to your attention a lack of stimulation, but when you are in a suitable environment you will experience it only momentarily and may not notice it all.

The environmental boundaries within which you will usually experience the positive feelings described above are largely defined by your personality traits. I refer to the space within these boundaries as your **optimal range**. When you are operating within your optimal range, you will be able to use your learning cycle without restriction, filtering and processing information at will and you will enter a state that psychologists call **flow**. When you are in a state of flow, it seems that you achieve your objectives almost effortlessly and you experience only positive feelings. The optimal range is represented in Figure 7 below by the central white area.

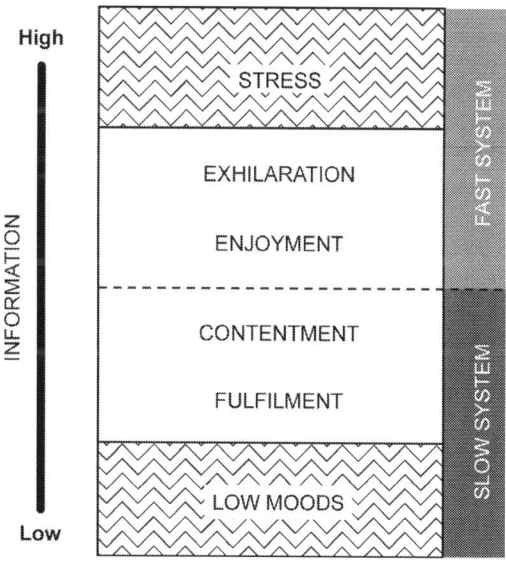

Figure 7. The optimal range, and stress and low moods zones

Negative feelings, stress and low moods

If you find yourself in an environment that forces you to operate outside your optimal range, you will experience stress or a low mood, and related negative feelings. Negative feelings are an indication that you are struggling to deal with a stressor in your environment, that you are performing tasks that require skills to which you are unsuited or which you do not possess, or that you are lacking stimulation. They serve as a prompt for you to confront, evade or hide from the stressor, and/or move to a more suitable environment.

I used Figure 7 on the previous page to illustrate the concept of optimal range. It contains two shaded zones, which you enter if you operate beyond your environmental boundaries – the **stress zone** and the **low moods zone**. I will now explain how the emotional system generates the following negative emotional responses: anger, fear, disgust, panic, chronic stress and frustration (which are associated with the stress zone), lowness, suppression, sadness and depression (which are associated with the low moods zone), and anxiety (which cannot be illustrated due to the diagram's simple nature).

When you experience a major stress event you will be jolted out of your current activity by shock. Shock may be accompanied by the feeling of surprise. If, however, an irritant or threat remains within your environment, anger, fear or disgust will mask the feeling of surprise. These emotions are products of your fight or flight mechanism and prompt you to confront, evade, hide from or disgorge a stressor. If the expression of one of these emotions and its accompanying actions does not effectively counter the stressor, your arousal level will remain high. Your fight or flight mechanism may then cause you to enter a state of **panic** in which case you will display erratic and unpredictable behaviour.

Panic is a sign of desperation indicating that your emotional system has lost control of a situation and cannot find a means of escape. It forces you into random acts in the hope that you will stumble upon a solution. You may attempt to avoid panic by restraining your arousal level. If you do so, you will be able to apply schemas or access your Slow System, thereby maintaining some degree of effectiveness. However, tension is created when you resist the promptings of your emotional system. We refer to this tension as **stress**. If you resist your fight or flight instinct, you experience a high level of stress, which I refer to as **chronic stress**. Because restraining your arousal level is difficult in such circumstances, you may alternate between states of panic and chronic stress. You will also experience chronic stress if you attempt to restrain the emotions of anger and disgust.

Anxiety and the associated feelings of apprehension and worry are also forms of stress. They arise when threatening information enters your environment while you are in Slow System operation and you decide to remain within that environment and to resist activation of your Fast System to deal with the threat. Such decisions are likely to occur when you are concerned to protect something or someone of high value, such as a child. In such circumstances, you decide to use the more accurate Slow System rather than accept the risks associated with using the Fast System. However, you experience a stress reaction in the form of anxiety because there is too much information in your environment for your Slow System to operate effectively.

Because anxiety is experienced at a lower arousal level than chronic stress it does not usually result in angry or aggressive responses. It is, though, likely to make you edgy and to cause you to exhibit controlling behaviour as a means of limiting the potential for harm or loss. If the information level in your environment keeps rising, there may come a point where you are no longer able to sustain Slow System operation and are forced to switch to Fast System operation. Once the Fast System takes over, the anxiety will dissipate as you engage appropriate schemas, although you may soon enter a state of panic or chronic stress if you do not possess appropriate schemas or the information level in your environment keeps increasing.

Sometimes when you are in Fast System operation, an obstacle that poses no significant danger interrupts your progress unexpectedly. Activating your Slow System in such a situation will slow you down so, instead, your body releases a sudden burst of anger. If the resultant aggression overwhelms the obstacle, you will be able to continue with your current activity. If it does not, or you are prevented from using aggressive behaviour by societal values or a desire to protect a person or object, you are likely to experience a stress reaction called **frustration**. You are also likely to experience frustration where you lack appropriate knowledge, skills or time to complete a task. For example, a man may feel that the quickest way to assemble a flat-pack wardrobe is to use his instinct rather than follow instructions. If he encounters problems in completing what he perceives as being a simple task, he is likely to get angry. He will not want to break the wardrobe, however, so he will restrain the instinct to use force or act aggressively. He will experience frustration as a result.

Frustration is a sign that you need to activate your Slow System to resolve a problem. If you resist doing so, you may release feelings of frustration through bursts of anger and aggression. A frustrated person may be aggressive to other people either because he perceives them as obstacles or because he is using them as a focal point for anger that he cannot direct at the real cause of his frustration. For example, a manager who is frustrated by the decisions of the board of his company may release frustration by shouting at junior work colleagues.

If you find yourself in an environment that provides you with insufficient stimulation or you remain in a low information environment after you have completed Slow System processing tasks, you are likely to experience restlessness and boredom. If you cannot relocate yourself to a more suitable environment, these feelings are likely to give way to **listlessness** and feelings of **lowness**, as your emotional system tires of trying to relocate you and gives up. Sometimes you force yourself or are forced by someone else to carry out a Slow System processing task when your emotional system is attempting to relocate you back to Fast System operation. Your arousal level will be suppressed in such circumstances and you will experience a stress reaction, which I term **suppression**. For example, a person who is high in opportunism and therefore able to operate in chaotic environments may force himself to tidy his house. As organisational skills are associated with the trait of low opportunism, a trait he does not possess, he is likely to experience suppression.

Although the learning cycle enables you to acquire knowledge, it begins with the experience of **loss** because a stress event represents the loss of functioning ability, security or support. If your Slow System cannot find an immediate solution, you will soon become tired, your arousal level will drop and you will feel sad. **Sadness** is a low mood and is most likely to occur when you lose access to a stimulating, supportive or protective force that cannot be easily replaced, for example in the circumstances of bereavement, imprisonment or redundancy. You will experience minor losses that result in smaller drops in arousal level and shorter periods of sadness on a day-to-day basis when, for example, a social event that you are looking forward to is cancelled or you lose a tennis match. You may also experience sadness in the form of **disappointment** when an expected benefit fails to materialise.

If you cannot find a way to compensate for a loss, you are likely to remain low for a sustained period and experience depression. **Depression** is characterised by continuing low spirits, reduced enjoyment of life and lack of purpose. It occurs when a person becomes trapped within cycles of ineffective Slow System processing such as excessive rumination. For example, a person suffering from depression may spend long periods of time alone trying to work out why a relationship broke down, regretting past actions or omissions, or simply feeling sorry for himself. When he is not doing so, he is likely to feel tired due to the energy he has expended and low due to the lack of stimulation in his environment. If he relocates himself to a more stimulating environment by engaging in activities that he would normally find enjoyable, he is unlikely to experience his usual level of positive feeling because of this tiredness and because his Slow System is likely to start ruminating in quieter moments. A person who is suffering from depression is also likely to experience stress where his loss has increased his vulnerability, for example where a protective parent passes away. Consequently, people who are diagnosed with depression often oscillate between states of depression, anxiety and chronic stress.

I will discuss the causes of depression in more detail in a later chapter. However, at this point, it is important to distinguish between depression and suppression. Depression is caused by a failure to resolve a major stress event, such as the loss of a loved one. It is likely to continue until the person can resolve the stress event, for example by finding a new partner or adapting to his changed circumstances. Suppression occurs when you carry out Slow System skills to which you are unsuited or which you consider to be unnecessary, such as when you are forced to obey a rule you consider to be pointless, It is not caused by major stress events and will usually dissipate once the suppressive forces and associated tiredness are relieved. When you experience a burst of energy and sense of achievement on completion of a task, it will usually be because you have overcome a challenge that has forced you into a suppressive state.

Your background and past experiences can be difficult to escape from. The cultures of your family, community, workplace and society restrict your freedom to some degree and impose obligations on you. You will experience significant losses from time to time. Negative feelings are therefore a fact of life. However, if they persist, they can seriously affect your health and relationships.

Many companies compel employees to work in high-pressure workplace environments that cause them to experience anxiety or chronic stress. Although these states are not healthy, the fact that they occur at mid to high levels of arousal means that the employees who experience them can often continue to work intensely and productively. When in such a state, a person will not have the time or space to use his Slow System to develop solutions to the problems caused by stressors and is not therefore likely to fully realise the damage that is being done to him or be able to consider the measures necessary to improve his environment. In other words, he is likely to remain trapped in the stressful environment, which may lead to longer-term health or relationship problems. Many other people are trapped in unrewarding job roles, which cause them to experience feelings of suppression and lowness, as a result of poor management styles, a lack of understanding of their natural attributes or their need to earn a living. They lack energy and enthusiasm and deliver a low level of productivity as a result.

While the immediate effects of stress hormones can be beneficial in the short-term, long-term exposure to stress may lead to high blood pressure, damage muscle tissue, inhibit growth and suppress the immune system. All forms of stress are tiring so your body needs more time to recover from stressful activity than when it is functioning normally. Depression can affect your eating habits, sleeping patterns and general ability to function. It is also tiring because intense Slow System processing is hard work. Both stress and depression can seriously affect a person's mental health and the health of their relationships.

In the absence of long-term solutions, people are forced to deal with negative feelings as they arise, finding releases to any stressors and seeking out stimulation when they feel low. For example, a man who is low in extraversion may retire to his shed to escape the frenetic nature of family life and a woman who is high in openness may visit an art gallery in her lunch break for some stimulation. We use also a wide range of mood enhancing substances to regulate our mood sand eliminate negative feelings. These ad hoc responses enable most of us to get through life, but they address the symptoms not the cause of our discomfort. However, if you understand how your emotional system works, you can more easily identify the causes of negative feelings and make adjustments to your lifestyle to avoid stress and low moods, or at least escape more quickly from them when you experience them.

The influence of personality

Trait biases, blind spots and no go areas

Any environment will contain information from each of the four personality spectrums. You will, therefore, have four optimal ranges. If you complete the PRTI test, your results will show a green band on each spectrum that represents your optimal range in relation to the type of information covered by that spectrum. Your optimal ranges will vary in position from spectrum to spectrum depending on your sensitivity, increasing or reducing the relative sizes of the stress and low moods zones, as shown in the example in Figure 8 opposite.

In Figure 8, the white dots correspond to the same level of arousal (the point at which a stress event is experienced). The black dots also correspond to the same level of arousal (the point at which restlessness is experienced). They are located at different information levels because of the different sensitivities of the profile holder to the four types of information. Another way of putting this is that information levels are objective as they relate to the environment, but arousal levels are subjective as they relate to an individual's levels of sensitivity.

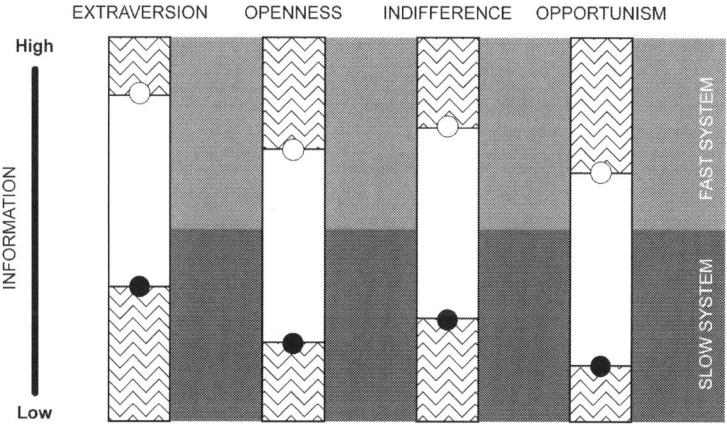

Figure 8. Arousal levels illustrated on an example personality profile

The fact that we have different sensitivities to different types of information means that the thresholds at which we experience stress or a low mood in any particular information environment will vary from person to person depending on the individual's personality traits.

A person with a high trait will be able to continue to use his Fast System without experiencing major stress events at high information levels. He will just feel more and more exhilarated as the information related to that trait within his environment increases. However, if the information level drops, he will feel bored very quickly because of his limited ability to use Slow System skills related to that trait. He is likely only to experience minor stress events so he will find it difficult to stay focused and is unlikely to experience a sense of contentment or fulfilment for very long. He will therefore seek out high information environments. As most environments contain average amounts of information, though, he is likely to experience suppression and lowness on a regular basis. Figure 9 overleaf illustrates the optimal range for a person with a high trait.

A person with a high trait will usually be able to exhibit behaviours associated with the reverse trait if conditions are favourable (i.e. when tasks need to be completed that only need basic Slow System processing). His window for doing so will be small, though, as is illustrated by the narrow area of Slow System functioning within the optimal range in Figure 9. For example a person who is high in opportunism may decide to quickly tidy his desk because he recognises that it will improve his efficiency. However, because his optimal range will not extend very far into the lower half of the spectrum, he will start to experience a low mood if the information level in his environment drops further or the task he is performing becomes more complex. He is therefore likely to resist carrying out a more thorough organisational process such as filing.

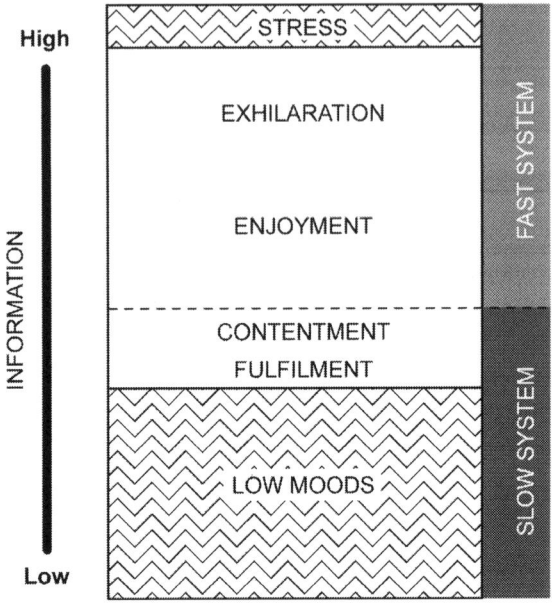

Figure 9. The optimal range in relation a high trait

A person with a high trait will try to resolve a stress event much more quickly than a person with a low trait would attempt to do in order to prevent him being dragged into a low information environment. He may take control of the situation and try to impose a solution, appearing dictatorial as a result. Therefore, although people with low traits most often exhibit controlling behaviours, a person with a high trait may at times appear more controlling than people in his team with the corresponding low trait. Also, the speed with which he comes to a conclusion may cause him to make errors that colleagues with the low trait would probably have picked up if they were given more time.

In contrast, a person with a low trait is unlikely to be able to use his Fast System to filter high levels of information relating to the corresponding spectrum without frequently experiencing major stress events and chronic stress. His ability to sustain a state of enjoyment or exhilaration when engaging in Fast System exploratory behaviours related to the high trait in that spectrum will be very limited. As most environments contain average amounts of information, he is likely to experience anxiety on a regular basis. He will, however, be able to operate his Slow System where there is a very low amount of information relating to that spectrum. In such circumstances, he will most likely just feel more and more content as he continues to perform Slow System skills related to the low trait in that spectrum, eventually experiencing a strong sense of fulfilment. These feelings will encourage him to locate himself in an environment that is favourable to the exercise of such skills. Figure 10 below illustrates the optimal range of a person with a low trait.

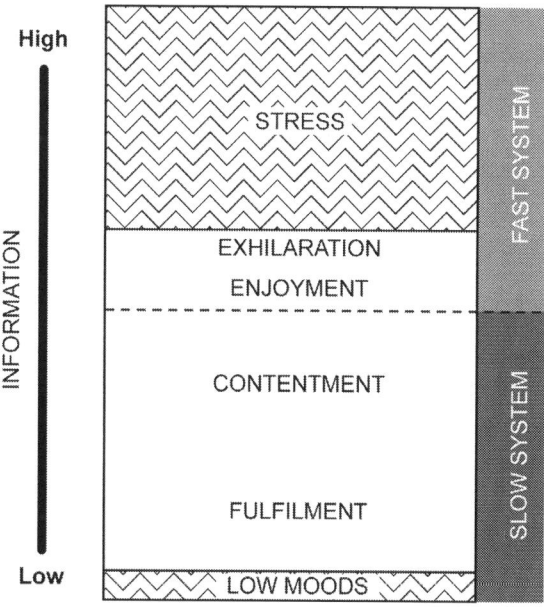

Figure 10. The optimal range in relation a low trait

A person with a low trait will be able to exhibit behaviours associated with the reverse trait if conditions are favourable (i.e. when he does not feel threatened by stressors relating to that spectrum). His window for doing so will be small, though, as is illustrated by the narrow area of Fast System functioning within the optimal range in Figure 10. For example, a person who is low in indifference is more likely to engage in competitive sport if he knows that there are rules that prevent competitors from being harmed. However, his arousal level will rise much more quickly than those around him because of his higher level of sensitivity and limited range of schemas. He may therefore appear more competitive than other members of his team. In reality, those team members will just be coasting. If the game becomes more confrontational and violent, they are likely to become animated as they experience more enjoyment, but the person who is low in indifference is likely to be pushed beyond his optimal range and experience major stress events leading to chronic stress or panic. He is therefore more likely to make mistakes. Similarly, in a quiet environment, the person who appears most animated within a group of friends may be the one who is lowest in extraversion.

His emotional system will be taking advantage of a rare safe environment to give free rein to his Fast System. However, because he will have a limited range of appropriate schemas, his actions and statements may be clumsy, inappropriate or exaggerated.

Most people will be biased towards the Fast System or Slow System to some degree in relation to each trait. Such a bias will give you advantages in some environments, but disadvantages in others. A person with a high trait is likely to lack the skills associated with the low trait in that spectrum, and a person with a low trait will lack the exploratory instinct that corresponds with the high trait in that spectrum. Trait biases therefore give rise to individual characteristics and personality traits, and orientate people towards particular roles. For example, a striker in a football team is likely to be higher in extraversion, openness and opportunism than a defender. This is because a striker will be surrounded by opposing players and will need to show creativity and adaptability to score. If he acts instinctively using his Fast System to deploy schemas, he is likely to be able to get to the ball ahead of a defender and use his creative ability to take advantage of opportunities. A defender works within a more organised system. He cannot make impulsive lunges towards the striker. If he does so, he is likely to give away a penalty or give an opportunity to the striker to go past him. Defenders therefore depend more on the Slow System skills of analysis, method and organisation.

The character that you display to others is therefore usually a balance between defensive behaviours associated with your low traits and exploratory ones associated with your high traits. A person who possesses four high traits will exhibit exploratory behaviours most of the time. In contrast, a person who possesses four low traits is likely to experience major stress events in average or high information environments. He will feel the need to perform defensive tasks on an on-going basis. For purposes of simplification, in this volume, I will sometimes refer to a person with predominantly high traits as high trait orientated and a person with predominantly low traits as low trait orientated. However, most people possess a mixture of high, low and middling traits.

Figure 11 opposite shows how a person's personality traits interact to orientate him towards a particular environment. The profile holder will naturally locate himself in an environment with a lot of changeable information as he is high in opportunism, but with a relatively small amount of physical information as he is low in extraversion. He might, for example, take on the role of freelance political commentator because it involves the analysis of the ever-changing world of current affairs, and would give him the flexibility and control he needs to work independently in a quiet place. It is likely that he would experience positive feelings and a sense of flow while performing this role. If, however, he were suddenly to be asked to present his findings in public, he would probably experience a major stress event because he would not be suited to being the centre of attention (an attribute associated with high extraversion). As a result, he might enter a state of panic or chronic stress. Alternatively, if he were to take up a role within a corporate organisation, he would struggle to cope with its structure and rules due to his high level of opportunism. He would experience frustration, restlessness, boredom or suppression as his emotional system attempted to relocate him to a more suitable environment.

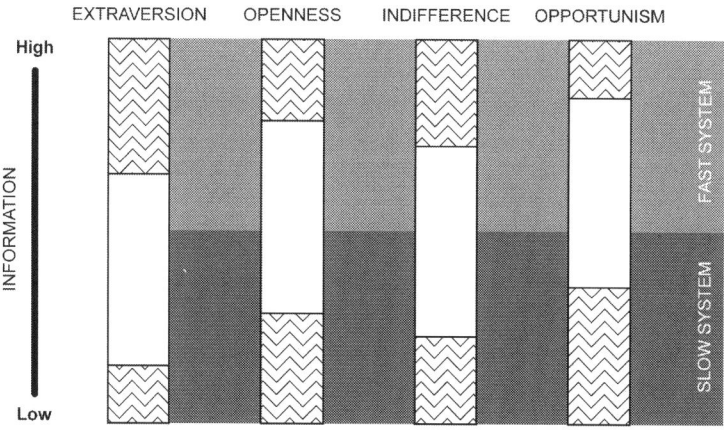

Figure 11. Optimal ranges for an example personality profile

Although a person with a high or low trait may develop skills that are associated with the reverse trait, he is never likely to be as accomplished as somebody whose personality traits more naturally suit him to doing so as he will experience negative feelings more often. A high trait orientated person will have a tendency to feel under-aroused and become frustrated or bored in average environments, and ultimately experience a low mood if he does not relocate to a more stimulating environment. A low trait orientated person will be easily over-stimulated in such circumstances, in which case he will feel threatened and insecure, and experience either anxiety or chronic stress. Such mismatches affect our ability to function effectively across the broad range of activities in which we engage on a day-to-day basis. They are most readily exposed to others when they result in listlessness, negativity, anxiety, or nasty or aggressive behaviour.

Prioritising emotional states

As The Personality Revolution's model of personality has four spectrums, a person's environment could predispose him to experience four different negative states; for example, boredom, chronic stress, anxiety and suppression. It is not possible to experience these states at the same time as they occur at different arousal levels. So how does your emotional system determine an order of priority for dealing with these states?

As survival is your emotional system's number one priority, it prompts you to tackle, hide from or evade the most serious threats within your environment first. It therefore ensures that feelings generated by the fight or flight mechanism (anger, panic, chronic stress, fear and disgust) overwhelm any other positive or negative feelings that you might otherwise be experiencing. Once you have successfully dealt with or avoided these threats, your arousal level drops and you seek out a safe space to carry out Slow System processing. You will be prevented from doing so effectively, though, if potential threats are causing you to experience anxiety. Your emotional system therefore prompts you to address these threats. Once you have done so, your arousal level drops further, prompting you to deal with any restrictive forces that are causing you to experience a low mood.

In summary, your emotional system prioritises negative feelings according to the level of threat they present, as determined by your arousal level, dealing with circumstances causing high arousal negative states first. Once you have dealt with all immediate threats and stressors, your emotional system will have succeeded in its immediate objective to position you in an environment that enables you to operate effectively. Negative feelings will subside and you will begin to feelings of contentment and fulfilment as you use your natural Slow System skills to develop and implement longer-term solutions to the stress events that you have experienced. Once this work has been completed, you will return to Fast System operation and be free to pursue activities that deliver enjoyment and exhilaration.

Because you are prompted to deal with threats before engaging with new information, your low traits will usually limit your ability to exhibit behaviours associated with your high traits. For example, a person who is high in openness will have the ability to filter large amounts of novel information. If, however, he is also low in extraversion, he is likely to be cautious within the physical world. If he enters an environment that contains large amounts of physical information, he will be over-stimulated and experience a major stress event. He will not be able to use his Fast System to pursue novelty-seeking behaviour in such circumstances so, if he sees a dish on a menu that he has not tried before, he is likely to be wary of it and will be inclined to choose a safer option. His novelty-seeking behaviour is therefore likely to be restricted to the realm of ideas. It is important to understand the restraining power of low traits because it greatly affects your direction in life. However, sometimes we neutralise it by engaging in avoidance.

Avoidance

A person with a very high trait will have a **blind spot** - an area of Slow System functioning that is very weak. He will try to avoid low information environments and tasks that are suited to the exercise of or involve the use of Slow System skills that are related to the corresponding low trait, because of the boredom or suppression that would otherwise result. He is therefore unlikely to develop skills associated with that trait. In contrast, a person with an extremely low trait will have a **no-go area** - an area of Fast System functioning that is very weak. He will avoid environments with high amounts of information related to the corresponding high trait, as exposure to such information is likely to cause him to panic or experience chronic stress. No-go areas, therefore, limit a person's ability to engage with the wider world.

As there are eight traits, there are four potential blind spots and four no-go areas. The blind spot of a person who is high in extraversion will cause him to avoid quiet places or activities requiring analysis whereas the no-go area of a person who is low in extraversion will cause him to avoid highly stimulating places and physical activity. The blind spot of a person who is high in openness will cause him to avoid methodical tasks and conventional environments whereas the no-go area of a person who is low in openness will cause him to avoid new experiences and interaction with people who seem different to him. The blind spot of a person who is high in indifference will cause him to avoid caring and collaborative environments whereas the no-go area of a person who is low in indifference will cause him to avoid competitive or tense situations. The blind spot of a person who is high in opportunism will cause him to avoid structure and routines whereas the no-go area of a person who is low in opportunism will cause him to avoid changing environments.

This form of avoidance makes sense in the context of a group because somebody with more suitable personality traits should carry out tasks that you find stressful or demoralising. In modern, individualistic society, however, most people lack support in some areas and need to carry out some tasks that they find unpleasant if they are to function effectively. If you avoid such tasks, your performance level is likely to drop and you will risk failing to achieve your objectives, delivering inferior products or services, or failing to meet the expectations of others.

Some people, though, avoid carrying out Slow System skills from which they could derive contentment and fulfilment so that they can take opportunities to experience more readily available feelings of enjoyment and exhilaration. Normally, you would need to eliminate stressors within his environment before adopting the high trait behaviours that deliver such feelings. However, if you can convince yourself that you have insulated yourself from such stressors, you are persuaded that somebody else is taking responsibility, or you mentally downgrade the threat level, you will be able to avoid doing so. For example, a parent might release more leisure time for himself by making an assumption that his daughter's school is providing all the educational support that she needs. In other words, you can trick yourself or be tricked into believing that you are living in a favourable environment when you are not, or fail to realise when threats are emerging.

Avoidance of high trait behaviours will deprive you of opportunities, reducing your productivity and expose you to the risk of being left behind technologically and outcompeted. When avoidance diverts you away from performing Slow System skills, you will continue to display high trait behaviours in circumstances where you would otherwise be prompted to focus on increasing your security. For example, you may continue to spend all your monthly income rather than investing money in a pension. However, if you ignore threats within your environment in the short term, they will often become more dangerous and may cause you greater harm in the longer term. In the pension example, by the time you reach old age, your ability to support yourself will be much reduced and you will be more likely to live out your final years in poverty. Over time, the exercise of avoidance of Slow System tasks is likely to leave a person with inadequate or out-dated skills. If you wish to sustain performance at a high level, it is therefore critical that you understand which tasks, stressors and environments you have a tendency to avoid.

Risk

New information introduces uncertainty into the equation of life and increases your range of choices, exposing you to risk. Your position on a personality trait spectrum is essentially a measure of your propensity to take risks. We tend to associate danger and risk with physical experiences, which relate to the spectrum of extraversion. You can, however, also expose yourself to risk by engaging with new ideas, or by locating yourself in a competitive or changing environment (which are related to the spectrums of openness, indifference and opportunism respectively).

A person who has a high trait will have a wide range of schemas that he can apply in environments where there is a great amount of information relating to that trait. This will enable him to act quickly without thinking through the consequences in advance. He will feel compelled to take risks by the feelings of enjoyment and exhilaration that he experiences when he does so. In contrast, a person with a low trait will spend much of his time assessing potential threats and factoring the results into his decision-making. His propensity to take risks will be reduced by fear of the consequences.

Although a person with a high trait will be inclined to take more risks by objective standards, his wide range of schemas means that he will be better able to cope in high information environments than a person with the corresponding low trait. He may miss an important element of detail, but he is likely to be able to achieve much more in a shorter time than the person with the low trait. The person with the low trait will be risk averse because he will find risk-taking stressful and often be too slow to take advantage of opportunities. He is also likely to be preoccupied with taking steps to maintain or increase his security. In other words, the amount of risk associated with a course of action and whether it is worth taking varies from person to person depending on his personality traits.

Because people who are high trait orientated take on greater levels of risk, they have the potential to become successful quickly. If such a person experiences a damaging setback but retains his capabilities, his exploratory nature is likely to help him recover his position. This is why it is quite common for somebody who has made a lot of money, and then lost it, to rebuild his wealth. In contrast, a person who is low trait orientated is unlikely to take the risks needed to make quick gains, so he is less likely to put himself in positions where a damaging setback may occur. His more conservative approach is likely to cause him to introduce safeguards that protect against a sudden collapse in his fortunes. If such people become successful, it is likely to be through the development and application of skills over a long period.

To help you understand the risk-taking approaches of people with high and low traits, imagine two spear fisherman, one who is high trait orientated and one who is low trait orientated. They are hunting for fish (the information). The sea is clear, but there are few fish (i.e. it is a low information environment). The fishermen will need to develop a strategy for spearing the fish and to show patience as they may go home empty handed if they act rashly. The low trait orientated fisherman will be suited to this task because he can use his Slow System skills to assess the likelihood of success and plan ahead. The high trait orientated fisherman, however, is likely to get bored because there is not enough stimulating information to occupy his Fast System. He may, therefore, become frustrated and take a risk by attempting to spear a fish that is beyond his reach and give it an opportunity to escape.

Suddenly, however, a large shoal of fish appears which massively increases the amount of information in the fishermen's environment. Because the high trait orientated fisherman has access to a wide range of schemas, he is able to take a general view of the situation, rather than focusing on detail. He will feel excited when swimming in the middle of the shoal and will be able to spear fish instinctively whilst doing so. In this situation, his more impulsive approach is more beneficial as it allows him to catch a lot of fish in a short period. Meanwhile, the low trait orientated fisherman will feel overwhelmed in the intense information environment. He will not be able to use his Slow System effectively because there will be too many fish around to carry out detailed assessments. His emotional system will recognise this impairment in functioning and interpret it as a threat, resulting in a major stress event. He will therefore retreat to quieter waters. The high trait orientated fisherman has an advantage because he will be able to finish fishing earlier and apply his energies to other activities. Use of the Fast System, however, exposes him to the risk of being compromised by an unforeseen change in his environment. If a shark is attracted to the area by the shoal of fish, he will be vulnerable to attack. The low trait orientated fisherman will be less vulnerable because fear and cautiousness will have already caused him to withdraw from the danger area.

As people vary in their sensitivity to information, a person will take on a greater level of risk in some areas than others. For example, a businessman who is high in indifference and low in openness is likely to be prepared to risk causing harm to another individual in order to win business, but be risk-averse in terms of innovation. Your particular combination of traits will set you up with your individual risk profile. In general, men are more inclined to take risks than women because they are on average higher in indifference. The trait of high indifference drives competition for the position of dominant male, and therefore mating rights, and promotes competition between different human groups. Fighters in war zones across the world still experience this primal force when putting their lives on the line. In peaceful, monogamous societies, men with high levels of indifference are likely to satisfy their appetite for risk in others ways that involve competition for dominance, such as participating in combat sports, playing war games or negotiating business deals. In contrast, the trait of low indifference discourages risk-taking by promoting harmony and collaboration.

You will gravitate towards environments that are suitable for your risk profile. However, sometimes you get trapped in inappropriate ones. For example, the culture of a group you belong to may encourage you to take what you view as excessive risks. Such a mismatch may cause you to experience stress or low moods on an on-going and long-term basis. However, once you understand your risk profile, you will be better placed to position yourself more appropriately within the group or find a more suitable alternative.

Learning styles

To learn effectively you need to engage with information in a way that suits your personality traits. In other words, your personality traits will orientate you towards a particular learning style. If you use your natural learning style you are likely to find learning a pleasant or invigorating experience. If you use a learning style that is unsuited to your personality traits, you will find the experience stressful or tiresome. You can work out your learning style by seeing which of the Fast System exploring tendencies and Slow System processing abilities set out in the table below you possess.

	HIGH	**LOW**
EXTRAVERSION	Hands On	Analytical
OPENNESS	Novelty seeking	Methodical
INDIFFERENCE	Competitive	Collaborative
OPPORTUNISM	Unstructured	Organised

If you locate yourself in an environment that is suited to your personality traits, you will be able to use your natural learning style. For example, a student who is high in extraversion and low in openness will be capable of filtering large amounts of information in the physical environment but will need to process new information methodically. He is likely to learn effectively in a workshop environment because it will enable him to take a hands-on, step-by-step approach. A student with the reverse traits will be capable of filtering large amounts of novel information but will need to process physical information analytically. This means that he is unlikely to engage physically with the environment until he has fully evaluated it. He will learn primarily by observing and thinking, and will be benefit from using teaching aids that can transmit a lot of varied information quickly, such multi-media presentations. These two students are not, therefore, suited to being taught in the same way or environment. If the first student is confronted by lots of new information in a classroom, he is likely to become stressed, as will the second student if he is forced to carry out manual tasks before being given time to think about how best to approach them. If the first student is forced to adopt an analytical approach, he is likely to become bored through lack of stimulation, as will the second student if he is required to adopt a methodical approach.

Most people will suited to dealing with average amounts of information and will be able to use different learning styles, depending on the nature of the information with which they are engaging. People in this mid-range use their Fast Systems and Slow Systems in a balanced way and build up a knowledge bank and suite of skills suited to average environments. This enables them to function well in most situations that they are likely to encounter and to maintain positive moods. People with high and/or low traits, however, will have a narrower range of learning styles and be suited to a more limited range of environments. As a consequence, they are more likely to find themselves in unsuitable learning environments in which case their acquisition of knowledge and skills will be inhibited because they will experience stress events, low moods and negative feelings when attempting to learn. People that are high in a trait are likely to feel frustrated, restless or bored when most people are feeling learning effectively. Those who are low in a trait will also struggle to learn, as they will be easily overwhelmed by new information and be prone to anxiety, chronic stress and panic. Individuals who possess multiple high and low traits will usually find it very difficult to find a suitable learning environment.

An understanding of the principles behind learning styles is particularly useful for people with extreme traits because it can enable them to identify the unusual environments in which they are suited to learn. They will not be suited to the generic teaching styles that have been developed for average people. Unfortunately, most people have little control over their learning environment at the time when they have large amounts of time to learn (i.e. when they are children). As a consequence, many students experience stress or boredom and avoid engaging with the learning process by switching off or creating a disturbance. They miss out on learning opportunities and this often limits their ability to achieve in adulthood. Schools and teachers should therefore adopt personalised approaches in relation to such children. Unfortunately, the cost of providing such tuition often deters schools and governments from investing in such children and many of them get left behind as a consequence.

Creativity

The word creativity describes the use of the learning cycle to develop new ideas, objects and experiences. Because literature, music and the visual arts are extremely flexible media, it is relatively easy for people to create works of art that are unique. However, we exercise creativity whenever we engage with and process information, and produce some form of original output as a result. For example, a plumber shows creativity when he plots the route of a new heating system in a house.

Creativity is usually associated with people with high levels of openness and opportunism because high openness compels people to engage with new experiences and ideas and high opportunism endows a person with flexibility and encourages rule breaking. Such people have the ability to filter large amounts of new information and to manipulate it without regard for existing interpretations or conventions. People who are low in openness and opportunism can be creative too. Any new idea or product developed by such a person is likely to involve less of a creative leap, though, and he will need to spend much longer processing the new information that he has generated than would a person who is high in those traits because he will feel a greater need to impose coherence and structure on it. For example, a scientist will show creativity when, for example, he suspects a link between a gene and a disease, but he may then spend several years carrying out experiments and research to validate it.

You can only be creative if your emotional system allows your Fast System to explore your information environment. When a person experiences a lack of creative inspiration, such as writer's block, he should therefore stop attempting to create and instead adopt exploratory behaviour for a while. Also, as your learning cycle will not function well when you are experiencing stress, you should locate yourself in a stress-free environment if you wish to develop new ideas and make other intuitive leaps. Consequently, brainstorming exercises work best when they are carried out in a non-judgmental environment and creative thoughts often come to us when we are relaxing or in bed.

As creativity describes the output of the learning cycle, it must involve some Slow System processing. New ideas, works of art or innovative designs are rarely of high quality or very useful until they have been refined or tested through the application of Slow System skills. People who are labelled as "highly creative" often fail to produce finished products because they lack the appropriate Slow System skills. For example, an artist who is high in openness and opportunism will not be suited to carrying out methodical and organisational tasks that are needed to get his artwork finished and to the point of sale. As a result, people whose exploratory instincts are limited often find it easier to produce artworks when working independently than those who are considered to be more creative. Professional artists usually seek the support of people who possess skills that they lack, such as agents. A conceptual artist may sub-contract the whole of the physical production of his artwork to a fabricator.

People who are highly exploratory in their behaviour and/or capable of producing fine detail often behave quite differently from most other people because they will have extreme traits that endow them with blind spots and/or no-go areas. They will be susceptible to stress and low moods in average environments, and their strong biases towards particular environments and limited range of learning styles may inhibit their development. As a result, although such a person may have the potential to produce work, deliver performances or take action that is considered by members of wider society to be a product of genius, visionary or heroic, in many cases his potential will remain unfulfilled or his work will not be recognised as valuable. Such people are therefore often viewed as eccentrics, wasters or troublemakers.

The impact of your wider environment

Mood swings and baselines

Although you can only experience one level of arousal at any time, your arousal level and feelings can change instantaneously as information enters or leaves your environment. A good example is air travel, where you can flip from boredom to fear when the plane experiences turbulence. Changes in information levels can also affect your mood.

People with middling traits will not usually experience pronounced mood swings because they are suited to operating in average environments. A person with extreme traits may, though, experience wild mood swings exhibit very changeable behaviour, especially if he possesses high and low traits. At times, he will be located in environments that suit his traits and he will experience extreme very positive feelings. However, as such environments are unusual these feelings will often be short-lived. As the information levels within his environment revert to normal, negative feelings will reappear.

As personality traits are lifelong characteristics and because most people operate within stable environments, people tend to have **baseline** levels of arousal in respect of each trait spectrum. Transitory information that they encounter in their immediate environment during their day-to-day experiences will move their arousal levels up and down from their baselines for short periods. For example, a person may get a buzz of excitement when he completes a task or feel disappointed if he loses a tennis match. However, he will normally return quickly to his baseline mood.

If all your baselines are located centrally within your optimal ranges, you will be primed to operate in a state of flow. You will be able to deal with situations that will moderately increase or reduce your arousal level without being pushed outside those ranges. If, however, one or more of your baselines is located near one of the boundaries of these ranges, it will take only a small environmental change to shift you into the stress zone or low moods zone. You are likely to experience negative feelings and bad moods more frequently in such circumstances and behave unpredictably. If one of your baselines is located in the stress zone or low moods zone, you will experience negative feelings most of the time. For example, a person who is high in extraversion but low in opportunism will be suited to a sales role in a corporation so if he secures this position, his baselines are likely to be centrally located within his optimal ranges. If, however, he decides to do a degree in marketing his baselines are likely to shift towards the boundaries of his optimal ranges as he will be obliged to spend more time on his own in a less structured environment. As a consequence he is likely to experience stress and low moods.

A person who has a baseline located in the stress zone will find himself stuck in a state of panic or chronic stress. He will be forced into fire fighting mode and will lack time and space to plan a way out. Many people who work in high-pressure environments or struggle with family responsibilities find themselves in this situation. A person who has a baseline located in the low moods zone will at least be able to access his Slow System to plan an escape. However, the fact it is so located will suggest that he lacks support from other people to resolve a stress event or overpower a suppressive force. In other words, his environment may prevent him from implementing any solution he comes up with, condemning him to a persistent low mood.

A person with a high trait who is trapped in an environment with low amounts of information relating to that trait may try to engineer an escape by throwing himself into a new project or generating a more favourable imaginary environment. For example, a person with a high level of extraversion will be adventurous by nature but may be forced to take a desk job in order to support his family. This is likely to cause him to experience suppression. He may then start to plan a foreign adventure. He will be able to generate strong positive feelings by envisioning a successful trip. However, he is likely to be brought back down to earth by the realisation that his plans are not feasible while he has family responsibilities. People who are high in openness and opportunism (typically highly creative people) find it particularly difficult to fit into traditional working environments as they are motivated by novelty and change. They feel trapped when required to act methodically or obey rules, and suffer from suppression as a result. They will have a tendency to act impulsively in order to change their circumstances. The projects that they begin, however, are often doomed to failure because such people do not possess the methodical or organisational skills that are needed to make their projects sustainable. People who are trapped in unfavourable environments and who temporarily succeed in generating highs by divorcing themselves from reality, but then drop into deep despair when the bubble that they have created bursts, are often diagnosed with bipolar disorder (also known as "manic depression").

Some people have lifestyles that cause levels of information within their environments to change on an hour-to-hour basis. For example, a mother with a career has to juggle her working role and childcare. Such people are less likely to have discernable baseline moods. The lack of predictability in their behaviour may make it more difficult for people around them to establish and maintain good relationships with them.

The Big Five personality model includes a spectrum called **neuroticism**, which is sometimes referred to as "emotional stability". These two descriptions refer to opposite ends of the spectrum (i.e. someone who is low in neuroticism will be high in emotional stability and vice versa). According to the Big Five model, we each have a default position on the neuroticism spectrum. In good times, your mood will brighten while at other times you will feel low, but you will return to this default position. People who are high in neuroticism are more likely to be moody and to experience negative feelings such as anxiety, worry, fear, anger, frustration, envy, jealousy, guilt, depressed mood and loneliness. Therefore, if your neighbour appears happier and more emotionally stable than you, it is likely that he would be positioned lower on the spectrum than you if you both took the Big Five personality test.

In my opinion, the creation of a neuroticism spectrum was misguided. You experience negative feelings either because you are located in an inappropriate environment or have experienced loss in some form. If your environment is difficult to change for the better or your loss is hard to recover from, one or more of your baselines are likely to be located in the stress or low moods zones. This would cause you to report consistent results in respect of neuroticism. However, this does not mean that neuroticism should be treated as a fixed personality trait. Indeed, it is unhelpful to make such a claim as it suggests to a person who scores high in neuroticism that the negative feelings he is experiencing are inherent in his make up rather than a result of an environmental mismatch, mistake or misfortune. He is therefore likely to be deterred from attempting to make the environmental changes that could return him to operation within his optimal ranges.

Confidence and optimism

Confidence is a measure of your belief in your ability to perform well within a particular environment. If you are located in an environment that allows you to operate within your optimal range for a sustained period, you are likely to be effective and feel confident. People who are high trait orientated tend to appear more confident than people who are low trait orientated because their exploratory natures and instinctive reactions are more noticeable. People who are low trait orientated usually appear less confident because they take time to process information in detail before making decisions. However, the latter can exude a quiet confidence when they locate themselves in environments suited to the exercise of their Slow System skills, for example when a lawyer opines in his office. In such an environment, a person who is high trait orientated is likely to feel less confident as he will lack the detailed knowledge and analytical skills to speak with authority.

If your performance level drops because you are located in an unsuitable environment, forced to undertake tasks to which you are unsuited or required to use skills that you have not developed sufficiently, you will lose confidence in your ability to some degree. If you are subject to a suppressive force, you will need to relocate yourself to a more suitable environment. For example, a person who is high in indifference is likely to be lacking in confidence in an environment that requires the use of empathy, such as a primary school, because he will lack that skill and experience suppression if he tries to develop it. He will therefore need to relocate himself to an environment focused around competitive activity, such as a professional sports club. In the case of a stressor, you will need to retreat to a safe space where you can resolve the stress event, enhance your skills and practice. For example, when a football striker experiences a goal drought, he is likely to lose confidence. Strikers operate instinctively because they need to act very quickly. When they are under pressure to score, though, they are likely to try too hard, using their Slow Systems to exert more control over the ball. However, this causes them to react too slowly and mistime the ball. Goal droughts are normally ended when the striker scores a lucky goal, which instantly increases his confidence, or after he has rebuilt his confidence through practice in the less pressurised environment of the reserve team.

You consciously and subconsciously assess your ability to survive and prosper in any environment on the basis of your previous experiences, your interpretation of your abilities, and what you believe other people think of you. These expectations and assessments increase or reduce your sensitivity to information and effectively shift your optimal range up or down the relevant trait spectrum. An upward shift represents an increase in confidence and a downward one a decrease in confidence.

Psychologists call negative self-assessments **limiting beliefs**. They cause a person to experience a stress event at a lower level of information than his personality traits would normally dictate, and therefore increase his susceptibility to panic, chronic stress and anxiety. This causes him to act more conservatively than he would otherwise do. Limiting beliefs can sometimes be perfectly reasonable, and indeed helpful. It is, for example, not sensible for a man of limited stature to get involved in a physical fight unless he has acquired some expertise in martial arts or has some other compensating attribute. However, many of us retain limiting beliefs that were acquired early in life and which have little basis in reality. For example, a person may assume that he has no musical ability because of a negative school report, but that report may have been the result of poor teaching.

People who grow up in supportive environments or who are naturally gifted benefit from the reverse dynamic. They can hold very positive opinions as to their abilities, which I will term **enabling beliefs**. They cause a person to experience a stress event at a higher level of information and therefore encourage him to act more adventurously than his personality traits would normally dictate. If a person is blessed with particularly high mental capacity or impressive physical attributes or has been educated to a high level, he is likely to experience less stress in his life than an average person because his superior abilities or attractiveness will help him to cope better with information in his environment. In other words, because he is unlikely to experience major stress events, he can dive into the unknown with the confidence that he will be able to deal with most threats that he is likely to encounter.

People without such advantages may also hold enabling beliefs if they grow up in privileged environments or are encouraged to believe that they will be successful. Even if such a belief is not founded on any natural ability, the confidence that it engenders may itself prove to be an asset, as it will make a person more attractive to others and encourage people to trust him. Such a belief, however, amounts to over-confidence. A person who is over-confident will be operating beyond his natural capability and is likely to make mistakes or errors of judgment. He will be prone to bullshitting and other behaviours that betray his lack of ability. At some point, he is likely to encounter a situation that he does not have the ability to cope with and which has serious consequences. Employers tend to favour confident applicants and employees. However, an employer should be aware that a person who displays confidence could hold an inflated opinion of his abilities and could, therefore, expose the employer's business to unnecessary risk.

It should now be clear that there is no such thing as a universally confident person. If you perceive a person to be confident, it is likely that either you are seeing him in an environment to which he is suited or that he is deceiving you, consciously or sub-consciously. In other circumstances, it is likely that he would lack confidence. For example, a soldier may be confident when surrounded by members of his platoon, but he may lack confidence when required to perform the role of husband or father.

When assisting a person who lacks confidence, it is necessary to assess whether that lack of confidence is well founded or due to the presence of an unjustified limiting belief. If a counsellor attempts to increase the confidence of a person who is ill suited to his environment, that person is likely to become over-confident and expose himself to increased risk of harm. For example, a person who is low in indifference will not be suited to operating in confrontational environments. If he is encouraged to be more assertive, he may function better in such environments in the short term, but he is likely to be out-competed by rivals who are higher in indifference in the longer term because he will not be able to perform to their level. However, if the counsellor takes the same approach with a person who has underestimated his ability, he may restore him to normal functioning.

Whereas confidence relates to your ability to perform within your current and anticipated environment, **optimism** is a general feeling that things will turn out well. People who are high trait orientated are naturally optimistic because they enjoy engaging with and exploring new information. They experience feelings of enjoyment and exhilaration when doing so and do not worry about what the future holds. In contrast, people who are low trait orientated tend to be **realistic** in their outlooks. This is because they are prone to experience major stress events in average or high information environments and therefore need to be more wary about the future. Low trait orientated people can still look forward positively, but they will first need to identify possible risks and be comfortable that suitable protective measures are in place. Consequently, their positivity will be constrained by a need to act cautiously, methodically, empathetically or in an organised way.

A realistic outlook may appear pessimistic to a person who is high trait orientated because he will feel constrained by the more conservative approach of the low trait orientated person. In contrast, a person who is low trait orientated is likely to see a person who is high trait orientated as complacent or reckless. As most people possess high and low traits, an individual is likely to be optimistic in some circumstances and realistic in others depending on his environment.

Both optimism and realism are associated with operation within your optimal ranges. However, if a person is forced to operate for long periods outside his optimal ranges, he will experience sustained negative feelings and is likely to look fearfully or with resignation into the future. If there is a present danger, he is likely to be experiencing chronic stress or panic and will struggle to look beyond the immediate threat. If he is experiencing a low mood, he is likely to adopt a **pessimistic** outlook.

People who have one or more high traits are particularly susceptible to pessimism as they are likely to experience states of low negative arousal more often than an average person. Bad things are more likely to happen to a person who is pessimistic, but only because his pessimism will be a reflection of a mismatch between his personality traits and his environment, and therefore his reduced performance level. Some people believe pessimism can be remedied by a determination to think positively. However, pessimism usually results from a suppressive force or an unresolved loss so these issues will need to be addressed if a sustainable solution is to be found.

Pessimism can be banished by **hope**. The act of hoping for a better future can be sufficient to lift a person out of a state of listlessness and increase his level of performance. Hope is, however, essentially a desire for positive change in circumstances where there are no realistic means of securing it. A person's circumstances are only likely to change for the better if hope is combined with actions aimed at securing such change. Authoritarian leaders try to extinguish hope amongst their enemies by ruthlessly dealing with any dissent. By reducing people to a state of hopelessness, such a leader deprives them of them of energy and motivation to overthrow him.

ASD and ADHD

Autism spectrum disorder (**ASD**) is a condition that affects social interaction, communication, interests and behaviour. It includes Asperger syndrome. The main features of ASD typically start to develop in childhood, although their impact may not be apparent until there is a significant change in the person's life. In the UK, it is estimated that about one in every 100 people has ASD. **Attention deficit hyperactivity disorder** (**ADHD**) is a term used to describe people who are inattentive, impulsive and/ or hyperactive. ADHD is the most common behavioural disorder in the UK. Estimates suggest if affects around 2 - 5% of young people. However, practitioners find it difficult to diagnose ASD and ADHD because they are defined quite widely, encompassing a wide range of symptoms. Also, although current medical practice dictates that ADHD cannot be diagnosed if it occurs solely within the context of a pervasive developmental disorder such as autism, there is no agreement as to the relationship between ASD and ADHD.

The picture becomes clearer if you look at ASD and ADHD in the context of personality traits. ASD and ADHD each describe a broad category of behaviours that are associated with very low traits and very high traits respectively. Autistic characteristics – introversion, narrow and intense focus, empathy and a dependence on structure - align with characteristics of people who are very low in extraversion, openness, indifference and opportunism respectively. Characteristics associated with ADHD – hyperactivity, lack of focus, lack of concern for the interests of others and impulsivity - align with characteristics of people who are very high in extraversion, openness, indifference and opportunism respectively. While a person with an extremely low trait will not display characteristics associated with a person who is very high in that trait, he may be high in another trait. In other words, there is no reason why a person should not have some genes that cause him to display characteristics of ASD and others that cause him to display characteristics of ADHD. This may explain why a false belief has arisen that autistic people lack empathy. A person may be autistic in respect of information relating to the spectrum of extraversion, openness or opportunism, but also possess the trait of high in indifference and therefore lack empathy. However, if a person is autistic in respect of information relating to the spectrum of indifference, he will be naturally empathetic. Such a person may not, though, be able to express empathy well due to poor social skills, a lack of understanding of his environment or the high level of stress that he is prone to experience.

A person with ASD will at times display disruptive behaviours of a type that are commonly associated with ADHD. This is because he will usually have a higher arousal level that the people around him and is therefore likely to experience anxiety, chronic stress or panic on a regular basis. Similarly, a person with ADHD may display withdrawn behaviours of a type that are commonly associated with ASD. This is because when he lacks stimulation, for example where is forced to remain in a low information environment, he will be susceptible to low moods. The key to understanding whether disruptive or withdrawn behaviour is associated with ASD or ADHD is appreciating the patient's mood. A person who is enjoying being disruptive is likely to have a high trait and therefore ADHD whereas a person who is experiencing negative feelings is likely to have ASD. Likewise, a person appears to be content in a low information environment is likely to have ASD, whereas if he appears down he may have ADHD.

Both ASD and ADHD are more commonly diagnosed in males than females, and in some studies the difference is very great. If one was to consider personality only, more women should have ASD than men because they are more likely to be low in indifference. It is likely that many females who are very sensitive to disharmony are not diagnosed with ASD because sensitivity and meekness are behaviours that traditionally have been seen as appropriate for females. Other reasons for the gender split have also been proposed including other genetic differences and the assertion that women and girls are better at masking or camouflaging their difficulties. Overly competitive behaviour is a characteristic of high indifference. It is not, therefore, surprising that childhood ADHD is more commonly diagnosed in boys than girls. Girls are more likely to work collaboratively than to compete with each other because of their lower levels of indifference. Girls with ADHD are, though, more likely to have an attention deficit than be hyperactive so they are more likely to slip under the radar where educational standards are poor.

Some scientists and pressure groups have linked ASD and ADHD to the use of particular medications, vaccines, cleaning products and pesticides. While there appears to be no evidence that vaccines have had an effect, it would surprise few people if the ingestion of manmade chemicals by mothers were proved to have an effect on the development of unborn children. Mating will sometimes combine genes in a way that produces disabilities. The behaviour of parents during conception and pregnancy, medical interventions and diets may contribute to ASD or ADHD in some cases.

Too many people in modern society are, though, being diagnosed with ASD or ADHD. Practitioners tend to focus their attention on fitting individuals into particular medical categories rather than looking for environmental causes for their behaviours. Parents tend to feel more comfortable once inappropriate behaviours are aligned with a particular condition as a diagnosis relieves them of feelings of guilt and allows them to pass some responsibility for their child's care to health professionals. However, the increase in diagnoses of ADHD most likely results from the sedentary and controlled environment in which we live. Increased focus on academic achievement at the expense of physical exercise and the development of manual skills, and an overprotective health and safety culture, prevent many children with high traits from engaging in explorative activities. It is also not surprising that more children are displaying behaviours associated with ASD. In modern, individualistic society, children are exposed to adult issues much earlier than in previous generations and often lack safe spaces in which they can develop their social skills. As a result, their emotional systems may cause them to withdraw from everyday life and focus on the development of Slow System skills, the exercise of which gives them comfort. A diagnosis of ASD or ADHD may be damaging to a child because it may embed limiting beliefs in his mind. It may also deter parents from making changes to their lifestyles that would help to create a more suitable environment for the child to develop within.

Some people have severe ASD or ADHD, which renders them unable to function independently within normal society. It is, however, too easy to ignore the positive aspects of these conditions. People with ASD or ADHD can still make valuable contributions to society. Historically, some societies tolerated and even venerated people with ADHD. For example, the Vikings put up with the disruptive activities of those of their number with uncontrollable, aggressive tendencies because they also excelled in battle. The word "berserk" comes from the Norse language and describes the activities of such people. Similarly, it is likely that some people with ASD would have found their way into monasteries where the controlled and safe environment would have allowed their exceptional eye for detail to be exercised in the production of highly decorated religious manuscripts. However, people who possess very low or very high traits, or have a combination of both, are much more unlikely to be able to function within society without interventions from mental health and other support services.

Many people possess a high or low trait that makes it difficult for them to fit in within certain environments or perform certain tasks. If this does not apply to you, it will certainly apply to a family member or friend. Although such people may display unusual or eccentric characteristics at times, they are generally accepted within society. Viewing ASD and ADHD from the perspective of personality traits can be enlightening because it allows us to consider the circumstances of people with these conditions without using the prism of disability. It enables us to recognise that such people possess abilities that are unsuited to the environment in which they are forced to inhabit. Instead of focusing on their weaknesses and marking them out as different, we should try to find ways to integrate them within society and make use of their attributes.

No man (or woman) is an island

It should be clear by now that the gifts our personality traits endow us with are balanced by deficiencies. If a person has a high or low trait, his ability to engage with certain types of information or perform certain tasks will be limited. Even a person who is located in the centre of each of the four personality spectrums will have weaknesses. He will find it relatively easy to cope with day-to-day situations, but is unlikely to make important discoveries or demonstrate great insight or wisdom. We, therefore, need to work with others if we are to achieve our goals.

In an effective group of people, group members will take on responsibilities and perform tasks that suit their personality traits. An appropriate balance will be achieved between exploratory and controlling behaviours. The optimistic outlooks of people with high traits will be restrained by the realism of individuals with low traits. In other words, a group culture with a particular risk profile will be established, the characteristics of which will reflect the environment in which the group operates and the group's objectives.

A person who has a high trait is likely to deal with threats associated with information relating to that trait as he comes across them because of his superior ability to filter such information. By doing so, he increases his productivity, but he also increases the likelihood of him missing an important detail that could have unexpected and damaging consequences. He will benefit from working with a person who is low in that trait and therefore capable of recognising and assessing such risks. People with low traits therefore play useful supporting roles. People who are low in extraversion identify risks in the physical environment through analysis; those who are low in openness identify risks posed by new processes and strangers by applying methodology and identifying inconsistencies; people who are low in indifference identify risks to relationships or individuals by using empathy; and those who are low in opportunism identify risks to structures by embedding routines or spotting organisational flaws. However, people with low traits need people with high traits to protect them from high levels of information so they can operate their Slow Systems effectively. If they lack access to safe spaces, they are likely to suffer from chronic stress, panic or anxiety. Therefore, the relationship between people with high and low traits is symbiotic. However, it is also much more nuanced than set out here because, as we shall see in the later chapter covering relationships, people with middling traits will often act as intermediaries between people with opposing traits.

Groups play a critical role in our lives. We have evolved to live in groups and use our talents and skills for the benefit of such groups. Even though most humans have transitioned from living in small groups to being citizens within national or international societies, our basic genetic programming remains unchanged. How we operate within groups differs from person to person depending on individual personality traits, but the need to commune still exists within us all. It is, therefore, necessary to look in more detail at the relationship between groups and personality. Before that, however, I will discuss the influence of the human mind on our feelings and behaviour.

6

THE POWER OF THE MIND

Decision making and problem solving

Logic and rationality

Historically, philosophers, psychologists and scientists have treated the human mind as a distinct unit, uninvolved in the generation of emotions. The mind was considered to be rational and controlling, whereas emotions were seen as spontaneous and unpredictable. We are still a long way from understanding how the human mind works at a biological level. It should be clear, though, from the previous chapters that your mind is fully integrated with your emotional system.

Humans and other animals are essentially decision makers and problem solvers. Your emotional system encourages you to explore and learn, but in a way and at a speed that is suited to your particular personality traits. You are constantly making decisions as to which information you should engage with and whether to take risks or act defensively. You acquire knowledge and understanding as a result of the learning process, and store it in your memory. Scientists use the term **cognition** to describe the processes by which our minds acquire and apply knowledge and understanding.

Your emotional system compels you to eliminate negative feelings and relocate yourself in an environment that will allow you to experience positive feelings on a sustainable basis. In other words, your primary objective in life is to find a way of operating within your optimal ranges so that your learning cycle can operate effectively. Humans have developed sophisticated thinking processes, but when you are experiencing negative feelings you will tend to revert to instinctive emotional responses to relieve them. If you experience a stress event, your fight or flight mechanism will be activated and your Fast System is likely to make decisions for you. You will use your Slow System processing capabilities once the immediate danger has passed. If you experience sadness, your emotional system encourages you to seek help from your supportive group. If you feel bored, it will prompt you to move to a more stimulating environment.

Once you are positioned within a suitable environment, you can start to use your learning cycle to explore and consolidate information. If you are in the exploratory stage, you will be using your Fast System to filter information and deploy schemas. Your decision-making will be guided by the feelings of enjoyment and exhilaration that you experience when you deploy a schema that fits well with your environment. If you are in the consolidation stage, you will activate your Slow System to process information. You will use your Slow System skills to assess logically the merits of different options, and choose the one that appears to be most beneficial. Your decision-making will be guided by the feelings of contentment and fulfilment that you experience when you resolve the associated stress event.

Logic can be defined as "reasoning conducted or assessed according to strict principles of validity" and **rationality** as "the quality of being based on or in accordance with reason or logic". Both logic and rationality are associated with use of the Slow System. Your ability to make rational decisions and solve problems using logic will, though, depend on your expertise, knowledge and processing ability as dictated by your personality traits. Expertise is developed through learning and practice. We gain knowledge through experience, observation, study and problem solving.

Each of the four low traits contributes towards logical thinking. Low extraversion prompts analysis, low openness encourages methodical approaches and low opportunism promotes organisation. Low indifference is less obviously associated with logic as it encourages empathy and caring. Some models of personality associate the reverse trait, high indifference (roughly equivalent to the "Thinking" trait in the Myers Briggs model or "Low agreeableness" in the Big Five Model) with logical thinking. This is because a lack of concern for the interests of other people helps a person to focus on systems, processes and inanimate objects, the actions of which are easier to predict than those of other people. This helps people who are high in indifference appear more rational. Also, people who are high in indifference experience less stress than those who are low in indifference and therefore sometimes better placed to make rational decisions. However, in reality, analytical thinking is associated with the trait of low extraversion. Humans have evolved to promote the survival of groups and are not equipped to survive independently from each other. In situations where a group is threatened, the group may need a leader who can act ruthlessly in the short term, but the group will be unsustainable unless vulnerable people who are capable of making future contributions to the group are protected and supported, especially its younger members. It is, therefore, rational to care for others.

Accuracy and completeness

The application of schemas enables you to take shortcuts. A person who employs schemas well may be described as having a **sixth sense**, appearing to have a natural ability to know about things before other people or make correct decisions when others cannot make up their minds. However, although schemas can improve your decision-making ability by freeing up capacity in your mind, they are unlikely to be 100% accurate. The more schemas that you create, the more likely that your Fast System will apply an appropriate one, but the fact that they have been created in response to previous stress events leaves scope for error.

You will be prone to making errors when you are highly stressed because chronic stress or panic indicates that you are operating beyond your optimal ranges. By remaining in the vicinity of the stressor, you deny yourself access to your Slow System. You will not be able to solve problems through the application of logic or create and adapt schemas. You will therefore be forced to apply ill-fitting schemas, your effectiveness will be reduced and you are likely to experience fear. You may also exhibit behaviour that is inappropriate, erratic or dangerous to others or yourself. You will have experienced the application of an ill-fitting schema if you have ever mistaken an inanimate object for a human figure when walking down a dark alley at night. In the absence of sufficient information to identify the object, your Fast System will have applied a schema associated with the most likely danger – a potential aggressor. You, therefore, thought you saw a person, but when you got closer, you realised it was a rubbish bin or a sign.

The Slow System tends to deliver more accurate results than the Fast System because it develops a bespoke solution. However, even when conditions allow you to activate your Slow System, it may still struggle to achieve an accurate result if it lacks access to relevant information, if you possess one or more blind spots or if you have not invested time and effort in developing Slow System skills.

Your Slow System can only make sense of the information that it has at its disposal. If you do not have enough information to resolve a problem, you will need to acquire further knowledge and then process it. For example, if you cannot assemble a tent, you will need to read the instructions. If you make decisions or calculations on the basis of incorrect, biased or incomplete information, the results are likely to be flawed. It is, therefore, important to keep exposing yourself to new information, and to process it effectively, to expand and refine your knowledge base.

Young people have less experience to draw upon than older people, but they will learn quickly if they are located in environments suited to their learning styles. Older people have a greater amount of knowledge that they can use as a basis for their decisions.

However, their energy levels drop as they age and they tend to embed themselves within static environments. As a result, they have a greater tendency to rely on existing schemas and knowledge. In a fast-moving world, these resources can quickly become out-dated. People of any age who avoid exposure to new ideas and experiences or fail to devote sufficient time to developing Slow System skills will, though, be prone to making errors of judgment.

If you possess a blind spot on a trait spectrum, you will not employ reasoning skills related to the low trait in that spectrum. As leading males are usually high in indifference, they tend to possess blind spots on the indifference spectrum. Therefore, male-dominated groups do not usually apply the caring element of rationality. This is why males tend to resort to violence and the projection of power to resolve problems, and to make decisions that lack compassion. Men have suppressed the voices of women over the whole of recorded history. As a result, the caring element of logical reasoning has been under-represented within human governance mechanisms. When men act aggressively, a vicious circle is created because the confrontational environments that they create make it harder for most women to operate beyond the domestic environment without experiencing major stress events. The influence of females generally (and that of males who are low in indifference) therefore further reduces within the wider group. As a consequence, it is very hard to negotiate an end to war once it has begun. Usually, conflicts only end when one side has overpowered the other or the parties have exhausted themselves.

You develop Slow System skills through training, experience and practise. If you have not invested sufficient time in developing them, you are likely to make processing errors. For example, people find it much harder to do mental arithmetic and similar tasks these days as they depend upon calculators and computers to carry out basic methodical processes. Consequently, a new employee in a sandwich shop without an electronic till is likely to struggle to work out the amount of change to give to customers.

You may need to make a decision or solve a problem before your Slow System has had the opportunity to complete its tasks. If you lack processing time, you are likely to be forced back into Fast System operation before you have eliminated all inconsistencies and errors. As your arousal level increases, you may experience anxiety or frustration and your ability to exercise Slow System skills is inhibited. This explains why you sometimes struggle to solve a problem only to find that the answer pops into your head later in the day while you're making a cup of coffee or when you are lying in bed. You put too much pressure on yourself to find a solution and this increases your arousal level. The moment of inspiration – an **'aha' moment** – occurs when you have relocated yourself to a low information environment that gives your Slow System space to process information subconsciously. When you struggle to recall information from your memory or work out a problem, it is therefore usually beneficial to take a break to give your Slow System the opportunity to trawl your memory banks or apply reasoning skills. If you are forced to return to a high information environment before you have completed Slow System processing, you are likely to experience chronic stress or panic if the relevant stressor remains within your environment. You are therefore likely to struggle to make a good decision or find a suitable way forward.

Decisions involve choices between options. The outcomes of these options will not necessarily be predictable as they may be influenced by people and events over whom and which you have little influence. Although you can increase the chances of a particular event occurring by taking action in support of the desired outcome, you can rarely be certain that it will occur when and how you want it to. The accuracy of your calculations will increase if you use your Slow System, others things being equal. However, the additional time you need to reach a Slow System decision may allow other factors to intervene that are out of your control and which render your conclusion inappropriate or obsolete. Accuracy can therefore come at a cost. Not all calculations need to be 100% correct. Sometimes, the big picture is more important. For example, a man may spend a long time working out the best way to approach a woman he finds attractive. Another man is, however, likely to dive straight in, instinctively recognising that establishing a basic relationship is more important in the first instance and that minor details can probably be sorted out later. Such an approach is likely to result in some failures, but also more successes.

Therefore, although decision-making is inherently risky, so is delaying or avoiding the making of decisions. People who are high trait orientated are likely to act impulsively and ignore details, moving forward quickly so that they can seize opportunities. They can see the big picture and are more likely to make good decisions in high information environments. As a result, their greater level of risk-taking may pay dividends. Sometimes though, their impulsiveness will get them into trouble, causing them to make serious errors or jump out of the frying pan into the fire. They are unlikely to take advantage of opportunities to check the validity of their decisions because they will experience suppression if forced to engage in deep processing. In contrast, people with low traits are inclined to make rational, considered decisions. They have a tendency to seek perfection, spending a long time processing small details to avoid making a mistake and reduce their anxiety levels. Such delay can, though, reduce their chances of success, giving people with higher traits who can see the big picture the opportunity to step in and reap the rewards, or prevent them from dealing with other important tasks that are necessary to move a project forward or meet deadlines. In high information environments, they will have a limited range of schemas to choose from, and are likely to become stressed, freeze or make inappropriate decisions.

People with high or low traits may though find particular niches where they can excel. Leaders and their groups will benefit from the input of generalists and specialists. In other words, we are more likely to make good decisions if we involve people encompassing the full range of personality traits within the decision-making process. The fact that humans have evolved to make decisions in groups is illustrated by the principle of the **wisdom of the crowd**, which states that the collective opinion of a group of individuals is more likely to be correct than that of a single person. This principle is embedded within justice systems in the form of juries. It only holds true, however, when people with a range of personalities are free to make decisions without influence from others. Where a dominant individual or sub-group emerges within a group, the opinions of other group members may be swayed or overruled. Where a sub-group consists of people with similar personalities, an unhealthy narrowing of perspective is likely to occur which has become known as **groupthink**. In an unusual environment, however, a person with extreme traits who is suited to that environment may be better suited to making decisions on behalf of the group because of his greater ability to operate effectively in such circumstances.

Sometimes, groups allow different options to be explored at the same time. If an individual follows his natural instincts rather than following the path of the majority of group members, he may make discoveries that ultimately benefit the group or take action that increases its security. If his efforts do not bring any rewards, the loss to the group is likely to be minimal in the context of the efforts of the remainder of the group. However, if too many people plough their own furrows, an individualistic culture will develop and the group will become incoherent and lose effectiveness.

The individualistic nature of modern society gives free rein to people with high traits and encourages people in general to make impulsive decisions for their own immediate enjoyment. However, if we expect to receive support and protection from groups, we should factor the interests of other group members into our decisions. Selfish decisions undermine groups and therefore disadvantage the decision-maker as well as other group members in the long-term. A balance is needed, though. Groups that tightly constrain self-interested behaviours tend to stagnate and lose competitiveness. The dynamics of groups will be discussed in more detail in the following chapter.

Facts, opinions and beliefs

Your ability to solve problems and make good decisions depends greatly on the quality of information to which you have access in your environment, memory and other knowledge resources. This information can be divided into three categories: facts, opinions and beliefs. A **fact** is something that is known or proved to be true. An **opinion** is a view or judgment formed about something, not necessarily based on fact or knowledge. A **belief** is an acceptance that something exists or is true, which does not rely on proof. Most people will know the difference between these terms without needing to read these definitions. However, it is often more difficult to distinguish between a fact, opinion and belief in real life.

You use your Slow System skills to form opinions about situations and other people. Once formed, you will save them as schemas. You may also take on the opinions of other people as schemas without questioning their validity. Opinions that are saved as schemas are helpful because they increase your ability to filter information, thereby allowing you to maintain Fast System operation. For example, you would instinctively trust a police officer to keep an eye on a pushbike for a couple of minutes, whereas it is likely that you would have to engage an analytical process before trusting a stranger in the same circumstances. This is because you have previously formed an opinion that police officers are trustworthy. We categorise people and form opinions about them because, if we were to assess the reliability of every person we come across using our Slow Systems, we would be overwhelmed with information and we would become much less effective. However, opinions serve us less well when they are based or incorrect, incomplete or out-dated information.

Beliefs go one step further than opinions. They leave no doubt or room for compromise in your mind. This certainty releases you from worry and allows you to spend more time and energy on other matters. However, the comfort and security that beliefs provide can cause their holders to defend them vigorously. Where beliefs are backed up by historic writings and centuries of practice, they can become embedded within societal culture, particularly where they are difficult to disprove, as is the case with religious beliefs.

We live in an information-rich world so, even if you have the inclination, you will often lack the time needed to check whether a statement is true. You need a compass to navigate this sea of information, so you identify sources of information that you consider to be trustworthy. You are likely to store information from such sources in your memory without questioning or testing it. If information comes from more dubious sources, you may reject it, carry out some research to validate it, or store it with reservations as to its accuracy. However, trusted sources do not always deliver accurate information. We naturally trust our parents, but sometimes they tell us falsehoods because it is convenient for them to do so or because they have not verified the information themselves. Wealthy individuals purchase news organisations with the intention of influencing the opinions and behaviour of ordinary people. Concern not to offend advertisers or government also constrains editorial freedom. Powerful cliques can also emerge within news organisations and impose editorial bias on their output. Sometimes, people or organisations tell outright lies. Such dishonesty is likely to result in them losing the confidence and respect of the public if proved. Many statements, though, have an element of truth but are presented in a way that is favourable to the publisher's interests. Often this is achieved by use of exaggeration or the failure to report facts that would lead the viewer to question the statement's validity. This latter approach has been described as being "economical with the truth". Truth is therefore often coloured by an opinion or belief.

Much of what we say falls into the category of opinion or belief, as we hold a lot of information in our heads that we cannot be certain is true. Opinions and beliefs are often influenced by a person's value system, which will be a product of his background, life experiences and personality traits. By expressing them, we hope to nudge societal culture towards our personal values, and therefore increase our chances of being effective and happy. Facts, on the other hand, can point to inconvenient truths that may compromise our ability to achieve such a state. Political debate often revolves around opinions and beliefs, rather than facts, because politicians tend to be ideologically driven and do not wish the impact of their message to be undermined by contradictory evidence or inconvenient truths.

The possession of a high trait inclines a person to have broad-based and flexible opinions in relation to information related to that trait. People with high traits are likely to make sweeping statements as they see the big picture and may get carried away with enthusiasm because they are enjoying themselves. Their actions tend to be driven by desire, not fear, so they will be inclined to adapt their opinions for personal gain. They are likely to feel frustrated or experience suppression when they are obliged to engage with detail or are constrained by strict values. They may, therefore, be dismissive of opinions of experts. Consequently, people who are high in extraversion like to position themselves at the centre of debates and are likely to adopt opinions that enhance their status or wealth. Those who are high in openness embrace new ideas and theories, and are therefore likely to appreciate other points of view. People who are high in indifference tend to promote arguments because, by doing so, they raise the tension level within their environment and increase their level of enjoyment. Finally, those who are high in opportunism tend to take contrary positions as they enjoy challenging societal rules.

In contrast, people with low traits tend to hold fixed values. They will be cautious in expressing opinions and will generally prefer to deal in facts. People who are low in extraversion use their analytical skills to give measured opinions and promote caution, those who are low in openness use their methodical skills to make their opinions more coherent, people who are low in indifference moderate opinions with compassion, and those who are low in opportunism will give opinions structure and try to establish them as rules. However, people with low traits can get bogged down in detail, attributing too much importance to factors that in the great scheme of things will probably have little influence on objectives and outcomes. This can slow down the opinion-forming process, reducing their ability to debate issues in real time. People with low traits are therefore usually more suited to presenting their opinions in written reports. They also tend to see things in simplistic, black and white terms, especially when they are stressed. In such circumstances, they are likely to resort to stereotypes, adopt uncompromising positions, find refuge in beliefs or react angrily when confronted with challenging opinions. For example, because scientists are usually low in openness, the scientific community has at times been guilty of conflating fact with belief and marginalising scientists who have challenged current assumptions. Charles Darwin kept his theory of evolution secret for 20 years for fear of the reaction of the scientific establishment because it contradicted Christian teachings. Therefore, even people who spend their lives developing expertise can be resistant to new information generated by other experts. Where such a person works in the same field, he may also dismiss new information for fear that his professional standing may be diminished.

Humans often seek out information that confirms their own opinions and beliefs, a practice that psychologists call **confirmation bias**. Doing so helps a person to convince himself that he understands the forces at play within his environment, thereby increasing his sense of security and confidence. The Internet enables people to engage in confirmation bias by joining social media groups that are aligned to their opinions and beliefs, but newspapers served the same purpose before its invention. People with low traits are more likely to resort to confirmation bias to relieve uncertainty as they find it distressing whereas people with high traits will be better placed to take advantage of opportunities that arise in uncertain environments.

Donald Trump is often dismissive of the opinions of experts. This is because his high traits encourage him to make decisions intuitively and his low level of openness causes him to be distrustful of new ideas. He is also subject to confirmation bias, as he seeks to justify his view of the world as expressed to American voters and searches for information that can help sustain his belief that he is being successful. However, he does depend on experts to get things done, particularly in his businesses. In such situations, he has confidence that they a help and not a hindrance to the achievement of his objectives.

Ambivalence, cognitive dissonance and mixed feelings

When your mind makes a decision, you will feel drawn to the course of action that it has selected. However, when you are faced with two or more options whose merits are evenly balanced, a state of psychological tension results, which you experience as a discomforting feeling. We label this state of uneasiness as **ambivalence**, although scientists refer to it as **cognitive dissonance**.

Ambivalence occurs when you experience positive and negative feelings in respect of a person, object, decision or action. It indicates that your Slow System has determined that the advantages and disadvantages associated with engaging with an entity or making a decision balance each other out. As a result, you fail to determine a course of action. For example, you may be in a shop comparing two blouses but find it very difficult to decide which one to buy. Your mind is unable to reach a conclusion because the two items are so closely matched and there is therefore no clear advantage to be gained from either one of them. As a result, you find yourself rooted to the spot in a state of mild discomfort.

You can overcome ambivalence by exposing yourself to information that can help your Slow System to decide between your options. Eventually, newly acquired knowledge will tip the balance towards one decision or another. Alternatively, you can adapt the criteria that you are using to make the decision. In the blouse example, you might realise that you had been trying to make a choice based on colour when it was more advisable to buy the one that fitted you best. Often, your mind will not go searching for new information because it has prioritised other actions or processing tasks. Also, relevant information may not be readily available, for example where the appropriateness of a decision is dependent on factors outside your control and can only be determined after the event. In such circumstances, making an arbitrary decision may be beneficial, as it will allow you to move forward or get on with more important things.

Cognitive dissonance is often used in place of ambivalence to describe the feeling that people experience when they simultaneously hold contradictory or incompatible attitudes, opinions or beliefs. For example, an employee may be required by his employer to take an uncompromising stance in relation to a customer complaint, but secretly may have sympathy with the customer. In these circumstances, the employee will probably feel uncomfortable and perhaps even guilty due to the presence of cognitive dissonance and may struggle to decide on a course of action. Such moral quandaries are difficult to resolve unless you adjust your values. In the scenario described above, the employee may decide that fairness is more important than loyalty to his employer, and favour the customer as a result. You may be aware of this adjustment process, but often it will occur subconsciously. In such circumstances, others may perceive you as being hypocritical or contradictory as you breach values that you have previously promoted or change your behaviour to relieve the dissonance.

Pressure of time will often cause you to make decisions without fully analysing and protecting against potential risks. **Mixed feelings** occur when you have made a decision, but your Slow System recognises that the selected course of action may have some negative consequences. You are likely to feel anxious when you experience mixed feelings because of the uncertainty associated with these risks. For example, you may decide that it is in your best interests to move to a different town to advance your career, but may experience mixed feelings because you will not be able to fulfil your responsibilities to your family when you are geographically distant. Mixed feelings serve as a warning mechanism, indicating that you may be acting inappropriately. You can overcome or reduce the intensity of mixed feelings by taking time to reconsider your decision, seeking assistance from others or throwing yourself wholeheartedly into the course of action you have selected.

Distortion of reality

Inaccurate and incomplete memories compromise judgment, problem solving and decision making. We tend to assume that the memories we recall are reliable representations of the circumstances that we encounter. This is not necessarily the case, however, because the primary purpose of our memory is to help us to perform optimally, not to preserve a historical record.

Our memories are compromised by the fact that humans tend to remember strong positive and negative events, but to forget less stimulating experiences. This is because your emotional system uses such memories to steer you away from danger and towards experiences that generate positive feelings. In other words, it places a greater value on information that helps you to operate within your optimal range. You may, therefore, struggle to describe a situation after the event if it did not result in a strong stimulus at the time. Your mind may fill in any gaps by deploying schemas or making reasoned deductions as to what happened. You may later assume the resultant memories to be accurate.

Older people are, generally, less accurate in their recollection of events than younger people. It would seem that this is partly due to their greater reliance on existing schemas. When an older person witnesses an event, he will be more inclined to use existing schemas to interpret it. His memory of the event may, therefore, be compromised by the application of a flawed schema. For example, a person's cultural experiences may lead him to associate young men in hoodies with the carrying of knives. If he sees a scuffle between two such men and a flash of light from a silver object, he may assume it was a knife when in fact it could have been a mobile phone.

You will find it difficult to remember minor details when you are experiencing stress because your fight and flight mechanism will be focused on the threats that are causing the stress. For example, people who are low in extraversion often find it difficult to remember the names of people when they are being introduced to them because the physical interaction involved provokes a stress event. In countries with traditional cultures, such as Saudi Arabia, the evidence of women is given less weight than that of men as it is considered to be less reliable. There is some justification for this distinction as the on-average lower level of indifference of women means that they are more likely to panic or experience chronic stress than men in circumstances where they or other people are at risk of harm. They are therefore more likely to make errors in interpretation than men when operating in hostile or dangerous environments. In reality, however, many men are low in indifference, and a significant number of women are higher in indifference than the average male. Also, many men possess other low traits that make them prone to experiencing stress. It is therefore unreasonable to make such a broad generalisation. As we shall see in the next chapter, alpha males have an interest in suppressing the influence of women, so they tend to take advantage of opportunities to do so.

If your self-esteem is likely to be damaged by the recall of a particular event, your emotional system may blank it from your memory or record it inaccurately to avoid future emotional harm. In other words, your emotional system can act as a spin-doctor, massaging the truth. A person who would otherwise feel guilty, embarrassed or ashamed about an action or omission may therefore subconsciously shift the blame on to somebody else. People with very high traits can struggle to maintain the high levels of stimulation and self-esteem that they need to feel good, so they are likely to remember events in ways that exaggerate their influence over them or portray them in a positive way. In contrast, people with low traits are often over-stimulated and frequently experience anxiety and chronic stress. They are therefore more likely to remember events in ways that relieve them from responsibility or reduce their prominence. These cognitive tendencies help to explain why Donald Trump says so many things that are factually incorrect, but favourable to him. He is high in extraversion, indifference and opportunism and will therefore be vulnerable to low moods. It is also likely that he is suffering from low self-esteem as he is a political outsider and has a low level of openness, which makes it difficult for him to get to grips with the wide-ranging, complex issues that governments now have to deal with.

The different ways that we handle information can result in mistrust, as is the case with the Trump administration and the White House press core. Most journalists will be lower in extraversion and higher in openness than Donald Trump. They will, therefore, be better able than Trump to see the pros and cons of complicated problems and will tend to find fault with his simplistic approaches. Journalists are also disturbed by Trump's looseness with the truth. Trump tends to get things wrong and contradicts himself because he is Fast System orientated and is therefore not inclined to study matters in detail or remember things that he considers inconsequential. He views himself as a decision maker and is used to employing other people to do the detail. His high trait orientation means that he also tends to repeat statements that he has heard from sources he trusts like Fox News without checking their accuracy. This tendency has been exacerbated by his need to find viewpoints and explanations that match his own. The low levels of openness and self-interested motivations of Trump and other people in his administration have caused them to engage in confirmation bias, seeking out "alternative facts" to justify their opinions and decisions rather than re-evaluating them. Trump's high level of extraversion also causes him to focus on the quality of his delivery rather than the factual content of his statements. He lives in the moment so he attributes little value to past statements and is inclined to remember them in a way that fits in with the stories he wants to tell.

Trump also lacks respect for the media because his low level of openness causes him to view criticism by people who he considers to be beneath him as acts of disloyalty. Having said that the media is not blameless. 24-hour news has reduced opportunities and incentives for journalists to thoroughly investigate and report on news stories and encouraged them to draw conclusions based upon limited evidence. More broadly, there is an on-going battle within society between people who have benefitted from the neo-liberal economic policies of the last 40 years and people who feel they have been left behind or ignored into which many news organisations have been drawn. Trump's actions are aligned with the latter reactionary element so news organisations that are defending the status quo are not inclined to give him a fair hearing whereas those that support his agenda willingly act as his mouthpiece.

Consciousness

We refer to the state of being aware of and responsive to your surroundings as **consciousness**. It is clearly advantageous for humans to have evolved a high level of consciousness. The broader your consciousness, the more likely you are to make good decisions, establish and maintain well-functioning relationships and achieve your long-term objectives. Consciousness is, though, very personal. It is your subjective representation of reality. Each of us sees the world differently depending on our personality traits and our experiences. When you encounter new information, you process it by reference to this perceived reality and use the results to adapt or embellish this perception. Your interactions with other people and other experiences, therefore, expand your consciousness. You encounter a unique set of circumstances during your life. Even when people share the same environment, variations in personality traits will mean that each person will filter out or avoid different amounts and types of information from or within it. Information that one person has discarded or avoided will be included within another person's consciousness.

The achievement of most objectives in life, including basic survival, requires people to work together in groups. It is therefore important for leaders, at least, to have a broad consciousness so they can understand the needs and desires of their followers and enemies. Where people within a group share the same interpretation, a **collective consciousness** emerges. Although we now associate the word "conscious" with a state of awareness, it is derived from the Latin words "con" (which means "together") and "scio" (which means to "know"). Literally, they describe a situation where people have common knowledge. Collective consciousness is important because it establishes a common understanding, encourages the adoption of shared objectives and values, and helps people to work effectively within a team.

The expansion of human consciousness may have been accelerated by the invention of tools. Tools would have enabled early humans to hunt other animals more easily. Their improved diet is likely to have resulted in increased brain size and functionality. The ability to store and pass on knowledge through language and writing has also had an enormous effect on our levels of consciousness. Knowledge allows us to expand our consciousness backwards to incorporate the past and forwards to envisage the future. This is very helpful in terms of setting objectives and avoiding repetition of mistakes and duplication of effort. Consequently, the study of history has been very important in terms of the development of human civilisation.

The Internet offers an opportunity for a massive expansion of personal and collective consciousness. It has made a vast range of information easily accessible and has enabled individuals to interact with people from different backgrounds and a variety of experiences and views. However, it has also allowed people to consolidate their existing opinions (i.e. engage in confirmation bias) by giving them access to groups of like-minded people. Consequently, social media and online groups tend to promote the development of feedback loops, which give their members a false impression of coherence and encourage self-righteousness.

The more that people broaden their individual consciousness, the more they overlap, expanding collective consciousness. Where a collective consciousness exists, it more likely that the decisions made by the leadership of the group will reflect the interests of the majority of its members. Ignorance encourages people to accept the status quo and makes them easier to manipulate. Authoritarian leaders naturally seek to limit the development of individual and collective consciousness because they find it easier to maintain order and pursue their personal objectives if they maintain members of the wider group in a state of ignorance of the wider world. The great challenge of modern times is to expand the consciousness of ordinary people across the world. If this can be achieved, populations will be able to appreciate the exploitative nature of the establishments that seek to control them and the virtues of working collaboratively with citizens of other nations to deliver a sustainable global society.

Consciousness remains unexplained from a biological perspective despite centuries of thought and investigation being applied to it. It has even been suggested that the answer lies within the mysteries of quantum mechanics. It seems, though, reasonable to suggest that consciousness is a collective representation of the knowledge and schemas you hold in your brain – a super-schema if you like. The remainder of this section assumes this explanation to be true. When you need to make a quick decision, you do so by reference to this super-schema. If you have more time, you can use your Slow System to test the accuracy of assumptions incorporated within this super-schema.

Recent research has revealed that mice store the same pieces of information in two separate parts of their brains – the long-term memory and the short-term memory. It may be that schemas and consciousness reside in the short-term memory and that new information is uploaded to it for the purposes of adapting and broadening this type of consciousness. Once the information has been consolidated within or checked against your perception of reality in your short-term memory, it is discarded or overwritten by new information. If you need access to that information after that, you will need to revert to the copy stored in your long-term memory.

As consciousness is a schema, it will incorporate a mixture of facts, assumptions and beliefs. You may build assumptions into your consciousness as a result of damaging emotional experiences. These experiences may be buried deep in your long-term memory and remain undisturbed. However, your current decision making may still be being influenced by them because they may be embedded within, or have informed the creation of, schemas. For example, a person who was abused as a child may no longer recall memories of the abuse by the time he reaches adulthood, but he may remain subject to limiting beliefs or exhibit undesirable behaviours as a result of the continuing deployment of schemas that are linked to such abuse.

Your self-awareness capability allows you to monitor and review your thought processes, feelings and behaviours. You also have the ability to consciously decide on courses of action, a capacity that is often described by psychologists as **executive function**. These powers are exercised by the **conscious mind**, a term that is used to group together the various cognitive processes that we are aware of. The conscious mind enables you to clarify objectives, monitor your progress towards them, and make adjustments to your behaviour when you go off course.

Although you will be conscious of some of your actions and behaviours, you will often complete tasks on autopilot using your Fast System. When you walk down the street or brush your teeth you do not usually give any thought to these processes as they are firmly embedded as schemas. Your Slow System also performs processing tasks beyond the reach of the conscious mind; for example, immediately before you experience an 'aha' moment. We attribute such actions to the **sub-conscious mind**.

Scientists and psychologists have not been able to come to any firm conclusions as to how the conscious and sub-conscious minds developed, operate or relate to each other, but the following explanation seems logical to me. Your Slow System's main function is to review your past performance, consolidate knowledge and improve your ability to cope with future challenges. It is capable of doing this subconsciously and it is likely that early humans would have been limited to this basic, reactive functionality. It would have operated in conjunction with the Fast System, which would also have operated sub-consciously. As the human brain evolved over hundreds of thousands of years, increased levels of consciousness opened up more opportunities. The Slow System developed new capabilities including the monitoring and reviewing of behaviour, feelings and thoughts in real time and the setting of objectives in the context of its host's abilities, current environment, past experiences and expectations of the future. The number and range of processing tasks it was required to carry out increased as a consequence. The mind therefore needed a mechanism to prioritise objectives and guide its host towards their achievement. Humans evolved the conscious mind for this purpose.

You will drift in and out of states of awareness. Sometimes, you will act with intention. In other situations, you will simply record events, or even fail to do that. For example, when you are driving you will usually be in a moderate state of awareness in which you will notice objects and events in your vicinity. At times, you will enter a higher state of awareness where you will assess your driving style or appreciate your mood (a state of self-awareness). At other times, you will completely lose awareness and realise later that you cannot remember that part of your journey. Your level of consciousness and the intensity with which you use your conscious mind therefore vary from moment to moment.

It is likely that **hypnosis** works by quietening the conscious mind, reducing self-awareness to zero, and thereby allowing the hypnotist access to the subject's sub-conscious mind. Then, by suggesting changes in behaviour or thinking, the hypnotist adapts schemas within the subject's mind, which results in changed behaviour or thinking once the subject is released from the trance. People who are Fast System orientated will be more susceptible to **suggestion** than those who are Slow System orientated because they spend more time in a state of low self-awareness. Hypnotists use stories and soothing language to promote relaxation, activate the subject's Fast System and gain access to his mind.

At times, you will experience an **inner voice** (also know as your "internal monologue" or "self-talk"). Your inner voice provides commentary, advice and motivational prompts and is the means by which your conscious mind directs your behaviour and focuses you on achieving your objectives. Where your Fast System and Slow System favour different courses of action, it may appear to be given your conflicting advice. Your inner voice is different from conversation with other people because, in the case of the latter, you factor in the likely reaction of your conversation partners and refrain from making certain statements or moderate your language as a consequence. As you do not need to exercise such restraint over your inner voice, its output can be biting and prejudicial, and it can encourage you to behave in ways that breach societal values. Most people see their inner voice as entirely natural and healthy. However, people who regularly experience negative feelings or are subject to limiting beliefs can find the prompts that it generates oppressive, unhelpfully critical or provocative. Some people experience the weighing up of options that goes on within the conscious mind before a decision is made as different voices and may attribute them to an external force such as a god or devil.

Although it is tempting to view the conscious mind as an executive decision maker, it is not reasonable to assume that the conscious mind is in control of the brain's other cognitive functions. The emotional system feeds prompts into the conscious mind, for example, when you experience pangs of regret. Memories appear at the forefront of your mind for no apparent reason. Nor is there any reason to believe that the conscious mind permits independent decision-making in the form of free will. It is likely that the decisions that you make and the behaviours that you display follow naturally and inevitably from the interaction of your personality traits and other characteristics with your environment, which includes your memories of past experiences and expectations of the future. Although you may feel that you are making decisions freely, given the same circumstances it is likely that your mind would make the same decision every time. Once you have read the following two chapters, you will be able to see how individuals are influenced by the dynamics of groups and how the interaction of personalities within them in the context of their environment delivers predictable results. This is why history tends to repeat itself.

It does not take a great leap of imagination to accept as plausible the mechanistic explanation of the human mind that I have just described. This explanation does present two challenges, however. Firstly, it implies that the decisions that you make are natural consequences of the interaction of your body with its environment and that your course in life is therefore determined by fate. Secondly, this explanation can be equally applied to other mammals and therefore challenges the religious belief that the human mind was created specially by God, and is an affront to our egotistical nature, which encourages us to believe that we are superior beings. Since Descartes first tackled this issue in the 17th century, philosophers, scientists and psychologists have struggled to justify consciousness in non-physical terms to avoid the conclusion that we are essentially machines with predestined paths. However, evolution and fatalism are more logical concepts than the existence of a god, and claims that we hold some special status in relation to other animals are being undermined by increasing evidence that chimpanzees, dogs and some other animals possess a degree of consciousness.

It is therefore likely that our perception of free will is an illusion. What is the point then in making any effort to improve your circumstances or change the world for the better if, in reality, you have no free will. If you are simply a machine following a predestined path, then what will be will be. However, if that is the case, you were always going to pick up this book and read it, and if, as a result of doing so, you make changes to your behaviour, those too will have been inevitable. There is little to be gained from thinking about the extent to which you have free will. What is important is that you recognise the value in expanding your consciousness and using your talents and skills to make positive contributions to society.

Psychosis

Some people perceive or interpret the world in a very different way from people around them. They are often described as having lost touch with reality and in extreme cases may be diagnosed with **psychosis** or experience a psychotic episode. Psychotic episodes are characterised by hallucinations, delusions or visions and disorganised thinking or speech.

Psychosis is very misunderstood. Many people incorrectly believe that the word 'psychotic' equates to 'dangerous'. In fact, very few people who experience psychosis ever hurt anyone else. Schizophrenia is a type of psychosis. Some people incorrectly associate schizophrenia with possessing a "split personality". There is a mental disorder characterised by the possession of at least two distinct and relatively enduring personality states, but this is called "dissociative identity disorder" (also known as "multiple personality disorder").

Psychosis occurs when a person is in Fast System operation and making connections between different pieces of information in ways that are new or unusual. Psychotic episodes can help people to understand the world or promote creativity. This is because the intuitive links made during these episodes can result in new ideas and broaden a person's consciousness. If the resultant conclusions or ideas are valid, but too advanced for their time, they are likely to be dismissed by others. For example, Leonardo da Vinci was respected in his time for his inventiveness because he lived in a liberal Renaissance city, but had he been born two centuries earlier, it is likely that his designs for flying and other machines would have been considered evidence of madness or blasphemous. However, many people who experience psychotic episodes jump to unwarranted or unjustified conclusions during them that cannot be substantiated in the cold light of day. People with low traits are more likely to make incorrect assumptions because of their limited range of schemas.

People who experience psychosis often feel misunderstood and frustrated because they tend to have their ideas and experiences dismissed by others. As psychosis involves disconnection with everyday life, it also has a disruptive effect, making it harder for a person to get things done and promoting tiredness and a sense of being overwhelmed. Some people experience strong positive feelings when they experience psychosis because it is associated with high information environments and use of the Fast System. However, others feel scared, threatened or confused. A high trait orientated person is likely to experience feelings of enjoyment or exhilaration when he has a psychotic episode because he is likely to be operating within his optimal range. A low trait orientated person is likely to experience major stress events and associated anxiety, chronic stress or panic. If he has made incorrect assumptions, he may experience **paranoia** – a persistent, irrational feeling that people are 'out to get you' or of constantly being monitored. Paranoia may be fuelled by confirmation bias as a person seeks to verify his beliefs.

7

THE STRUCTURE AND CULTURE OF HUMAN GROUPS

In modern society, people tend to believe that they can dictate their destiny, but we need the help of others to survive and prosper. Your achievements are made possible by the contributions of other people, many of which you take for granted. However, some people have objectives that conflict with yours, or adopt behaviours that impede your progress. You will be affected and influenced by the actions and values of members of the groups to which you belong. These groups will encourage you to accept responsibility, impose obligations upon you and set behavioural parameters. Your environment is therefore shaped by the people with whom you come into contact and by the groups that you belong to or encounter.

Most models of personality focus on identifying a person's personality traits and matching them to appropriate job roles. While this approach is usually helpful, it fails to take account of the influence of groups on our performance and mental health. In primeval times, humans would have belonged to one extended family group and gravitated towards suitable roles within it. In modern society, though, a person will belong to multiple groups of differing size and makeup, which will each have their particular purposes, structures and values. In some ways, this variety makes it easier for people to find suitable roles and environments, but the looseness of their connections to these groups leaves many people feeling out of place, unprotected or lacking in support.

A group is a collection of different personalities. This chapter explains how these personalities interact with each other and their environment to deliver predictable results in terms of group dynamics. Your personality traits may locate you in a specific place within a group structure and suit you to a particular culture. Alternatively, they may locate you in an intermediate or extreme position and prime you to act as a stabilising or disruptive force. Once you appreciate where you naturally fit in, you will be able to position yourself more appropriately within groups, and exert a greater influence over their values.

Many of the behaviours that you display and the feelings you experience are related to the structure and culture of the groups to which you belong. If you fit well within a group, you are likely to be effective and to experience positive feelings consistently. If you feel out of place, unprotected or lacking in support, you are likely to experience stress or low moods and display inappropriate behaviours. For example, you are likely to experience negative feelings if your employer does not value your contribution or provide you with appropriate support. Feelings and behaviours associated with groups will be discussed in the next chapter.

Group values

Your emotional system guides you towards environments that allow you to operate within your optimal ranges and behaviours to which you are suited. Your ideal environment may, however, not be conducive to the achievement of the objectives of a group to which you belong, and the behaviours that you would naturally exhibit might cause harm to other group members or impose unacceptable restraints upon them. High traits encourage people to be greedy, capricious, ruthless or impulsive, depending on the trait. Joyriding and queue jumping are examples of high trait behaviours that promote positive feelings within an individual, but which are perceived as being damaging to society. Possession of a low trait may cause a person to restrict adventurous activities, close down debate, restrict competition or introduce strict rules of behaviour, again depending on the trait. Examples of such behaviour include imposing fundamentalist religious rules, behaving in an authoritarian manner, and being a spoilsport, killjoy or jobsworth.

Although high traits encourage individualistic, self-interested behaviours, they also bring benefits to groups when channelled in the right way. They prompt exploratory behaviour, which helps a group to expand, acquire new resources and develop technologically. People who are high in extraversion are likely to be adventurous, acquisitive and sociable, and will therefore be able to identify new resources for groups. Those who are high in openness are likely to develop new ideas and seek out new experiences so they enable groups to innovate. People who are high in indifference compete intensely and therefore help to maintain the competitiveness of a group in relation to other groups. People who are high in opportunism are naturally flexible and help groups to survive in changing or unpredictable circumstances by taking advantage of opportunities.

When channelled correctly, low traits prompt defensive, controlling behaviours that promote stability within a group by strengthening the group's structure and restricting the expression of potentially damaging high trait behaviours. A person with a low trait will generally attempt to stop a person who is high in that trait from taking what he sees as excessive risks. Most of us possess at least one low trait and therefore have a mechanism that helps us limit our own and other people's risk-taking. People who are low in extraversion serve as a useful brake on the exuberance and materialism of those who are high in extraversion by using their powers of reflection and analytical skills to weigh up pros and cons and promote fairness. People who are low in openness identify risks in engaging with novelty and interacting with strangers, and help to bring coherency to the new ideas and ventures of people who are high in openness by adopting methodical approaches. Those who are low in indifference create harmonious environments by restricting the expression of competitive instincts by people who are high in indifference where they could result in harm to vulnerable people. People who are low in opportunism develop rules that require people who are high in opportunism to operate within organised frameworks, thereby preventing the emergence of anarchic forces.

As there are four different personality spectrums, a group may encourage the expression of high trait behaviours associated with one spectrum of information, but restrain those associated with another. For example, competition may be encouraged but opportunistic behaviour be restrained. The success of a group will depend on its ability to adopt a risk profile that is suited to its environment. If high-risk behaviours are not sufficiently restrained, the group may be weakened or fracture. For example, a general who takes excessive risks on the battlefield may be defeated and leave his country open to conquest. If high trait behaviours are too constrained, however, the group will stagnate and will eventually be out-competed by other groups. For example, a company that cuts its research and development budget is likely to fall behind its competitors and become unprofitable. Each group will have its own distinct character, which will be strongly influenced by the environment it inhabits and the personality traits of its leaders.

A culture will emerge within a group that reflects the prevailing high trait and low trait behaviours. The group will promote values that are aligned to this culture. These values keep the behaviour of group members within acceptable limits and encourage them to engage in activities that benefit the group as a whole. A value system helps to build trust. Trust allows you to concentrate your attentions on your primary objectives without having to worry about other people undermining your security. It therefore enables individuals and groups to operate effectively. Group members who display high trait behaviours that breach group values are usually marginalised or punished as their deviancy threatens the integrity of the group. People who display low trait behaviours that are more cautious and controlling than those imposed by the group's value system generally have little influence because most group members will ignore their attempt to exert control. The general nature of values can make them difficult to enforce against those who breach them so they are often codified into laws.

Values shift over time as the environment in which a group operates changes and as group objectives are redefined. In times of peace and prosperity, group members will usually feel secure and therefore favour Fast System, high trait behaviours. In times of hardship and conflict, people generally look to increase their levels of security and therefore spend more time using Slow System skills and exhibiting low trait behaviours. A group's values are also likely to shift when the balance of power changes within the group. Where people with a particular set of personality traits gain control of a group, they will set new objectives that accord with their personality traits and group values will tend to shift towards their personal values. Sudden shifts in values can also occur when major environmental changes occur, such as natural disasters. At any time, certain traits will be dominant within a group's culture, others will be exerting an influence and some will be powerless.

The Personality Revolution's Circle of Power

Shifts in the culture of groups can be illustrated on **The Personality Revolution's Circle of Power**, which is illustrated in Figure 12 opposite. A group's culture will either span the equivalent of four traits on the circle or stretch across five traits without completely spanning the traits at the start and end of the sequence. The high traits, which are associated with exploration and freedom, are located in the right half of the circle and the low traits, which are associated with defensiveness and control, in the left half. The fact that the high and low traits in each spectrum are located opposite each other means that, as a group's position shifts around the circle, the characteristics of one trait will become more evident at the expense of those of the reverse trait. This also means that wherever a group is located, it will be represented on each of the trait spectrums. Traits that sit next to each other promote complementary behaviours. The central trait or traits within the span (the dominant traits) will be the most influential within the group because it or they will be supported by the traits either side of it or them.

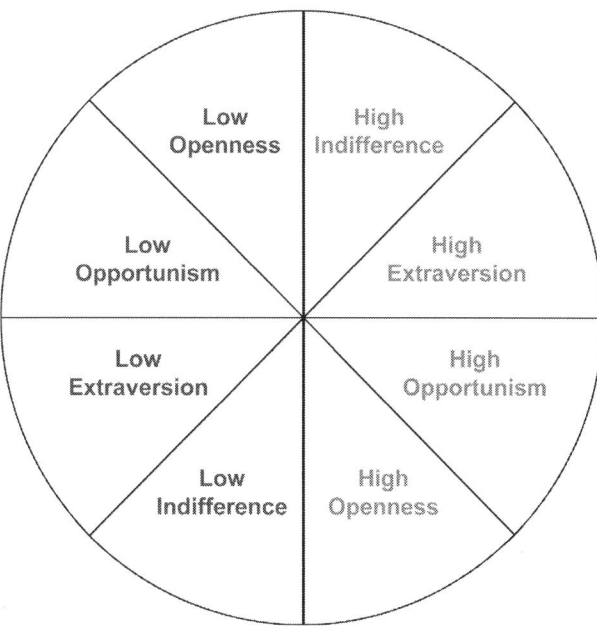

Figure 12. The Circle of Power

Because people tend to have middling traits, the natural balancing point for a group with a typical distribution of personality traits will lie in the centre of the Circle of Power. Environmental factors will, however, cause a group's culture to shift away from this point. Even if the environment in which the group operates would naturally cause the group's culture to be located at this balancing point, the fact that group leaders tend to have more extreme traits than average members usually results in a shift away from the centre.

If your personality traits match the culture of your group, you are likely to find yourself in a favourable environment that enables you to be very effective. If they are in complete conflict, you are likely to find life difficult and have little influence. However, as The Personality Revolution's Model of Personality gives rise to 16 different combinations of personality traits, most people will not possess four adjacent traits on the Circle of Power. Such a person will always possess some traits that are in favour and some that are not. He will therefore never feel completely in tune with the values of the group, but is also unlikely to feel like a complete outsider. He may play a stabilising role within the group, as his behaviour is likely to inhibit shifts towards extreme cultures.

I suggest that you now assess where you fit within the Circle of Power. If you have taken the free PRTI personality test at **thepersonalityrevolution.com**, your results will include a diagram plotting your traits on the Circle of Power. Later in this chapter, I describe four cultures that are associated with different positions on the Circle of Power. I also explain how shifts occur around it. First, however, it is necessary to understand the underlying structure of human groups.

The primal group structure

Diversity and teamwork have enabled human groups to survive within challenging environments and powered their ascent to the position of dominant mammal on this planet. Each person needs the input of other people with different skills to fulfil his own potential and to maximise the benefit to his group. Together, these attributes amount to a sum greater than their parts. Our early ancestors would have lived together in small groups of about 150 people. A group of this size would have been large enough for a wide range of talents and skills to be represented within it.

A specific organisational framework has evolved within human groups to promote effective teamwork, which is founded upon personality traits. I call it the **primal group structure**. The complexity of modern society has resulted in the creation of many groups with atypical distributions of personality traits. Even so, the primal group structure will emerge to some degree within them.

The primal group structure is similar to the organisational structure that exists within other primate groups. The nature of this structure and the distribution of power within it vary from species to species. Chimpanzee groups are ruled by a dominant male and establish all-male hierarchies. Females have a low status and depend on males for protection. In contrast, in bonobo groups, females greatly influence male behaviour. It has been suggested that these differences in behaviour between chimpanzee and bonobo groups arose because bonobos live in a more favourable environment, being shielded from competition with gorillas by the Congo River. The spread of human groups across the globe has, though, forced them to adapt their cultures to suit new environments and changed circumstances. The form of the primal group structure that emerges in a human group will therefore largely depend on environmental factors.

The primal group structure is divided into a number of sub-groups, which I will now discuss. A person's position within this structure will be dictated by his personality traits and his gender. For the moment, you should try to ignore the fact that in modern society men and women work side by side and socialise together. Mixed gender groups will be considered later.

The primal hierarchy

Competition between males results in the emergence of a **dominant male**. The position of dominant male is valuable because it bestows mating rights, access to resources, and high status. The dominant male must be capable of physically overpowering rivals. However, he must also show ruthlessness. Contenders for the position of dominant male, who I refer to as **alpha males**, therefore possess the traits of high extraversion and high indifference.

A normal-sized human group is too large for one male to control alone. Therefore, although a dominant male may be aggressive towards individual group members at times to demonstrate his ability to overpower them, he will not be able to maintain his authority without the assistance of others. The dominant male therefore enrols other alpha males within the governance structure of the group. These males have an interest in accepting such positions because close association with the dominant male gives them superior access to resources. They are, however, likely to be tempted to usurp the dominant male by greed and a lust for power. The dominant male will, therefore, need to secure their loyalty, a characteristic that is associated with the trait of low openness. He will also need to establish control over other males in the group. He, therefore, needs his key supporters to fit into and take senior positions within an organisational structure. To do so effectively, they will need to be low in opportunism. People with this trait tend to understand systems, including the network of relationships within a group. Males who possess the four traits of high extraversion, high indifference, low openness, and low opportunism therefore naturally form a tight-knit, mutually supportive governing elite, which I refer to as the **establishment**. I term these four traits collectively as the **establishment traits**.

The dominant male and the establishment bring benefits to other members of the group by securing resources, making territorial gains and defending the group from attack by other groups. To achieve these objectives, the dominant male needs the support of a loyal and coherent body of males within the group. The natural balance of personality traits within a group delivers a subset of males suited to serve as troops and workers, which I call the **rank and file**. In the context of a society, the rank and file roughly equates to the working class. The behaviour of members of the rank and file is characterised by a low level of openness. Unlike members of the establishment, they do not possess high levels of extraversion and indifference so their loyalty will not be compromised by a desire for power and wealth. They are primarily concerned with maintaining and increasing their own security.

When alpha males from one group come into contact with alpha males from another, they compete for resources, and particularly mating rights over females. Competition is brutal. It is a zero-sum game. Ultimately, there can only be one winner. The passing on of high-quality genes to the next generation is more important than the survival of individual males. Consequently, alpha males are reluctant to compromise in such circumstances. It is in their best interests to eliminate or emasculate males in other groups so that they can increase the number of women under their control. Males from other groups, therefore, present not only a physical danger to a group's males but also an existential threat to their group. Fear of this outcome encourages members of the rank and file to be loyal and helps to bond them together. However, members of the rank and file are also fearful of males within their group who behave differently to them. Their low level of openness causes them see non-conformist behaviours and characteristics as threatening because it undermines the coherency of the group. They, therefore, tend to marginalise or suppress the activities of creative individuals, immigrants and people with unconventional sexual preferences.

Most other species of mammals do not kill members of their species. A losing participant will usually be permitted to withdraw. This makes sense in terms of ensuring the survival of the species. However, the development of weapons enabled human leaders to develop killing machines in the form of armies. Although members of the rank and file are not normally very competitive, they are likely to follow a charismatic leader into battle. Testosterone aids this warring dynamic. A male's testosterone level will rise when he finds himself in a competitive situation, promoting feelings of enjoyment and exhilaration and blunting fear.

People who are low in openness tend to support leaders who can set out clear plans because of the difficulties they have in dealing with wide-ranging and complex arguments. As dominant males are usually high in extraversion and low in openness (traits possessed by Donald Trump), they enjoy being the centre of attention and share the rank and file's fear of novelty and difference. They are therefore capable of speaking enthusiastically and in simple, traditional terms to their audiences, and thereby instilling confidence and belief in them.

The dominant male will often highlight or exaggerate the existence of potential threats to secure the compliance of the rank and file and other group members. In other words, he will use fear as a means of control. Also, as behaviours associated with low openness are more apparent in people who have limited educations, the dominant male and establishment will usually try to prevent members of the wider group from acquiring knowledge. If they cannot stop the flow of information, they will spread misinformation. Where conflicting opinions and facts are circulating, people who are low in openness are likely to become stressed because of their limited ability to cope with ambiguity. Their fear levels will rise, and they will be more inclined to place their trust in the current leader, being a known quantity.

A **command chain** naturally emerges beneath the establishment in the form of a hierarchical structure through which the dominant male controls and directs the rank and file. The dominant trait of males within this command chain will be low opportunism, as this trait promotes a need for structure and encourages a person to develop organisational skills. A male's position within the command chain will, though, be determined by his levels of ambition, competitiveness and loyalty, which relate to the traits of high extraversion, high indifference and low openness respectively.

The establishment, command chain and rank and file together form the **primal hierarchy**. In summary, a male's position in the primal hierarchy will depend on which of these traits are most prominent within his personality. Members of the establishment will be particularly high in extraversion and indifference, members of the command chain will be low in opportunism, and members of the rank and file will be low in openness. Members of the establishment are naturally inclined to engage males from other groups in conflict over resources, the rank and file will instinctively support the dominant male within their group to enhance their security, and the command chain will provide organisational structure. The primal hierarchy is therefore essentially a machine that harvests resources from the environment in which it operates. It has evolved to be mobile, enabling groups of males to hunt and fight in challenging environments. Its loyal and organised nature enables it to be deployed in a direct and forceful way by the dominant male. He will use the primal hierarchy to accumulate resources through military conquest, by exploiting natural resources and by manufacturing wealth-generating products. The primal hierarchy also defends the group. Although the actions of a successful dominant male will benefit the group by providing its members with increased access to resources and security, the dominant male will primarily act in his own interests. He will therefore instinctively employ the primal hierarchy to increase his status and wealth, and to neutralise those who may present a challenge to his authority.

The primal hierarchy naturally emerges in any human group with a standard distribution of personality traits. Materialistic, competitive and connected men will rise to positions of authority and create an establishment. These establishment members will exploit the organised nature and loyalty of the command chain and rank and file to strengthen their position. The primal hierarchy is very evident in modern society within corporate structures, governmental bodies, and armies and police forces. Authoritarian regimes establish strong primal hierarchies, as their leaders instinctively consolidate their positions by monitoring and controlling other group members.

The relationship between the dominant male and the establishment is symbiotic, but also unstable. The dominant male will need the help of members of the establishment to maintain control over the group. However, members of the establishment present a threat to the dominant male as their competitive instincts instil in them a desire to usurp him. They experience a conflict between their desire for power, status and resources and their need to be part of an organised and coherent group. To retain power, the dominant male must ensure that their need for security overwhelms their lust for power. The dominant male secures their loyalty by promoting a sense of fear and distributing patronage. He will make examples of establishment members who step out of line, punishing them harshly, while rewarding loyal subjects. The dominant male will not have the physical strength to be able to overpower all other establishment members if they work together so he will need to prevent them uniting against him. He will therefore keep members of the establishment jockeying for position by bestowing rewards on some and holding out the prospect of enrichment to others. If he achieves the right balance between fear, patronage and competition for position, the risk-reward ratio will not be positive enough for a potential usurper to mount a challenge to him or work with others to unseat him.

Over time, members of the establishment will accumulate wealth, which they will seek to protect. The risk of losing such resources in the event of an unsuccessful challenge will further deter them from mounting a coup. The need of members of the establishment for structure also causes them to resist change and strengthen their relationships within the establishment. They view the resultant networks as a means of accessing wealth, power and protection. Consequently, members of the establishment tend to marry people from other establishment families, and sometimes forced by relatives to marry their own cousins. Establishment events are characterised by displays of wealth and formal protocols, which serve to re-enforce their status and exclude other group members. A threat to a member of the establishment from such a person is met by a closing of ranks in his support because the trait of low opportunism causes members of the establishment to protect their networks of contacts and the trait of low openness promotes loyalty. This explains why members of the establishment often avoid prosecution when they commit crimes. Other members of the establishment are too protective of their positions, and their associated rewards and protection, to risk being ostracised as a result of reporting the crime or giving evidence. Members of the command chain and rank and file keep quiet too because they fear losing their jobs or some other act of retribution if they report it. In the 1970s and 1980s, influential television presenters like Jimmy Saville took advantage of the establishment culture within the BBC, hospitals and local authorities in the UK to abuse large numbers of children.

The dominant male must keep the support of the rank and file if he is to retain power. If he becomes too greedy and deprives the rank and file of basic necessities, he risks losing the support of its members. In such circumstances, members of the rank and file may transfer their allegiance to another alpha male. It is therefore important for the dominant male not to allow members of the establishment the freedom to develop independent power bases within the primal hierarchy. Leaders of groups often give potential challengers positions of responsibility that give them an interest in maintaining the status quo or tie them to the policies of the leader. The leader will also want to monitor their behaviour. This explains the phrase "Keep your friends close, and your enemies closer."

A populist or fascist may rise to power where the rank and file feel unprotected. He will usually play on the rank and file's instinctive distrust of immigrants and foreign powers, heightening their fears, and channel the resultant anger towards the current leader and establishment. Populist and fascist leaders have a particularly low level of openness, which allows them to connect strongly to members of the rank and file, but also makes them very sensitive to disloyalty. As a result, they will purge, banish or execute senior members of the primal hierarchy who they perceive as potentially threatening, replacing them with people they consider to be more trustworthy, typically family members, cronies or military personnel (as Donald Trump has done). Such people are, though, likely to have similar views and limitations to the leader, or will at least keep quiet and obey orders. Therefore, over time, the leader is likely to become as isolated from the wider population as the previous incumbent and be sustained in power only by his authoritarian leadership style.

In modern society, establishments have embraced technology in their pursuit of profit, eliminating or downgrading traditional working-class jobs in the process. This has made many members of the rank and file fearful. Consequently, working-class people have been transferring their allegiance away from the mainstream parties that have been supporting this dynamic to populist politicians and parties. This is one of the dynamics behind Brexit and Donald Trump's rise to power. The second volume of this work explains the influence of personality on modern economic, social and political structures and the reasons behind the rise of populist politicians in more detail.

In exceptional cases, the rank and file may revolt and replace the dominant male and establishment with a communist leadership structure as occurred in Russia in the early 20th century. Although such a revolution may be powered by egalitarian ideas, the laws of group dynamics usually result in establishment males rising to leadership positions once a new power structure is created. Consequently, behind the veneer of communist values, established communist regimes tend to take the form of authoritarian dictatorships.

The tight-knit nature of the establishment makes it difficult for a potential challenger to develop a supportive group around him without news of his plans finding its way back to the dominant male. The dominant male will accumulate as much useful information as he can about potential challengers and enemies. Leaders of groups with strong primal hierarchies therefore often direct resources towards surveillance of group members. The dominant male's need for information and natural ruthlessness will incline him to use duress to extract information from individuals so torture tends to be a favoured tool of dictators.

The dominant male will need to keep information, including his plans and strategies, secret to prevent competitors benefiting from them. Members of the primal hierarchy treat information as intrinsically valuable as it potentially confers competitive advantage, hence the phrase "Knowledge is power". They tend only to release it on a need to know basis. The primal hierarchy is suited to the control of information due to its organised and loyal nature. Its hierarchical structure enables information to be transferred reliably and with clarity upwards or downwards, as it is gathered or as orders are given.

The establishment's strength lies in its control of the known world. It is protective of the wealth that is has acquired and therefore generally seeks to maintain the status quo. Innovation is dangerous as it threatens to introduce de-stabilising influences that may lead to the transfer of power and wealth away from the establishment. The low level of openness of members of establishment causes them to distrust new ideas and products and to protect the value in their existing assets. The establishment suppresses creativity by restricting the generation and spread of knowledge.

As a result, members of establishment in developed countries tend to have their wealth tied up in traditional industries, particularly the oil industry. Their low level of openness naturally inclines them to dismiss manmade climate change as a fraud and to distrust new methods of energy production, but their financial interests also give them a strong reason to prevent or slow down a shift towards sustainable energy production. The secrecy and command structure of the primal hierarchy and its distrust of new ideas also mean that hierarchical, male-dominated organisations tend to stall technologically and to become trapped into silo thinking.

Most people are not members of the establishment, but they live within systems that have been created or rigged by the establishment for the enrichment of its members. They usually do not realise this fact, as they are pre-occupied with what they perceive to be their own interests and objectives. The establishment ties them into such systems by encouraging the development of such perceptions, by keeping them busy enough to prevent them from realising how they are being exploited or by promoting fear of the consequences of stepping out of line. As members of wider society become more educated, they are more likely to notice and question any unfair distribution of group resources. Therefore, educating the masses only serves a useful purpose for the establishment when it involves developing skills that generate wealth or strengthen the primal hierarchy. Establishment politicians therefore try to limit the scope of education to the development of skills that are useful to corporations or the armed forces by removing arts and humanities subjects from the curriculum.

Because members of the establishment are driven by a desire for power, wealth and status, and are ruthless by nature, they will be inclined to use methods that other group members would consider unfair, corrupt or immoral, or which are harmful to others, to achieve their objectives, such as insider dealing, deception, manipulation and favouritism. As power and wealth rest within the primal hierarchy, its members are susceptible to bribery by other members of the group or by people from other groups. They may demand facilitation payments or kickbacks for providing access to important people, commercial opportunities or governmental consents. Bribery and other corrupt practices tend to be endemic in governmental systems in developing countries and within poorly regulated bureaucracies like the European Union. In the absence of a contrary force promoting honesty and integrity, such as an obligation to behave transparently, people working within these structures who possess establishment traits are likely to be tempted to boost their status and wealth by engaging in corrupt practices. They may even see such action as a legitimate way of supplementing their incomes. However, members of the establishment often crack down on corrupt practices by non-establishment members of the primal hierarchy as embezzlement, theft and fraud deprive them of resources that they view as their own. Consequently, while company directors and bankers are rarely prosecuted for financial crimes, ordinary employees often receive long sentences for such offences.

Progressive males

The primal hierarchy evolved because groups needed a system and structure that could help them secure resources and protect their members from anarchic forces and external threats. If the group dynamic that gives rise to the primal hierarchy did not exist, police forces, companies and governmental bodies would be unable to function. However, left unchecked, members of the establishment abuse the power that the primal hierarchy gives them, increasing inequality, reducing productivity and suppressing innovation and freedoms.

Men who possess one or more of the traits of low extraversion, high openness, low indifference and high opportunism (the reverse of the establishment traits) potentially present a challenge to the authority of the dominant male and the establishment because they will not be constrained by the conventions or rules of the primal hierarchy (in the case of low openness and low opportunism respectively) or are likely to attempt to restrict their materialistic or domineering behaviours (in the case of low extraversion and low indifference). I refer to these four traits as the **progressive traits**, as they help to maintain free markets, liberal democracy, and fair and compassionate societies, and the males who possess them as **progressive males**.

The primal hierarchy responds to the threat presented by males with progressive traits by marginalising them. As a result, these males will often have lower status than members of the primal hierarchy, become isolated and be vulnerable to abuse. This explains why many younger men with progressive traits struggle to fit into peer groups and often experience mental health problems. At times, however, the establishment will need to access the talents and skills of progressive males. By serving the establishment, these men can increase their status and tap into its resources.

Males who are low in extraversion often struggle to function effectively in the physical world. They will not have a desire to acquire resources and status, although they may see wealth as a means of increasing their security. As they are likely to experience stress if they are required to participate in group-based activities, they naturally distance themselves from the primal hierarchy. However, they instinctively promote fairness within groups and restrict the ability of establishment members to accumulate wealth and resources. They may anger or frustrate establishment members as a consequence, Men who are low in extraversion tend, though, not to be able to assemble and motivate a potentially dangerous group of supporters around them and are naturally cautious, so they usually present little physical threat to the establishment. Their positioning on the edge of groups enables them to be objective and use their observational skills for the benefit of the primal hierarchy. Their measured opinions make them ideally suited to the role of adviser, and this can enable them to achieve high status, although the maintenance of such status will be dependent on the goodwill of the establishment members whom they support.

Males who are high in openness enjoy new experiences and engaging with new ideas and people who are different. These behaviours threaten to reduce the coherency of the primal hierarchy and the wider group, and therefore present a threat to the establishment's grip on power. New ideas can encourage dissension within a group and confuse the rank and file, and inventions can undermine the wealth-generating interests of establishment members. The fickle nature of men who are high in openness means that they may be disloyal or release confidential information to competitors. They therefore tend to be distrusted by members of the primal hierarchy. They can, however, be useful to the establishment because their creative ability can enable a group to innovate and out-compete rival groups by, for example, inventing new weapons. They can also help to boost a leader's status and authority by creating great works of art or spectacular buildings for him. People who are high in openness are therefore sometimes pushed to the margins of society or persecuted, but at other times embraced and rewarded. An effective establishment leader will make use of the capabilities of males who are high in openness while limiting their ability to exert a wider influence.

Males who are low in indifference find conflict distressing, so they do not function well in competitive or hostile environments. As status in male groups is to a great extent determined by competitive ability, men who are low in indifference usually have lowly positions within them. They tend to adopt conciliatory or submissive approaches and their sensitivity to harmful circumstances and disharmony leaves them open to abuse and susceptible to mental health problems. When they work together, they can place limits on the actions of the dominant male and establishment by establishing a culture that promotes peace and harmony. Historically, they have used the power of religious belief to aid their cause. Males who are low in indifference can, however, be helpful to the establishment by promoting collaborative behaviours and serving as mediators.

Males who are high in opportunism tend to function well where they are free to act spontaneously. They gravitate towards low regulation environments where they can make money opportunistically or be creative, for example as traders, thieves or artists. Members of the establishment are poorly equipped to cope with such environments due to their low levels of opportunism. They seek certainty and stability to protect their positions and wealth. The establishment, therefore, creates structures and systems that marginalise males who are high in opportunism. When there is a strong primal hierarchy in a group, males who are high in opportunism tend to be ineffective because of the difficulties they find in engaging with structure and organisation. They become more useful, however, when this structure degrades or breaks apart, for example, in a market economy, battle for succession or intergroup conflict, or following a natural disaster. Their opportunistic nature and flexibility allows them to quickly adapt to, and take advantage of, the new circumstances.

The establishment is small, as a low percentage of males will possess all four establishment traits. An even smaller number possess all four progressive traits because most men are high in indifference. Many men will, though, possess a mixture of establishment and progressive traits. People who on balance have more establishment traits are likely to align themselves with the establishment and may have ambitions to ascend the primal hierarchy. However, the possession of one or more progressive traits and their resultant behaviour will prevent them from being accepted within the establishment.

Many males will be high in indifference and possess at least one progressive trait. Such men may present a challenge to the dominant male and establishment because their competitive instincts will combine with the destabilising or restraining effects of their progressive traits. This is best illustrated by considering the behaviour of national leaders. Countries are large groups and group dynamics apply to them in the same way as smaller groups.

The establishment continually attempts to increase its control over markets and citizens so that it can channel the wealth that they generate into the pockets of establishment members. It achieves this by creating large companies with monopolistic powers, manipulating tax systems and forcing people to work within systems. People who are high in opportunism and indifference react against this consolidation process as they value the freedom to compete. They challenge rules that restrict their freedom or prevent them from exerting dominance over those around them. Their resistance to being organised and controlled provides a counterbalance to the controlling actions of the establishment.

Attempts by people who are high in opportunism and indifference to work together are usually doomed to fail. Although they may identify common objectives, their inability to operate within structures and systems and their desire to exert their dominance leads to internal conflict. This is even more likely to occur when people who are high in opportunism are also low in openness because this trait encourages people to develop fixed opinions and view the display of independent action by a colleague as disloyalty. Donald Trump possesses these three traits and this explains why he has fallen out with many of the people who helped to get him elected. Such men often display bitterness, frustration or anger when they come across other people who are obstructing their path and may isolate themselves from other men so that they can feel a sense of freedom and power in the territory they have defined as theirs. They therefore tend to gravitate towards sparsely populated, rural areas.

Men who are high in openness and indifference, like Steve Jobs who co-founded Apple, have the ability to develop new products and services. Where they operate independently of existing corporations and systems, they present a threat to them. Where a person is high in opportunism, openness and indifference, he is likely to be very entrepreneurial and may set up rival organisations that are capable of re-configuring the marketplace. This dynamic is sometimes referred to as **creative destruction**. Men who are high in openness and indifference will have a tendency to fight for the right to express their individuality and ideas. Where they are successful, they reduce the coherency of society and promote variety and the enjoyment of difference, making it more difficult for the establishment to exploit the general population. Educated, middle classes emerge in such circumstances and the rank and file is weakened as a consequence.

The values of the USA and particularly the UK have been strongly influenced by people with the traits of high indifference, high opportunism and high openness. As a result, the establishments in these countries have been forced to grant individuals a considerable amount of personal freedom. However, men with these traits want freedom on their own terms. In particular, they will not have any desire to extend the rights they carve out to women, as they will wish to retain the rights associated with the status of dominant male within their relationships. They will often oppose the introduction of laws that protect women and children from abuse or give women equal status to men to maintain their ability to impose their will on their families.

In countries without a tradition of free markets and democracy like Russia, the dominant male and establishment continue to derive their power from the rank and file and use it to suppress creative and libertarian forces. Where the primal hierarchy remains strong and cohesive, the establishment maintains a tight grip on wealth and power, adopting authoritarian approaches. Innovation and trade are stifled as a result, reducing competitiveness in world markets, limiting economic growth and eroding military capability. However, people who are high in indifference and low in extraversion may restrain the establishments in such countries. In a society where there is a lack of wealth generating opportunities, either through trade or colonial expansion, the influence of men who are high in extraversion will be reduced. More cautious, measured and strategic approaches are likely to be appropriate. Such a culture favours men who are low in extraversion and suited to roles within legal, security and other regulatory systems. It is, therefore, no surprise that Vladimir Putin is low in extraversion and high in indifference.

In summary, power in male groups naturally resides with the establishment, and when this is the case, the group will be located at the top of the Circle of Power. However, at times the group will shift clockwise around the circle towards a more liberal culture, or anti-clockwise towards a more conservative one. Because a minority of males are low in indifference, this trait plays little part in determining the culture of male groups, and therefore it is very unlikely that a male group will move to the bottom of the circle.

The female collective

The greater physical strength and higher levels of indifference of males enable them to out-compete females and suit them to hunting and fighting. The female's on average lower level of indifference and her childbearing capability naturally incline her to care for children and reduce her ability to cause harm to other people or animals. In contrast to the primal hierarchy, which focuses on the accumulation and exploitation of resources, the fundamental objective of females is to create an environment suitable for the rearing of children and to release resources from the control of the establishment for their benefit. To achieve this, they naturally operate in a sub-structure that I call the **female collective**.

A majority of women possess the progressive trait of low indifference. This prompts women in general to restrict the expression of competitive instincts and promote collaboration, caring and harmony. Most women instinctively help each other to deal with the challenges of pregnancy, childbirth and looking after children. Those who lack that instinct still have an incentive to help others out, as they are likely to need support from other women at some point. Although there is no gender difference in respect of the other three progressive traits, behaviours associated with these traits are more apparent within the female collective than the primal hierarchy. This is because they assist with the task of bringing up children. Young children require constant attention and restrict their mother's mobility. Historically, therefore, women focused their attention on domestic activities and the harvesting of crops and fruit close to where they lived. This lack of mobility encouraged the female collective to adopt sustainable practices that helped to protect its environment. Females would also have had to conserve their food sources because alpha males would have reserved the best quality meat for themselves. As the trait of low extraversion promotes fairness, sharing and frugality, women who possess this trait are useful in such circumstances. Also, the observational skills that people with this trait possess enable them to look out for physical dangers to children. The trait of high openness promotes broad-based learning and tolerance, which aid the development of children so women with this trait are given more freedom to act on their novelty-seeking instincts than their male counterparts. High opportunism endows a person with flexibility, which is a useful asset when faced with the many challenges of looking after children, so women with this trait are also more valued by the female collective than the primal hierarchy.

The progressive traits therefore dictate the default culture of the female collective. Women with these traits are therefore fully accepted within the collective whereas their male counterparts are excluded or marginalised by the primal hierarchy. The orientation of female groups towards the progressive traits means that they tend to be much more willing to embrace creativity and tolerate non-conformity and expressions of individuality than male groups. As a result, the female collective is less cohesive and organised than the primal hierarchy. It is held together by the mutual need for support and an obligation not to harm others, not by physical force, greed, systems or loyalty.

As the female collective's purpose is the protection and development of all children within the group, it is redistributive by nature. Wealth and resources tend to be seen as a means to an end, rather than a source of power and status. A female's status amongst males can be enhanced if she establishes a strong relationship with the dominant male or a member of the establishment. In primeval times, achieving favoured status could have given a female priority access to food. Now it might bring a luxurious lifestyle and high social status. Achieving high status amongst males will not usually enhance a woman's status within the female collective unless she uses her superior access to resources for the benefit of the female collective or takes advantage of her position in some other way to advance its interests.

The information sharing systems and power dynamics within the female collective tend to be much more complicated and unstable than in the primal hierarchy. Behaviours associated with progressive traits result in the creation of an information network rather than a command and control hierarchy. The culture of sharing that exists within the female collective extends to the exchange of information. Sharing information helps females to uncover the secrets of the establishment, opening up access to resources. Information, therefore, spreads much more widely in female groups than in the male ones. The communication of information through networks is less precise and organised than within a hierarchical structure. As a consequence, women tend to spend much more time communicating with each other than men do, and there is no guarantee that every woman in the network receives information that is relevant to her or an accurate version of the original message. This can result in inefficiencies, miscalculations or failures. Within typical female environments, such consequences can usually be accommodated. This is because women have the safety net of knowing that other women in the group are bound by the obligation not to cause significant harm to others. Mistakes, disagreements and betrayals of trust can therefore usually be remedied, and parties can be reconciled without major damage occurring. This safety net gives women the freedom to be more outgoing in female company than they would be in the presence of men. This behaviour is in stark contrast to that of male groups where errors, failings or breaches of trust can result in death or loss of resources due to the nature of job roles in the wider world and the competitive nature of individual males. Networked structures are therefore not suitable for companies managing nuclear facilities and other organisations whose failures could have catastrophic consequences. The greater dangers that males face cause them to be more guarded in their conversation than women, often avoiding discussion of business or personal issues.

Some women possess all four establishment traits. They will instinctively pursue wealth and status and attempt to increase the coherency and strengthen the structure of the female collective. Their personality traits suit them to membership of the primal hierarchy, but their gender differences prevent them from being accepted by its members. As a result, they will attempt to create hierarchical structures within the female collective. A dominant female and a quasi-establishment may emerge as a consequence, but they will be much less powerful than their male equivalents. The female collective's commitment to fairness makes it difficult for a dominant female to set herself up as the focal point of attention and resources. The collective is harder to control than the primal hierarchy, as it is more tolerant of new ideas and nonconformity than the primal hierarchy, and allows individuals more personal freedom. Its information sharing practices and the freedom it grants to its members make it impossible to establish effective command and control structures. Although the dominant female will be high in indifference, she is unlikely to be as ruthless as a dominant male and will lack his physical strength. She may, however, use verbal attacks or emotional manipulation to get her way. For example, she may portray situations in ways that induce guilt in the minds of other group members. Such strategies are, however, unlikely to be received well by other members of the female collective due to the harm that they cause to the individuals concerned. The female collective's preference for harmony makes it harder for the dominant female to impose her will. Consequently, she will need to take more account of the wishes of ordinary members of the female collective than the dominant male does of members of the primal hierarchy.

A dominant female may take advantage of the looser information networks that exist within the female collective to spread misinformation that benefits her cause. However, such networks usually work against establishment interests as they allow members of the collective to check the validity of statements with other members of the collective. As a result, the female collective can develop a viewpoint independently of the dominant female. If she behaves unreasonably in the eyes of the female collective, she is likely to find herself side-lined. She may not be overtly challenged because of the lack of appetite for confrontation within female groups, but if a quiet consensus is achieved amongst members of the collective, her power will evaporate as allegiances are transferred to a new leader. Female groups are therefore democratic in nature whereas male groups are authoritarian.

Females with higher levels of indifference do, however, serve a useful purpose in female groups. Consensus building can slow down decision-making so it helps to have people who are less concerned about hurting other people's feelings than the average female if you wish a timely decision to be made. An excessive focus on maintaining harmony within the female collective can also result in a closing down of debate and a culture of political correctness so it helps to have women who are prepared to speak their mind. A concern to keep children from being harmed can result in over-protective behaviours, which may ultimately disadvantage children and the wider group by preventing or delaying the acquisition of life skills and acceptance of responsibility. It is therefore useful to have some women who are less sympathetic.

As with other ape species, young females would have transitioned to other groups in primeval times. This dynamic helps to maintain genetic diversity. The female collective accepts females from other groups because of its tolerant culture and the common interest that its members have in looking after children. An attractive new female would have provoked some jealousy amongst the group's females, but because males would not have been restricted to a single female, they would have had no reason to discard existing mates. In modern, monogamous societies, however, the fact that alpha males are expected to commit to one female at a time means that their current wives or girlfriends have greater reason to feel insecure and to keep them away from more attractive women.

Females have less to fear when encountering males from other groups than their male counterparts. This is because alpha males see them as assets. In the primeval context, if the female collective's current protectors were overwhelmed, its members would have assimilated into the conquering male group. By transferring its allegiance to a new group of males, the collective would have secured access to the superior genes that enabled that group to achieve victory. In reality, such conquest would have had traumatic consequences for females within the group. Males to whom they were emotionally attached (including their male children) would have been killed, driven away or enslaved, as males have no interest in securing the survival of genes from males belonging to rival groups. This instinct remains today as demonstrated by the fact that stepfathers are significantly more likely to abuse their stepchildren than their natural fathers.

Women are also likely to experience emotional or physical harm when anarchy breaks out in a group or where they are left unprotected in times of conflict. Where the primal hierarchy is weakened or destroyed, opportunistic males are able to take advantage of unwilling females so women are much more likely to be raped in conflict scenarios. Therefore, in times of significant threat, members of the female collective look to men with establishment traits for protection and are forced to be subservient to them in exchange. In more peaceful times, they have less need to submit to such men and can instead form relationships with men with progressive traits who are more likely to share their objectives and allow them to play a role in wider society.

The desire of women to see their children grow up into effective and happy members of society causes them to be hopeful by nature. As they age, women who have had children are likely to become more influential and secure because they will usually find themselves at the centre of a supportive unit of relations. In contrast, males tend to become increasingly fearful once their physical power begins to wane and other younger males in the group (including their sons) begin to outcompete them. They are aware that sudden changes within their environment may result in losses in wealth and authority that are likely to be irreversible. As a consequence, males tend to become more conservative and defensive in their behaviour in their later years and join with other males in the same position to constrain and direct the actions of younger men. The smaller size of families and geographic dispersion of family members in modern society has, however, deprived many men and women of such support.

The default culture for the female collective is located at the bottom of the Circle of Power. In times of peace and prosperity, the female collective allows females who are high in extraversion more freedom to exercise their outgoing and materialistic behaviours. A more liberal culture emerges within it that encourages personal gratification, which is represented by a shift anti-clockwise around the Circle of Power. When resources are scarce and the environment is more uncertain, a more conservative culture is likely to emerge. The collective will become more structured and conformist with matriarchal figures imposing order, resulting in a clockwise shift of culture to include the traits of low opportunism and low openness. A dominant female may be high in indifference, but because a minority of females possess this trait, it plays little part in determining the culture of female groups. Therefore, it is very unlikely that a female group will move to the top of the Circle of Power.

Males with three or four progressive traits will be more suited to the structure of the female collective than the primal hierarchy. However, they will be excluded because of their gender. This is because men, in general, present a threat to the harmony of the female collective and their children due to the priority they give to securing mating opportunities with females. They will therefore generally be excluded from the information sharing and support networks that females establish.

Illustrating the primal hierarchy and female collective

The differences in structure between the primal hierarchy and the female collective are illustrated simplistically in Figures 13 and 14 below and overleaf. The primal hierarchy is a pyramid shape because of its hierarchical nature. The leader and the establishment are at the top above the solid line. Below this tight group is the command chain and rank and file. The command chain is shown as one row of boxes, but in reality it has multiple levels. Men with progressive traits (the dark boxes) are marginalised. The dotted line indicates that the primal hierarchy will make use of the talents and skills of individual progressives.

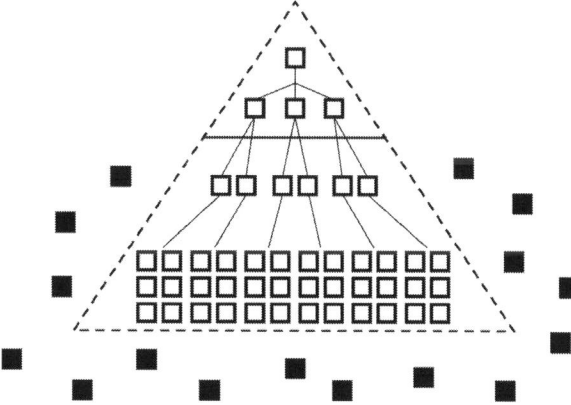

Figure 13. The structure of the primal hierarchy

The structure of the female collective is flatter and more uneven than that of the primal hierarchy due to its networked structure. Power is more evenly distributed and shifts more easily than in the primal hierarchy so the dominant female is less of a focal point. Women with progressive traits are fully integrated within the female collective so there is no need for a dotted line.

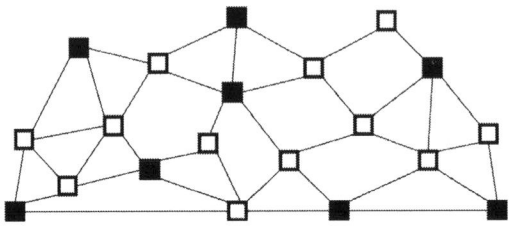

Figure 14. The structure of the female collective

To summarise, the eight personality traits in The Personality Revolution's Model of Personality form a natural and circular sequence on the Circle of Power. The establishment traits are located at the top of the circle and the progressive traits at the bottom. The establishment traits will usually be dominant within male groups. The most influential establishment traits are high indifference and low openness, which is why I have located them at the top of the circle. High indifference endows a capacity for ruthlessness. Low openness encourages a narrow focus, group bonding and fear of other groups of males. These traits give the primal hierarchy coherence and competitive drive, which are key to the projection of power. They are flanked by the traits of high extraversion and low opportunism. High extraversion promotes a desire for status and resources and therefore provides physical objectives for the competitive drive of the establishment. Low opportunism gives a male group structure, which increases its effectiveness as a unit. The establishment traits, therefore, orientate male groups to compete for resources against other groups and give rise to an **establishment culture**, as illustrated in Figure 15 opposite.

The remaining four traits are progressive traits. They promote the values of freedom, tolerance, compassion and fairness, and collectively give rise to a **progressive culture.** They represent the default setting for female groups. Within the female collective, the traits of low indifference and high openness are most influential and are located at the bottom of the circle. The trait of low indifference promotes peace and harmony and is most evident within the domestic environment over which the female collective naturally has control. High openness is associated with exploration of new ideas and experiences and the sharing of knowledge. These traits are flanked by the traits of low extraversion and high opportunism. Low extraversion promotes fairness and sharing, and high opportunism encourages flexible responses.

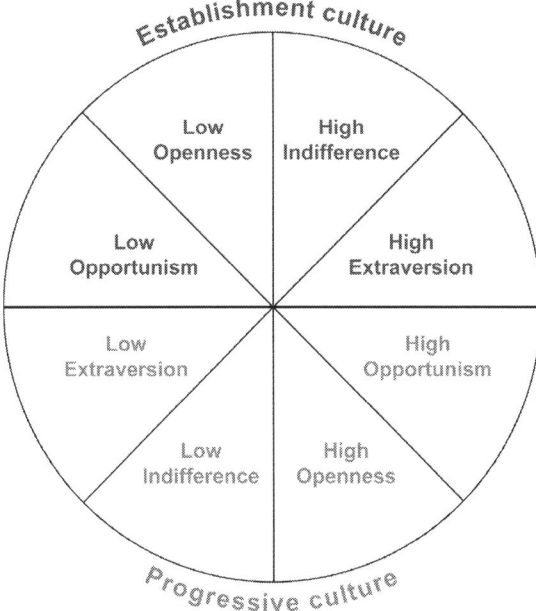

Figure 15. Establishment and progressive cultures
illustrated on the Circle of Power

Because the default cultures of the primal hierarchy and the female collective are related to specific personality traits, these sub-groups can be plotted on the Circle of Power, as illustrated in Figure 16 overleaf. This diagram is very simplistic. As there are 16 basic personality combinations, only a small proportion of a typical population will possess all four establishment traits or all four progressive traits. Most people will have a mixture of high and low traits and will display behaviours associated with the primal hierarchy in some respects and behaviours associated with the female collective in others. Also, extreme traits are relatively rare. Most people possess middling traits and therefore are pulled towards different cultures depending on the nature of the current environment. The establishment, command chain and rank and file are plotted on the diagram according to the traits that most characterise their behaviour. The sizes of the segments in the upper half do not relate to the actual number of people within each of these categories. In reality, the establishment is small because a member of it must clearly possess all four establishment traits to fit in. The rank and file is a much larger group because it is defined by the possession of a single trait – that of low openness. With regard to the other spectrums, its members may possess middling traits. However, the possession of a progressive trait marks a person out as a progressive male. Because such males are linked together only by their exclusion from the primal hierarchy, they are not classified as a sub-group in this model and therefore not illustrated on the diagram.

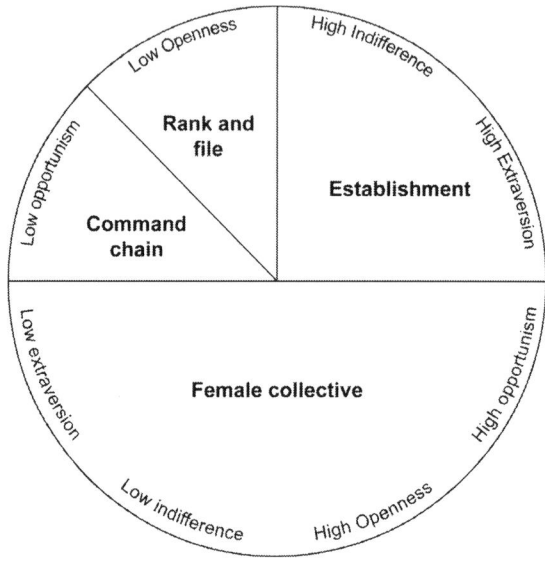

Figure 16. The primal hierarchy

Mixed gender groups

The primal hierarchy and female collective do not operate in isolation. They have a symbiotic relationship. Establishment males cannot regenerate the primal hierarchy with young men without females. Meanwhile, females need to secure access to the resources of the establishment and protective capabilities of the primal hierarchy for the benefit of the group's children. The primal hierarchy and female collective also share social space. Each sub-group therefore influences the behaviour of the other to some extent. There is also a tension between the two sub-groups. Establishment males seek to control fertile females so that they can secure their genetic legacy and prevent women from influencing members of the primal hierarchy. Females try to obtain resources and protection while minimising their loss of freedom.

The interaction of the primal hierarchy and female collective creates a wider group culture. The position of this culture on the Circle of Power will be determined by the relative strength of these sub-groups and environmental conditions. If the dominant male and establishment impose their will over the female collective, an establishment culture results. If the female collective is more influential, a progressive culture emerges.

In an establishment culture, the establishment uses the primal hierarchy to accumulate resources and project power against other groups. The primal hierarchy ranges widely, extending the group's territory where it is successful. Males view females as objects for sexual gratification, procreation and childcare, and afford them no influence over worldly matters. They restrict females to the domestic environment and childcare. Women in establishment cultures are therefore denied basic rights such as the right to own property, vote or associate with men without supervision by a guardian.

In a progressive culture, the power of establishment males is constrained by the female collective. Competitive instincts are suppressed, and this enables females to operate effectively alongside males. Females are not tied to a single male and may have multiple sexual partners at the same time. Males take on more responsibility for domestic tasks, giving females the opportunity to engage with the wider world. Females are therefore able to access education, develop new interests and roles and participate in decision-making on worldly matters. Behaviours associated with the female collective become more evident in the wider group resulting in the emergence of a tolerant, compassionate culture and a peaceful environment.

The extent of the influence of the female collective within a group will largely depend on the physical threat level within its environment. Females are unsuited to competing with males and are vulnerable to the use of physical force by them. In times of inter-group conflict or anarchy, the influence of the female collective will be very limited because the male competitive instinct will be aroused along with feelings of fear. Males tend to exert their physical dominance or group together for protection. The primal hierarchy is strengthened and, as a result, an establishment culture emerges. Women are forced to accept a subservient role because of their lesser physical strength, the ineffectiveness of their consensus-building and peace-making skills in such environments, and their inability to conform sufficiently to be accepted as equals by members of the primal hierarchy. In situations where a group does not face threats from other groups, but is threatened by food shortages due to natural causes, group members will need to share resources and innovate to survive. These behaviours are associated with the female collective so the collective becomes more influential. A progressive culture therefore emerges.

Two intermediate positions exist on the Circle of Power between establishment and progressive cultures. Where conditions are benign, members of both sexes are drawn towards exploratory, individualistic behaviours, and the primal hierarchy and female collective become less influential, resulting in an **individualistic culture**. Where the environment is more challenging, men and women focus on performing Slow System skills for the benefit of their sub-groups. The rank and file and more socially responsible members of the female collective join forces and become the dominant influence at the expense of the establishment and liberal progressives. A **collectivist culture** therefore emerges. These intermediate cultures are illustrated in Figure 17 below.

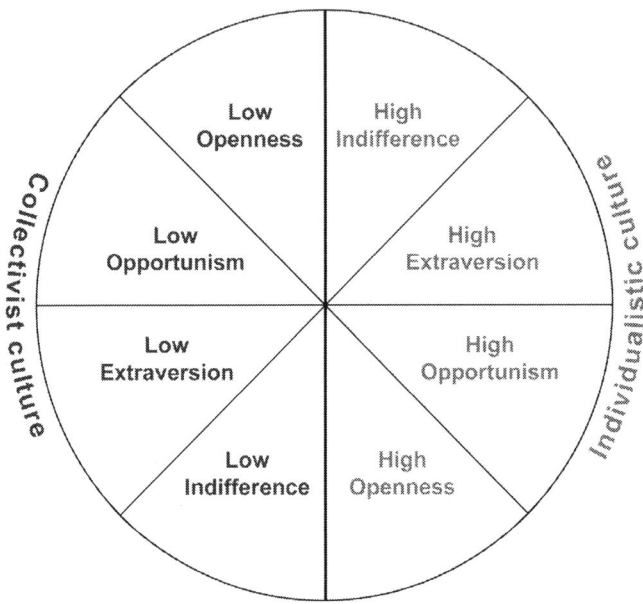

Figure 17. Collectivist and individualistic cultures on the Circle of Power

In a collectivist culture, although men and women have equal status, roles are allocated according to gender. Men perform jobs in the armed forces, commerce and industry whereas women are restricted to health, education and domestic responsibilities. In individualistic cultures, however, men and women compete on a level playing field. This allows women with establishment traits to perform roles traditionally associated with the primal hierarchy and men with progressive traits to perform roles associated with the female collective. For example, a woman with a relatively high level of indifference and a low level of openness is likely to be more interested in processes and mechanics than caring for people. In an individualistic society, she will find it easier for to secure a job role in engineering or another process-related industry. Similarly, men who are low in indifference will be more readily accepted within the nursing profession, which is traditionally reserved for members of the female collective.

Cultural shifts around the Circle of Power

In any mixed gender group, there will be an on-going tension between high traits and low traits, and between the interests of the establishment and the female collective. These forces are located equidistantly from each other on the Circle of Power so there is a natural balancing point at the centre. As most people are located towards the centre of the personality spectrums, group culture will tend towards this central position. In average conditions, a group that contains a typical distribution of personality traits (including a society) will be most effective when its culture is located in this position. However, environmental factors and the actions and objectives of influential people can cause groups to adopt establishment, progressive, collectivist or individualistic cultures. As circumstances change, the group is likely to shift around the Circle of Power and adopt a new culture.

In any group, there will always be traits that are dominant, bordering traits that are exerting some influence and traits that are marginalised. Group culture will shift towards one of the bordering traits if the environment in which the group operates changes and the talents and skills associated with such trait are suited to the new environment. It may also shift if a new leader with different traits ascends to power. However, a challenger to an existing leader is more likely to be successful if his group's environment has changed and his attributes are suited to this new environment. In other words, members of a group are likely to support a challenger when he appears to be more capable than the existing leader. Because particular traits are associated with the establishment, command chain, rank and file and female collective, these sub-groups will be empowered when values shift in their favour and marginalised when they move away.

Where a group's environment remains the same for an extended period, people whose traits match the prevailing culture tend to entrench their positions. The group's culture may become more extreme as a result, moving away from the natural balancing point at the centre of the Circle of Power. In such circumstances, people with the reverse traits will become increasingly disadvantaged and are likely to find it difficult to express their discontent effectively. People who have entrenched their positions are likely to resist the influence of environmental factors that would otherwise prompt a shift in culture. They may, though, become complacent and fail to notice, or avoid dealing with, potential threats. Whichever is the case, their position will be weakened over time and they will be vulnerable to conquest or a revolution. If successful, group culture is likely to suddenly shift to one that is more appropriate for the current environment.

Conquests and revolutions are rare. Normally circumstances change gradually and group culture shifts around the Circle of Power in response. I will now explain how a group's culture can shift around the circle. To assist with this explanation, in the version of the circle in Figure 18 below, I have placed a key characteristic associated with each trait in its respective segment.

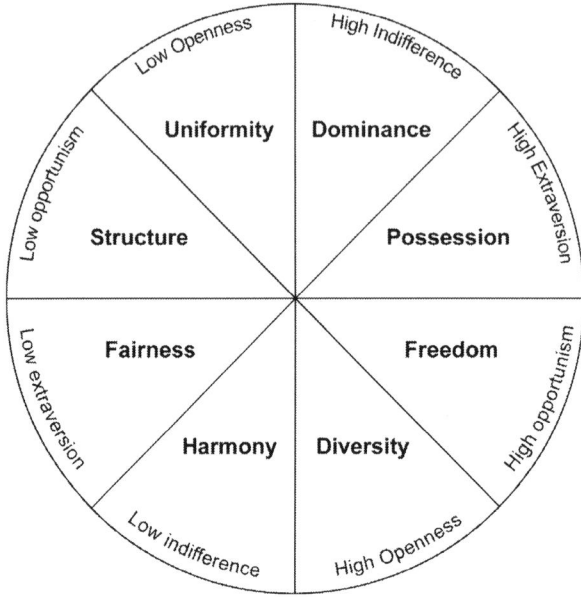

Figure 18. Characteristics associated with particular traits

Let us assume that a group's culture currently spans the four high traits. The group will be characterised by exploratory behaviours, giving rise to an individualistic culture. Group members will have a great amount of personal freedom, and the group will embrace innovation and diversity. Individuals will be permitted to compete for dominance, possess wealth and resources and display exhibitionist behaviour. However, the freedom given to individuals within an individualistic culture to pursue self-interested behaviours causes the group to disintegrate. People with low traits feel increasingly insecure as the structures they depend upon for support and protection are undermined by the general pursuit of self-interested objectives. A controlling intervention is therefore likely, resulting in a shift around the circle either clockwise or anti-clockwise. I will deal with anti-clockwise movements first.

Novelty seeking behaviour results in the creation of a wide range of new ideas, products and experiences. However, diversity causes members of the rank and file to experience anxiety and chronic stress, so they look for security in traditional environments. They are attracted to leaders who offer a return to a simpler and more uniform society. As individualistic cultures encourage the exertion of dominance, it is likely that a potential leader with a high level of indifference and low level of openness will be waiting in the wings. If he establishes a power base in the rank and file and secures power, group culture will shift to include the trait of low openness. It is easier to organise a group that has a high level of coherency, so people who are low in opportunism gain more influence in such circumstances. A leader is likely to entrench his position by making the primal hierarchy more organised and imposing rules on the wider group. He will therefore strengthen the command chain. The group therefore becomes more structured and adopts an establishment culture.

Establishment families may become so wealthy and entrenched that they cease to engage in aggressive power plays or materialistic endeavours and concentrate instead on the protection of their existing assets. In such circumstances, people who are cautious in their use of resources and measured in their decision-making (i.e. those who are low in extraversion) will become more valuable. Group culture shifts further around the Circle of Power as a result. Group members are less likely to be physically or emotionally harmed by other group members where the group operates cautiously and fairly. People who are low in indifference and who promote harmony become more influential in such circumstances. At this point, a collectivist culture characterised by defensive, controlling behaviours emerges.

The behaviour of people who are different is likely to be tolerated within a harmonious environment. People who are high in openness therefore benefit in such circumstances. As diversity undermines uniformity, group culture shifts anti-clockwise again. It is hard to create a set of rules that accommodate a wide variety of beliefs and behaviours, so a group becomes less organised when its group members acquire more personal freedom. This benefits those who are high in opportunism and the group culture shifts further to a progressive culture. However, where people have a lot of personal freedom, it is easier for them to use it to pursue increased status and behave materialistically. People who are high in extraversion are therefore released to explore the world. This behaviour increases the availability of resources and encourages people, and particularly men, to compete for those resources. The group, therefore, completes the full circle and once again adopts an individualistic culture.

Group culture can also shift in a clockwise direction. Starting again from an individualistic culture, a group's environment is likely to be peaceful where people with different backgrounds and values mix together and tolerate each other's behaviour. People who are low in indifference therefore become more influential and focus on preventing harm to others when a group displays behaviours associated with the trait of high openness. It is easier for people who are low in extraversion to enforce principles of fairness in environments where abuses of power are prevented. At this point, a progressive culture emerges. People who are low in extraversion naturally look to people who are organised to help them achieve their objectives so people who are low in opportunism gain influence and impose more structure within the group. A highly structured group brings people into closer contact with each other and makes it easier for those wishing to impose uniformity to do so, increasing the influence of those who are low in openness. This results in a shift to a collectivist culture. People who are high in indifference can more easily exert authority over groups that are uniform so they tend to become more powerful in such circumstances. A dominant leader will instinctively try to extend his group's territory, increasing the resources available to the group. This gives people who are high in extraversion more opportunity to acquire status and wealth. An establishment culture results. People with status and wealth tend to feel self-sufficient and therefore desire more freedom, so people who are high in opportunism gain more influence. As people gain more freedom, they will be less concerned about differences with other people and diversity will increase. At this point, the group's culture has turned full circle back to an individualistic one.

Sometimes the forces at play within a group or society can pull a group in both directions around the Circle of Power at the same time. This is occurring at the moment as the primal hierarchy and the female collective are strengthening their positions in response to the insecurity caused by the individualistic culture that has prevailed globally over the last forty years. The society we are living in is proving unsustainable and establishment and progressive forces are engaged in a struggle that is essentially a battle of the sexes.

Dealing with an unfavourable culture

As different cultures favour particular personality traits, your ability to be effective and experience positive feelings will depend to a considerable degree on the level of synchronicity between the culture that currently exists within your group and your personality traits. If your personality traits match the dominant traits within the group, you will have the potential to become a successful and influential figure because your natural behaviours will align with the values of the group. People with traits that are out of favour are likely to feel like outsiders, lack influence and experience stress or low moods.

If you are experiencing negative feelings as a result of the culture and power dynamics within a group, you have four choices if you wish to improve your state of mind. You can try to change the culture to suit your personality traits, hope circumstances will change for the better, relocate yourself to another group with a more favourable culture, or accept that you have no alternative but to accept your unfavourable positions. These options correspond to the solutions available to the fight or flight mechanism – confrontation, hiding, evasion and submission.

Hiding, and its close relation avoidance, does nothing to counter the underlying causes of negative feelings. Indeed, they give stressors space to become more threatening. Leaving a group is superficially attractive as it allows you to instantly escape from the dynamics within it that are causing you discomfort. However, there is no guarantee that any new group that you join will not have or develop a similar culture to the one that you have just left. Also, it is unlikely that your existing group will be entirely detrimental to your progress in life, so you will lose the support and protection that it does provide you with, which may have taken many years to acquire, if you choose to leave. Although you can replace a job or online group relatively easily, you will find it much harder to replace a family or friendship group. The breakdown of such bonds can negatively affect your future performance and your physical and emotional wellbeing. Also, some groups are very difficult to leave, particularly a society. Although many people now migrate from one country to another, language differences and cultural and immigration restrictions can present significant obstacles.

In some instances, therefore, you may only be able to improve your situation significantly if you succeed in changing group or societal culture. A single person cannot usually change the culture of a group through his own will. He will need the support of others who share his values or who are prepared to trust his judgement. A leader will be in a highly influential position and is potentially a greater agent of change than an ordinary group member. However, unless the group is very small, he will only be able to shift its culture significantly if he has established a strong support base within it or has a means of enforcing change. In other words, he will need to either court popularity or adopt an authoritarian approach. If ordinary group members or citizens wish to shift the culture of a group or society they will need the weight of numbers, so they must work together to convince others within the group of the virtue of their objectives.

If you are in the unfortunate position of possessing traits that are not suited to your current environment and lacking supportive colleagues, you may need to accept that it is not possible for you to change your group's culture. If you reach an accommodation with yourself, you are likely to be able to operate more effectively within it and release some of your negative feelings. If you are unable or unprepared to make such an accommodation, you will need to show resilience although you may employ regulatory techniques or resort to drugs to reduce the intensity of the negative feelings that you are experiencing. Accommodation, resilience and regulation are discussed in more detail in a later chapter.

The battle of the sexes

In primeval times, females would have exerted a significant influence on the establishment, even within establishment cultures. The female collective would have played an important role in the selection of the dominant male and the maintenance of his authority. This is demonstrated in primate groups by the fact that dominant males are usually fine physical specimens, not simply masters of competition. Females have a dual interest. They need their young to be protected, but they are also driven to seek out the best genes. The female collective would have encouraged males that it determined to be of mating quality to pursue dominant male status by adopting behaviours that enhanced their confidence and self-esteem. Females would have also helped a dominant male to maintain togetherness within a group by performing activities that promote harmony and creating an environment in which the primal hierarchy could recover from their exertions. Any withdrawal of goodwill by female members would have undermined his position.

As the number of humans on the planet was much smaller than it is today, some groups would have found themselves in the isolated locations that favoured the emergence of progressive cultures. However, as human civilisation developed, and particularly once men began to develop tools, the primal hierarchy became more powerful relative to the female collective. As humans multiplied, increased proximity to other groups resulted in competition for resources and the conquest and assimilation of rival groups. Weapons increased the ability of men to compete for territory in armed warfare. Advances in transportation and communications allowed them to travel further away and transact their business out of sight of females, who were obliged to remain within the domestic environment. Leaders and other senior figures set up systems that allowed them to exercise their greedy instincts and behave in an authoritarian manner. In other words, as the female collective's influence over the establishment declined, establishment cultures became embedded.

As human groups increased in size, it became impractical for establishment males to claim exclusive ownership rights over all females within a group. Other males were able to develop sexual relationships with females and eventually long-term monogamous relationships became the norm. The authority of the dominant male is undermined where men who are not members of the establishment and particularly members of the rank and file marry and establish families of their own. This is because a marriage essentially marks the creation of a new human group and gives husbands the opportunity to set up their own personal fiefdoms in which case they begin to compete with the dominant male to some degree and dilute his power. In other words, the nuclear family replicates the dynamics of the primal group by establishing the man as the dominant male. Husbands therefore assumed control over their wives and guided the development of their sons, sometimes enrolling them into family businesses. They were also able to trade their daughters for profit or other advantage by obtaining a bride price or establishing a useful relationship with another family through an arranged marriage and payment of a dowry.

The wives of non-establishment men find it easier to exert influence over their husbands than those women who are married to members of the establishment because their husbands are likely to be less ruthless or less controlling than members of the establishment. Establishment leaders sought to prevent their soldiers from falling under the influence of women by housing them in barracks and keeping them mobile. International football managers often take a similar approach, barring players from seeing their girlfriends and wives when they are preparing for and participating in competitions. Such leaders also sought to suppress women by limiting their access to education and setting down rules of conduct in religious texts, most notably an obligation to obey their husbands. Even though, males gained some independence through marriage, the dynamics of the primal hierarchy still operate within a society so an establishment leader would have found males within his group more reliable than females and would have depended on them to constrain their wives and daughters. In countries with strong establishment cultures, men are still expected to perform this role and are encouraged to engage in practices that make it easier to do so, such as female genital mutilation. If a woman under a male's control disobeys him or breaches cultural values, the shame the man feels may cause him or male relatives to punish her. In extreme cases, this results in honour killings.

The adoption of monogamy, therefore, weakened the genetic and physical influence of the dominant male and establishment. However, the cohesiveness of the female collective is reduced in groups where long-term monogamous relationships are the norm because its members are separated physically from each other. When women enter into such relationships, their ability to support each other and stand together as a united force is reduced. Also, the link between the female collective and the dominant male and his resources is broken. This reduction in influence over the dominant male is, however, balanced by increased influence over individual males. A close one-to-one relationship with a man makes it easier for a woman to influence his behaviour, especially if he is not an alpha male. Women who marry tolerant or trusting men, and their daughters, are more likely to be given the freedom to learn and participate in wider society than those who are controlled by establishment men. Where members of the rank and file and the female collective join forces in marriage, they place limits on the exploitative behaviours of the establishment and a collectivist culture will emerge. Examples include countries with long histories of monogamous culture or assertive rank and files, like China and France. During the mid 20th century, collectivist cultures were commonplace in the developed world as governments implemented economic and social policies based on state ownership of economic assets and the provision of universal public services.

The development of market economies following the Industrial Revolution allowed some women to escape the domestic environment. Whereas men with establishment traits are inclined to keep women separate from men, entrepreneurial men tend to see them as a useful labour resource. Consequently, women were drawn into the working world. The adoption of universal suffrage in Europe and the USA in the early 20th century greatly empowered women and since then they have steadily been increasing their influence. They have entered the workforce in large numbers and now perform job roles that have been historically seen as the preserve of males, while their partners make a greater contribution in the domestic environment than their predecessors would have done.

Access to education and the job market have propelled women to a position of near equality with men in modern society and a significant number of women have achieved leadership positions that were formerly the preserve of men. Recent technological advances have improved communications and made it easier for women to network with each other at a distance, thereby strengthening the female collective. Gender equality laws and universal education systems have embedded liberal, progressive values within Western society, such as tolerance and the right to terminate unwanted pregnancies. Practices associated with the female collective such as seeking collaborative, win-win solutions have become more evident within traditionally male organisations. Win-win solutions, as opposed to winner-takes-it-all or zero-sum game approaches, recognise the value of seeking outcomes that maximise the return for each party. However, while women are fighting harder than ever to secure equality in the workplace and social arenas, their interests are being undermined economically.

A progressive culture can be undermined by the traits of high extraversion or low opportunism as these traits sit either side of the progressive traits on the Circle of Power. High extraversion promotes materialistic behaviour. It is the Achilles heel of the female collective because it encourages women who possess it to submit to men.

A woman who desires material goods that she cannot afford will naturally look to an establishment male to provide them. If she is not married to one, which will be more likely than not, she may encourage her husband to compete for position and income as if he was. Society, therefore, becomes more competitive and there is a shift towards an individualistic culture. The trait of low opportunism promotes organisation and structure. Members of the female collective will be inclined to create rules to embed their values within a group and restrain the actions of people who are high in indifference and extraversion, for example, product safety laws. Rules, however, give people who possess the establishment trait of low opportunism greater influence, increasing bureaucracy and limiting freedom of action. They also give opportunities to people who are low in openness to increase conformity within society, resulting in a shift towards a collectivist culture.

Towards the end of the 20th century, the governments of Ronald Reagan in the USA and Margaret Thatcher in the UK championed materialism, introducing free-market economic policies which undermined the progressive values of fairness and compassion, and caused those countries to develop strongly individualistic cultures. These neo-liberal policies have combined with technological innovations have enabled the emergence of a new global establishment. Contemporaneously, the European Union, United Nations and international trade organisations developed rules-based bureaucratic systems in an attempt to prevent the harmful actions of opportunistic businesses and governments. These organisations developed collectivist cultures. The behaviour of members of this establishment is now undermining both individualistic and collectivist cultures around the world, resulting in a global shift towards an establishment culture. However, if it is given the opportunity, the establishment will introduce structure and systems into a group with an individualistic culture that channel wealth to the establishment more efficiently. Members of the global establishment have created companies and the global economic system for this purpose. This liberal economic framework has allowed multinationals free rein to outcompete local and national businesses. In a country with a collectivist culture, the establishment will promote competition for resources by releasing assets held by the government and other bodies into markets. The global establishment has achieved this very effectively in the UK by lobbying for privatisation of industries that were established or nationalised by socialist governments in the mid 20th century and reductions in the amount of money spent on public services and social security.

As a result, we are experiencing a shift towards an establishment culture. This shift has been masked to a considerable extent by progress that liberal social campaigners have made in areas such as trans-gender rights and the appointment or election of increasing numbers of women to positions of power. It is, though, very real and such progressive gains will be lost if the global establishment gains complete control of the global economy. As women tend to be more concerned with social and domestic issues than economic ones, the female collective has not yet woken up to this threat. Instead, it is disadvantaged members of national primal hierarchies and local and nationally orientated opportunistic business people who have reacted against the economic consequences of globalisation. This has empowered populist leaders whose aim is to establish their own national power bases.

If a group is to develop or maintain a culture of progressive values, it is essential that the environment in which the group operates is peaceful and stable. If members of a group feel threatened, establishment cultures can reappear very quickly. In such circumstances, it is likely that group members, and particularly members of the primal hierarchy, will feel insecure and support a leader with establishment traits who has the ability to compete in the physical world and, therefore, the capacity to protect the group. Ultimately, personal freedom and the emotional wellbeing and safety of group members would all be put at risk if the group is outcompeted or overwhelmed. Psychologically, therefore, group members of both sexes tend to be prepared to surrender some of their freedoms and accept more brutal approaches when the group is subject to an external threat. Unfortunately, the emergence of nationalist leaders is likely to result in more conflict, as they attempt to assert their authority and compete for scarce natural resources on the international stage. These leaders are already using their power to undermine civil rights that have been hard won over centuries.

The rise to power of reactionary male politicians and increasing power of the global establishment has therefore caused a shift towards establishment cultures and the associated behaviours of greed and authoritarianism. If this dynamic is not checked, it will lead to war and environmental damage on a catastrophic scale. A battle for power and influence is taking place in households, workplaces and social environments between the male establishment and the female collective. Although laws have been introduced to prevent discrimination, the behaviours associated with the primal group structure will often be exhibited in the shadows. For example, establishment males may block the progression of females in the workplace, creating a glass ceiling, and females may take advantage of the female collective's superior communication networks to establish a collective position and place limits on the competitive behaviours of the establishment, as is currently occurring in relation to sexual harassment at work. Women, however, need to extend this battle into the economic arena if they are to counter the establishment dynamic and move the world towards peace and sustainability. This struggle is a major theme in the second volume of this work.

Political viewpoints

We are constantly managing internal conflicts between our personal values and group or societal values. Sometimes we speak our minds and challenge the behaviours of other people. At other times, we avoid difficult situations or put up with negative feelings in order to avoid confrontation. In a democratic country, though, people have the opportunity to influence the culture of their society at a societal level by engaging in politics.

Although you will usually be preoccupied with managing your immediate environment, it is important to spend time considering the big picture. If the political party in power espouses beliefs and principles that conflict with your personality traits, you are likely to experience a decline in your effectiveness and happiness as it puts its policies into practice. People tend to vote in accordance with their beliefs and values. Social background can, though, cause individuals to become tribally committed to a party, especially in countries with low levels of education or deeply embedded class systems. People whose traits conflict with the value system of the party to which they belong will serve as a counterweight to some degree, helping to prevent the party adopting extreme policies. However, they are likely to experience stress or low moods frequently due to the conflict between their personality traits and their party's policies. It is, therefore, useful to understand where your personality traits position you politically.

Although people are encouraged by the media to see political movements on a spectrum of left and right, they actually fit within a circle (the Circle of Power), as illustrated in Figure 19 overleaf. The three main political movements – conservatism, socialism and liberalism – overlap so many people find themselves torn between parties related to two of these movements. A significant number of people will possess a mixture of traits that does not neatly align with any of the movements. Also, most people have middling personality traits, so they will tend to adopt moderate political positions. They will be swing voters and are likely to vote for the party that appears to be most competent or which appears to have solutions for the issues that are most pressing at that time. Parties, therefore, usually do better in elections when they adopt cultures that are close to the centre of the Circle of Power and governments tend to be more popular when they adopt a pragmatic approach.

The **conservative** movement protects establishment interests. It pursues capitalist policies that channel wealth towards the establishment. If such policies were pursued to the extreme, the population would be trapped within a state of quasi-feudalism, but democracy or a revolution normally ensures that conservative parties moderate their approach or are removed from power before this occurs. Its leadership behaves in an authoritarian way, closing down debate and enforcing whips. It views elected members and the wider party as a machine for the projection of power. In other words it replicates the primal hierarchy. Historically, the conservative movement has depended on the support and labour of the rank and file to achieve its objectives. Male members of the working class, who roughly equate to the rank and file, will be inclined to support the establishment as they share the establishment's interest in promoting uniformity and strengthening the primal hierarchy. The central traits of conservatism are high indifference and low openness as they enable the establishment to project the power of a loyal and coherent body of men.

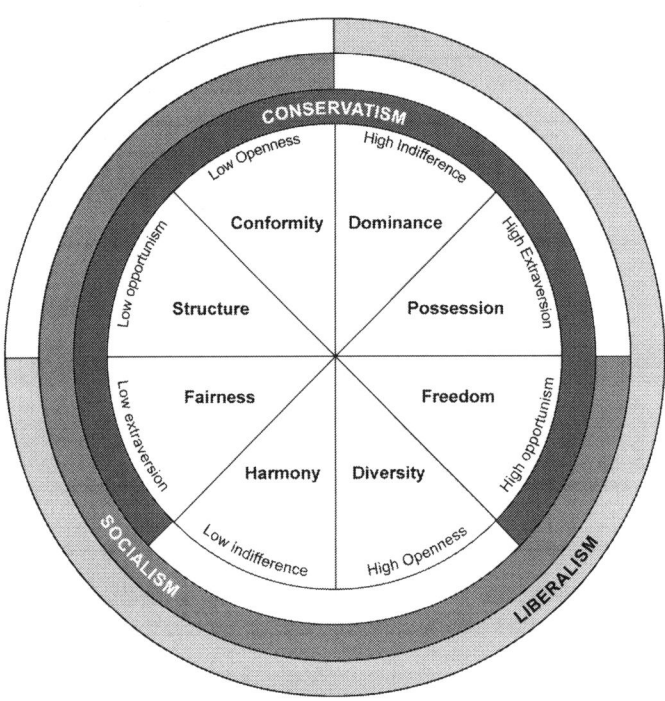

Figure 19. Political movements on the Circle of Power

Members of the rank and file are, though, susceptible to influence by people who are low in indifference and extraversion where they feel they are not being looked after by the establishment. People who possess one or both of these traits, a majority of whom will be female, serve as a counterbalance to alpha males and attempt to restrain their materialistic, self-interested objectives. People who are low in extraversion focus on making practices and the distribution of wealth within a country fairer while those who are low in indifference promote campaign for peace and harmony, and look after weaker members of society. These traits are the central traits within the **socialist** movement and orientate this movement around the principles of social justice and compassion.

High opportunism and high openness are the central traits within the **liberal** movement. Liberalism emerges in countries with strong market economies because people who possess theses traits thrive when they have freedom of action and the opportunity to trade and innovate. They help to keep market economies vibrant by preventing the establishment from introducing monopolistic practices and systems. Free markets help to create and spread wealth, resulting in the emergence of middle classes. The middle classes tend to place a greater value on education than members of the rank and file as they see it as a means of advancement and personal development. Education also promotes behaviours associated with high levels of openness, so middle-class people tend to be more tolerant and open to new ideas than members of the rank and file. New ideas help to stimulate economies so the middle classes expand further at the expense of the working class in educated, open societies. The traits of high opportunism and high openness are the bulwarks of liberal democracy as they encourage the people who possess them to fight for freedom of expression and other individualistic rights. The liberal movement, however, lacks coherency and structure because these characteristics are associated with the traits of low openness and low opportunism respectively. The resultant difficulties that liberal parties face in agreeing coherent policy positions can render them ineffective in the political arena.

Liberalism is often seen, mistakenly, as a centrist movement as commentators usually place it between right and left on a spectrum. We have seen, though, that the true political centre is at the centre of the Circle of Power. This explains why many people with liberal values are currently so confused about the reactionary politics we are currently experiencing. They have not realised that the liberal culture that has existed within the Western world over the past 40 years represents an extreme position in terms of personality and has marginalised and caused discomfort to many people, particularly those who are low in openness.

If the establishment is to keep power in a democracy, it must persuade people who are not members of the establishment to vote for conservative parties. In countries with traditional cultures, conservative parties tend to look to the rank and file for support. In liberal democracies, the reduced size of the working class forces them to look beyond the rank and file and seek the support of the aspirational middle classes and libertarians. They try to attract business people who are high in opportunism by promising to reduce regulation. These people will be torn between conservatism and liberalism and tend to pull conservative party policy towards more liberal positions when they join them in large numbers. However, conservative parties rarely embrace people with liberal social values as such people undermine conformity and often hold views that conflict with traditional religious beliefs. Conservative parties can also attract people who are low in extraversion whose natural caution causes them to seek to protect their assets. If such people gain significant influence within a conservative party, its policies will be focused on increasing fairness within society. When a conservative party shifts towards this more collectivist culture, it is likely to steal votes from socialist parties.

These dynamics can work the other way around in which case liberal or socialist parties attract votes away from conservative parties. When the culture of a socialist party shifts to include the traits of low openness, a collectivist culture will emerge. The rank and file and "hard" or "regressive" left" will gain influence at the expense of liberals, and communist ideas may become popular. When the culture of a liberal party shifts to include the trait of high indifference, an individualistic culture will emerge within it and neo-liberal economic policies will be championed.

The liberal and socialist movements also overlap, and do so more substantially than in respect of conservatism on the Circle of Power. People who occupy the overlapping space, which is characterised by behaviours associated with all four progressive traits, are usually known as social democrats although they share this space with many members of the green movement. They balance the rights of the individual to act freely with a responsibility to care for others and distribute resources fairly. In modern society, this translates to an entrepreneurial, but regulated, market economy with redistributive taxation policies and a strong commitment to public services.

The structure of conservative parties reflects the primal hierarchy. Conservative leaders place a high value on loyalty and organisation. Many politicians within these parties will be high in extraversion and indifference, which will cause them to seeker higher status, power and wealth. Their manoeuvres for power will usually be carried out surreptitiously. However, when a leader dies or is weakened, rivalries and ambitions become more apparent and candidates for succession will emerge. At this point, differences in opinion that have been kept in-house are likely to be exposed to public view. Leadership battles can be bloody affairs as rivals compete for power, but conservative parties will usually pull themselves back together quickly once a leader has been selected. The new leader will enforce order by taking advantage of the authoritarian powers at his disposal and the conforming tendencies of party members

Political parties that are characterised by progressive traits are less structured and more and welcoming of new ideas than conservative parties. These characteristics make them more accepting of internal dissent, and their members more inclined to disagree with each other in public. They also tend to make progressive parties appear disorganised and incoherent. However, as most members will be low in indifference, they will feel a need to reach a consensus and abide by democratic processes and this compensates for the lack of structure and coherency.

The nature of group dynamics means that people with establishment traits tend to ascend to positions of power within progressive parties, in which case behaviours associated with the primal hierarchy will begin to emerge. Union leaders may adopt authoritarian approaches, "hard left" activists may demand conformity, and politicians with outgoing personalities may be drawn towards wealth and status. This tendency has been exacerbated by the emergence of career politicians. They are more likely to target wealth and status and to be prepared to sacrifice principles for purposes of promotion or enrichment than politicians with independent incomes. In the last 40 years, a political class has developed in the UK and other Western countries that is self-serving and neglectful of the interests of voters.

Sometimes, however, a person who possesses predominantly progressive traits succeeds in becoming the leader of a progressive party. This is most likely to occur where a voting mechanism empowers ordinary group members and a large proportion of those members are female. In such cases, the relationship between the leader and establishment within the party is usually very difficult, as the leader is likely to pursue objectives related to his personality traits and the party's core values rather than act in the interests of the party's establishment. In the case of a democratically elected leader, it is likely that his policies will be in tune with the needs and desires of the party's members, so the establishment will find it difficult to remove him. This dynamic has been operating within the British Labour Party since 2015 when Jeremy Corbyn was elected as leader. Corbyn came to power after large numbers of new members joined the party. 422,664 people voted in the election and women made up 47% of the membership at that time.

Corbyn possesses three progressive traits. His low level of indifference means that he instinctively tries to build consensus and refuses to use aggressive and abusive language against his political opponents, although the stresses of Brexit caused him to call Theresa May, the British Prime Minister, "stupid" under his breath in Parliament in a display of frustration. His low level of extraversion causes him to treat people fairly, and to look at situations objectively and in a measured way. The traits of low indifference and low extraversion cause him to promote policies based upon social justice, but they also incline him to experience stress in competitive, physical environments, such as political debating chambers, so he finds it difficult to project charisma. His high level of opportunism also makes him appear disorganised and limits his ability to deliver well-structured speeches. As a consequence, he has been criticised by those in his party and beyond who expect a more forceful style of leadership. However, in the 2017 general election, he was able to gain the support of a large section of the general public who respected his honesty and integrity. Now that it has been demonstrated that he is capable of winning a general election, the dissenting voices in his own party have quietened to a significant degree.

The higher level of indifference of the average man inclines him towards competition and to be suspicious or dismissive of attempts by progressive parties to promote harmony. It is therefore essential for progressive parties to communicate effectively with women and to persuade them to vote. However, where men feel neglected or abused by the establishment, they are likely to be drawn towards the hopeful messages of progressive parties. The establishment will do all it can to prevent anybody with progressive traits from achieving a position of power. If such a person is elected, it will attempt to unseat him, diminish his authority or corrupt him. As members of the establishment are not inclined to behave fairly, they will be prepared to use smear campaigns, blackmail or other coercive tactics to get their way. The coherence of the conservative movement enables it to focus the voices of its members on an individual, policy or organisation, and the potency of such efforts is often capable of influencing the media and members of the public towards their agenda. For example, Conservative politicians in the UK currently feel very vulnerable due to splits in their party over Brexit. They are very aware that Corbyn presents a serious threat to their hold on power, and establishment interests in the UK and beyond. Therefore, they are working to undermine him. Almost every interview they give or statement they make begins with an attack on Corbyn. However, people who are low in extraversion and indifference tend to be incorruptible because they do not value status, wealth or power. They are also unlikely to allow themselves to be dragged into slanging matches or other behaviour that the public would consider inappropriate. The Conservatives are therefore finding it difficult to land a knockout blow.

Social mobility

The relative positions of group members within human groups are constantly changing as members gain knowledge, take on new roles, grow older, experience changes in health, and benefit from or suffer the consequences of their decision-making and environmental factors that are out of their control. You may start out incorrectly located as far as the primal group structure is concerned by virtue of your family background or early life experiences. However, generally speaking, as you progress through life, the cumulative effect of your actions and behaviour, as dictated by your personality traits, will cause you to gravitate towards a position within the group that reflects your natural position within the primal group structure. For example, if your traits position you within the establishment, but you are born to a father who is a member of the rank and file, your status and wealth is likely to increase substantially through your lifetime as you rise through the ranks towards your natural position. In contrast, a son who has progressive traits, but who has an establishment father, is likely to lose status and wealth as his opportunistic, creative, cautious and caring behaviours distance him from the establishment and the primal hierarchy.

A person who finds himself higher up the social hierarchy than his personality traits would otherwise dictate will be susceptible to complacency or feelings of fear and jealousy. If he feels comfortable in his position, he is likely to relax and enjoy himself. If he feels insecure in his position, he is likely to be constantly looking over his shoulder for potential threats to his unwarranted status. As a result, he may exhibit controlling or aggressive behaviours. These feelings and behaviours will be discussed in more detail in the next chapter.

Your physical attributes or deficiencies, level of intelligence and life experiences may influence your position, elevating you above or relegating you below your natural position. You may also be maintained in a position, or prevented from moving to a more appropriate one, by the status and wealth of your parents and the quality of your education. Social mobility is also influenced by a group's culture. A particular culture will favour some behaviours, characteristics and sub-groups at the expense of others. Some people will, therefore, feel undervalued and be prevented from making the most of their talents and skills while others will be primed to be successful.

The behaviour of other group members also locks you in a position with your group to some degree. You will contribute to the information in their environment and will therefore provide them with stimulation. You may also be a source of support or protection for them. For example, a person may enjoy exerting power over you, benefit from your labour or be comforted by your presence. Such people are likely to feel uncomfortable if you attempt to reposition yourself. This is one reason why friends and family can be less supportive than you expect when you announce an intention to move your life on. Your repositioning may cause them to experience a loss of enjoyment or negative feelings.

Leading figures within groups tend to introduce class systems that restrict the natural gravitational pull of the primal group structure. In particular, since the creation of property rights, members of the establishment have used their resources to protect family members with different personality traits and therefore perpetuate their families' wealth, high status and access to superior education. These class systems restrict social mobility and prevent some people from moving towards their natural place within society. However, the gravitational pull of personality continues to operate within these classes. As members of the establishment naturally rise to the leadership positions within groups, they will usually assume control of groups within the class that they find themselves. This is why trade unions and other bodies that were created to protect the working class are often led by people who behave in similar ways to wealthy elites, abusing their positions to enrich themselves and engaging in unfair, dishonorable or abusive practices to maintain their hold on power.

Where a person finds himself incorrectly positioned within a group, but in a position of influence by virtue of his family's status, he may be able to exert a counterbalancing effect that helps to break down class structures. For example, people with progressive traits who are born into establishment families may work to restrain the expression of establishment behaviours from within. Consequently, in most parliaments there are elected members from wealthy backgrounds representing liberal and socialist parties. In general, though, a group will be most effective if people are correctly located in terms of the primal group structure. Measures to increase social mobility, promote learning and redistribute wealth are essential elements of a successful society because they help people to find roles that suit their personalities and to reduce friction within the system caused by inherited wealth and social connections. Where a society has small income differentials between job roles and a flexible social structure, people are encouraged to find positions that suit their personality traits rather than to focus on the generation of income. They are likely to be effective and experience good mental health as a result. In contrast, where there are large income differentials, a person may be stigmatised by his peers for accepting a position that they deem to be beneath his social status, or he may be forced to perform a well-paid, but unsuitable, role in order to provide for his family. He will therefore experience negative feelings, stress and low moods on a regular basis.

People who possess the traits of high extraversion and high indifference desire wealth and status and act ruthlessly to secure it. Society should allow these **strivers** to pursue this aim to some degree as their efforts can help promote competition and innovation. However, the interests of large numbers of citizens will be compromised if the pursuit of wealth becomes a group value as large income and wealth differentials will open up in society. Most people are primed by their personality traits to pursue non-monetary objectives, such as caring for others or maintaining the security of organisations or their nation. People who have middling traits, who form the majority, will wish to live life in a balanced way, gradually increasing their income and status as they acquire knowledge and experience while contributing to the maintenance of support systems for the vulnerable and less fortunate.

Societies with clearly defined class structures are very resistant to change because the upper classes use their power and wealth to protect their positions. They will try to hide the extent of their wealth and their extravagant and ruthless behaviours from the public. However, when they are exposed, their authority will be undermined within society and they will be required to moderate their behaviour. They will usually be able to maintain their privileged positions by making relatively small adjustments or compromises. The UK's establishment has consistently adopted this approach and this has delivered a stable political environment for hundreds of years. If progressive political parties are elected to government more significant reforms may be implemented. Redistributive measures such as progressive taxation are likely to be introduced. Equality laws and positive discrimination may be used to advance the interests of groups who tend to be discriminated against, such as women and racial minorities, and to achieve a change in culture. Where group members are subject to excessive control, regulations may be removed to allow people more freedom to find their natural place. Sometimes, however, the establishment adopts an uncompromising position, prompting a revolution. If they attain power, the leaders of the revolution may take more drastic action to rebalance the group's culture and increase social mobility. In contrast to the UK, dictatorial leaders, complacent establishments and revolutions have been a feature of the history of mainland Europe. These different approaches are still evident today. The unwillingness of the European Union's establishment to accept the need for reform is one of the reasons UK citizens voted to leave that institution in 2016.

When politicians try to promote social mobility, their interpretation of this phrase is strongly influenced by their personality traits. Conservatives tend to view social mobility as an exercise in releasing strivers from the social restrictions they face in expressing their materialistic and competitive instincts. They usually define aspiration narrowly in terms of wealth and status. Politicians with liberal values see education and freedom of action as the primary ways of improving social mobility. They embrace diversity and innovation, encouraging people to explore their talents and use them in creative ways. Social democratic politicians tend to focus on improving the lives of disadvantaged or vulnerable people by making systems fairer and more sympathetic to their circumstances. To hard left socialists, social mobility tends to be a class-based concept through which they seek to narrow the differences in wealth and status between the establishment and working class. In other words, they are less concerned about the social mobility of individuals and more concerned about the distribution of power between the subgroups within the primal group structure.

Finding your position

The version of the Circle of Power in Figure 16 below gives an indication of the roles associated with different traits. You may have one particularly high or low trait in which case you may identify strongly with one of the roles within the circle. You will, though, have four traits, so you may feel pulled towards more than one role. Each job role within society will be suited to a particular balance of traits and fit into the primal group structure at some point.

Figure 20. Roles associated with particular traits

Identifying your natural position within the primal group structure will help you to determine your ideal job role and develop a strong sense of purpose. If you are a member of the establishment, you are likely to be suited to exerting authority within an organisation. If you a member of the rank and file, you will be suited to roles that require methodical skills and enable you to establish close bonds with other males. If you are a male progressive you may be suited to being a trader, creative, mediator or analyst depending on which progressive traits you possess. If you are female, you are likely to feel rewarded if you use your talents and skills to advance the interests of the female collective. You may, therefore, be interested in caring or teaching roles, or roles within which you can limit the potential for males to cause harm. However, I have explained the primal group structure in a very simplistic way for ease of understanding. Most people will have middling traits and a majority of people will not fit neatly into one of the primal group's sub-groups. The boundaries between these sub-groups are in reality blurred and there are many graduations and variations within the primal group structure. As a consequence, society generates a large number of different roles and most people have the flexibility to perform a range of them.

There is not enough space in this book for an in-depth analysis of the traits associated with different job roles. In any case, many people possess middling traits that would allow them to perform a wide variety of roles. A few people have a vocation - a strong feeling of suitability for a particular career or occupation. Most people, though, need some life experience before they can make such decisions. Some people are not suited to perform specific roles for long periods. Instead, their talents lie in recognising and taking opportunities. People should therefore be encouraged to explore different options.

Obliging a young person to choose a career when he has no practical experience on which to base his decision is unreasonable and places unnecessary pressure on him. The personality test results of young people are less reliable than those of adults because they are still developing biologically and because they spend their time in family and school environments that differ greatly from adult workplaces and social spaces. It is therefore important for parents and schools to help children to understand what is involved in particular roles and to give them opportunities to meet people who perform them. They must also recognise that their role is primarily to identify a child's talents and help him to develop skills to which he is suited, not to dictate his career. Some roles, such as that of doctor, involve intense and lengthy training and require those who perform them to take decisions about their future career early in life. However, many skills are transferable so it is not necessary for a young person who is a generalist by nature to identify a particular industry in which he wishes to work at an early stage. It will be more important for him to identify and develop his natural abilities. As the African proverb says: "it takes a whole village to raise a child". Unfortunately, in modern society, the nuclear family, the prevalence of single parent families and child protection policies prevent many children from interacting with appropriate role models.

In modern, individualistic society, we are encouraged to focus on our own ambitions. However, you cannot achieve anything alone. You need to understand whom your personality traits suit you to working with and how your ambitions relate to their objectives and those of the overarching group or organisation. The primal group structure is particularly useful in helping people to understand how they can operate effectively in groups. It can also help you to determine which cultures you are suited to operating within. If you do not understand the group dynamics that are operating in your environment, the structures that are needed to deliver a project or achieve a goal, and the role you are suited to playing, you are likely to hit obstacles, miss out on opportunities or find yourself marginalised. However, if you find a suitable role in a group with supportive colleagues and a favourable culture, you are likely to be effective and experience a sense of flow.

Developed countries have diverse economies with a wide variety of job and social roles, and organisational structures. Their citizens now have many more opportunities to find positions that are suited to their personality traits than their ancestors had. However, many of the groups we belong to and organisations we work for are too small or unbalanced from a personality perspective. As a result, they fail to operate as effective teams and expose members and employees to stress due to a lack of appropriate support. As we have seen, unfavourable group cultures and restrictions on social mobility also prevent people from finding their natural positions. A recent survey suggested that 65% of adults in the UK wish that they had pursued a different career. In reality, many of these people will be in careers to which they are suited. It is just that they are working for companies with unsuitable cultures or which do not offer them appropriate support.

8

FEELINGS, THOUGHTS AND BEHAVIOURS ASSOCIATED WITH GROUPS

Your emotional system guides you towards environments in which you can operate effectively. Your environment will, however, be shaped by the groups to which you belong. To experience positive feelings, you need to be positioned appropriately with a group. You also need support and protection from other group members. If you receive such assistance and are allowed to pursue your objectives unhindered, you will be able to operate within your optimal ranges. If you are out of position or your objectives conflict with the culture of a group, group members may decline to assist you or restrain or marginalise you. In each case, you are likely to experience stress, low moods and negative feelings such as envy, low self-esteem and loneliness. These states and feelings may be accompanied by physical discomfort due to lack of access to food, health care or appropriate accommodation. This chapter discusses feelings, thoughts and behaviours that are associated with interactions within or between groups.

Feelings associated with positioning within groups

The longer you remain within an environment that causes you to experience negative feelings, the more you will grow to **dislike** the people within it who are causing you discomfort and any person who is preventing you from leaving that environment. Your emotional system uses the feeling of dislike to bring the source of your discomfort to your attention, thereby encouraging you to address the issue. If you are unable to take effective action, the intensity of such feelings is likely to increase and you may experience **hatred**. Hatred is likely to prompt aggression, which is a means of removing the stressor from your environment.

If your progress towards your natural position within a group (or the position you perceive you should occupy) is inhibited, you are likely to be envious of those who are performing your ideal role or successful in your eyes. **Envy** is a feeling of discontent or covetousness with regard to another's advantages, success, or possessions. It occurs when you envisage the positive feelings you would experience if you occupied the coveted position, but are prevented from doing so by societal culture, circumstances beyond your control or your own limitations. Envy is therefore a form of suppression. **Jealousy**, in one of its two meanings, is similar to envy, but it is experienced at a higher level of arousal. Whereas envy is a calculating, Slow System state, jealousy is a Fast System, reactive state and is therefore likely to result in sudden flashes of anger.

Once a person succeeds in positioning himself within a group in a way that delivers positive feelings, he is likely to resist any forces that threaten to unseat him. If he believes that his position in a group is vulnerable, he may experience jealousy in its alternative sense, which may be defined as suspicion or fear of rivalry or unfaithfulness. Jealousy is a stress reaction that occurs when a person fears that he may lose possessions or other things that give him enjoyment or status within a group. It is most often associated with the fear of the loss of a sexual partner, but it is also common in companies and other hierarchical organisations where people are protective of their positions. Because it is associated with a fear of loss, it is most likely to be experienced by a person who finds himself in a beneficial position that is not justified by his personality traits or attributes; for example, where his status is inherited.

Leaders of groups and countries who wish to strengthen their power base or engage in militaristic expansion tend to whip group members and their subjects into states of fear, jealousy and hatred. By doing so, such a leader will be able to increase his subjects' dependence on him and channel their anger and aggression towards his adversaries or targets. He may also increase his popularity by issuing nationalistic propaganda, boosting his subjects' confidence by making them feel superior to citizens of other countries.

You are also likely to dislike or hate somebody who causes you to experience disappointment or a serious loss; for example, where somebody is promoted ahead of you or attracts a sexual partner away from you. Where you have experienced loss as a result of another person, you may feel a compulsion to exact **revenge**. Revenge is a Fast System behaviour associated with anger and is unguided; for example, when hotheads form lynch mobs. **Retribution** is a more measured, Slow System response associated with getting even. It is more likely to restore balance to a group whereas acts of revenge may spiral out of control. The Old Testament validated retribution by permitting "an eye for an eye". Retribution underlies the concept of blood money where financial compensation avoids the need for further loss of life. Once formal justice systems were established, prison sentences, fines and community service reduced the need for individuals to seek retribution.

Sometimes you are unable to exact revenge or secure retribution because of your own weakness or the existence of restraining values or laws. In this case, your anger is likely to emerge as **bitterness**, a Fast System emotional response. If you hold back a desire for revenge or retribution, you are likely to become frustrated. This can result in you adopting spiteful behaviour. **Spite** is a malicious, usually petty, desire to harm, annoy, obstruct or humiliate another person. It is an angry response which just about remains within the bounds of acceptable behaviour. Over time, your anger is likely to subside and bitterness will be replaced by a feeling of **resentment** as you use your Slow System to review the causes of your loss and work out solutions for implementation in the longer term. You may have to wait a long time for an opportunity to get even during which time you may experience a great deal of resentment. As a result, if you finally obtain retribution, you are likely to experience strong positive feelings, hence the saying "revenge is a dish best served cold".

The nature of group living means that people are forced to share spaces with people who are potentially harmful or who have caused them to experience harm or loss in the past. You may feel **contempt** for such a person. Contempt will distance you psychologically from him. It is a Fast System response and combines the emotions of anger and disgust. While the person still presents a threat, you may treat him with **scorn**, which is the vocal expression of contempt. When you are not in his company, you will engage your Slow System to find ways to neutralise any on-going threat that he presents. Once the threat has been neutralised, either by the creation of a new schema that increases your security or imposition of restrictions on the offending person's behaviour, any further encounters with that person are unlikely to trigger a major stress event. You are then likely to express **disdain** towards the offender. Disdain is a similar emotion to contempt and scorn, but it is experienced at a lower level of arousal. It expresses a belief that a person is unworthy of consideration – literally, beneath contempt.

You may forgive a person who has caused you harm. **Forgiveness** is a voluntary process whereby a victim lets go of any expectation of, or right to exact retribution. It releases you from negative emotions that could otherwise continue to harm you if no retribution is achieved. Forgiveness may be given unilaterally, but the offender usually needs to show some remorse for a person to be able to forgive. Forgiveness helps groups to escape cycles of violent revenge; for example, where truth and reconciliation tribunals are set up, as occurred in post-apartheid South Africa. However, forgiveness may be interpreted by the perpetrator as submissive or tolerant behaviour and encourage him to continue with inappropriate or harmful behaviour.

People who are low in extraversion and high in indifference are most likely to seek retribution from other group members, as these traits are associated with fairness and ruthlessness respectively. A judge with these traits is unlikely to have any sympathy for an offender. People who have the reverse traits - high extraversion and low indifference - are most likely to forgive. As such a person will enjoy being the centre of attention, he will be inclined to sacrifice the opportunity of getting even in order to restore his social circle. His compassionate nature and need to promote harmony will also cause him to refrain from harming the offender where possible.

A group may punish you if you breach a group value by causing you to experience **shame**. You may feel ashamed either when your actions are brought to public attention, or when you consciously or subconsciously realise that you have offended a group value. Shame lowers your status within the group and prompts you to adopt behaviours that are likely to restore your reputation. In establishment cultures, a man's status is closely linked to his control over, and the behaviour of, his family. Consequently, if a family member brings shame on the family and causes the head of the household to lose face, he (or more often she) may be ostracised or subjected to an honour killing. **Embarrassment** is a less socially offensive form of shame. It occurs when you breach a group value without causing serious harm or damage and is part of the learning and assimilation process that a person goes through when joining a group.

You experience **guilt** when you contravene a group value that is associated with one of your low traits. It is a feeling of responsibility for an act or omission that exposes other group members to potential harm and prompts you to take remedial action. As women tend to be lower in indifference than men, they are more likely to feel guilty when they neglect caring responsibilities. As there is no gender difference in relation to the other spectrums, a man or woman could just as easily feel guilty if he or she attempts, for example, to smuggle drugs through customs at an airport. If you allow a threat to cause harm and it is too late too reverse the damage, you will feel **remorse**, rather than guilt. Some criminals, usually males, are incapable of showing remorse as their very high levels of indifference make them incapable of empathising with other people.

At other times, you will experience **regret** rather than guilt or remorse. Regret is a sense of dissatisfaction that arises when you miss or deprive yourself of an opportunity to experience positive feelings, especially enjoyment and exhilaration. It therefore tends to be experienced more by people with high traits and is a self-interested rather than a group-orientated emotional response. Your emotional system embeds regrets as schemas to help you avoid making the same mistakes again. They are therefore likely to reappear in your conscious mind from time to time and tend to be very difficult to erase. Men are more likely to experience regret than women when they experience loss in competitive environments; for example, when they miss out on a sexual conquest, because of their higher levels of indifference.

Many of the actions and behaviours of others that we find annoying breach unwritten codes of conduct; for example, abusing hospitality or swearing in public. If repeated on a regular basis, they can generate resentment and other negative states amongst group members, undermine group values and reduce the effectiveness of the group. Societies have therefore developed reciprocal greetings, "please and thank you" routines, and other social courtesies that help to relieve these tensions and enable people to get along. If a person fails to comply with such behavioural expectations he is likely to find life more difficult than it would otherwise be, so generally most people abide by them. Collectivist societies place a high value on maintaining such routines. In individualistic cultures, however, people are less likely to view people they meet as members of their group and therefore less likely to recognise any benefit from devoting time to the development and implementation of such routines. Consequently, anti-social behaviour is more common in such cultures.

Sometimes, we use humour to inform people that they are breaching group values or attempting to position themselves inappropriately within a group. When a friend is behaving unreasonably, you may gently mock him to help him realise his mistake or bring him down a peg or two. Sarcasm, which is the use of vocal inflection to mock or convey contempt, performs a similar purpose, but is more biting than mockery. When you use it, you draw your conversation partner's attention to the fact that he has failed to realise that his behaviour has caused you or other people to experience negative feelings. Satire is an artistic form in which vices, follies, abuses, and shortcomings are held up to ridicule, with the intent of shaming individuals, corporations, government, or society itself into improvement.

Behaviours associated with group dynamics

Conformity and compliance

We all grow up and live in social frameworks that guide and constrain our actions. From the moment we are born we are affected by the way our parents treat us. As we grow older, we adopt behavioural patterns associated with our schools, social circles, workplaces and wider society. At times, you will abide by group values, keeping within the bounds of social acceptance or taking a course of action that is considered 'best practice'. At other times, you will pursue a personal objective when you know that others will disapprove or take action that is unusual or contrary to your group's values.

We can find adherence to group values comforting. When you adopt behaviours that align to the values of a group and experience positive feelings as a result, you **conform**. For example, a person who is low in openness is likely to feel uncomfortable if faced with choosing between different styles of clothing. However, if he joins the police, he will experience positive feelings when he puts on the uniform as conforming in this way removes the stress associated with choice and strengthens his bonds with other group members. Likewise, a rugby player who is high in extraversion and indifference will enjoy intense, physical competition and will therefore naturally respond to his coach's demands for more aggression. You may also conform when you submit to a stressor. Such acts of submission are unlikely to completely eliminate negative feelings, but assuming the stressor accepts your act of submission, chronic stress is likely to give way to the less intense feelings associated with suppression.

Sometimes the behavioural expectations of a group will conflict with your need to increase your own personal security or desire to pursue your own objectives. Where a person acts in accordance with such expectations, and experiences negative feelings as a result, he **complies**. You comply with group values because you either see potential benefit in doing so or fear losing status, freedom or resources if you do not. Sometimes, when you are stressed or feel that you can act with impunity, you will break rules by acting impulsively. Usually, however, if you know a rule exists, you will use your Slow System to carry out a cost-benefit analysis before deciding to break it. If the benefits exceed the cost, you are likely to go ahead.

Compliance is an everyday aspect of life, as we need to retain membership of groups if we are to benefit from the protection and support they offer. For example, a person who is low in extraversion may join in activities on an adventure weekend that scare him, for fear of being dropped from a friendship circle. You will experience stress when you comply, as you will be operating outside your optimal ranges. People who have one or more extreme traits often feel this tension, as they are most likely to experience a conflict between their personal values and the values of their groups because most groups adopt balanced cultures. The more extreme a person's personality traits, the more regular and intense these negative feelings are likely to be.

We comply because we fear punishment for non-compliance. This may be in the form of violence. For example, a male mammal will often submit to another male once it becomes clear that he is weaker to avoid serious injury or death. However, it may also take the form of a fine, a loss of reputation, a deprivation of rights or resources, imprisonment, marginalisation or ostracism. For example, a person who is high in extraversion is likely to comply with speed limits that he would otherwise be inclined to break for fear of losing his licence. Non-compliance may be instinctive, for example when a person's Fast System causes him to confront a stressor, or considered when your Slow System carries out a cost/benefit analysis following a stress event and determines it is appropriate.

In their teenage years, many young people behave in ways that breach the values that they have been brought up with. For some of them, rebellion will be a reaction to the subjugation of their core personality by the discipline of parents and schooling. In other words, it will be an act of deliberate non-compliance. Such rebellion is seen as a rite of passage, and is part of the process of developing one's own individuality. For many, though, their behaviour is driven by a desire or need to be accepted within new social groups, membership of which they perceive gives higher status, protection or other benefits than their families. Gaining acceptance into a new group can be a tricky process. You need to gain the trust of existing group members so you naturally behave in ways that help you to fit in. New and prospective members therefore tend to comply with, to the extent they do not naturally conform to, the values established by the group's leaders, in order to gain acceptance. In the context of young people, these leaders will often be students with more anarchic or challenging temperaments. As they transition into adulthood and these groups lose importance, most young people revert to more normal behaviours.

You are more likely to comply when you can see that your act of compliance will lead to future benefits and strengthen a group from which you anticipate needing assistance. We appreciate the value of groups more once we recognise our own mortality and take responsibility for loved ones. From that point on, we are more likely to compromise our personal values and objectives for the benefit of others who may be able to offer us protection or support. As a person will have fewer opportunities to, and less energy to create or join, new groups in later life, it is less likely that he will be prepared to accept the loss of status and support associated with non-compliance. People therefore tend to become more compliant as they age. Having said that, some people delight in breaking free from the systems associated with employment and bringing up children, and take advantage of the departure of children from the family home or retirement to exercise more independence.

Because high traits tend to promote individualistic behaviours, most values encourage the expression of low trait behaviours. Therefore, a low trait orientated person will spend more time conforming to group values than complying with them. The reverse is true for high trait orientated people. As a consequence, a collectivist culture is likely to be perceived as having strong values and an individualistic culture as lacking values. However, in some cases high trait behaviours are adopted as values, for example in a liberal society where people are expected to display tolerance towards people from different races. A person who is high in openness will naturally conform to this value because he will enjoy new experiences, but a person who is low in openness is likely to feel threatened by people who are different so, if he abides by this value, he will be complying. Similarly, in an establishment culture, men are expected to show bravery. A person who is high in extraversion and indifference is likely to enjoy warfare so he will naturally appear brave, but a person who has the reverse traits will have to show true courage to overcome his fear of the battlefield.

A leader will usually be given more freedom to deviate from group values than the average member because leaders are primarily judged by their ability to protect and provide for the group. He will, though, take advantage of the dynamics of compliance and conformity to maintain order within his group. He will introduce codes of conduct, rules or laws backed up by punishments, and may also exaggerate external threats to strengthen group members' instinct to conform and secure greater compliance by them. Leaders also influence people's behaviour by offering or threatening to withdraw benefits. A carrot and stick approach is effective because it gives a person the opportunity to experience positive feelings and a need to escape negative feelings. Sometimes, particularly with children, we create specific incentives and penalties to achieve compliance. In many cases, though, members of groups create these motivating factors naturally through their interactions. A man may, for example, get into the habit of being helpful around his house to avoid being nagged by his wife and so that he can meet up with his friends for a beer without being criticised.

You will belong to multiple groups with different values. When you encounter a situation where these values clash, you will experience cognitive dissonance as your Slow System attempts to resolve the associated stress event. The behaviour of an individual changes when he is in a group that he perceives is offering him protection, for example one with a charismatic leader. Membership of such a group increases a person's confidence, allowing him to lose his inhibitions, enjoy himself and experience feelings of exhilaration. In other words, he will spend more time in Fast System operation, lose self-awareness and be more likely to conform to high trait behaviours exhibited by people around him. In this state, which psychologists use the term **deindividuation**, a person may cease to be restrained by broader societal values. For example, people are more likely to drop litter when in a crowd. A leader may take advantage of deindividuation in battle or other scenarios where it is helpful to have unquestioning and enthusiastic support. The different behaviours we adopt when acting as individuals and as part of a group can cause us to display double standards or hypocrisy.

Attempts to control the behaviour of an individual may cause him to experience anger or frustration, leading to displays of violence or impatience, or a low mood, which may lead to grumpiness, irritation or listlessness. As people with extreme traits are most likely to exhibit behaviours that deviate substantially from accepted norms, they will often find themselves in a no-win situation. They can either follow their natural instincts and be subjected to some form of punishment by other group members, or comply with group values and experience strong negative feelings.

Sometimes, groups need individuals to break rules and conventions to gain knowledge and make progress in other ways, or to achieve a shift of group values following an environmental change. Without such challenging behaviour, a group is likely to lose effectiveness. Therefore, the question of whether a person's behaviour is right or wrong is often a subjective matter, and a group's view of a perceived breach of values may change with hindsight. For example, Nelson Mandela was considered to be a terrorist by many white people in South Africa and beyond. However, as more people became aware of the iniquities of apartheid and Mandela demonstrated his leadership capabilities and integrity, he became a highly respected figure within national and international politics.

Avoidance and responsibility

You depend on other people with different traits to perform tasks that you find stressful or boring, and to create an environment in which you can operate effectively; for example, police officers, nurses, refuse collectors, traders or farmers. We tend, though, to focus on our own roles and objectives, whether these be personal or group-orientated. We do not give much thought to the actions or omissions of others unless we can see that they directly affect our circumstances or the achievement of our objectives. This is because we have evolved to perform particular roles and to interact primarily with people with related roles within the context of the primal group structure. This structure operates like a machine so no person needs to understand what everybody else in the group does. As long as each person is performing his natural role adequately, the group should operate effectively. However, this does mean that we live in bubbles and are oblivious to many of the actions and experiences of other group members.

These bubbles overlap, resulting in the formation of relationships and shared experiences. The effectiveness of a group will depend to a great degree on the strength and nature of the relationships within it. In a well-balanced group, group members will generally be able to exist sustainably within their bubbles because other people will be providing them with appropriate protection and support. Where such protection and support is lacking, people will be faced with the choice of either performing tasks that will cause them to experience negative feelings, or reconfiguring their environments and lifestyles to avoid the need to perform such tasks. Your emotional system is likely to prompt you to take the avoidance option unless it concludes that the task is necessary to achieve an important objective or that it is in your interests to comply with a group value or command. This is because avoidance allows you to continue to experience positive feelings in the short term.

If a group has a typical balance of personality traits, its culture is appropriate for its environment and group members are correctly positioned within it, there will be little need for a group member to employ avoidance tactics, as he should be performing within his optimal ranges. If the structure is weak, people are poorly positioned within it or there is an unsuitable culture, avoidance will be more common. This will negatively affect the group, as threats to the group will not be dealt with, deficiencies within the group will not be addressed and its skill base will deteriorate. Consequently, the group will become less effective and more vulnerable to external attack or disintegration.

A shift of group culture represents a collective change in behaviour within a group. Such a change encourages the performance and avoidance of particular tasks. Shifts occur because people with middling traits have the ability to switch between use of their Fast System and Slow System easily, and can favour one system or the other depending on the circumstances. These cultural shifts are usually prompted by a change in the nature of the group's environment and enable groups to adapt to new challenges presented by that new environment. For example, if a group is militarily strong and has an opportunity to acquire more territory and resources, it is likely to adopt an establishment culture. It will make sense for most people within that group to devote less time to promoting harmony because the group's objective is to establish dominance.

Establishment cultures cause people to avoid novelty, change, and the exercise of analytical and caring skills. Collectivist cultures cause people to avoid novelty, change, physical experiences and competition. Progressive cultures cause people to avoid physical experiences and competition, and the exercise of methodical and organisational skills. Individualistic cultures cause people to avoid the exercise of analytical, caring, methodical and organisational skills.

As a group's environment changes, group members will increasingly encounter stressors that threaten to burst the bubbles they are occupying. People who are suited to the new environment will embrace it. People who are not will tend to engage avoidance tactics so that they can continue to experience positive feelings. However, as they do so, their bubbles are likely to get smaller and smaller and their effectiveness will decrease as they focus on avoidance rather than performing useful tasks. They will block themselves off from the wider world and their ability to work in a team will be eroded. Eventually, their bubbles will burst and they will either experience a breakdown or be forced to take responsibility for restoring their fortunes and those of their group.

Continued avoidance will therefore damage a group, especially if the group has adopted an extreme culture. This is evidenced in modern British society. There has been a strong individualistic culture for 40 years and individualistic behaviours are therefore widely exhibited. However, a weaker economy and ageing population mean that there is a greater need to invest in public services, persuade more people to take on caring responsibilities, use resources more efficiently and distribute wealth more equitably. In other words, a shift towards a more collectivist culture needs to occur. This shift is beginning to take place within the British population, but has been derailed politically by disagreements and obfuscation in relation to Brexit policy. Even if a government with a more collectivist approach is formed in the near future, the skills deficit that exists within the population will mean a sudden improvement in the country's fortunes is unlikely. Successive governments have encouraged people to pursue high trait activities that deliver enjoyment, such as travel, conspicuous consumption, individual creativity and the pursuit of wealth rather than focusing on the development of skills and a sustainable society. Consequently, there is a shortage of scientists, engineers, doctors and other professionals and tradesmen who perform roles that hold society together.

Vested interests will also inhibit a group from responding to environmental changes. People who have done well under the existing culture will usually resist any reallocation of resources that weakens their authority or otherwise undermines their interests. They are likely to continue steadfastly with the practices that have delivered success to them in the past and avoid or discredit new ideas and practices. For example, people whose wealth and power depend on the exploitation of fossil fuels refuse to accept that climate change is man-made or any need for the world to adopt more sustainable practices because they will undermine their position by doing so. In the context of a group with an individualistic culture, people with high traits will have vested interests because they will wish to protect their access to enjoyable experiences. Many middle class British people who are campaigning to remain in the EU referendum fit into this category as they are seeking to protect their freedom of movement and access to interesting and financially rewarding experiences.

Sometimes, a section of a group or society whose members are characterised by specific personality traits can become dislocated. **Dislocation** divides a group, allowing some members (often the most privileged ones) to freely engage in behaviours that breach the values of the wider group. The sub-group behaves as if it were a new group, establishing its own values and pursuing its own objectives. The separation is, however, artificial because, in reality, the sub-group is incapable of functioning without assistance from the wider group. It takes advantage of the benefits of membership of the wider group, but neglects its responsibilities to that group. Inevitably, at some point the wider group regains some influence over the sub-group, usually when the actions of its members have become intolerable or members of the sub-group have become complacent. This is essentially the dynamic behind revolutions. Marie Antoinette may not have actually said "Let them eat cake", but this quotation aptly demonstrated the dislocation between the establishment in France in the 18th century and the impoverished population.

In small, tight-knit groups, it is likely that most people will realise when a threat to the group emerges. It will therefore be hard for them to avoid helping to combat it. In large, disparate groups, however, it will be harder for a person to recognise such threats and relate them to his daily experience of life. He will find it easier to engage in avoidance as a result. Consequently, avoidance by individuals is most common in countries with individualistic cultures like the UK and to a lesser degree the USA. It is, however, easier for people in such cultures to adopt new behaviours and begin the culture shift process. In contrast, it is hard for an individual to follow a different path from other group members in a collectivist culture so practices become embedded and the group stagnates. France is a good example of a country that has engaged in this collective avoidance, resisting the introduction of innovations that would undermine its traditions.

We can all think of situations where we have chosen not to engage with groups or avoided taking responsibility. Some people accept positions of responsibility, but perform their duties inadequately, neglecting obligations that they find tiresome while reaping the accompanying rewards, particularly high status and salary. People take responsibility at different times in their lives, and often such action is prompted by a life-changing event, such as the birth of a child. Taking responsibility need not be arduous. If you accept a responsibility to which your personality traits are suited, you are likely to experience a sense of purpose and feelings of fulfilment when performing tasks associated with it. However, taking responsibility for tasks to which you are unsuited and which expose you to stress requires courage and selflessness. It becomes easier to take responsibility when you appreciate how groups provide you with support and protection. In individualistic cultures, however, people tend to lack a sense of responsibility because they have loose connections to groups and tend to avoid thinking about the future threats. For example, in the UK the average man would now be very reluctant to put his life on the line for his country, but during the First World War, when the UK had an establishment culture, large numbers of working-class men volunteered to defend the nation.

People with middling traits will be suited to taking on general responsibilities while people with extreme traits will be suited to more specific or wide-ranging ones. People with low traits are very sensitive to information. They will react to threats that people with the corresponding high traits consider to be inconsequential. They will therefore make the decision to avoid or take responsibility at an earlier stage. If they take responsibility, they will attend to details that others might miss. Because people who are high trait orientated can operate more effectively in high information environments, they are less likely to appreciate the existence of threats to their group so they will take longer to accept responsibility. However, if they accept responsibility, they will be able to identify threatening themes and dynamics and develop more wide-ranging responses, as they will be capable of seeing the big picture. In a successful group, each member will therefore undertake responsibility for particular tasks. The more you broaden your consciousness, the better able you will be to appreciate dangers within your environment and envisage solutions, and the more suited you will be to taking on a leadership role.

The loose nature of groups in modern society, the fast pace of life, and expectations of protection and support from the state, have given large numbers of people a sense of security and enabled them to avoid taking responsibility. Many people are too busy to think about the future. There is often a time lag between damage to a person's protective and supportive structure and his appreciation of this fact. For example, a person may not realise that the health service he depends on is disintegrating until he falls ill. Also, some issues seem too remote from people's daily lives for them to feel any need to address them. This applies particularly to people with low traits because of the difficulty they have in seeing the big picture. We are living in an era when human civilisation as we know it is threatened by climate change, degradation of our natural environment, authoritarianism and an unsustainable global economic system. Unfortunately, these issues are too ephemeral for most people, particularly those who are low in openness, to cause them to radically change their behaviour.

Sometimes, an event can occur that is so potentially damaging that the bulk of a population recognise the need to take responsibility. Typically, this occurs in times of war or natural disaster. However, much of the damage to our natural environment that is occurring now is shielded from us by governments and multinational companies, or occurring in distant places or invisibly or at a microscopic level. Therefore, by the time we realise the true extent of the harm we are causing, it is likely to be too late. Great leaders can, though, persuade people to take responsibility by distilling and expressing the nature of a threat in a way that broadens the collective consciousness. We desperately need visionary leaders who are capable of persuading the global population of the necessity of moving quickly towards a sustainable global society to emerge within the political arena. Unfortunately, at the moment, narrow-minded populists, whose focus is exploiting resources, are in the ascendancy.

Tolerance, respect, honesty and integrity

The fundamental values that promote the success of groups are tolerance, respect, honesty and integrity.

No person possesses all the talents and skills he would need to survive and prosper independently so you will need the support and protection of people with different traits. These people add colour and emotional richness to your world, but, as they have different traits, they also cause you to experience negative feelings at times. Group members therefore need to show each other tolerance and respect if they are to work effectively together.

When a person with a low trait tolerates behaviours associated with the corresponding high trait, he restrains his instinct to control such behaviour. In doing so, he is likely to experience anxiety or chronic stress, as he will be exposing himself to higher levels of information than he is naturally comfortable with. Similarly, when a person with a high trait respects the sensitivities of those who possess the corresponding low trait by keeping his high trait behaviours within the bounds of acceptability, he is likely to experience boredom or a low mood.

Your emotional system will only put up with such feelings if it has a reason to do so. Tolerance and respect are therefore founded upon mutual understanding, an appreciation of other group members' talents and skills, and a shared commitment to group objectives. Where one of these requirements is missing or poorly developed, dissatisfaction, hostility or conflict is likely to occur. For example, a person who is low in indifference may feel hurt if he receives an email from a senior manager that does not start with a greeting. If he is high in indifference, the person sending the email is likely to be asserting authority (although he may just feel he is too busy to engage in social niceties or be conforming to the communication style within the leadership team). Such a mismatch in communication styles may appear innocuous, but it could provoke feelings of hurt in the person who is low in indifference that, over a period of time and combined with similar behaviours, could develop into dislike or hostility. If, however, the person who receives the e-mail recognises that the sender's assertive style helps to win the company business and pay his wages, he is likely to be more tolerant of the offending behaviour.

Because you cannot be everywhere and do everything that needs to be done, you will need to trust other people to look after your interests. If you do not have people that you can rely on, your performance level will drop. You will either be forced to micromanage other people or spend time performing tasks to which you are unsuited. Trust is founded upon honesty and integrity. **Honesty** is the expression of truthfulness, sincerity or frankness, whereas a person behaves with **integrity** where he consistently adheres to a set of moral and ethical principles. Integrity is therefore associated with performing consistently and reliably. People who are low extraversion are most likely to be honest because they lack a desire for status and material possessions. Low openness encourages loyalty, which is a form of reliability. A person who is low in indifference can usually be depended on not to cause you harm and low opportunism promotes reliability in an organisational sense. High traits promote dishonesty and unreliability, as they are associated with desire and wanting. These feelings encourage people with high traits to pursue personal gratification and tempt them to breach group values and their commitments to others. A breach of trust by a person who is high in indifference is particularly serious because he is unlikely to be concerned about any harm that he may cause to other people as a consequence. Of course, most people have a mixture of high and low traits. Such a person is likely to be more trustworthy and reliable in some aspects of his life than others. For example, a person who is high in extraversion and opportunism, but low in openness, is likely to be a loyal friend, but may be tempted to steal from you if he is presented with an opportunity and believes that crime would not be detected.

People with low traits tend to be trusting and naïve when they are young because they do not appreciate the risks that people with high traits are prepared to take in order to enjoy themselves. If, however, a person with a low trait experiences a significant breach of trust, he may become deeply suspicious of people with high traits when he encounters similar situations in the future. He will have trouble seeing the big picture so he will find it difficult to distinguish between those whom he can trust and those whom he cannot. People with low traits tend to feel insecure and value the protection they get from groups. This greater reliance on groups deters them from breaching trust or obligations although they may not follow through with commitments where they fear for their personal security. Trust is also relative. The greater the potential rewards, the more likely a person is to breach trust. You are likely to trust most people with a dollar or a pound, but will be much choosier if you are entrusting your life with somebody.

You will have a tendency to drop your guard in the company of people who appear to offer you protection or who cause you to experience feelings of enjoyment or exhilaration. However, you should not assume that such a person is acting in your best interests. Where a person's environment allows him to operate within his optimal range and he feels he is making good progress towards his objectives, his demeanour is likely to be pleasant and he is likely to exude confidence and positivity. However, he may be pursuing a self-interested agenda that is detrimental to your own interests. In contrast, a person's aggressive or awkward behaviour may actually be caused by a reaction to, or his attempts to deal with, a stressor that also threatens you, but which you have not yet recognised.

We are therefore susceptible to being misled or deceived by confidence tricks played by fraudsters. For example, people who are high in extraversion and indifference can remain positive and confident in physically confrontational environments. This is a good thing if they are on your side in a battle, but this attribute also makes it easier for them to exploit other people, which they are naturally drawn to do. It is therefore wise to be suspicious of any person, such as an establishment politician, who seems at ease in confrontational situations. It is likely that such a person will be prepared to cause you harm if he can advance his own interests by doing so. In contrast, we are likely to discount warnings given by people who appear to be struggling to cope with their current environment and distance ourselves from campaigners who seem agitated. For example, a member of your group who is low in extraversion and indifference is likely to put the interests of the group ahead of his own. However, he is also likely to experience chronic stress or panic in physical and confrontational environments so he will be inclined to display anger when those around him are being more level-headed. Subconsciously, you are likely to interpret such behaviour as evidence that he lacks the ability to protect you in your current environment and therefore disregard him or distance yourself from him.

Group members therefore face a dilemma. The people who are most capable of protecting them and securing resources for the group (members of the establishment) are also the people who are most likely to exploit or deceive them. Those who are most likely to treat them fairly and with compassion are least capable of protecting them from, and competing successfully for resources against, other groups. As a consequence, when people feel threatened by outsiders, they tend to place their trust in the establishment and conservative parties and when the threat level is low they are more likely to support progressive parties. This is why conservative parties promote fear and progressive parties encourage hope, and why the financial crisis of 2008, the subsequent economic malaise in Western countries and the actions of ISIS have resulted in a global shift towards leaders with establishment traits.

The strength of a person's connection to a group also affects his levels of trustworthiness and reliability. If he is well integrated within a group and respected by its members, he is likely to be trustworthy as he will find it difficult to breach trust without his reputation being damaged. He will also find it easier to trust people, as he will have others on whom he can depend if he is let down. However, if he sells a car through a newspaper advert to a stranger, he is more likely to be untruthful than if he sells it to a family member because his behaviour is less likely to be discovered by people that he knows and he will not depend on the stranger for future support or protection. Familiarity allows you to assess a person's integrity. If you deal with a member of another group, his high traits are likely to lead him to breach trust and his low traits are likely to make him fearful and wary of you. Also, in the event of a conflict of interest, he may put loyalty to his group before honouring an obligation to you. People are therefore often reluctant to deal with strangers. Where people belong to multiple groups, conflicts of interest may arise frequently. A person may breach an obligation to one group where he acts in the interests of another group. The forces of conformance and compliance can act sub-consciously upon us so we are not always aware when we are committing such a breach. If a person is to operate with integrity, he must therefore be careful to consider potential conflicts in advance. Most public and professional codes of conduct require disclosure of such a conflict and withdrawal from decision-making processes relating to it.

In modern, individualistic society, we belong to multiple groups, and the connections we have to them are often loose. This promotes uncertainty as to whom you can trust and weakens your sense of obligation to and responsibility for others, making it more likely that you will breach trust or behave unreliably. In terms of cost/benefit analysis, there is more risk and less prospect of reward in assisting another person. Where a person has been repeatedly let down by others or the pervading culture undermines values held by him, he may become cynical of other people's stated intentions. A person displays **cynicism** where he is distrusting or disparaging of the motives of others. People are more likely to be cynical of the intentions of other people when they have loose connections to them because they will not have had the opportunity to thoroughly assess their reliability.

If a society is to function well, the vast majority of citizens within it must commit to honest behaviour and to behave with integrity in their dealings with other people. Political parties, especially establishment ones, contain a disproportionate number of ambitious people who are seeking power, wealth and higher status and who will be prepared to compromise societal values and behave in self-interested ways if they think they can get away with it. If corruption becomes endemic, it is very difficult to re-establish honest practices as politicians, police officers and government officials are also likely to be corrupt. However, as people who are high in extraversion and indifference consider it important to maintain their position in society, they tend to be less prepared to engage in corrupt behaviour where it is likely to result in reputational or financial loss. Transparency therefore helps to promote honesty and integrity. Members of the establishment try to prevent other group members from monitoring their activities and disclosing their unprincipled behaviour by buying or closing down media organisations, influencing or coercing their editorial teams and threatening, imprisoning or killing journalists. Where they cannot restrict the flow of potentially damaging information, they make it harder for members of the public to interpret it by undermining the credibility of such organisations and promoting fake news.

It is difficult to strike an appropriate balance between privacy and freedom of information. It is damaging to society to allow individuals too much privacy. In recent years, privacy laws have limited the ability of photographers and journalists to photograph and comment on the activities of public figures and ordinary individuals, even when such people are behaving in ways that run contrary to moral codes. These restrictions undermine the values of honesty and integrity. If people know that their behaviour could be reported in news articles and stored forever in publicly accessible online files, they are much more likely to comply with expected behaviours. However, it is generally accepted that people should be given an opportunity to reform themselves. Permanent access to records of past misdemeanours on the Internet would make it harder for them to re-establish themselves as well functioning members of society. The European Court has introduced a "right to be forgotten" whereby people can ask for information about them to be removed from the Internet after a certain period of time. In applying this to people who have committed crimes, courts have to balance the public's right to access the historical record, the precise impacts on the person and the public interest.

The balance between privacy and freedom in a group will reflect the group's culture. In countries with establishment cultures, security services and companies are allowed considerable freedom to access personal data and monitor behaviours of individuals. However, wealthy members of society are allowed to keep their finances private, with tax returns remaining confidential and the use of tax havens tolerated. In countries with progressive cultures, people are allowed a great amount of privacy in terms of their social behaviours, but they are forced be much more open about their wealth and income as this promotes fairness and social responsibility.

The Internet and computers have enabled individuals and organisations to obtain, store and process large amounts of information about individuals' personal lives. Blackmailers, companies and governments use such information to make money or exercise control. Data protection laws have been introduced in most developed countries to restrict the activities of corporations, but governments, security services and police forces are constantly seeking ing to gain increased access to information about their citizens via the Internet, CCTV and DNA recording so they can exert more control over them. Countries with authoritarian regimes target non-conformist elements and minorities including migrant workers, political dissidents and ethnic or religious minorities. The global shift towards more authoritarian behaviour is also affecting liberal democracies, though. The British police and intelligence services have taken advantage of fears of terrorism to extend their powers to monitor the behaviour of citizens and access their data. Police officers can use technology to extract location data, conversations on encrypted apps, call logs, emails, text messages, passwords and internet searches from mobile phones without seeking permission from a court and 26 of the UK's regional police forces admit to using this power.

The discriminatory dynamic

When groups become large and disjointed, members are likely to develop prejudices. A person displays **prejudice** when he has a preconceived opinion about somebody else that is not based on reason or actual experience. Prejudice may cause a person to **discriminate** against group members with particular characteristics. When there is a strong cultural value of fairness, minorities can benefit from positive discrimination. Discrimination is, however, usually encountered in its negative form and you should attribute this meaning to it for the purposes of this volume.

Discrimination is a product of fear and is therefore more likely to be exhibited by people with low traits. The essence of discrimination is an inability by a person to quantify the risk in a particular data set. In high information environments, people with low traits are forced to rely on flawed schemas and they therefore subconsciously know that they are liable to make errors. Their reaction is to label the whole data set as dangerous and reject it. This is what happens when, for example, a woman says: "All men are bastards". Because she is low in indifference, she is unable to distinguish between men who are likely to cause serious harm and those who may simply be lacking in sensitivity, so she rejects them all.

A person may encourage discriminatory behaviour to strengthen his position within a group or where he fears losing status within a group. He may enhance his sense of belonging and status within a group by identifying people who are different, and then demeaning, marginalising or victimising them. By isolating such people, he psychologically increases the coherency of his core group and strengthens his bond with it. Such behaviour is usually classed as bullying when carried out on a single individual, but as discrimination when a group exhibits it. Children often discriminate against individuals who are different or uncool because such behaviour enhances their sense of belonging to groups that they perceive to offer higher status. Class systems encourage people to discriminate against people from lower classes.

Discrimination is most obvious when it is practised by people who are low in openness because this spectrum relates to sensitivity to new experiences and ideas, and the fear of difference. People who are low in openness look for security in groups of people with clearly defined values and strong bonds of loyalty. The tight-knit and uniform nature of these groups creates a barrier to entry for anybody who is different. Because immigrants are so obviously different, their presence in significant numbers promotes fear amongst people who are low in openness, resulting in the emergence of anti-immigration, nationalist and racist attitudes. Members of the primal hierarchy, and particularly the rank and file (which roughly translates to working class males) are prone to anti-immigrant sentiments due to their low levels of openness.

People who choose alternative lifestyles, adopt non-conformist behaviours or are different by virtue of their physical or mental characteristics present a threat to the coherency of a group and are therefore often targets of discrimination. The more that people conform and comply within a group, the more obvious people who do not or cannot do so become and the more vulnerable they are to violent or verbal attack, marginalisation or other discriminatory behaviours. Consequently, people who are different find life very difficult in authoritarian countries like Russia.

Discrimination may stem from unreasonable opinions and therefore be founded on prejudice, but may result from the existence of a genuine threat. For example, some practices associated with Islam conflict with Western, liberal values. In particular, the wearing of a niqab or burqa constrains a person's ability to express their individuality and establishes a barrier that inhibits social contact. People often confuse racial discrimination with discrimination on the grounds of culture. It is totally unreasonable to judge people according to their race because genes related to race have a very small effect on a person's behaviour. However, it can sometimes be reasonable to discriminate against a group of people in order to prevent them from exerting a negative influence. For example, we discriminate against people who join groups whose leaders consider it is acceptable to use violence to achieve their aims. The boundaries between acceptable and unacceptable behaviour can, though, be very difficult to draw, especially when it comes to religious beliefs and practices.

Sometimes, sub-groups within a society set up barriers between themselves and wider society. This may be a result of historic persecution, religious beliefs or alternative lifestyles. The sub-group can become characterised by certain behaviours that are valued within the sub-group's culture, and over time inbreeding can re-enforce the resultant culture by shifting the balance of personality traits within the group towards traits associated with those behaviours. When this happens, a cultural clash is likely to result and continue indefinitely. For example, gypsy groups and other nomadic peoples are characterised by the trait of high opportunism because a travelling lifestyle requires the ability to act flexibly. However, this trait also encourages rule breaking and therefore such groups often find themselves at odds with settled populations.

Progressive governments and organisations try to eliminate prejudice and discrimination. There is a current trend of "no-platforming" in universities in the UK and USA where people holding views regarded as unacceptable or offensive are prevented from contributing to a public debate or meeting. However, it is damaging to democracy to restrict freedom of speech. Some people argue that it is better for people with abhorrent values to have the weaknesses in their arguments and beliefs exposed in debate. Also, as prejudice stems from fear, it is a signal that sections of a population are feeling insecure. The emergence of discriminatory language and behaviours should therefore prompt governments to address the underlying economic and social issues that are causing such insecurity. Where a culture of "political correctness" emerges or governments impose strict anti-discrimination laws, marginalised people who are prevented from expressing their views may resort to violence or develop underground organisations that are difficult to monitor.

The presence of people who are different within a group presents an opportunity for those who are high in indifference to exert their dominance. Authoritarian leaders have taken advantage of such opportunities throughout history to increase their power. They have sought to differentiate their followers, ethnic group or native countrymen from other members of society who they consider as dangerous or disposable, or from citizens of other states. By so doing, they strengthen the primal hierarchy, create a cohesive force that is more easily controllable, and shift the blame for the ills of society on to groups of people with no ability to fight back. They also increase fear levels by highlighting and exaggerating the potential threat from other groups. This helps them to persuade members of the rank and file to participate in their expansionist wars. Such behaviour may not be deliberately manipulative as authoritarian leaders will usually be low in openness and will therefore instinctively display discriminatory behaviours.

The female collective is less discriminatory than the primal hierarchy because it is characterised by the trait of high openness. There is, though, no significant gender difference in respect of the openness spectrum so the more tolerant nature of the female collective depends to a great degree on its members' confidence in their own security. As we have seen, its members have less reason to fear males from beyond their group than males in their group. The average female's low level of indifference also makes it difficult for her to appreciate how violent and uncaring some males can be, and therefore her more tolerant behaviour will partly result from naivety.

When taken to extremes, discriminatory attitudes can cause one group of people to see another group as worthless or sub-human and to exploit or harm them as a consequence. **Dehumanisation** deprives a person or group of positive human qualities. It enables soldiers and guards to harm other people in ways that would otherwise offend their values. If they dehumanise a sub-group, establishment leaders, regimes and governments can more easily persuade ordinary members of society to participate in their subjugation or elimination, as Hitler did in Nazi Germany in respect of Jews, homosexuals and gypsies. The Israeli military is a current example. It dehumanises Palestinians in the eyes of its soldiers. This enables the Israeli government to use its troops to oppress the Palestinians in the West Bank and Gaza and pursue a policy of confiscation of Palestinian land.

Men who are high in indifference discriminate against women because they present a threat to them and undermine their status when they enter the workforce and gain influence beyond the domestic environment. If they are forced to treat women as equals, they experience a loss of dominance and feelings of frustration or lowness. Members of the primal hierarchy also instinctively recognise that women are less trustworthy than fellow members because their primary loyalty is to the female collective.

Members of the female collective do discriminate against men where they fear they will present a threat to the harmonious environment that they have created. As most men are high in indifference, they may be justified in doing so on occasion. Because women find it difficult to weed out dangerous men from those who can help them to further their objectives, they tend to form protective all-female groups, such as women's business forums. These groups enable them to support each other and share knowledge that they consider valuable without fear of it being exploited by men. However, dominant females often use this discriminatory tendency to maintain power within female groups. Where females are allowed to associate with powerful and influential males, some of them adopt submissive behaviours out of fear or in exchange for protection and resources. This weakens the authority of the dominant female so it in her interests to reduce or eliminate such opportunities.

Members of groups can be particularly aggressive to members of other groups with similar aims or characteristics. This is because their similarity causes uncertainty in members' minds as to which group they should belong. They experience cognitive dissonance as their minds battle to make a decision in the absence of conclusive evidence one way or the other. This is why charities find it so difficult to work together and why local derbies are so fiercely contested. Because of the large number of charities in existence, any charity is usually competing against another for the same resources to meet very similar objectives. Football fans resolve this cognitive dissonance by committing wholeheartedly to a particular club, wrapping themselves in its colours and adopting its customs.

As much of the information that we encounter is filtered or processed subconsciously, we are not fully in control of the formation of opinions or our consequent actions. Even people who are committed to fighting discrimination will sometimes have a discriminatory thought as a schema created many years previously, perhaps even in childhood, is resurrected. Some discriminatory thoughts will, though, be the result of rational calculations made by your Slow System in the present time. As discrimination is a means by which groups seek to protect their own culture and values, individuals will often not view their actions as discriminatory. We therefore tend to allow discrimination to influence our judgments and decision-making, especially when we are stressed or fearful. This can have very serious consequences, particularly in justice and law enforcement systems where officers tend to be low in openness. For example, in the USA, police arrest black Americans for drug crimes at twice the rate of whites, according to federal data, despite the fact that whites use and sell drugs at comparable or even higher rates. Racism, homophobia and other views that are considered undesirable in modern society will therefore never be fully eliminated. A continual education process is necessary to keep these primal instincts under control, but it is important for progressive leaders not to go too far and lose the ability to defend their group's culture from other cultures that threaten to undermine it.

Evidence shows that efforts to break down discriminatory attitudes by encouraging interaction between individuals of different backgrounds often fail. Although a person may succeed in establishing a good relationship with an individual from a group in respect of which he holds a discriminatory belief, this interaction is unlikely to cause him to adapt the schema underlying such belief if it is deeply embedded. A person may therefore be friendly with his Asian newsagent, but be hostile to Asians as a group. Individually, his interests lie in establishing a relationship, but he perceives that Asians as a group threaten his job and cultural identity. To tackle discrimination effectively, it is therefore necessary to improve the security of the people from which it is emanating.

Good and evil

Although most people have middling traits and groups tend to adopt centrist values, you will sometimes revert to an extreme or dichotomous position to emphasise a point or clarify a confused situation. This is most likely to occur when you are suffering from stress and need to simplify your environment or are trying to explain a concept or value to a person with limited intelligence or a low level of education, such as a young child. Religious leaders often revert to the concepts of good and evil in an effort to introduce clarity into situations that they find morally confusing. The dichotomy of good and evil also helps to fix values in the minds of people with low levels of education and people with low levels of openness because they appreciate simple explanations and clear values. Some religions have personified evil in the form of Satan, devils or djinns to help establish boundaries in people's minds. A similar dichotomy was created between heaven and hell, establishing a destiny of either salvation or damnation.

However, as a group's values will shift in response to environmental changes, there can be no absolute definition of right and wrong that holds true over time. For example, the death penalty was once widely used, but has been abolished in most developed countries. Also, the complexity of human interactions makes it very difficult to set down principles that will reliably distinguish between right and wrong. Where a person has to choose between two alternative courses of action which both cause some degree of harm, moral judgments can be very difficult to make. Consequently, countries have developed judicial systems that take account of the particular circumstances of a case. Also, most people have middling personality traits so they will fall somewhere in-between saints and sinners. The major religious institutions have evolved to recognise this complexity and view evil simply as a term that describes the absence of good or God's influence rather than a force in its own right. Christianity has in the past incorporated the Devil into its teachings to a greater extent than any other religion, but such references play little part in mainstream Christian practice and belief. Most faiths make allowances for people who do not lead exemplary lives; for example, Catholicism developed the concept of Purgatory.

Religious institutions can, though, lose credibility and support if they compromise their principles. The Church of England, for example, now permits women to be clerics and has a tolerant approach to birth control and homosexuality. Such compromises and adjustments to traditional teachings disturb believers who are low in openness, as does the diverse nature of modern, liberal society. Such people tend to be drawn towards fundamentalist beliefs, taking the wording of early religious texts literally. Where they feel out of place and insecure, they are vulnerable to recruitment by radical groups like ISIS (also known as ISIL and Daesh) that promise to introduce a more uniform and controlled culture, especially where they have cultural connections with members of such groups or have limited education or intelligence.

The possession of a low trait inclines a person to see issues in black and white terms. Such a person will be attracted to clear values because he will struggle to cope with ambiguity and will therefore be prone to experiencing anxiety and chronic stress. By adopting black and white approaches, he minimises the scope for uncertainty and confusion to arise in his mind, thereby reducing the potential for stress. The nature of the clarity such people seek will depend on their personality traits. People who are low in extraversion draw a sharp distinction between what is fair and unfair, people who are low in openness need values to be coherent, those who are low in indifference are inclined to see things in terms of what is harmful and what is not, and people who are low in opportunism need an organised set of rules to follow. In contrast, the possession of a high trait will enable a person to introduce more subtlety, flexibility and variation into this interpretation of values and his behaviour. Such people may also adopt extreme positions, but they will do so to maximise their personal freedom and increase the amount of information within their environment so that they can experience feelings of enjoyment and exhilaration, not to increase their security.

Throughout history, the dichotomy of good and evil has been used to distinguish between behaviours that are beneficial to groups and those that are damaging. Good and evil are primarily associated with the spectrum of indifference. People who are low in indifference will be inclined to care for others, show compassion and promote harmony, and are therefore seen as good. Those who are high in indifference will be inclined to compete for power, dominate others and act ruthlessly in their own interests, and will tend to be viewed as evil. Evil is most obvious when combined with greed, but any high or low trait behaviours in the spectrums of extraversion, openness and opportunism can be corrupted by the trait of high indifference, resulting in evil behaviour. For example, a trader who is high in indifference and opportunism will be inclined to take opportunities to make a profit even if he knows that the products he is selling are harmful. Similarly, a husband who is high in indifference and low in openness is likely to feel a need to punish his wife severely for any perceived disloyalty. In contrast, although a woman who is high in extraversion and low in indifference will be inclined to be greedy, she will be restrained from displaying such behaviour in circumstances where harm to other people would result. People who are low in indifference can, though, commit evil acts. When such a person is very scared or suddenly experiences a major loss, he will be operating in his stress zone and may resort to Fast System behaviours such as aggression and revenge.

Some people are innately evil. They are very high in indifference and incapable of feeling guilt or remorse, which is the key characteristic of **psychopathy**. This characteristic enables psychopaths to remain cool in environments where most other people feel tense, and they may appear confident and even charming as a consequence. Their lack of empathy inclines them to be manipulative and commit crimes. Some of them will possess all four high traits and will be inclined to ruthlessly pursue their desires. Most, though, will have at least one low trait that inclines them to exert control over their environment, which of course includes other people.

Having a psychopathic disposition is not, though, in itself enough to prompt a person to commit evil crimes. He will also need to feel unconstrained by its values and laws or be dislocated from society. This may be because he is very confident in his own abilities, belongs to a group with a weak value or justice system, or has been marginalised by society to a point that he feels he has nothing to lose. For example, a leader may become so dominant that he feels he can act with impunity, or a person with paedophilic tendencies who lives in an individualistic culture may take advantage of the lack of community in a neighbourhood to enter it and abuse children. A person may also display evil behaviour as a result of being incorrectly positioned in terms of the primal group structure. As the primal hierarchy is more hierarchical than the female collective, there is more scope for males to find themselves out of position, but establishment females are likely to feel frustrated at the lack of opportunities to display their natural behaviours within the female collective.

The trait of high indifference inclines a person to pursue his objectives ruthlessly. Although such a person may cause harm to other people, this is normally a by-product. Sometimes, however, harming or controlling other people becomes the actual objective. A person who is high in indifference will derive enjoyment from dominating other people. If he possesses a low trait he is likely to feel a sense of contentment when he exerts control over others. Such a person will, though, need to discover that such actions are pleasurable before they become embedded in his behaviour. Consequently, a person who has committed an evil crime is likely to have been influenced by a negative culture that has exposed him to harm or enabled him to witness another person deriving positive feelings from harming others. For example, a boy may realise that his father is gaining a sense of power and satisfaction from abusing his mother, and therefore behave the same way to his wife in later life. Environments and circumstances that prompt hate, fear, jealousy, revenge, abuse and exploitation therefore greatly contribute to the display of evil behaviour. Children growing up in these environments will be influenced by the pervading negative culture. It is very difficult to break this cycle as those who have the most interest in doing so have the least power.

Some people possess a gene that can make them particularly violent and aggressive. It seems that this **warrior gene** is switched on when a young person who possesses it is exposed to harsh treatment. Men with this gene would have been useful to primitive groups that were subject to external threat or internal disorder because they would have been able to offer their groups greater protection and been more ruthless in restoring order than men without it. However, this gene can trap groups into cycles of conflict as young people who are exposed to violence grow up with the gene activated. People with the warrior gene who were abused as children are more likely to be disruptive influences within society than those who had normal childhoods. This may go some way to explaining why impoverished neighbourhoods experience more violence, although such neighbourhoods will also be more likely to attract drug addicts and dealers, provide refuge for the criminally minded and lack educational and career opportunities, all of which all likely to contribute towards higher levels of violence.

One study concluded that 5.5% of black men, 0.9% of Caucasian men, and 0.00067% of Asian men carry the warrior gene. The racial variations in its occurrence may explain why countries in the Far East have on the whole had more peaceful societies than those in Europe and Africa. However, it is not always a good thing to have a small number of men with the warrior gene. Where a leader abuses and exploits other group members and there is a lack of men with the warrior gene within the group, it is less likely that he will face a challenge to his authority. Violent, authoritarian regimes may therefore become entrenched, as occurred in Cambodia with the Khmer Rouge. On the other hand, many countries with predominantly black populations in Africa have struggled to escape cycles of violence. It may be that the distribution within the white population is particularly suited to democratic forms of governance. However, many other factors have an influence on the stability of a society, including colonial history and the exploitation of resources by multinationals.

As a majority of males possess the trait of high indifference, most males will be drawn towards evil behaviour at times. Usually, though, they will stay within the bounds of acceptable behaviour because they will be restrained by the value systems and cultures of the groups to which they belong or because they find niches where dominating behaviours are considered useful to groups. For example, chief executives of large companies often have psychopathic tendencies. The typical male may commit misdemeanours or engage in mischief making, but he is unlikely to cause significant harm unless he is enrolled into a system or structure in the form of the primal hierarchy and that hierarchy is controlled by an evil leader. The primal hierarchy is a machine for accumulating wealth and exert dominance. Members of the establishment use it to exploit resources and people, start wars and adopt authoritarian approaches to governance. Establishment culture is characterised by desire, hatred and ignorance, which are the "root of all evil" in Buddhist teaching. In contrast, the female collective does not usually tolerate evil behaviour. Its members are drawn towards goodness, compassion, fairness, tolerance and freedom, and therefore promote progressive cultures.

The dynamics of personality mean that members of the establishment will naturally ascend to positions of power and influence that enable them to accumulate resources. However, other members of the group will also benefit where an establishment acquires new resources from beyond the group. Therefore, whether a person considers an act to be evil or not will depend to some degree on whether he is benefitting from it and the extent to which he has sympathy for members of other groups from whom resources have been acquired. An act that is considered evil when carried out on an ordinary group member may be considered worthy when carried out for the benefit of a group. For example, murder is prohibited, but the killing of an enemy of the group in war is likely to be considered acceptable and may even be celebrated. The ruthlessness of the establishment also enables it to create and manage functional units of people. We need such structures within armed forces, businesses and other organisations to protect and provide for us, and competition between such groups can promote innovation, and increase productivity and efficiency. Therefore, provided establishment behaviours are moderated by progressive values, they can be a force for good.

In contrast, although people who possess all four progressive traits will be good by nature, such behaviour will not always be beneficial to a group. When confronted by an aggressive external force, a person who is low in indifference is likely to try to reach a compromise. Such an approach is likely to be perceived as weakness by the aggressor, and may lead to anarchy or conquest. One of the best examples of such weakness occurred in 1939 when British Prime Minister Neville Chamberlain adopted a policy of appeasement towards Adolf Hitler's regime in Germany. On his return from the Munich conference he triumphantly stated: "I believe it is peace for our time", but this was soon followed by further German aggression. The other progressive traits also serve to weaken the primal hierarchy within a society and therefore make a country more vulnerable to attack.

Members of the primal hierarchy tend to be attracted to organisations with evil intent because they potentially offer the opportunity to be part of a dominant force and to increase their sense of security. Some people who are low in indifference and high in openness struggle to understand why wars break out because they cannot appreciate why one person would kill or harm another. They fail to realise that war, fighting and other dominating or competitive behaviours excite people who are high in indifference, rather than horrify them, and that a low level of openness promotes fear of strangers and compels people to seek protection within armed units. Holding a gun gives a man with establishment traits a sense of enjoyment and contentment because it gives him a sense of authority and control.

When a group leader is strong, he will attempt to minimise competition within the male sub-group and focus the competitive instincts of its members on conquest and the accumulation of resources. However, where he is weak, males will start competing with each other for position. Those who are high in indifference but lack competitive ability or are restrained by other forces may take advantage of opportunities to abuse, exploit or exert control over vulnerable people in order to eliminate their feelings of loss or disappointment and to secure the positive feelings associated with the exertion of power. This may take the form of domestic abuse, or verbal or physical attacks on the disabled, homeless and members of other vulnerable groups. The Chinese philosopher Confucius referred to such a person as a small man, saying: "What the superior man seeks is in himself; what the small man seeks is in others". The primal hierarchy has largely disintegrated within UK society due to its individualistic culture, and the dominance of multinational companies and a long period of austerity have deprived many men of opportunities to compete successfully in the workplace, so it is not surprising that attacks on homeless and other vulnerable people in the UK have been increasing.

For most of the 20th century, the USA acted as the policeman of the world, keeping countries with despotic leaders in check. These leaders were essentially locked in a global primal hierarchy and forced to obey the dominant male. The USA's influence has waned, however, as a result of the emergence of China as a superpower, the antagonistic approach of Vladimir Putin and the apparent impotency of America in the Middle East. Barack Obama avoided confrontation where he could while Donald Trump appears unconcerned about the behaviour of leaders within their own countries. As a consequence, the USA appears weak and leaders with authoritarian instincts are acting upon them. Some, no doubt see Trump as a role model or at least like mind. The dynamics of personality mean that these leaders will be inclined to compete with each other for status and resources. Further down the primal hierarchy, males with establishment traits are watching Trump's confrontational leadership style and rejection of progressive values and seeing it as a green light to behave in similar ways in their communities and workplaces. The lack of a strong dominant male on the world stage is, therefore, promoting behaviours that are likely to lead to conflict, abuse and exploitation.

It is not just people who are high in indifference who are likely to abuse others. Sometimes people who are low in indifference will do so, especially if they have a strong desire to achieve higher status. People with low traits have a small environmental window in which they can operate their Fast Systems and experience feelings of enjoyment. If they find an environment in which they can do so, they can become very protective of it. They may force people around them to behave in ways that maintain that environment. Despite these bullying efforts, the narrowness of their Fast System window is likely to cause them to experience stress frequently and display anger and aggression as a result. Therefore, although people with high traits are naturally forceful, it is often the possession of a low trait that triggers nastiness in a person.

Members of a group who are likely to be subject to abuse will be inclined to support a leader who is willing and able to control abusers. However, as leaders of groups tend to be high in indifference, they are unlikely to offer such protection out of compassion. Instead, they will demand loyalty, support and submission. As we have seen, the establishment will naturally marginalise men with progressive traits and repress women. The female collective depend on men with progressive traits to restrain such males because they lack physical strength, competitive ability and access to male groups.

Historically, progressive males who were low in extraversion and indifference sought to restrain the evil instincts of establishment leaders and those who naturally follow them (i.e. other members of the primal hierarchy) by developing moral and religious codes based on fairness and compassion. As members of the primal hierarchy appreciate conformity and structure, they increased the coherency of their religious beliefs and created organised institutions and rituals. Therefore, even though Jesus' behaviour and teaching suggest that he possessed progressive traits, the Christian church developed a collectivist culture. Over its long history, it has, though, been strongly influenced by establishment and progressive forces. In the 500 years following the death of Jesus, Christians clarified and codified their religious texts and practices, before splitting into several church units including the Catholic Church in Europe. Over time, the Catholic Church was able to extend its influence across whole populations and gain influence over national leaders and establishments across Europe. However, national leaders were also able to use the structure and coherency of the church to exert control over their citizens. Early European monarchs gained influence over their national churches by claiming to be divinely appointed. The influence of national leaders over the Catholic Church declined as a strong establishment (the Papacy) emerged within it centred on Rome. This led to conflict between the Catholic Church on the one hand and reformist clerics backed up by some national leaders on the other, and a proliferation of new Christian faiths.

Islam was more organised and demanding of conformity than Christianity from the start because it emerged in reaction to the liberal, polytheistic culture that existed in Mecca at the time of the Prophet Muhammad. In Islam's formative years, political and religious power rested one person, known as the caliph, who ruled over the entire Muslim world at that time – the "ummah wahidah", which means "one community" or "one nation" in Arabic. This ended as a result of a schism in 632. Two traditions emerged and their followers became known as the Sunni and the Shia. Political power also became separated from religious authority as separate nations began to emerge. However, the ummah wahidah remains a powerful aspirational force for many Muslims as it was referred to in the Quran and offers those who are low in openness the possibility of a return to a simpler life.

The West's recent experience of Islamic fundamentalism has caused many people to see Islam as ruthless and domineering by nature. However, this interpretation fails to account for the confrontational environment in which Mohammed was forced to operate. His group of followers were attacked many times by neighbouring tribes in Islam's early years. It also fails to recognise the strong emphasis on compassion within the Qur'an. For example, when Muslims start something new they recite the words "Bi Ism-i-Allah al-Rahman al-Rahim", the translation of which is "in the name of Allah who is compassionate and merciful". A lack of knowledge of history also means that most people do not know that for much of the medieval period, the Ottoman Empire allowed Christians and Jews to practise their faiths while European monarchs and the Catholic Church persecuted those with non-conformist beliefs.

The power that religious organisations have over populations still creates tension between secular and religious leaders today, although common ground tends to be found between leaders with authoritarian tendencies and religious organisations that are focused on traditional, establishment values. In Russia at the moment, President Putin and the Russian Orthodox Church are working closely together as the strengthening of traditional values currently suits both of their agendas. In the USA, the Republican Party is strongly influenced by conservative, fundamentalist Christian groups.

Wars are usually started by leaders in pursuit of greater power and wealth. In societies where religious beliefs are widely held, these leaders often seek to justify acts of war on religious grounds. Differences in beliefs present opportunities for confrontation and conquest, and the enhanced status that accompanies victory is magnified when it is achieved in the name of God. In modern, secular society the promotion of democracy now serves as a justification for the military adventures of establishment politicians. It is very difficult for any belief system or individual to remain unsullied by exposure to the power dynamics of the physical world, hence the saying: "he who sups with the Devil should have a long spoon".

Although men who possess some progressive traits are likely to oppose or undermine the establishment, they still tend to view themselves as superior to women if they are high in indifference. Men who attain positions of power tend to be high in indifference, even in religious settings. Also, people who are low in openness tend to draw a clear boundary between male and female roles in society. As a result, for most of recorded history women have been treated as second-class citizens by religious institutions and scriptures, and in most cases still are. Despite this, they have had a considerable influence over the morals of wider society by encouraging their husbands and children to show compassion and act responsibly.

Children learn to distinguish between right and wrong within the domestic environment, for example in role-playing games. In modern society, however, young people are exposed to the wider world with its attractions, threats and dangers much earlier than in previous generations. The media, and the entertainment and advertising industries, play a role in determining their values. Sometimes they pull people towards evil behaviours, such as materialism and violence. At other times, they help to delineate the boundaries between good and evil, for example in the case of crime dramas. Although people can be nudged sub-consciously to make small behavioural changes, most of us will experience a stress event when we are at risk of contravening a value that has been deeply embedded at an early age by parents or schooling, or which relates to one of our personality traits. As a result, we can develop fantasies without translating them to real life. Therefore, although playing violent video games and watching hard-core pornography can desensitise some men to the horrors of war and increase the likelihood of them causing harm to their sexual partners, for most men they provide a harmless outlet for behaviours that might otherwise emerge in more harmful scenarios.

Men who are high in opportunism and indifference are often described as anti-establishment because they object to the organising behaviours of the establishment. However, they want to be freed from such control so they can exert their authority over others, often their immediate family, and compete freely with other men. As the female collective is orientated around the trait of low indifference, it is the true anti-establishment force. This is why establishment males seek to restrain the influence of women, passing laws and developing values that oblige them to remain within the domestic environment and be subservient to men.

Human civilisation faces great challenges in the form of climate change, increasing inequality and the re-emergence of authoritarianism, all of which relate to the dominating behaviours of establishments. Establishments thrive where fear and hatred are commonplace. In such circumstances, members of the primal hierarchy show aggression and defensiveness. This undermines the influence of progressive forces, as we are seeing across the globe at present. The forces of good, including kind-hearted religious people, the female collective and the progressive movement must reverse this dynamic by capturing the hearts and minds of the rank and file and other group members. The key to success for progressive forces is to convince males with one or more progressive traits their interests lie in restraining the power of establishments rather than empowering them. They need to reduce these males' fear of other groups and nations, and encourage them to believe that they can survive and prosper without an establishment leader. This can only be achieved if many more people with progressive traits devote time to reducing inequality, conserving resources, promoting peace and understanding, caring for others, developing green technologies, investing time and money in their communities, and convincing electors that they can move to a sustainable world without compromising their wellbeing. People with progressive traits will naturally pursue these objectives, but they find it hard to work together effectively as coherency and organisation are establishment characteristics. They will be dependent on the open-minded nature of people who are high in openness and collaborative behaviours of people who are low in indifference to bring people together.

If good is to triumph over evil, however, people with progressive traits will need to join forces and operate within a global progressive movement. The film series that most closely illustrates the battle for control between the establishment and progressive forces is Star Wars. The Galactic Empire is a dark force led by a ruthless leader. Its storm troopers represent the rank and file. They are highly organised and their uniformity is emphasised by the wearing of masks. In contrast, the Rebel Alliance promotes freedom and harmony, and is made up of a disorganised and incoherent set of fighters led by a woman. It is therefore representative of progressive forces. George Lucas, the creator of Star Wars, invented the concept of the Force - a mythical energy field that allowed the series to further explore the dichotomy between good and evil. Lucas said there is a choice between good and bad, and "the world works better if you're on the good side".

The expression of feelings

You express your feelings by speaking and using facial and other body movements. Many of these actions are instinctive and you perform them without noticing. Sometimes you restrain their expression to remain within socially acceptable or legal boundaries, to maintain the health of key relationships or to protect you from harm. When you are busy, frustrated or stressed, or drop your guard, you may say or do something instinctively that you later regret.

People who are high trait orientated tend to express their feelings freely because they usually feel secure in their environment. They spend most of their time in Fast System operation and have a wide range of schemas to choose from. Depending on which high traits a person possesses, his feelings may be expressed in an outgoing way, using varied language, assertively or spontaneously. The possession of a low trait causes a person to exercise restraint. He will use his Slow System to exert control over his use of language and behaviour. Depending on which low traits he possesses, his feelings may be expressed in a measured way, methodically, gently or in an organised way. Because people with low traits feel less secure than people with high traits, they tend to be wary of releasing information in case it is used against them. Where they experience fear, they may freeze, retreat into the shadows or psychologically distance themselves from other people, making them appear aloof, as their fight or flight mechanisms kick in. As low traits promote group-orientated behaviours, people who possess them will be deterred from saying or doing things that might damage their groups and are likely to view extravagant or exaggerated expressions of feeling by people with high traits as selfish behaviour. For example, a person who is low in extraversion may label a person who is high in extraversion who is broadcasting his unhappiness a "drama queen". A person who possesses a mixture of high and low traits is likely to be expressive in some environments and to exercise restraint in others. For example, a person who is high in opportunism and low in indifference is likely to behave excitedly in situations where things are changing very quickly; for example, positions in a horse race, but may restrain feelings of anger in a confrontational environment for fear of being overpowered or abused.

A person's propensity to express his feelings will be influenced by the culture of the group and the conformance and compliance dynamics within it. Individualistic cultures encourage the expression of feelings. People therefore tend to become self-centred and may compete for attention. In contrast, collectivist cultures promote restraint. Although they encourage sympathy for people who experience emotional distress, there is an expectation that those individuals will behave reasonably and proportionately, and place the group's needs above their own. Extravagant displays of emotion are therefore discouraged. In establishment cultures, the emphasis is on achieving material objectives rather than looking after individuals. Consequently, males who are outgoing and assertive are championed, and aggression is acceptable as long as it is channelled in a controlled way. Men who are more cerebral or compassionate are expected to comply with these values, hiding any negative emotions behind a stiff upper lip. Females are given more freedom to express their emotions than males in establishment cultures because they are kept away from decision-making, but they tend to be considered as fragile and unreliable as the expression of fear or unhappiness is seen a sign of weakness. In progressive cultures, people are encouraged to be open about emotional distress so that they can be cared for, but they are expected to do so in a measured way.

Women tend to find it easier to express their feelings in female company than men do in male company because it is not culturally acceptable within the female collective to cause harm to others. In contrast, male groups are built around competition and men who are high in indifference will be tempted to take advantage of signs of weakness emanating from other men. Men will therefore tend to hide their feelings to avoid being ridiculed, exploited or abused. Women are therefore usually more animated than men when socialising with members of the same sex. However, a woman is likely to be more restrained in a male-dominated environment because she will fear exposing herself or people she cares about to danger or abuse, or being seen as fragile or unstable. A woman who is distressed at work may therefore retreat to the privacy of the female toilets to cry when she feels upset. Men who are low in indifference will be naturally empathetic and are likely to help other people who are in distress. However, in establishment cultures, they will be reluctant to reveal these characteristics so other men are unlikely to benefit from their support unless they are very close friends. A man is most likely to confide in another man and receive support where he has established a strong bond of loyalty with him. Men will be reluctant to show weakness in front of a woman because men are generally expected to protect women and because women are more likely to breach confidence due to their inclination to share information.

Mental health conditions associated with group dynamics

Protection and support

People are tied to groups by their need for protection and support. People with high traits need support from people with low traits to achieve their exploratory objectives and experience the associated feelings of excitement and exhilaration whereas people with low traits need protection from people with high traits so they use their Slow Systems safely and experience a sense of contentment and fulfilment. In a well-functioning group, people with different traits will work together, offering protection and support to each other, to achieve the group's objectives. However, if connections within a group are too loose, high trait orientated individuals will be tempted to take advantage of any increased freedom they have to pursue selfish objectives rather than perform their protection duties and low trait orientated individuals are likely to hide away rather than carry out supportive tasks. In both cases, conformance and compliance to the group's values will reduce and the group's ability to fulfil its objectives will be compromised. Where a group is too small or unbalanced, people will be obliged to carry out unsuitable tasks. They are likely to experience stress and low moods on a regular basis, and these states may cause them to exhibit unpleasant or inappropriate behaviours, or limit their ability to perform.

People with high traits will usually be dissatisfied to some degree with their environment and will try to spend more time exhibiting high trait behaviours and to increase the intensity of such experiences. A person who is high in extraversion will seek out physically stimulating environments, a person who is high in openness will search for novelty, a person who is high in indifference will crave power and a person who is high in opportunism will look for changing circumstances. These behaviours can have destabilising or other harmful effects on groups and cause group members with low traits to experience stress if they are uncontrolled. Greed and inequality are associated with high extraversion; incoherency and non-conformity are associated with high openness; domination and abuse are associated with high indifference; and disorganisation and anarchy are associated with high opportunism.

People with low traits often retreat into safe spaces to escape threats that might cause them to experience major stress events. By hiding away, a person can trick himself into believing his environment is more favourable to him than it actually is and avoid the need to use his Slow System skills to support his group. A person who is low in extraversion will try to avoid physical stimulation, a person who is low in openness will try to locate himself in a uniform environment, a person who is low in indifference will try to embed himself in a harmonious environment, and a person who is low in opportunism will try to avoid changing environments.

A vicious cycle can be created, whereby the behaviour of high trait orientated individuals increases the amount of information within a group's environment, forcing increasing numbers of low trait orientated individuals to feel unprotected and to hide away. This leaves fewer low trait orientated individuals to exert a controlling influence on people with high traits so their efforts become less effective, allowing high trait orientated individuals to indulge themselves even more. The number of people taking responsibility for the health of the group therefore reduces to a point where such people become overstretched or are forced to take on unsuitable roles. This dynamic leads to an individualistic culture and the group splits into small, loose and unbalanced sub-groups that are ignorant of, or antagonistic towards, each other. This is very evident in the USA and the UK where people increasingly want to be heard, but are not prepared to listen. 75% of Americans have cut off contact with a friend or relative because they dislike his political stance. The inefficiencies created by this individualistic dynamic are making large numbers of people feel insecure, reducing productivity and incomes, increasing inequality, making it easier for people to exploit and abuse others, and greatly impacting on mental health.

Loneliness and isolation

Loneliness is a sad feeling caused by a lack, or the loss of, companionship. Whereas you can normally relate sadness to a specific loss, loneliness is a more general feeling reflecting an absence of company. Social isolation increases the chances of experiencing loneliness, but an individual can still feel lonely when he has people around him. Loneliness is likely to be experienced within a group context where a person is incorrectly located in terms of the primal group structure. Although loneliness is a low mood, a person who experiences it will often lack protection and support in which case he is also likely to suffer from stress at times.

In modern society, people have tended to withdraw from community activity and prioritise personal enjoyment. People living in individualistic cultures are less likely to have children because they prefer to allocate their time to other activities and find it difficult to establish long-term relationships. Large numbers of middle-aged and older people are living alone as a result of divorces or separations. Many families have therefore disintegrated or lack sustainability. Large numbers of people work alone or in small groups. Individualistic behaviours are usually initiated when times are good and the people concerned feel secure. However, as people age, experience misfortune or appreciate their own mortality, they need more support and protection. Many middle-aged people who have lived relatively carefree lives are now beginning to feel more insecure as they realise that they may lack resources, good health or emotional support in later life. Many older people are living alone as a result of the dispersion of their families, often with complex health problems.

Isolating factors such as ill health, disability, low income, bereavement, retirement, care responsibilities, fear of crime, poor public transport and the breakdown of communities increase the chances of experiencing loneliness. Over the last four decades, neo-liberal policies have increased the power of directors, wealthy investors and large corporations at the expense of the social fabric of communities and nations. Companies have taken advantage of liberalised employment laws and the weakness of unions to reduce job security and other long-term benefits that they previously provided to employees. As a result, individuals are more likely to lose their jobs suddenly, have their wages reduced or be reduced to poverty in old age or due to illness. Austerity measures introduced by the UK government following the financial crisis have resulted in the withdrawal of funding to community-orientated facilities such as libraries, community centres, and arts and cultural institutions. As a result, social opportunities are increasingly only accessible through the payment of money, either directly in entrance fees or indirectly by the purchase of food and drinks. Declining levels of disposable income in the poorer sections of society mean that many people find such costs unaffordable. Cuts to bus services have made it harder for people to access the facilities that remain.

At the same time, technological advances have made it easier for people to entertain themselves at home without engaging physically with other people. The Internet, in particular, is making it easier for people to avoid physical social contact and situations where they might be required to take responsibility. Hollywood films once provided people with an occasional opportunity to escape reality. Online, cable and satellite television services now enable people to waste enormous amounts of time that they could be spending reconnecting within their local communities. We generally think of technology as a communication enhancer. However, many everyday technological products reduce our social connections. The Internet enables people to purchase the goods and services that they need remotely without engaging with local traders. Labour-intensive manufacturing industries, which used to provide opportunities for working-class men to establish bonds of loyalty with other men, have either been mechanised or transferred to developing countries, and many people now use DIY tools to carry out tasks at home rather than engaging tradesmen. Cars, headphones and sunglasses enable people to go about their business with minimal contact with members of wider society.

Users of social media get an inaccurate representation of their friends' lifestyles and mental states because people mostly post details of positive experiences in their lives. This may cause a person who is viewing from an isolated position to feel inadequate or that he is missing out. The Internet has also provided bullies with new private channels through which they can abuse people who are isolated. Bullies and trolls have been empowered by social media and websites that allow them to contribute anonymously or by using pseudonyms and by a lack of effective policing.

When conditions change for the worse, group members are eventually forced to address issues that affect their security. New dynamics emerge within the group that encourage them to adopt behaviours that strengthen the group. The financial crisis of 2008 may come to be seen as one such turning point. However, people will tend to engage in avoidance and sustain their self-interested behaviours for as long as possible. When they finally realise they need to contribute, they are likely to lack the skills needed to do so. Also, it takes a long time to create strong groups, as members need to build trust with each other and develop a sufficient amount of mutual dependence to cause them to recognise that they have common objectives and to accept responsibility for the health of the group. Therefore, many people are likely to experience loneliness, stress and low moods on a continuing basis as a result of a lack of support and protection.

Loneliness occurs disproportionately amongst those who are over 50 because it is more difficult for a person to rebuild his supportive group after that age. A person's chances of reproducing will be much reduced so he will be dependent on his children, if he has them, to increase the size of his immediate family. Our sexual urges encourage us to build a wide social group in order to gain access to potential mates. A person will, though, become more selective when making friends once he recognises that his chances of forming a new sexual relationship have reduced substantially, or his sex drive wanes. In the absence of the masking effect of sex hormones, he is more likely to be dissuaded from forging relationships by annoying habits or differences in opinions. As building strong relationships usually requires considerable effort, declining energy levels also impact on a person's ability to make new friends.

Women tend to find it easier than men to make friends with people of the same gender in later life. This is because they instinctively work together to create harmonious environments and therefore have a common interest in supporting each other. In contrast, men tend to see other men as potential threats. They usually need to go through trust building exercises before establishing social relationships with each other. The instability of modern working environments means that men have less opportunity to build solid relationships with each other. The ready availability of enjoyable, individualistic activities means that men are less likely than in previous generations to belong to golf clubs, masonic lodges, working men's clubs or other organised groups that used to provide them with social networks and promote trust building. Male bonding opportunities have also been reduced as a result of men taking on more domestic and childcare responsibilities, and spending more time socialising with their partners, than in previous generations.

People do not need to be alone to feel lonely. People who are out of position within a group in terms of the primal group structure or marginalised by other group members are likely to feel lonely. Also, where a group breaks into cliques or sub-groups, a person may find that he is excluded. Young people usually have lots of people around them, but some individuals will feel very lonely at times. Childhood friendship groups are often very unstable and children that do not fit in or who have low status are often discriminated against or bullied. Social media can exacerbate these problems as it encourages children to measure their popularity by the number of likes they get, enables them to create exclusive online groups and provides bullies with private channels to abuse and manipulate their victims. Children can therefore feel isolated within their own families. Modern schools are often very large with many hundreds of students so it is easy for individuals to feel lost or be neglected. Increasingly, young people lack support and protection in their home environments. Parents may neglect their responsibilities to their children because they are busy at work, experiencing mental health problems or simply preoccupied with their own lives. Often, parents' ambitions for their children, as determined by the parents' personality traits, background and experience of life are at odds with the desires and needs of their children. Any child is likely to experience poor mental health if he lacks protection or support. The loss or absence of a mother or father through death, separation or neglect can therefore be damaging to a child, but so can be growing up in a family unit characterised by arguments, violence or unhappiness.

Because girls are on average lower in indifference than boys, they tend to suffer more where there is disharmony in the home. However, their collaborative nature means that they usually establish supportive relationships at school. Girls tend, though, to have a lesser level of commitment to the female collective, and to be more self-interested, than women, as they do not have children to look after. In all-girls schools, the absence of boys means that the female collective lacks a focal point for its energies. Also, girls who are higher in indifference have a greater opportunity to exert dominance over or abuse others in such schools. In general, boys are better able to cope with tension at school and parental conflict because of their higher levels of indifference. However, boys who are low in openness and opportunism will feel insecure if they are not part of a closely bonded and organised male group. They are likely to experience anxiety or chronic stress if they lack father figures and may join gangs for protection. In all-boys schools, an establishment culture will naturally form unless the head teacher works very hard to stop it. Boys with progressive traits are likely to be marginalised or bullied in such schools as these traits cause them to adopt behaviours that conflict with the culture of the primal hierarchy. Boys who possess the trait of low indifference are particularly vulnerable to bullying and emotional harm as most of their peers will be higher in indifference. They are most likely to feel a sense of belonging in harmonious and collaborative environments so they are suited to mixed sex schools.

Depression

You will feel low when you experience a loss. Your arousal level drops and you experience feelings of sadness. These feelings prompt you to reflect on your loss and take remedial steps. When a member of your family and friendship group dies or leaves, or a work colleague resigns or retires, you will therefore naturally take action to strengthen your group. If you live in a close-knit family group or work in a supportive team, you will benefit from the protection and support of relatives or colleagues. Feelings of loss and sadness are felt broadly across such groups, especially in the case of the death of an important person. This shared sense of loss results in a collective grieving process. Mourning, funeral wakes and leaving parties help people to come to terms with loss. They strengthen groups by bringing family, friends and work colleagues together. While members of the group are in this subdued state, they are prompted to activate their Slow Systems and use their analytical, methodical, empathetic and organisational skills to consolidate and re-enforce the group. Once this task is achieved, their arousal levels increase, feelings of sadness dissipate and the group resumes normal functioning.

In the absence of a strong group, it is harder to recover from loss. Your lack of support and protection and your limited skillset will restrict your ability to move forward. For example, if a person who is high in extraversion and opportunism and low in openness and indifference experiences bereavement, he will instinctively use his Slow System skills to cement loyalty bonds and promote harmony. He is unlikely, though, to adopt behaviours that could help increase his security where they are related to his blind spots, such as adopting a more cautious approach to his finances or strengthening the structure of his family and friendship circle. He will naturally leave these tasks to other people who are more suited to performing them. In the absence of people who are prepared to offer such support, he is likely to move between periods of activity when he is performing Slow System skills ineffectively and periods of inaction during which he will experience a low mood. However, he may be unable to perform any group strengthening activities if he lacks a protective environment. In such case, he may hide away, be paralysed by fear or experience chronic stress.

When a person experiences a low mood due to a loss and is unable to complete the tasks necessary to recover, he is likely to be diagnosed with depression. In this state, you remain stuck in the resolution stage of the learning cycle and alternate between ineffective Slow System processing and tiredness. You are likely to withdraw from society to carry out this processing. Without appropriate support or exposure to new information that could help you escape from your predicament, you are likely to ruminate excessively. It is, though, impossible to cut yourself off from the outside world completely. If you lack people to protect you, you will be more vulnerable to external threats and therefore anxiety and chronic stress. If you lack support, you are more likely to be forced to undertake Slow System tasks to which you are unsuited and to experience suppression. Depression is therefore often experienced contemporaneously with stress in general.

Individualistic cultures encourage people of all ages to neglect Slow System behaviours including protecting against future loss and hardship. This weakens families and communities and causes people to rely more on their partners or employers for support than their ancestors did. Therefore, when a person loses somebody who is close to him or his job, he is more likely to have to face the experience alone or with limited support from friends and family. Many people therefore lack protection and support. This explains why depression is so prevalent in modern, individualistic society.

The relationships that we now establish and maintain are often very superficial or tenuous, especially those formed online. You may have a large group of friends on Facebook, but for the most part these relationships provide you with illusory support. They trick you into believing that you have a strong support network and this allows you to spend more time enjoying yourself. In reality, however, if it were to be put to the test, it is likely that you would find that you could rely on only a small subset of your online friendship group. The more time a person spends online, the less time he has to build physical relationships in his local area, which are likely to be stronger in the long-term. In modern society, we have therefore substituted tightknit family and community groups with all their complications, restrictions and obligations for a much looser network that allows us more freedom, but leaves us more vulnerable.

The fact that friends and relatives tend to be scattered further afield than in previous generations means that less people are available to help when a person is experiencing loss. People are often separated from loved ones by many miles and families spread themselves across different countries and continents. We are very sensitive to the physical presence of other humans. Facial expressions and behaviours, such as sad faces and crying, attract our attention and encourage us to provide additional support to the person experiencing loss. We are, therefore, much less likely to recognise when other group members are fearful or require assistance when we are not in their physical presence, hence the saying "out of sight, out of mind". We also tend to assume that somebody nearer or with more appropriate skills will take responsibility. In other words, we are inclined to engage in avoidance when given the opportunity.

Of course, the vast majority of people live close to other people who need support. Unfortunately, the disintegration of communities that has occurred in the past 40 years has left many citizens with little sense of obligation to neighbours and other people living in their locality. Communities are largely held together by a fear of what lies beyond them. The relative peace and prosperity that developed countries experienced in the late 20th century reduced fear levels and encouraged people to travel more and break ties with the geographic communities in which they grew up. New relationships can be difficult to establish because of the time that relationship building takes. Also, as you will see in the chapter on relationships, your personality traits suit you to a particular relationship building style. Many people have a low trait that causes them to display an element of caution. The fast pace of modern, individualistic society means that such people often do not act quickly enough to take advantages of social opportunities or recognise the existence of common needs or objectives.

By the time a person realises that his group has become too loose or small to provide him with the protection or support he needs, it may be difficult for him to strengthen it, as humans have not evolved to form new relationships when they are recovering from loss. You are most likely to be attractive to new people when using your Fast System. This is because it helps to be adventurous, open, competitive and/or opportunistic if you are trying to connect with strangers. However, these behaviours expose you to increased risk so your emotional system will deter you from engaging in them until you feel secure. A person who suffers major damage to his group may therefore get caught in a Catch 22 situation that traps him in a depressive state.

General practitioners are channelled into prescribing antidepressants as a solution to depression by pharmaceutical companies and because of the lack of funding for talking therapies and activities focused on promoting wellbeing. The amount of antidepressants dispensed annually in England rose by 25 million between 1998 and 2012, from 15 million prescription items in 1998, to 40 million in 2012. In the US, 11% of people over the age of 12 take antidepressants. These drugs artificially shift a person back within his optimal range. They can break the depressive cycle by enabling people to socialise and make new friends or by stopping excessive rumination. Too often, however, they deter people from making the changes that are necessary in their lives to return them to normal functioning. These drugs silence the patient's instinctive prompts to strengthen his support structure. Their prescription has therefore encouraged large numbers of people to continue to pursue damaging individualistic lifestyles and contributed to the breakdown of families and communities.

Governments of developed countries are struggling to generate the tax revenues needed to support demand for welfare benefits, adult social care and healthcare. It is therefore essential for governments to persuade people to be more pro-active in managing their own health and helping others, both at work and in their communities. They must therefore restrict the dispensing of antidepressants and redirect monies into counselling services and community building initiatives. Such action is not, however, in the interests of multinational pharmaceutical companies whose business models depend on mass consumption.

Suppression and depression are often confused. Sometimes, a person is forced to exercise Slow System skills to which he is unsuited; for example, when a child who is high in extraversion is forced to study quietly, in which case he will experience suppression. At other times, people voluntarily undertake suppressive activities; for example, when a person who is high in opportunism remains in a job requiring strong organisational skills in order to provide for his family. Stress is tiring so if a person's lifestyle causes him to spend long periods of time in a state of suppression, he will alternate between feelings of low arousal stress and tiredness. He may therefore appear to be depressed.

Suppression differs from depression in that a change of environment or a release from obligations will quickly restore a positive mood. In other words, the low mood associated with it is caused purely by environmental conditions that are unrelated to the strength of the person's support structures and therefore no repair work is required to his groups. Consequently, when a person who is suffering from suppression goes on holiday, he is likely to feel liberated and enlivened. In contrast, depression occurs when a person is trapped in the Slow System stage of the learning cycle and will not therefore be resolved by a simple environmental change. Depression and suppression therefore have different remedies. A person who is suffering from depression should focus on activities that will help him recover from the loss, which in the first instance means strengthening his connections with, and improving the security of, his family and wider group. In contrast, as suppression is the result of mismatches between a person's personality and his environment or activities, solutions must be focused around changing that person's environment or role.

Depression is two to three times more common in people with a chronic physical health problem (such as cancer, heart disease, diabetes or a musculoskeletal, respiratory or neurological disorder), occurring in about 20% of this group. Many of these people will in fact be suffering from suppression rather than depression. It is difficult to be optimistic about the future if you have an incurable condition. Humans are, though, remarkably good at adapting to a loss of function. Where a disabled person experiences negative feelings, it is often because of on-going pain, because his disability prevents him from performing useful tasks and causes him to lose his sense of purpose or because he loses status or is deprived of resources as a result of the disability. These are suppressive forces. However, people who are seriously ill or disabled are also susceptible to depression where they lack a strong group or their conditions restrict their ability to maintain strong connections to groups.

Low self-esteem

Self-esteem is a person's subjective emotional evaluation of his own worth. However, your level of self-esteem is to a great extent a measure of your value to the groups to which you belong, as perceived by you. If you feel valued, you are likely to experience a high level of self-esteem; if you do not, you are likely to experience a low level. Your self-esteem will therefore be raised by praise and other appreciative acts by fellow group members, provided you believe them to be sincere, and reduced by disrespectful or belittling behaviour by others towards you. Low self-esteem is evidence of poor mental health and may manifest itself in feelings of hopelessness, self-criticism, anger towards yourself, or worrying about your level of ability.

If you are physically and mentally able, correctly located in terms of the primal group structure and have supportive colleagues, and your personality traits are aligned with the culture of your group, you are likely to perform well. People around you will respect you, and you may be treated favourably by the leaders of the group. You will therefore feel valued and have a high level of self-esteem. If you have a disability or deficiency, or have been deprived of the assistance you need for a sustained period, for example in the educational environment, you are less likely to be valued by your group, particularly one focused on achieving economic objectives. The same applies if you perform poorly or adopt inappropriate behaviours because you are incorrectly positioned within your group, you are forced to perform unsuitable tasks or your values conflict with your group's culture. In such cases, you are likely to have a low level of self-esteem. Therefore, low self-esteem may be evidence of a genuine lack of usefulness as a result of age or disability, or may be a result of a conflict between his environment and personality traits.

Even if you deliver good results, you may receive little recognition or be undermined by negative comments if your face does not fit or you threaten somebody else's position within the group. This is most likely to happen where there is an extreme culture or a lack of social mobility. In the former case, people with certain traits set themselves as an elite within a group and favour their own kind. For example, people who are high in extraversion and openness, but low in opportunism, tend to create cliques where membership is based upon strict adherence to the latest trends. Where there is a lack of social mobility, people from higher classes will tend to look down on people beneath them and try to prevent individuals from lower classes whose personality traits suit them to promotion up the hierarchy from achieving it. Individuals who are subject to such restraints may experience self-doubt, develop limiting beliefs and experience low self-esteem.

A person will usually lose self-esteem if he ceases to make a positive contribution to a group. This is one reason why low self-esteem is common amongst unemployed and retired people. Your value to a group will be determined by your past contribution, your current input and the extent to which your talents and skills are needed to meet the environmental challenges and objectives of the group. The balance between these factors will be influenced by the culture of the group. Establishment cultures encourage respect for wealthy, powerful and older people because they promote hierarchical structures that focus on the acquisition and accumulation of resources and because they encourage people to look back to the past for guidance. They also encourage respect for members of the primal hierarchy, especially those in positions of authority such as policemen. Compassionate, peace loving, honest and fair people are considered to be weak or obstructive in such cultures. Progressive cultures encourage respect for people who have demonstrated a commitment to fairness and those who care for others. People who attempt to exert authority over others or display greedy behaviour are held in low regard. As progressive cultures promote creativity and personal development, they tend to value younger people more than older people and attribute little value to traditions or job roles performed by members of the primal hierarchy. Individualistic cultures encourage people to live in the moment and be self-interested so they value opportunistic, creative wealth generators and attribute less value to history, established organisations, older people or people who perform roles that strengthen groups. Collectivist cultures encourage people to respect the past and treat people fairly and compassionately. People within them who display self-interested behaviours or who lack experience or skills are considered to be disruptive or lacking in usefulness.

A person will also lose self-esteem if his personality traits cause him to view his actions as pointless even where others value his contribution. In this scenario, he will be not located correctly in the primal group structure or the culture of his group will be obliging him to pursue objectives that he does not agree with. He will feel that he is not making the best use of his talents and skills and he may lose self-respect as a consequence Therefore, although most people will be able to increase their usefulness to a group by adapting their behaviour and complying with group values, a person may suffer a loss of self-esteem when doing so.

Low self-esteem is an enduring state that builds up over time as a person is unable to find a way of contributing to a group in a way that he and other group members view as useful. People can increase their levels of self-esteem by associating themselves with high status individuals or teams. A football fan will have his self-esteem raised to some degree if his team wins. Other people bask in the reflective glory of celebrities or wear branded clothing to increase their self-esteem. Psychologically, such allegiances give a person a sense of belonging and provide short cuts to higher status, but they offer no broader benefit to him because his relationship with the team, celebrity or brand will be based on a commercial transaction, not shared interests. High self-esteem is only of real worth to an individual when it reflects an appreciation by other group members of his contribution to that group or it is generated as a result of him performing his natural role.

A person who has made a valuable contribution to a group is likely to experience a sense of pride. **Pride** is a positive feeling and a sign of high self-esteem. However, it may encourage a person to become over-confident or complacent, hence the phrase "pride comes before a fall". Sometimes people are beneficiaries of favourable circumstances that allow them to occupy positions in a group or society that are undeserved. Inherited status or wealth, or good fortune, rather than innate talent or hard work, maintains them in their positions. Where such a person sees the benefits that he is receiving as rights rather than privileges, he will develop a sense of **entitlement**. For example, a person who is born into a wealthy family may feel entitled to walk into a well-paid job, and a person who receives benefits from the state, but who makes no positive contribution to society in return, may express indignation at the prospect of them being withdrawn. A sense of entitlement encourages the display of Fast System behaviours such as greed and arrogance because it causes people to become over-confident. It is an indication that a person's level of self-esteem is higher than justified by reality. Entitlement is most likely to occur in groups with individualistic cultures because group members receive less feedback about their own worth from other people and have more freedom to avoid responsibilities to others where such culture prevails. When a person who displays a sense of entitlement is challenged about their behaviour, he will experience a major stress event and may react angrily because his emotional system will recognise that he is not capable of sustaining his unduly beneficial position in the group through his own endeavours.

Some people are gripped by self-doubt or a fear of failure when taking action in front of other people because they envisage a loss of self-esteem. Such hesitation and lack of confidence may indicate that a person does not have the ability to complete the task or that disadvantageous circumstances make completion of the task difficult. It may, though, result from a lack of assistance from other group members or the existence of an unfavourable culture that is likely to cause group members to ridicule or criticise him unfairly. When you experience self-doubt, your Slow System is questioning the wisdom of your proposed course of action, having calculated your chances of success and assessed the likely benefits. It indicates to you that it may be advisable to redefine your objective, improve your skills or build a stronger, more supportive team around you before moving forward.

People with low levels of self-esteem often refrain from participating in activities that could increase their self-esteem in the longer term if they risk embarrassment in the short-term. This is one reason why people tend to be reticent in trying new things within group contexts (for example, learning a new artistic skill). When a person lacks confidence, he is likely to hang on to use of his Slow System so that he can monitor his actions and environment. This will prevent him from using any relevant schemas that he may possess to perform tasks, slowing him down. It will also expose him to anxiety, which will limit his ability to use his Slow System effectively. This explains why people who are negatively stereotyped by others tend to conform to the stereotype. Their self-esteem is reduced, causing them to lose confidence and perform below their capability.

A person is likely to experience stress and listlessness when he has a low level of self-esteem. Others may perceive his resultant behaviours as being damaging to the group. He may therefore be marginalised or disparaged. His level of self-esteem is likely to be further eroded as a result. A loss of self-esteem can therefore result in a downward spiral towards a state of despair. A person who has been marginalised by other group members will be vulnerable to bullying. Bullies are therefore attracted to people who have low self-esteem. The damage inflicted by the bully is likely to distance the victim further from the group, especially if the bully is manipulative. A person with a low level of self-esteem can therefore become trapped in a vicious circle that leads to him ceding control of his life to the bully.

Where a person increases his self-esteem, it may be at the expense of another person's. For example, an employee may increase his self-esteem by criticising a colleague's work presentation, but this is likely to reduce the presenter's self-esteem if the comments are not made in a constructive way. Such point-scoring behaviour is frowned upon in a collective or progressive culture because of the harm it causes to the person who is being criticised, and may therefore ultimately cause the critic to lose self-esteem as well. In an establishment or individualistic culture, however, it may be seen as a normal part of the competitive dynamic that is encouraged in such cultures.

As low self-esteem represents a loss of value, it may lead to depression. Studies have confirmed this link, but also found that the reverse does not apply; depression does not lead to low self-esteem. This is probably because depression causes a person to focus on resolving his loss and not to look more broadly at how other people in the group view him or assess his progress towards his objectives as dictated by his personality traits. Also, in tight knit groups, other group members will often share an individual's loss to some degree, in which case they are likely to be sympathetic towards him.

Some counsellors attempt to restore their clients' self-esteem by building up their sense of self-worth or encouraging them to think more positively or be more assertive. This reframing process can help a person whose confidence has been undermined by bullying or other abuse. However, where the real cause of low self-esteem is poor positioning within a group structure or an unfavourable culture, such techniques are unlikely to have a lasting effect. The client will remain vulnerable due to his lack of support and protection. If he is to restore his self-esteem in such circumstances, he will need to show determination and reinforce his self-belief through helpful self-talk as he will frequently be encountering evidence that justifies his low level of self-esteem when he interacts with other group members. The long-term solution to low self-esteem in such cases is usually the acquisition and application of skills of benefit to the group, relocation to a group with a more favourable culture or the addition of people to your group who are prepared to provide you with support and protection, for example by finding a more supportive partner.

Intrusive thoughts

An **intrusive thought** is an involuntary thought, memory or idea. We are often distracted by unexpected thoughts, but many of them are pleasant so we have no cause to question them. We tend to notice intrusive thoughts when they contravene our morals or the values of wider society or when they relate to distressing experiences in the past. For example, you may feel a desire to harm somebody else or experience a pang of regret. We all experience intrusive thoughts from time to time, but some people do so more frequently and in a more distressing way than others. They may view them as evidence that they are worthless or sinful people. Most people are unlikely to act on intrusive thoughts that are compelling them to harm others as they will be restrained by their personal values and the values and laws of their groups. Such thoughts may even make them feel guilty or ashamed.

Intrusive thoughts are sometimes generated by your emotional system to guide your behaviour. For example, you may experience a sudden desire to harm somebody if that person presents an obstacle to your progress or has caused you to experience loss. Feelings of guilt indicate that you are neglecting your responsibilities to others in some way. People who are suffering from stress or low moods, and who are therefore resisting, or being prevented from, changing their environment or behaviour, are likely to experience unpleasant intrusive thoughts. These thoughts will result from a failure to recover from serious loss, or a lack support or protection from groups. People with extreme traits are most likely to find themselves in unsuitable environments so they tend to experience intrusive thoughts more powerfully and often than people with middling traits.

Your emotional system stores strong positive and negative experiences in your memory and uses them to guide you towards appropriate actions and environments. You are likely to recall strong negative memories when you are operating outside your optimal ranges and strong positive ones within them. For example, where your emotional system anticipates a stress event, it may recover a negative memory to dissuade you from continuing with your current course of action. If a person has a traumatic experience, his emotional system is likely to become particularly sensitive to potential stressors. As a result, he will be susceptible to feelings of anxiety and chronic stress. His emotional system may use memories of that traumatic experience to deter him from engaging with potentially damaging information, especially in the immediate aftermath of the event. Some people continue to experience vivid flashbacks on a regular basis. They may be diagnosed with Post Traumatic Stress Disorder as a result.

Before humans developed an advanced state of consciousness, they would have acted mostly on instinct. They would not have been in a position to consciously analyse why a particular memory was being recalled or to dwell on their thoughts. The emotional system would, therefore, have been free to recall memories that were unrelated to the current situation, solely to trigger appropriate emotional responses. However, the acquisition of consciousness has interfered with the workings of this mechanism. A person may assume that the presence of intrusive thoughts indicates the presence of some form of mental illness that needs to be resolved when in fact his mind is simply issuing him with an emotional prompt to guide him back to an environment and activities that will generate positive feelings, or solve a problem. If he ruminates over the meaning of such thoughts rather than taking action to change his circumstances or provide his brain with useful information that could help solve the problem, he is likely to perpetuate his negative state.

Sometimes intrusive thoughts are more than just emotional prompts. In quiet periods when you feel relaxed and have time available for processing, your Slow System may re-open unresolved cases and bring them to your conscious mind to encourage you to focus on finding a solution. If the related stress events had traumatic consequences, you are likely to experience fear when addressing them. Consequently, demons that have been suppressed tend to emerge at night when you are alone. In the daytime, your emotional system is likely to conclude that you can use your time more productively so it may stimulate you with an energising burst of anger when your Slow System starts to ruminate over an intrusive thought. The complex nature of modern society can make it difficult to link emotional prompts to appropriate remedial actions and gives people more opportunity to engage in avoidance. For example, a man might feel guilty for not spending enough time with his son following a divorce, but blame his behaviour on work pressures or throw himself into enjoyable activities to rid himself of this feeling. However, such intrusive thoughts are likely to return until he takes steps to increase contact with his son.

People who are low in extraversion are more likely to get trapped in inactive states of rumination because this process involves analytical thinking, which is their forte. People who are high in extraversion naturally engage with the physical world and avoid using analytical thought processes. They are more likely to counter an intrusive thought by undertaking an activity that is likely to distract their attention from it or moving to a more energised environment. They are therefore less likely to get trapped in ruminative states, but they are also less likely to discover or address the causes of the intrusive thoughts so they are likely to return repeatedly.

Personality disorders and other diagnosable conditions

I am not a psychiatrist and do not pretend to have specialist knowledge in the areas of 'personality disorders'. I feel, however, that the approach to personality set out in this book may be helpful to some people who are diagnosed with such conditions and their relations.

The Oxford Dictionary defines **personality disorder** as a: "deeply ingrained and maladaptive pattern of behaviour of a specified kind, typically apparent by the time of adolescence, causing long-term difficulties in personal relationships or in functioning in society".

Psychiatrists have established ten diagnosable personality disorders, which have been divided into 3 clusters:

- Cluster A: "odd or eccentric" (paranoid, schizoid, schizotypal)

- Cluster B: "dramatic emotional or erratic" (histrionic, narcissistic, antisocial, borderline)

- Cluster C: "anxious and fearful" (obsessive-compulsive, avoidant and dependent).

Cluster A personality disorders relate to behaviours that cause a person to distance himself from other people or groups because either he likes being alone or feels that other people are harbouring negative attitudes towards him or intend to harm him in some way. These behaviours are associated with people who have particularly low traits. They are likely to be quickly overwhelmed in average and high information environments, experiencing major stress events as a consequence. Their limited ability to filter information will make it difficult for them to see the big picture or determine the trustworthiness of other people. As a result, they may jump to unreasonable conclusions, experience paranoia and or buy into conspiracy theories. They tend to distance themselves from other people to minimise their exposure to potential threats, either physically by adopting solitary behaviours or psychologically by displaying coldness or emotional detachment. In other words, their lack of protection causes them to seek refuge in isolation. The chances of a person experiencing one of these disorders is increased where a person has experienced a traumatic event as a result of the actions or omissions of another person or group and has not regained his ability to trust people.

Cluster B personality disorders are characterised by high trait behaviours. People diagnosed with them tend to hold exaggerated opinions of their attractiveness, intelligence or importance. They feel that other group members are not showing them enough respect or giving them enough attention. As a result, they may engage in attention-seeking behaviours, such as monopolising conversations or playing the role of victim, or develop fantasy worlds. A person with one of these disorders will have failed to integrate himself within a group in a way that enables him to use his talents, as dictated by their personality traits, for the benefit of that group.

Cluster C personality disorders relate to behaviours that are adopted in order to manage anxiety levels such as obsessive orderliness and perfectionism. A person who experiences one of these disorders will feel that he lacks protection from a group. This may be because his group is too small or loose, perhaps due to a traumatic event, or has an unfavourable culture, or because he is incorrectly located within it. It may also be because he possesses a particularly low trait or is disabled or has another condition or behavioural pattern that has caused him to be rejected or marginalised by his group. Such a person will therefore be unsure of his ability to cope with his environment. He may have long-standing feelings of inadequacy and be very sensitive to negative comments made about him. These feelings may lead to social inhibition and the avoidance of work, school, and any activities that involve interacting with others. Unlike people with Cluster A disorders, those with Cluster C disorders feel a need to remain connected to their group. They may fear being abandoned or separated from important individuals in their lives. As a result, they may become dependent on, and be submissive to, particular people who they perceive as protectors.

A person who is diagnosed with a personality disorder may need to take drugs to enable him to function within society. His personality traits may be so extreme that he will never be able to adapt his environment in a way that relieves his negative feelings. However, if a doctor focuses on drug treatment rather than seeking to identify and address stressors, environmental mismatches and weaknesses within his patient's groups, he is likely to disempower his patient, making it harder for him to use his own abilities and initiative to alleviate his condition. His patient may relinquish any hope of overcoming the condition through his own efforts and become completely reliant on medication or his psychiatrist's advice. Also, diagnosing a person with a personality disorder may distance him further from his group by marking him out as different. If we attribute negative feelings, thoughts and behaviours to environmental mismatches or a lack of protection or support, it becomes more difficult to label them as personality disorders. Once a person appreciates that he has an extreme version of a personality trait that many other people share in a more moderate form or that he has failed to recover from a traumatic life experience, he is likely to feel more connected with society and be less likely to accept being labelled as mentally ill.

Increasingly, people who are experiencing mental health issues attempt self-diagnosis. The Internet provides access to a vast amount of information about medical conditions and the human problem-solving mechanism causes people to try to match their symptoms to recognised conditions. However, they will be doing so with limited knowledge and no training so they are liable to make errors and jump to incorrect conclusions. This is a particular problem for young people as they lack experience of life.

If a person understands that any negative feelings and damaging behaviours that he may be experiencing or exhibiting are likely to relate to the interaction of his personality traits with his environment, weaknesses in his groups or an event that has caused him to experience loss, he will be empowered to make changes to his environment, thinking processes or group structure that may return him to normal functioning. As most mental health issues are founded upon stress or low moods, young people should be taught how to recognise these feelings and relate them to environmental factors, groups and loss. Such an approach would help to demystify mental health and enable young people to realise that it is common to experience stress and low moods and that, in most cases, there are approaches they can take and techniques they can implement, either by themselves or with the support of others, to improve their mental health.

It is likely that many other psychological conditions are related to personality. Although a condition may not align neatly with a particular personality trait, it may be related to the experience of fear and therefore sensitivity to information. For example, social anxiety can be triggered by any low trait depending on whether the person experiencing it fears that a social environment will be too crowded, varied, confrontational or unstructured.

The adoption of controlling or defensive behaviours is a natural response in an environment where there are potential threats. For example, a person who is low in indifference may feel the need to use his mediation skills to calm a tense atmosphere while a person who is low in openness may go to the aid of a friend who gets into a fight out of a sense of loyalty. However, where a person lacks a group to support, he will struggle to apply his Slow System skills for the benefit of others. As a consequence, he is likely to use these skills on himself or apply them to unproductive tasks. Exerting more control over his immediate environment or own body helps to give a person a sense of security and compensates to some degree for the lack of a strong supportive group.

People who are low in indifference will usually have low levels of testosterone in which case they are more likely to experience pain. If they are also low in extraversion, they will are likely to notice changes in their physical environment, including their bodies, and are likely to analyse the resultant information. As a consequence, people with these traits are particularly prone to hypochondria. As they are naturally frugal, low in extraversion may hoard items in case they come in useful in the future. People who are low in openness seek to control intellectual information and therefore tend to absorb themselves in activities that require a methodical approach or which increase the amount of uniformity in their environment, for example by cleaning obsessively or building up collections of similar items. People who are low in indifference may focus on their own emotional distress and wallow in self-pity or dote over their pets. People who are low in opportunism seek to limit the scope for change and can therefore become preoccupied with structure and orderliness. People can be helped to escape from such behavioural traps if they are encouraged to use their Slow System skills for the benefit of others. For example, a person who is low in indifference could be encouraged to take on caring responsibilities within his community, and a person who is low in opportunism could be encouraged to take on an organisational role. When they use their skills in this way, people increase their sense of security and experience feelings of contentment and fulfilment. If, however, a person is prescribed drug treatment to reduce his anxiety levels, society will be denied such valuable contributions and he may experience side effects from the treatment.

People who are prone to anxiety will often develop mechanisms that allow them to maintain low levels of arousal and therefore avoid triggering apprehension and worry. A person may, for example, double check that his front door is locked when he leaves his house. However, if you artificially increase the level of threat posed by a particular situation by focusing your attention on it, you will increase your susceptibility to a stress event. Therefore, a person may go for many years leaving the house without checking whether the iron was switched off. If one day, he forgets to switch it off, he may catastrophise the situation, imagining the consequences of a fire, and therefore heighten his on-going fear level in respect of such possibility, resulting in anxiety. He may begin to check whether the iron is switched off as he leaves his house in the future. In doing so, he relieves the immediate anxiety but the comfort this action delivers may cause him to repeat such behaviour with it eventually becoming compulsive. Such behaviour may be diagnosed as obsessive-compulsive disorder.

Some people release stress through **tics**, which are fast, repetitive muscle movements that result in sudden and difficult to control body jolts or sounds. Tics do not usually have serious consequences and normally improve over time, but they can be frustrating and interfere with everyday activities. Examples of tics include blinking, wrinkling the nose, grimacing, coughing, grunting or sniffing, or repeating a sound or phrase. Because tics are related to stress, they often occur in situations where people attempt, or are forced, to comply with social norms that cause them to experience chronic stress or anxiety. When people experience high levels of stress, swearing often provides a release. Tourette's syndrome is characterised by the display of tics and people often associate it with swearing, but this is rare and affects only about 1 in 10 people with the syndrome.

People who experience very high stress levels may experience dissociation. Dissociation occurs when your emotional system psychologically distances you from reality so it is often experienced by people who have been diagnosed with Cluster A personality disorders. It deadens your feelings, and may cause you to forget stressful events in your life, feel that the world around you is unreal, view your actions and experiences as if you were an observer not a participant, or adopt a different identity.

Unfortunately, the individualistic nature of modern society means that many people do not belong to groups that can provide them with suitable roles or adequate protection or support. A vicious cycle has been established whereby people avoid using their Slow System skills for the benefit of others, thereby weakening group structures within society and further loosening the connection between individuals and such groups. The weakness of groups makes individuals more vulnerable to stress events and more uncertain as to their positions within groups and the motivations of others, increasing the likelihood of them exhibiting behaviours associated with personality disorders or other psychological conditions. However, any extreme culture will increase the prevalence of poor mental health in a society.

Eating disorders, self-harm and suicide

Where a person in unable to exercise control over his emotions through psychological means, he may develop an eating disorder, resort to self-harm or even commit suicide.

An eating disorder is a medical diagnosis based on a person's eating patterns, weight, blood test results and body mass index. The most well known are bulimia nervosa, anorexia nervosa and binge eating disorder. A person with bulimia may binge because he feels upset or worried. He may then feel guilty or ashamed after binging and want to get rid of the food he has eaten by making himself vomit. A person with anorexia will not be eating enough food to get the energy he needs to stay healthy. This condition is often connected to very low self-esteem, negative self-image and feelings of intense distress. A person with binge eating disorder will feel that he cannot stop himself from eating, even if he wants to. He may rely on food to make him feel better or to hide negative feelings. However, many people have a very difficult relationship with food that impacts on their mental health but would not result in diagnosis of one of these conditions.

Self-harm occurs when a person hurts himself as a way of dealing with feelings such as anger, shame, sadness, loneliness and guilt, or painful memories, or overwhelming situations or experiences. He may see it as a way to turn invisible thoughts or feelings into something visible, change emotional pain into physical pain, avoid traumatic memories, reduce overwhelming emotional feelings or thoughts, establish a sense of being in control, punish himself for his feelings and experiences, stop feelings of numbness, disconnection or dissociation, create a reason to physically care for himself, or express suicidal feelings and thoughts without taking his own life. After self-harming, a person may feel a short-term sense of release, but the cause of the distress is unlikely to have gone away so self-harming tends to become a recurrent behaviour.

About 25% of people with an eating disorder also self-harm. Sometimes one condition replaces the other. If a person tries to give up self-harming when he is not psychologically ready, another self-destructive symptom may replace it to help him to cope with, screen and release the intense negative feelings he is experiencing. He will need to address these feelings and find ways of dealing with them to break free of the harming cycle. The relationship between eating disorders and self-harm is complex and can differ from person to person. Most people who suffer from one or both of these conditions will, though, have experienced a significant loss or lack appropriate protection or support from such groups. It is, therefore, important for any practitioner who is treating a patient with an eating disorder or who self-harms to identify and help him overcome the environmental challenges that he will be experiencing.

Suicidal feelings can range from being preoccupied by abstract thoughts about ending your life, or feeling that people would be better off without you, to thinking about methods of suicide, or making clear plans to take your own life. A person who contemplates suicide may be overwhelmed with negative thoughts, feel useless or unwanted, or experience unbearable pain that he cannot imagine ending. Where a person is suffering from an incurable, painful disease, it is easy to understand why he may consider suicide. However, people with good mental health often view suicide as an irrational action. Suicide is, though, a logical way to end persistent negative feelings and therefore it is not surprising that the Slow System considers it as an option. When it carries out a thorough assessment of the situation, however, it is likely to prefer other courses of action. A person may derive strength from imagining or preparing for the act of suicide and then resisting it. Such behaviour can help him to focus more intently on his purpose in life and reason for living. Therefore, although many people experience suicidal thoughts, relatively few are at serious risk of acting upon them.

Some people do go on to commit suicide. In many of these cases, it is likely that Slow System processing has been too brief or performed with insufficient supporting information. A person may be trapped in a high pressure situation and be unable to exercise his Slow System skills properly, and make a rash decision as a consequence, or he may not have immediate access to information that would enable him to view his circumstances in a more positive way. People who have a low level of self-awareness or are stressed and stuck in Fast System operation are likely to be more susceptible to suggestion. Parents and governments should therefore be concerned about the ease with which young people can access material that urges them to engage in self-harm or commit suicide.

People are therefore in greatest danger when they isolate themselves from other people who could help to energise them, relieve the pressure they are under or help them to reframe their situations. The Samaritans and other groups that offer immediate online and telephone support are therefore very important and have contributed to a significant reduction in the UK's suicide rate in recent years. People who are at risk benefit greatly from talking therapies. However, they are expensive to provide and some people are reluctant to seek help.

In British society, men above the age of 50 are most likely to commit suicide because they grew up in a culture where men were expected to be strong providers and not to display weakness. People who have served in the armed forces are particularly vulnerable due to the establishment cultures in these organisations, their exposure to traumatic events in conflict scenarios and the difficulties they find in accessing appropriate mental health support once they enter civilian life. Shockingly, in 2013 the United States Department of Veterans Affairs released a study that covered suicides from 1999 to 2010, which showed that roughly 22 veterans of the US Army were dying by suicide per day (one every 65 minutes).

9

PERFORMANCE

The secret of success

So far in this book, I have stressed the importance of locating yourself in an environment that suits your personality traits. In particular, this means performing appropriate roles and being part of a well-functioning team that has values that are consistent with your own. The extent to which you can achieve this, however, is often limited by factors beyond your control, especially in the early stages of your life.

Your childhood environment and the culture of the society in which you live have an enormous impact on your ability to achieve. The positions and cultures we find ourselves in do not necessarily match up with the attributes that are gifted to us by our personality traits. We are influenced by parents, schools, employers and the media and comply with their values, rules and directions to some extent. The framework imposed on our lives by our backgrounds and current circumstances is often difficult to escape from. People from disadvantaged backgrounds face a struggle to overcome educational deficiencies and low expectations. Intelligent, well-educated people can also find it difficult to find their place in society because they tend to have fewer obvious weaknesses than the average person and to be channelled into careers that are socially respected or financially lucrative. A person trapped in such a scenario may appear very capable to other people if he employs his talents conscientiously, but may feel unfulfilled and unhappy inside. Inappropriate positioning, weaknesses in his supportive groups, unfavourable group cultures and restrictions in social mobility can, therefore, cause a person to experience negative feelings over a long period and inhibit his progress.

To be successful, you need a considerable amount of luck. In his book "Outliers", Malcolm Gladwell used a series of examples to show how particular high achievers benefitted from being located in environments that were ideally suited to their personalities and which allowed them to exercise their talents and develop their skills to the maximum. Gladwell describes the great amount of good fortune that Bill Gates, co-founder and public face of Microsoft, benefitted from in his early life. Gates is highly intelligent, and a hard worker, but he was born into an environment that allowed him to make the most of his talents. His parents recognised that he needed a school that could challenge him intellectually. Fortunately, they were wealthy, so they were able to send him to Lakeside, a school in Seattle, which catered to the city's high-powered families. It just so happened that the school had invested in an extremely advanced computer when Gates was 13. This allowed him to learn programming skills. At this time (in 1968) only a handful of children on the planet would have been presented with this opportunity. He then took advantage of a series of other opportunities to develop his abilities during his childhood and early adulthood. By the time he dropped out of Harvard University after his second year to found a software company, he was one of the most experienced programmers in the world. He was also very fortunate to be born in 1955, within two years of the birth dates of Paul Allen (the co-founder of Microsoft), Steve Jobs (co-founder of Apple) and many other leading lights in the software industry, and to have had Paul Allen as a childhood friend. When the personal computing revolution began, which is generally considered to be the date of publication of a magazine review of the Altair 8800 personal computer in January 1975, Gates found himself with experience in programming which could only be matched by a very small number of people who just happened to be close associates or acquaintances of his. Gladwell goes on to show in a series of examples how success tends to come to a smart, focused individual who finds himself in the right place at the right time.

Of course, we are not all meant to be experts or achieve great feats. Many people have middling personality traits that suit them to regular jobs or bringing up children, and perform these roles successfully without attracting much attention. We all know people who always seem to be happy and appear to deal with the transactions of life effortlessly. It is likely that they have been located within supportive and protective groups with favourable cultures for most of their lives. However, few people will be fortunate enough to live their whole lives in the state of Nirvana. Most of us experience difficult times along the way. You may find yourself in an unsuitable environment, take on obligations to which you are unsuited, or experience loss or disappointment. We are exposed to a more varied range of challenges than our ancestors would have been due to the interconnectedness and complexity of modern society. People who possess extreme personality traits or have failed to recover effectively from a traumatic loss are likely to experience feelings of stress and low moods on a daily basis as they comply with group values or face the consequences of breaching them, or fail to secure support and protection from other people.

Successful people usually deal with negative feelings in ways that enable them to avoid being thrown off course or held back significantly. You will naturally employ these techniques to some degree, but there will usually be scope for improvement. You put up with negative emotional states in the short term to achieve objectives in the long-term, a capability generally known as **resilience**. Sometimes, you accept that an objective is not achievable and reach an **accommodation** with yourself that enables you to redirect your energies towards more realistic objectives.

You can increase your effectiveness by working to understand, develop and enhance these techniques. Also, it is important to recognise when your emotional system has been subconsciously employing them, as their use can prevent you from making more substantial changes to your environment and lifestyle that could enable you to operate more sustainably within your optimal ranges. In other words, these techniques can trap you into reactive decision making. I describe a person who understands his role in life, has a high level of awareness of his feelings, thoughts and behaviours, and is capable of employing the techniques described above effectively to achieve his objectives as **emotionally literate**. An important element of emotional literacy is the appreciation of the fact that people have different motivations, values and levels of commitment. If you have a high level of emotional literacy, you will be able to recognise and manage other people's emotional states for your and their benefit.

Emotional literacy is sometimes used interchangeably with the phrase "emotional intelligence", which was popularised by Daniel Goleman in his book of the same name published in 1996. There has been a lot of psychological research in this area, and there are multiple definitions of both of these terms. Researchers and psychologists have tended to view emotional capabilities in terms of measurable abilities, trait-dependent preferences or learned skills. In my opinion, each of these perspectives is relevant. People differ in their responses to external stimuli, and such differences can be measured. These differences largely result from the individual nature of their personality traits. You can, however, develop emotional management skills by learning from experience or through study. I prefer the word "literacy" because I do not think it is appropriate to use the word "intelligence" to describe skills that can be learned.

Most people would benefit from gaining more control over their emotional responses and improving their decision-making. If you understand your personality and appreciate how your emotional system works, you will be able to direct your energies more effectively, limit the effect of potentially damaging instincts, and build stronger relationships. You will also be able to get back on track more quickly when you experience loss. Increasing numbers of people are experiencing serious, long-term mental health issues as a result of the environments that we now inhabit and the weakness of their groups. For such people, improved emotional literacy could greatly improve their health and wellbeing. You may not be able to change your environment immediately, for example where you have family responsibilities or need to acquire new skills, and recovery from loss can take a long time, but whatever your circumstances, increasing your level of emotional literacy is likely to assist your in achieving your objectives and maintaining a positive outlook.

Emotional regulation

You learn and recover from loss by completing the learning cycle. In challenging environments, it can be difficult to keep your learning cycle functioning. You can improve its performance and maintain progress towards your objectives by employing techniques and taking substances that influence your emotional responses, a practice I refer to as **emotional regulation**. You can regulate your emotions in four ways – by managing the amount and type of information that your mind is required to filter and process, by controlling your arousal level, by reframing situations or by adjusting your sensitivity to information by using stimulants and depressants.

Managing information levels

Your emotional system will naturally prompt you to change your environment or seek support or protection from other people if you experience negative feelings. It can, though, be difficult to change your wider environment because external forces, including group dynamics, dictate so much of it. As a result, you will constantly be making minor adjustments to your immediate environment to improve or maintain your emotional state. For example, you may cross the street to avoid somebody who is likely to cause you to experience negative feelings.

Your Fast System will make many of these adjustments by applying relevant schemas. Your Slow System will make adjustments for new situations where it has time to do so. For example, if you have had a hard day at the office and a friend calls and asks if you want to join him for a beer, you may instinctively say yes. However, if somebody you do not know very well invites you to a party at the weekend, you may use your Slow System to weigh it against other options.

Because we have evolved to live in groups, we naturally use other people to help regulate our moods. For example, when two work colleagues meet at a coffee point at work, one may initiate a conversation to provide him with some enjoyment and the other person may join in willingly in order to relieve the stress he has been experiencing in the meeting from which he has just escaped. The feelings two people experience when they interact will depend on their personality traits, which are fixed, their background and experiences, and their circumstances at that moment, which can be very changeable. If you have access to a wide range of people with different personality traits, you should be able to find somebody who is capable of promoting positive feelings within you, whatever your mood. Our primeval ancestors would have lived in large family groups so they would have had access to many different personalities. In modern society, families are smaller and more geographically dispersed, but we have developed networks of friends and acquaintances to compensate.

We now have access to a multitude of activities and experiences that allow us to regulate the amount and type of information within our environment independently of other people. People use television programmes, computer games, social networking sites, music, hobbies, pets, gambling and pornography to relax or energise themselves, as they feel necessary. For example, if you feel stressed you might watch a nature programme. If you are bored, you might listen to some energising rock music. Smartphones are now many people's first choice of emotional regulation because of the instant access to information and varied methods of communication that they offer.

Adjusting your arousal level

Sometimes you are not able to make minor environmental adjustments and are forced to deal with the situation that you find yourself in. In such circumstances, you risk exposing yourself to stress or a low mood and associated negative feelings. However, if you learn how to monitor and control your arousal level, you will be able to minimise the impact of stressors and suppressive influences on your performance.

In modern society, it is rarely beneficial to enter a state of panic or chronic stress or allow yourself to become angry or frustrated. If you do so, your level of functioning will drop, you will experience strong negative feelings, and you may react aggressively. For example, some footballers experience a 'red mist' during matches, which may cause them to commit violent acts. This usually occurs when an opponent challenges a player when that player is already in a state of high arousal. Because he will be in Fast System operation in such a situation, he will find it difficult to restrain aggressive impulses. Such behaviour is particularly likely where a player lacks restraining schemas derived from a strong value system. Another player or a referee will usually be needed to calm down the situation. If you can keep your arousal level under control in pressurised environments, you will be able to prevent your emotional system prompting inappropriate behaviours, and you may be able to retain access to your Slow System.

Let us consider a presentation scenario. Presenting to an audience can be a stressful experience for people who are not high in extraversion. You can keep control of your arousal level during a presentation by breathing deeply and slowly, standing upright and clenching your core stomach muscles. Talking in a measured and deliberate fashion helps you to keep control. If you familiarise yourself with the auditorium in advance and visualise an audience within it, the chances of a sudden spike in your arousal level will be reduced. Such spikes can cause major stress events and cause you to freeze, resulting in mental blocks. You can also use avoidance tactics by, for example, avoiding eye contact with audience members or focusing your attention on a particular individual, thereby psychologically removing the rest of the audience from your environment. If you are presenting jointly with other people, you may be able to escape from a stressor momentarily when a colleague is speaking by recalling a memory of a soothing experience.

Retaining access to your Slow System is important because, when you do so, you will be able to maintain operation of your learning cycle and make calculated decisions. For example, a military leader will benefit from being able to access his Slow System in a conflict situation because it will enable him to adapt his strategy in the light of new information. If he can maintain a moderate level of arousal in the heat of battle, he will be able to make considered decisions when others are, literally and figuratively, losing their heads. Although people who are high in extraversion may feel excited in battlefield situations due to their intensely physical nature, they will have limited ability to use their Slow Systems for analytical purposes. Military leaders therefore often have lower levels of extraversion than many of their troops. They will, though, need to use emotional regulation techniques to stay cool in physically challenging situations.

We expect police officers to act proportionately. In potentially stressful situations, they need to be able to maintain the capacity to use their Slow Systems so they can make rational decisions. Police forces in the US have reduced the number of fatalities caused by policemen by adopting techniques and strategies that keep their arousal levels low. For example, by moving from two-man to one-man patrol cars, officers have been encouraged to be more cautious and call for back up before intervening. Such tactics allow officers to keep control in situations that previously may have pushed them over the edge into uncontrolled, aggressive acts.

The value of maintaining a low arousal level is recognised within sporting circles. If a sports person can keep his arousal level down within a match, he will be able to retain access to his Slow System and develop new strategies if his pre-prepared plans are not delivering results. When tennis players win key points, they and their coaches often react with a slow fist pump and other controlled responses designed to increase confidence without increasing the player's arousal level. The fitter a person is, the easier it will be for him to maintain a low level of arousal so the best players tend to devote a lot of time to cardio exercise.

Sometimes, however, situations are so stimulating that it is impossible to retain access to your Slow System. You will then be forced to fall back on the use of schemas. Efficient armies spend a lot of time embedding battlefield routines in the minds of soldiers as schemas, which they will instinctively deploy in challenging circumstances. Similarly, in high-pressure moments within a match, a sports person's arousal level will rise and he will switch to Fast System mode. He will have very limited ability to access his Slow System to develop alternative strategies. Even if he does have access to his Slow System, the speed of play may make it impossible for him to use it to make decisions quickly enough to be effective. Sports coaches therefore put players through practice drills to embed strategies within their minds that can be deployed as schemas. This helps them to react instantaneously where necessary; for example, on the return of a fast tennis serve.

You can also employ emotional regulation techniques to increase your arousal level when it drops to a point at which you experience a low mood by, for example, engaging in physical activity, recalling exciting experiences from your memory or finding ways to increase the risk level associate with the task you are facing. With regard to the presentation example above, you might use the audience to increase your arousal level by encouraging them to ask difficult questions. Arriving ill prepared or just in time would also raise your arousal level, but these are risky approaches to take.

When you experience very strong emotions in a particular circumstance, an emotional response can become **imprinted** in your memory. A reoccurrence of such circumstance will prompt its recall. You can take advantage of this imprinting mechanism by mentally linking actions with positive experiences so that, when you repeat the action in the future, the positive feelings are resurrected. This will enable you to summon up positive feelings at will. If you repeatedly recall the memory while performing the action, you will eventually imprint the feeling. For example, you might link positive memories from a beach holiday to the action of pressing your thumb and second finger together. Recalling positive experiences that have been imprinted in this way helps to distract your emotional system from stressors and suppressive influences within your environment and return your arousal level to a point within your optimal range.

Reframing your situation

You can eliminate or reduce the impact of stress or low moods by **reframing** your circumstances. If you adjust the weight you are giving to the various factors that are informing a decision and then re-evaluate your situation, your arousal level is likely to change and your emotional system may issue a different emotional response. You might introduce new information or take time to clarify your understanding of certain factors as part of this reframing process. Reframing therefore involves operation of the learning cycle and the expansion of your consciousness.

You can reframe the nature of the threats in your environment, the challenges that you face and the opportunities that are open to you. For example, you may envisage somebody you would like to impress knocking randomly on your door to provide you an incentive to complete some household chores. Similarly, if you are stressed, you might view your situation with a wider perspective and realise that the threat you face is not as serious as you initially thought. In this case, you will be discounting the risks associated with failure. You can also increase your level of confidence in relation to the carrying out of a task by reassessing your capabilities. By doing so, you enable your mind to deploy schemas more effectively, thereby reducing the likelihood of experiencing stress.

Sometimes, we focus so intently on our personal problems that we neglect to look more widely at the broader causes of our discomfort or fail to establish useful relationships with people who could be part of the solution. Reframing your situation can help you escape such episodes of self-absorption and the stress and depressive moods that accompany them. Once you gain a broader perspective, you will be able to reconnect with society and begin to take action with others to change your environment for the better.

Reframing can present dangers, however. If you are providing your mind with information that allows you to re-evaluate the nature of a threat more accurately, then you will be increasing your effectiveness, but if that information is incorrect or you attribute inappropriate values to the factors you need to consider, you may trick your mind into taking on excessive risks or being overly cautious. A counsellor may increase a person's confidence and self-belief using reframing techniques, but this will not change the underlying threat level.

Sometimes, the simple act of appreciating the reason why you are feeling stressed or low is enough to cause an adjustment to your arousal level and return you to a positive state. The resultant clarity allows you to move to the next stage of the learning cycle. For example, your arousal level will drop in overcast weather conditions, partly because lower levels of light reduce the vibrancy of colour in our visual environment. This loss of stimulation causes some people to experience low moods. Psychologists have shown that people can be returned to a positive mood simply by being made consciously aware of the weather conditions. This information enables their Slow Systems to resolve the cause of the stress event or loss of stimulation and prompts a return to normal functioning. This is probably why British people talk about the weather so much. The UK has particularly changeable weather patterns, so its inhabitants are more likely to experience mood changes due to weather. By pointing out the existence of adverse weather conditions to each other, they help their sub-conscious minds to carry out this resolution process.

Mood enhancers

You can relieve negative feelings and increase your level of positive feeling without changing your environment by taking stimulants, depressants or other mood enhancing substances. These mood enhancers can make activities or environments that would normally result in stress or a low mood enjoyable, or increase the intensity of a positive experience. However, people who take them may become addicted to them. Addiction is defined as not having control over doing, taking or using something to the point where it could be harmful to you. We commonly associate it with drugs, but you can become addicted to almost anything that delivers positive feelings to you, including activities like gambling or using a mobile phone. An addiction can also serve as a distraction, enabling an individual to avoid dealing with issues. An addict who is deprived of the opportunity to take the substance or engage in the activity to which he is addicted will experience unpleasant feelings. He may also experience physical withdrawal symptoms.

Stimulants, such as cocaine and caffeine, increase your sensitivity to your environment, making you more aware of the information within it. They therefore heighten your arousal level and increase the likelihood of you exhibiting Fast System behaviours. As a result, they tend to promote enjoyment and exhilaration, and sometimes induce euphoria. Stimulants can also temporarily improve mental and physical functioning, increasing alertness, endurance and productivity. **Depressants**, such as cannabis and alcohol, reduce your sensitivity to your environment, making you less aware of the information within it. They therefore lower your arousal level and increase the likelihood of you exhibiting Slow System behaviours. They reduce the intensity at which a person operates, so they can help to combat anxiety and chronic stress. They can also help to relieve pain as they act as sedatives and promote muscle relaxation. Depressants are often used recreationally to reduce social anxiety.

The effect of stimulants and depressants on a person will though depend on his personality traits. Stimulants promote feelings of enjoyment and exhilaration in people with high traits. This is because a person with a high trait has great elasticity within his Fast System in respect of information relating to that trait and, as a result, is unlikely to experience negative feelings in environments with high levels of such information. A person who is high in extraversion is therefore likely to feel a sense of euphoria after taking cocaine in a crowded environment. However, a person who has a low trait and who therefore has limited ability to use his Fast System to filter information relating to that trait is likely to experience a major stress event if he takes a stimulant in the same situation. Consumption of stimulants by people with low traits can cause them to transition quickly to a state of hyper-alertness and chronic stress. For example, where a person who is low in openness takes a stimulant in a place full of strangers, he may suffer increased social anxiety or even experience a panic attack or paranoia. Unsurprisingly, therefore, the use of stimulants increases the chances of a person experiencing a psychotic episode.

In contrast, a depressant will promote feelings of contentment and fulfilment in people with low traits. This is because a person with a low trait has great elasticity within his Slow System in respect of the processing of information relating to that trait and, as a result, is unlikely to experience negative feelings when engaging it for that purpose. For example, a person who is low in opportunism is likely to become more and more contented as he drinks alcohol in a formal social environment. However, a person who is high in opportunism and who therefore has limited ability to use his Slow System to process information relating to that trait is likely to feel bored or lethargic if he takes a depressant in such an environment.

Stimulants and depressants can, though, also help people to perform tasks and operate in environments to which they are unsuited. If a person with a high trait is experiencing a low mood because of environmental factors, he will be able to relieve these by taking a stimulant. For example, he may consume a cup of coffee. By increasing his arousal level, he will be able to move from the low mood zone into the relevant optimal range. As a result, he may experience contentment rather than suppression. Similarly, if a person with a low trait experiences anxiety or chronic stress in a particular environment, he will be able to reduce the likelihood of suffering a stress event by taking a depressant. By reducing his arousal level, he will move from the stress zone into his optimal range. For example, a person who is low in indifference is likely to feel stressed in an environment where he is exposed to competitive forces, such as a boxing match. If he has an alcoholic drink, however, he may find the experience enjoyable once its sedative effects start to take effect.

Stimulants and depressants will therefore have different effects on a person depending on his environment. For example, a person who is low in extraversion may fall asleep after drinking alcohol alone at home at lunchtime, but drinking alcohol later that evening in a crowded bar may make the experience more enjoyable. In the first instance, his arousal level would already be low because he is in a safe environment. Alcohol would further reduce it and therefore induce sleepiness. In the bar, however, the presence of people and loud music is likely to cause his arousal level to increase to a point where he experiences chronic stress. In this case, drinking alcohol would reduce his arousal level, thereby eliminating the associated negative feelings.

Our reactions to stimulants and depressants are complicated by the fact that we have different levels of sensitivity across the four personality spectrums. Where a person who has a high trait and a low trait takes a stimulant, he may switch between feelings of elation and stress if the information levels in his environment are unstable or where he changes his location. For example, a person who is high in extraversion and low in openness may consume a caffeine-based energy drink to boost his arousal level when he is carrying out an analytical task, a behaviour associated with low extraversion that would normally cause him to experience suppression. If, however, he then participates in a debate involving new ideas, he is likely to experience anxiety, as his low level of openness makes him unsuited to dealing with novelty. If the stimulant is still in his system, his arousal level will be heightened further, possibly to a point where he experiences chronic stress or panic. In contrast, if he was to take a depressant when engaging in a brainstorming session, he is likely to find the experience more enjoyable as he will be better able to cope with new ideas, but he would suffer from a greater degree of suppression if he then returned to the analytical task.

Fatigue and illness affect your arousal level. In these states, your arousal level will drop (unless you have a fever), prompting you to rest or go to sleep. Use of depressants in such circumstances will make you sleepier and, if you attempt to stay awake, lead to negative feelings. Stimulants will increase your arousal level, relieving feelings of tiredness and allowing you to continue to function without experiencing negative feelings. Consequently, as an evening social function progresses, people often switch from depressants like alcohol to consumption of stimulants, such as coffee or caffeine-based energy drinks.

At work, our options to change our environment are usually more limited than in our social lives, so people often resort to stimulants or depressants to counter negative feelings and tiredness. For example, many people charge themselves up in the morning with strong, stimulating coffee while others escape out the back door during breaks for a relaxing smoke. However, increasingly, people use stimulants or depressants in domestic and social environments. You only have to walk into your local newsagent or liquor store to realise how many people are engaged in a constant battle to regulate their feelings, at home and work. These shops have become 21st-century pharmacies, dispensing not only a huge variety of alcoholic beverages, but also a multitude of other mood enhancers including chocolate, high-sugar and caffeinated drinks, and cigarettes. Most people use food in some way to regulate their arousal level. Sugary foods act as stimulants, increasing a person's arousal level and energising them, whereas fatty foods depress it, resulting in feelings of relaxation. We are attracted to foods with high sugar or fat content because we subconsciously or consciously recognise their ability to produce positive feelings.

Some substances can act as both stimulants and depressants. Tobacco acts as a stimulant when smoked quickly in small doses, but as a depressant when consumed more slowly in larger quantities. Consequently, a smoker who wishes to be stimulated will take many small puffs, whereas one who wishes to relax will take longer drags. Alcohol initially acts as a stimulant, but after about an hour it has more of a depressant effect. A person, therefore, needs to keep drinking to maintain the stimulant effect. A person will experience feelings of enjoyment and display risk-taking Fast System behaviours such as gregariousness, sexual freedom and aggression when the stimulant effect is dominant. However, he will start to exhibit Slow System behaviours, such as introspection and caring, as the depressive effect takes hold. He may show aggression in this state too due to his increased sensitivity to threats, or tiredness. Cannabis can also act as a stimulant in some people, causing anxiety or chronic stress and sometimes paranoia, although it is not clear why.

There is a third category of mood enhancers called **opioids**. It includes codeine, heroin and morphine. Opioids are not a means of managing arousal levels. Instead, they enable a person to escape temporarily from their current reality. They are primarily prescribed for the relief of physical pain, but patients often become addicted to them and struggle to cope without them once their prescriptions are terminated. The euphoria that these drugs induce attracts recreational use, but people also resort to them to relieve emotional pain. It is estimated that 23% of individuals who use heroin develop opioid addiction. Because of their association with addiction and fatal overdose, most opioids are controlled substances. However, in the USA many people are addicted to opioids as a result of the liberal prescribing practices of doctors in that country. In 2012, 259 million prescriptions were written for opioids. 80% of new heroin users started out misusing prescription painkillers. Of the 20.5 million Americans over 11 years of age that had a substance use disorder in 2015, 2 million had one involving prescription pain relievers and 591,000 had one involving heroin. Fentanyl, a synthetic drug up to 100 times more potent than morphine, has been responsible for a surge in overdose deaths in the USA in recent years.

The final category of mood enhancer is **hallucinogens**. This type of drug alters your perception of reality by changing the way the nerve cells in your brain communicate with each other. They include LSD, psilocybin, and MDMA. Continued use of hallucinogens can lead to speech problems, memory loss, anxiety and low moods. In rare cases, people may be left with psychosis or flashbacks. Hallucinations are unusual or false perceptions of objects or event, whereas paranoia involves an idea that others perceive to be invalid. However, they are both associated with high arousal levels and therefore in all probability the Fast System pattern recognition function.

Mood enhancers can help a person to get through difficult times and achieve objectives that he finds challenging. They also make it easier for a person to function within groups that have values or laws that restrict his instinctive behaviours. As people are less likely to resort to violence or vandalism where they find it easy to regulate their moods, easy access to mood enhancers contributed to a fall in crime and antisocial behaviour in developed countries like the UK before the financial crisis of 2008. However, when people use mood enhancers on a regular basis to access feelings of enjoyment, they inhibit operation of their learning cycle, avoid using their Slow Systems to develop skills and are less able to apply themselves to tasks for sustained periods. Fast System behaviours become more prevalent and people neglect planning, strategic thinking and caring for others. The use of mood enhancers therefore promotes individualistic behaviours, encourages people to delay addressing threats to their security and deters people from finding healthier and more sustainable solutions to environmental mismatches and losses.

As mood enhancers reduce a person's incentive to change his circumstances for the better, you will be more inclined to put up with the status quo if you use them. Where they are widely used in a society, people are less likely to challenge government policies that are having, or are likely to have in the future, a negative impact on their lives. Campaigning groups seeking to tackle injustices and promote responsible behaviour therefore do not attract as much support as they would otherwise do. The widespread prescription of anti-depressants to women is particularly damaging to society as it reduces their motivation to take steps to restrict the harmful behaviours of establishment men that are increasing inequality, driving climate change and promoting conflict.

This section has only considered the effect of mood enhancers on the emotional system. Each substance will have its own individual character due to particular chemical make-up, which may affect the human body in other ways. Most mood enhancers have negative effects on physical health in the longer term. For example, excessive caffeine consumption has been linked to Type 2 diabetes and high blood pressure. People who use food to regulate their arousal levels are likely to suffer from obesity and other health problems resulting from poor diets. People who take mood enhancers regularly may become less sensitive to them and require increased doses to produce the same effect over time, increasing the health risk. Consuming stimulants and depressants at the same time can be damaging because the overall effect on the emotional system will be balanced and therefore increase the likelihood of excessive consumption. Where drugs are freely available on the black market, users leave themselves vulnerable to contaminated supplies or overdoses. A drug addict will often become focused on securing his next hit and may resort to criminal acts to fund his addiction. This narrow focus and desperation makes them vulnerable to abuse, exploitation, poverty and homelessness. Newly developed synthetic drugs are often much stronger than natural ones and are therefore more likely to result in overdoses or unexpected feelings and behaviours. Spice, a synthetic form of cannabis, is currently causing havoc in UK prisons as inmates are obtaining and abusing it in large numbers.

Resilience and recovery

Resilience

You cannot always relieve negative feelings by using emotional regulation techniques. Sometimes, you will need to put up with them to achieve objectives, fulfil responsibilities, or comply with group values or instructions. It requires mental and physical strength to put up with the stress, low moods and fatigue that you experience when you operate outside your optimal ranges. The capacity to soldier on in adverse circumstances is known as **resilience**.

You naturally develop resilience through your life experiences. When you were young, your siblings and friends would have tested your limits of tolerance. Parents and schools would have obliged you to comply with behavioural norms and rules. You would have been forced to study subjects and perform roles to which you were unsuited. In adulthood, you need to show resilience at times in order to achieve your objectives. You may find yourself out of place in terms of the primal group structure, or the culture of your group may conflict with your personality traits. Your group may be too small to provide you with all the protection and support you need. If, when such circumstances arise or events occur, you battle through the negative feelings that they prompt, you will extend your range of operation. You will learn from the experience, and if you encounter similar situations in the future, you will experience reduced levels of negative feelings. In other words, if you move out of your optimal ranges and learn to tolerate negative feelings, you will become a more resilient individual. There is much truth in the statement: "What does not kill you makes you stronger".

Resilience is an attribute that is acquired when a person lacks protection or support from other people. We have evolved to work together to achieve our objectives. Humans resort to resilience where they create unbalanced groups, fail to invest sufficiently in technology or skill development, or lack sufficient numbers of personnel. Resilience therefore compensates for weaknesses within teams of people and other human groups. It also endows a person or group with flexibility and makes him or it better able to cope with unexpected situations.

If an individual wishes to achieve a complex objective without support from others, he will need to show a high level of resilience, as the nature of personality traits means that he will be weak in certain areas. People who compete in individual sports at the highest level are required to show resilience on a day-to-day basis. Historically, coaches have focused on improving skills associated with their players' natural attributes. This, however, only takes a player so far. Players target the weaknesses of their opponents, and modern technology delivers detailed performance statistics that make it very easy for coaches to identify such weaknesses.

The pursuit of challenging objectives and the deliberate acquisition of skills in areas where you are not naturally gifted can help you to become a more rounded and effective individual. You cannot hope to find an environment entirely suited to your personality. Resilience helps you to get through temporary periods of adversity that might otherwise prevent you from achieving your objectives, destabilise your life or damage your mental health. It can also give you the strength to fight against unfavourable group cultures. However, if you are forced to display resilience for long periods, the stress or low moods that you will experience will damage you, mentally and physically.

When you operate outside your optimal range, your learning cycle will not be operating efficiently. A person who is required to display resilience over a sustained period is therefore less likely to be successful than a person who is suited to performing the role or tasks that he has undertaken. A person who experiences chronic stress will struggle to develop his skills because he will find it difficult to activate his Slow System to create or adapt schemas. A person who experiences low moods will lack new information for his Fast System to filter and his progress will be inhibited. This does not mean, however, that such states are completely unproductive. A person who is experiencing chronic stress will be operating at a high level of arousal and capable of deploying existing schemas at a fast rate. He will therefore be able to carry out tasks that he already knows how to perform at a high tempo. This industriousness will compensate to some degree for his reduced learning capability. Eventually, however, a person operating at such high-stress levels is liable to encounter a situation that pushes him over the edge into a breakdown scenario. A person who is suffering from a low mood or suppression will be able to perform Slow System skills to which he is unsuited, but at a slower pace and less accurately than somebody who is naturally suited to doing so.

The mental and physical effects of showing resilience can be particularly damaging when it is associated with the loss of a close relative or another important individual because resilience tends to be sustained for a long time in such cases. In times of war, people tend to be very resilient because of the greater losses of human life, but the burden they carry forward is heavy too. Whereas relief from negative feelings caused by environmental factors can be achieved simply by changing your environment, feelings of loss can only be relieved by replacement or restitution of the lost person or item. In many cases, this option is not available. Resilience and depression therefore often go hand in hand.

You develop resilience in circumstances where you experience stress or low moods. You are not likely to put yourself in such situations unless you envisage a positive outcome in the future. People are therefore only likely to develop resilience where they are forced to perform unsuitable tasks by others or environmental challenges, or they are focused on achieving important objectives. In other situations, they are likely to engage in avoidance or emotional regulation. Resilient people will therefore often have developed this capability as children or in response a traumatic experience. People who grow up in very protective and supportive environments will not have the opportunity to develop resilience. As a result, such a person may struggle to cope with the consequences of a sudden environmental change or cultural shift. Some people describe young people in Western society as "snowflakes" because they perceive that they have grown up in an unduly favourable environment free from war and material hardship. It is certainly true that many Millenials have limited Slow System skills as a result of growing up in an individualistic society. However, many of them are experiencing high levels of stress due to the uncontrolled nature of this society and are forced to put up with strong negative feelings due to their lack of emotional literacy skills and inability to adapt their environment.

A person can become habituated to inappropriate environments if he develops a very high level of resilience. In such circumstances, he may be prevented from taking the steps that are necessary to move him to a more suitable environment and therefore fail to achieve his potential. Complying behaviours can become so entrenched that a person may believe that they are representative of his personality. He may, therefore, give incorrect answers to questions in personality tests, re-enforcing this error. Where a person with a high trait consistently displays behaviours associated with the corresponding low trait or vice versa, I describe him as possessing an **imposter trait**. A person with an imposter trait will frequently experience chronic stress, anxiety or suppression. Although he may not recognise his experience as abnormal, the symptoms of stress or a low mood - negativity, an abrupt communication style, impatience, frustration, intolerance and listlessness - will often be visible to his work colleagues and family. People with imposter traits tend to be particularly critical of others who fail to meet their standards. The huge amount of effort that they expend in complying causes them to demand the same amount of commitment from others. Ironically, therefore, their harshest words are often directed at those who have similar traits, and weaknesses, to themselves. As a result, they undermine people who are cultural companions in terms of personality.

Relaxation and energy releases

The state of relaxation occurs at the end of each learning cycle. This may last for a fraction of a second or a much longer period. It allows the body to recover before launching into further exploratory behaviour. If you are operating within your optimal ranges, you will be only need short periods of relaxation. If you are operating in a stressful environment, you are likely to feel tired after completing a task and will need longer to recover. If you have been subject to a sustained period of chronic stress, you will have built up a backlog of unresolved stress events that need attention in which case you will not be able to truly relax until you have used your Slow System to resolve them. If you have been experiencing suppression, you will need to overcome the resultant tiredness, but you will have no stress events to resolve so you will then be able to adopt exploratory Fast System behaviours.

You need to locate yourself in a low information environment if you are to relax. Yoga and other similar "mind and body" exercises are particularly good forms of relaxation because they strengthen and loosen the body's muscles, and quieten the mind, preparing you for your next challenge. You can also relax by engaging in activities that are pleasurable, but not too demanding. For example, if you have had a stressful day at work, you may watch a nature programme when you get back home. You can artificially create a suitable environment to relax in by using stimulants or, more likely, depressants. However, they may affect physical health if taken over a long period. Physical exercise is perhaps the most flexible and the healthiest way to induce relaxation. It has a stimulating effect in short bursts, which can re-energise you. Over longer periods it has a depressing effect and therefore helps you to relax.

You can change your environment for the better temporarily by engaging in leisure activities. Leisure activities may involve relaxation, but they make you feel better primarily because they allow you to retreat into an environment in which you can exercise your learning cycle within your optimal ranges. As you will not be experiencing stress or a low mood, you will be able to experience positive feelings and recharge your batteries while carrying them out. Modern, individualistic society offers a wide range of leisure activities including arts and cultural experiences, gardening, collecting and other hobbies, travel and sport. However, the pleasurable nature and wide availability of leisure activities in modern society causes many people to avoid putting in the effort that is needed to fit into more rounded and useful social groups, such as communities. In other words, they can prevent people from developing social skills.

There are sports and positions within teams to suit most personalities, so most people can find a sporting activity that they like and enjoy. They may require the exercise of Fast System behaviours, such as physical interaction, creativity, competition and spontaneity, or the development of Slow System skills, such as tactical analysis, refinement of technique, co-operation and practice. People who are high in extraversion like the buzz of high-intensity exercise, physical contact and playing in teams whereas those who are low in extraversion prefer a slower burn and are suited to individualistic and endurance sports. People who are high in indifference will be highly competitive and are likely to enjoy combat sports. Those who are low in indifference tend to prefer exercise that involves relationship building or indirect competition. They may remove the competitive element completely and simply exercise in the gym. People who are high in openness are likely to be creative while those who are high in opportunism will be flexible. These characteristics make them less likely to "fit in" or practice though, so people with these traits tend to gravitate towards individualistic sports like tennis and are likely to fail to sustain commitment to a team or exercise routines. Professional sportspeople tend to be low in openness because of the methodical nature of training. People who are low in openness also tend to be attracted to gym work because of its routine nature and to team sports due to the group bonding opportunities that they present. People who are low in opportunism feel comforted by the structure that sports teams and clubs offer.

Rugby is renowned for its team bonding and has a very structured format so it naturally attracts players who are low in openness and opportunism (i.e. members of the primal hierarchy). Creative players often find it difficult to fit in unless creativity is valued within their country's society or their rugby traditions, as is the case with France. Football is a much more flexible and open game and therefore is more suited to people who are high in opportunism, although it has become a lot more structured in recent years as coaches have used technology to develop more systems of play. As in rugby, the amount of creativity that is acceptable to coaches and fellow teammates is influenced by cultural values. Historically, the Brazilian national team played a relaxed and exhibitionist style, reflecting the outgoing and individualistic culture of its country, whereas England's team, whose players were drawn from closed, working-class communities characterised by the trait of low openness, often played in a simple, predictable way. Modern football is, though, more structured and young people are exposed to more varied influences, so Brazilian players play in a more restrained and organized way while English players have improved their technical skills and are showing more creativity.

Forced relaxation techniques provide only temporary relief. They will not eliminate the causes of stress so many people only experience brief respite before returning to stressful jobs or roles. They will need to make changes to their wider environments or strengthen their groups if they are to prevent the reoccurrence of negative feelings. Leisure activities usually take up more of our time than exercises focused on energy release or relaxation. They are a luxury and can waste valuable resources where they have no broader purpose than promoting positive feelings within the individual. In individualistic societies, many people spend time pursuing leisure activities when they could be using their abilities for the benefit of their families and communities. If you find appropriate roles in your workplace and community, you will be primed to experience positive feelings and will feel less need or desire to pursue leisure activities.

Accommodation

Most children at some point realise that their parents do not have the resources to satisfy all their material desires. When people enter the job market, the reality of working life often falls short of their idealistic visions. Many people start families with partners whose attributes and qualities fail to meet their expectations. It is impossible to live your life without experiencing some form of irreplaceable loss. Even the luckiest individuals experience bereavements and suffer a decline in their physical ability if they live to middle or old age. When you come to terms with your inability to achieve an objective or recover from a loss, you make an **accommodation** with yourself. Accommodations enable you to devote more time to useful activities and achievable objectives.

If you refuse to make an accommodation, you are likely to dwell on the past and blame yourself or others for the misfortune you have experienced. While reviewing past behaviour is a natural part of the learning cycle, you can only influence the course of events in the present and future. A preoccupation with the past is likely to prevent you from moving forward and shaping your environment in a way that allows you to operate within your optimal ranges. You may experience depression in such circumstances.

Making an accommodation can be challenging, as it will involve overcoming feelings of anger and disappointment, and may lead to a loss of status and self-esteem. It therefore requires courage and humility. However, if you forgive yourself and others who you hold responsible for your failure or loss, and move on, you are likely to feel liberated. The discomfort associated with making accommodations can be eased by the expression of **gratitude**. Being thankful for the events, circumstances and relationships that have enabled you to experience positive feelings during your life helps you to reframe your perspective, shifting your focus away from your personal failures and disappointments.

People with middling traits are not likely to have to make many accommodations because their objectives in life will be relatively closely matched to average achievement levels. When they do make accommodations, they are likely to be minor and involve only mid discomfort. It is more likely that people with high or low traits will have to make accommodations because they will find it harder to locate themselves in suitable environments. They will also find it more difficult to make accommodations because they will usually be required to compromise significantly and therefore expose themselves to stress or low moods, and strong negative feelings. People who possess high traits are optimistic by nature and tend to set challenging objectives. They will often avoid accepting defeat by switching quickly to a new objective. People who are low trait orientated may cut themselves off from society rather than make accommodations that will require them to experience anxiety or stress on an on-going basis and are likely to see their continuing efforts to control their environment ignored by others. People who possess a combination of very high and low traits are likely to set objectives with a high degree of difficulty that other people consider to be unrealistic and unimportant. They may choose to struggle on against adversity, ploughing a lonely furrow rather than accept the stress and low moods that they would otherwise experience in normal life. If ultimately such a person is successful, he may reap the benefits and die happy, but this is a high-risk strategy, as he will probably lack the support and protection he needs to achieve his objective and therefore be at high risk of isolation, loneliness and poor mental health.

Accommodations are harder to make where a group's culture places a high value on the outcomes that are being compromised. In such circumstances, a person may feel obliged to continue to pursue objectives that are not suited to his personality traits, such as keeping up with the materialistic lifestyles of his neighbours. Similarly, where a person has an on-going responsibility, he may be required to continue to perform tasks to which he is unsuited for a long time. In such cases, you may be able to release the pressure you are under by making an accommodation. For example, a man who is unsuited to providing resources for a family by himself is likely to feel relieved when he accepts that fact. Once he has made that accommodation, he is more likely to be prepared to accept help from others and his family is likely to be in a better position as a result.

Sometimes, people make accommodations in advance. By mentally accepting potential losses, you can free yourself from the fear of failure and channel your energies more effectively towards achieving your objective. Such accommodations help you to be courageous. For example, when a person comes to terms with the risk of losing his life, he can present a potent force on the battlefield.

In establishment cultures, people find it harder to make accommodations because high status is valued and society is more hierarchical. They are, therefore, protective of their positions. Establishment cultures are also more competitive and abusive so a person who makes a mistake or displays weakness is likely to be punished or exploited within them. Consequently, people fear revealing their inadequacies and seek to shift blame on to others. In contrast, the compassionate nature of progressive cultures encourages people to make accommodations. People have less to lose because they operate within a more networked structure and benefit from support from other people.

Making an accommodation is a process of realisation, acceptance and forgiveness. It is carried out by the Slow System and involves reflection, understanding and compassion. Accommodation, therefore, represents a triumph of learning over instinct and helps to expand a person's consciousness. Human civilisation is experiencing a challenging period as it attempts to adapt to technological change and other forces associated with globalisation. If we are to achieve a sustainable global society, many more people need to realise the harm that their desires and fears are causing to other people and our natural environment, and adapt their behaviour accordingly. The question is whether enough people will expand their consciousness sufficiently to appreciate the impending dangers that human civilisation faces in time for them to make the accommodations to their lifestyles that are needed to avoid catastrophe.

Finding your purpose

Motivation and drive

We all want to be motivated. We know how good it feels and how much we can achieve when we are in this state. Businesses also need their employees to be motivated. As a consequence, a whole industry related to motivation has grown up to service the self-help market and corporate world. However, many people have a poor understanding of what motivates them and those around them, and too often line managers are focused on implementing procedures rather than addressing motivational issues. In such situations, individuals tend to lack a sense of purpose, and organisational productivity and efficiency levels decline.

Since Abraham Maslow first set out his hierarchy of needs in his book "Motivation and Personality" published in 1954, many theories of motivation have been proposed. There is a demand for a unified, coherent explanation, particularly from businesses seeking simple solutions that can be rolled out to their employees in a generic form. The problem is that we are all individuals with different personalities and life experiences. As a consequence, what motivates us varies from person to person.

Maslow mapped out a journey from preoccupation with survival to a state of fulfilment. In his model, a person works his way up the hierarchy by satisfying physiological needs, securing his safety, finding love and belonging, and building his self-esteem. If he succeeds in making it to the top, he reaches a state of "self-actualisation", which Maslow defined as a state of personal growth in which a person is maximising his potential. However, although Maslow realised that we are programmed to satisfy our needs before progressing to our wants, his model did not account for the different personalities of individuals. Also, although he recognised that we have a need to belong, his model did not factor in the influence of groups and their differing cultures. The Personality Revolution's model of personality is more rounded and flexible and offers insights into these aspects of motivation. It does not define a hierarchy of needs. Instead, it recognises that people have different sensitivities to specific threats and they have often have to deal with multiple stressors. You prioritise these stressors according to the effect they have on your arousal level. Essentially, therefore, you have your own personal hierarchy of stress.

Your decision-making processes are founded upon a need to relieve negative feelings and a desire to experience positive feelings. You will, therefore, be naturally drawn towards activities that make you feel good. If you locate yourself in a suitable environment, you will experience a state of flow. While you are in this state, you will be able to operate effectively for a sustained period and you will experience feelings of enjoyment, exhilaration, contentment and fulfilment. When you are experiencing a state of flow, you will feel **motivated**. However, sometimes you will pursue an activity intently or with vigour even though you are operating within an environment that is causing you to experience negative feelings. In such circumstances, you will derive your high level of motivation from the visualisation of a more rewarding future or a feeling that you are making progress towards a longer-term objective. For example, if you see that working hard in an unsuitable job will allow you to build up enough funds to buy a house, that objective may enable you to sustain your effort level. If you are incorrectly positioned within a group structure, you may identify, and attempt to transition to, a more suitable role. If the culture of your group is not suited to your personality traits, you may attempt to change it to one suited to your personality traits. I describe a person who is able to remain motivated while in an unsuitable environment as **driven**. A person who is driven will have a high level of resilience.

When you notice that a person is exhibiting high levels of motivation, it is likely that he possesses high or low traits. Such people stand out because of their unusually exploratory or controlling behaviours. When they are successful, they tend to achieve high status or notoriety or find niches in society that enable them to express their talents and skills in ways that deliver exceptional or unusual outcomes. Most people, however, have middling traits. As a result, they will be suited to more ordinary roles, and their achievements will be less obvious. This does not mean that such people are not motivated. We are not all meant to be leaders, saints, experts or innovators. Groups are held together by people with middling personality traits who can perform the basic tasks of life such as labouring and childcare, and who feel rewarded when they do so.

You may compare yourself unfavourably to a person who appears to be highly motivated and assume that there must be some failing in your make-up. In reality, it may just be that the "more motivated" person has personality traits that direct his energies differently or that he is less suited to his environment and unhappier than you are, and therefore more driven to change his circumstances. If you make such a comparison, though, the very fact that you are doing so suggests that you are experiencing negative feelings. You may be incorrectly located in respect of the primal group structure, have weaknesses within your supportive group or feel insufficiently valued by other group members. You may lack the drive needed to change your circumstances because you cannot see a way to reposition yourself to a more conducive environment. In such circumstances, you are likely to experience a low mood and listlessness.

When a person suffers loss, he will usually be able to recover if he has developed his talents and skills to do so, is a member of a strong team around him and his group's culture is favourable to his personality. If he lacks support or protection, he may be able to drive himself to restore his position. However, sometimes it is very difficult to recover from loss; for example, when a key person in your life dies. In this instance, a person may redirect his energies towards alternative objectives in an attempt to eliminate the intense feelings associated with the loss. I refer to this behaviour as **loss transference**. Loss transference can be a powerful force and can spur people on to achieve great things. People often find themselves complying with the values of group in order to remain connected to it or avoid damaging relationships. The stress and unhappiness generated by a significant loss and the need to eliminate those feelings may help a person to break or remodel such connections in a way that allows him to take up a more appropriate role or behave more naturally.

Writers on motivation often make a distinction between intrinsic and extrinsic motivation. Intrinsic rewards are generated naturally when you operate within your optimal ranges. If you experience positive feelings as a result of performing a role, you will be intrinsically motivated to continue performing well. An employee will, for example, receive an intrinsic reward if he gains satisfaction from learning a new skill or from being given more autonomy. A person who achieves a high level of intrinsic motivation therefore becomes self-motivating. Intrinsic rewards are maximised when an organisation recruits people to positions to which they are suited by their personality traits and establishes cultures and sub-cultures that correspond to the values of its employees. As intrinsic rewards occur naturally when a person is working, an organisation that focuses on delivering intrinsic rewards to its employees should be able to reduce its staff costs. It will, however, need to invest in systems and promote cultures that allow intrinsic rewards to be generated.

In contrast, extrinsic rewards are not derived directly from the performance of a task but are awarded on the basis of performance or in recognition of some other valuable contribution. They include pay rises, promotion, bonuses, extra holiday and other benefits. The cheapest form of extrinsic reward is praise. Praise boosts your confidence and self-esteem when you believe it to be given sincerely. It may increase an employee's sense of belonging and level of commitment, and prompt him to work harder. However, despite being free, praise is massively underused in working environments. There are three reasons for this. Firstly, managers naturally expect employees who work under them to complete the tasks that they have been allocated because they are required to do so under their employment contracts, and may face disciplinary action if they do not. Secondly, if a manager praises a subordinate, he is in effect raising that person's status within his work group and undermining his own authority to some degree. His position will therefore become less secure and he may experience anxiety as a result. Thirdly, people towards the top of competitive hierarchies tend to be high in indifference in which case they will have little concern for the emotional health of employees and see a lack of ruthlessness as weakness. People who are low in extraversion tend, though, to feel uncomfortable receiving praise in public because it singles them out for attention. They are also more likely to analyse the motives and sincerity of the person who is giving the praise whereas people are high in extraversion are likely to embrace it unreservedly. People who are low trait orientated and therefore drawn towards behaviours that strengthen groups often feel uncomfortable receiving praise because they feel they are just doing their job.

Promotion is an extrinsic reward, but if used correctly it helps people to achieve their natural level in an organisation and therefore enables them to access a greater level of intrinsic reward. Other extrinsic rewards improve a person's performance in work by providing him with benefits in his broader life. A holiday enables a person to temporarily relocate himself to a more favourable environment and culture, and pursue leisure activities. Money is a very flexible extrinsic reward as it can be applied to satisfy a wide range of desires and needs. Financial rewards and promotion are particularly attractive to people with materialistic status-seeking tendencies and to those who measure their competitive ability in monetary terms (i.e. people who possess the traits of high extraversion and indifference). Business owners and company directors often fall into this category, so they tend to assume that such rewards are the best way of motivating people. Money is also a strong motivator for people who are struggling financially or who have few assets, including most young adults.

However, companies that regularly give extrinsic rewards inevitably create expectations of further reward as employees develop a sense of entitlement to their higher status or improved financial position. For example, if a person receives a bonus one year, he will expect to receive it again in the next year. Financial rewards therefore tend to lose their motivational impact unless they are increased year-on-year, which is unsustainable for most businesses. Opportunities for promotion are by their nature limited. Also, employees adapt their behaviour to secure extrinsic rewards. Consequently, they behave unnaturally, experience fewer intrinsic rewards and become less able to motivate themselves. For example, a person may apply for a promotion to increase his salary even though he is unsuited to taking on managerial responsibilities. Where extrinsic rewards are given, they are usually more effective in the long term when they are awarded to a team rather than individuals, as team members are less likely to develop a sense of entitlement than if they received the reward exclusively. Team rewards also encourage group bonding, foster a sense of belonging and promote collaboration.

Which extrinsic or intrinsic rewards you respond to or experience will depend on your personality traits. You may be motivated by high trait rewards such as wealth, power, prestige, new experiences, creativity, competition or freedom, or low trait rewards such as the need for safety, conformity, friendship or structure. For example, a person who is high in indifference is likely to be motivated by the opportunity to compete with colleagues for bonuses (an extrinsic driver) or a job role which involves competing for business with rival companies (an intrinsic driver). A person who is low in indifference is likely to feel rewarded if the company he works for supports a local charity (an extrinsic driver) or makes him responsible for promoting a collaborative atmosphere at work (an intrinsic driver). As the bulk of any population will be suited to cultures near the centre of the Circle of Power, most people will respond to a range of motivating factors. People with high or low traits (typically those performing atypical or specialist roles) will, though, respond strongly to some rewards and weakly to others. It, therefore, makes sense for an organisation to offer a comprehensive range of rewards. However, if people are recruited to roles that suited them, there will be less of a need to provide extrinsic rewards.

Some people are very difficult to motivate within an organisational context. They are likely to possess extreme traits or have suffered abuse, exploitation or been excluded from groups in the past, or both. They may have mental health problems as a result, be disruptive or ineffective, and their presence within an organisation may have a demotivating effect on other group members. Such people will have no reason to expect to receive the assistance they need from others in the future so they lack a reason to engage with or trust other people, or comply with societal values. Living on a group's margins is often difficult. A person can easily be forgotten, and will find it difficult to access the resources that he needs to survive. People in this situation are therefore often unhappy and may be forced into desperate acts to relieve their negative feelings or simply survive, such as drug taking and robbery. Some of them find alternative groups that give them protection and support; for example, criminal gangs, but many lead transient, lonely and stressful lives.

Corporations will try to avoid recruiting such people and are likely to dismiss employees who develop such behaviours. Societies, however, have to deal with the challenges that they present. Controlling people who are inclined to contravene group values and looking after people who avoid or are unable to take their share of responsibility is costly. The ability of an organisation or society to find useful roles for them to perform is an indication of its strength. A well-balanced group should be able to reach out to such people and provide them with pathways to engage with, and operate effectively within, the group. They will have talents and skills that the group may need to access from time to time. If a significant number of group members become marginalised, it is likely that the group has adopted an extreme culture.

People who are disruptive and inclined to criminal antisocial behaviour can be reintegrated back into society. However, they need to be given a stake in it for this to be achieved. People with high traits will be inclined to act in self-interested ways and will not naturally adopt behaviours that strengthen groups, but they will usually seek the respect, support or allegiance of other people or the freedom to use their talents. They will be inclined to abide by group values if they believe they have a reasonable prospect of securing these benefits. Young males with criminal, psychopathic tendencies may be gradually reintegrated back into society through programmes that reward them with increased social acceptance. However, it is important not to fall into the trap of believing that people with high traits can develop the sense of responsibility and group-orientated behaviours associated with low traits. They will be dissuaded from doing so by the experience of frustration and low moods. One rehabilitative program went badly wrong when a number of murderers were released from a US prison after being encouraged to empathise with other people. Rather than developing empathy, which they were incapable of doing due to their high levels of indifference, they used the knowledge they gained to exploit and abuse others more effectively.

Child abusers are particularly difficult for society to deal with. They experience high levels of positive feeling when they abuse and often perceive the risk of being caught to be low, especially where they are in positions of authority or are able to instil fear or guilt in their victims and associates, so it is difficult to reverse the result of their cost-benefit calculation. On release from prison, child abusers are likely to be rejected by their communities because of the on-going risk they present. However, ostracism causes them to adopt transient lifestyles, making it more difficult to monitor their activities and easier for them to offend again elsewhere. Long-term imprisonment is usually the public's preferred solution, but it is very costly. As most abusers commit their first offence within their usual environments, the most effective way to prevent child abuse is to increase the likelihood of them being caught. Making children aware of the offence and convincing them that the police and other authorities will take their concerns seriously if they raise them is the best way to achieve this.

People who are low trait orientated generally present less of a threat to society than high trait orientated people, as they will usually see no overall benefit in breaching group values. If they have been marginalised, they will feel vulnerable and insecure. They will not be seeking respect or personal rewards. Instead, they need to be given protection and support if they are to be re-integrated into society. They therefore need to be embraced and given opportunities to use their skills for the benefit of society.

Where criminals remain unreformed and people continue to live on the streets, it is most likely to be because educational deficiencies, drug addictions or mental health issues have not been addressed, or insufficient life skills support has been offered to them. Societies need to invest considerable sums if they are to reintegrate people who have been marginalised back into society. However, the powerless status of such people makes them dependent on the goodwill of voters and taxpayers. In countries with establishment and individualistic cultures, greed and a lack of compassion mean that governments are reluctant to allocate the necessary resources. Some people, though, become habituated to marginalised status and do not respond to offers of help to re-integrate them back into society. They may become used to rough sleeping or institutionalised within prisons, or see prison terms as a normal part of their criminal careers. If their attitudes are to be changed, they need to be treated more harshly to increase their incentive to engage. Prisons, though, do not usually have the funding or flexibility to develop individual regimes for prisoners, and hard labour and laws banning begging are not considered appropriate in countries with progressive cultures. It is therefore not be possible to design an appropriate carrot and stick approach for every inmate or vagrant.

It is not just people with extreme traits or unfortunate backgrounds who can be difficult to motivate. When environmental circumstances change, a group will need to shift its culture to encourage behaviours that promote the success of the group in the new environment. There is, though, usually a lag in this behavioural change as group members who have experienced good times in the old environment will tend to engage in avoidance or feel entitled to status, resources, freedom or protection to which they have had access. It takes time to break down this resistance and orientate people towards the achievement of new group objectives. The financial crisis of 2008, and the dangers associated with climate change, damage to our natural environment and uncontrolled migration, have initiated such a shift. Liberal-minded and materialistic individuals are, though, reluctant to accept that limits need to be placed on freedom of movement and the consumption of resources because they will restrict their ability to enjoy themselves.

Ambition and a work ethic

Ambition and a work ethic are probably the two most valued qualities in business. They are defined as follows by the Oxford English Dictionary:

Ambition: a strong desire to do or achieve something

Work ethic: the principle that hard work is intrinsically virtuous or worthy of reward

Ambition is a powerful motivational force associated with a state of high arousal and 'wanting'. It is, therefore, a high trait characteristic. A high trait will encourage its holder to seek out activities that give him a sense of enjoyment and exhilaration. This exploratory behaviour may be unguided in which case it will give rise to a generalised desire to achieve. If it becomes more defined, it will form into an ambition. The ability of people with high traits to see the big picture and their inclination to look to the future helps them to develop ambitions. In contrast, low trait orientated people tend to be cautious, focus on detail and seek reassurance from the past so they tend not to be very ambitious.

A work ethic is a more stable attribute associated with a lower state of arousal and 'needing'. It is, therefore, a low trait characteristic. People with low traits need to control their environment to avoid excessive stimulation and stress. They do so by processing information, and reducing the risk associated with it. This generates feelings of contentment and fulfilment. The exercise of control through the performance of Slow System skills is the basis of a work ethic. The possession of a low trait, however, does not automatically mean that a person will possess a work ethic. He may instead have spent his time avoiding potential threats so that he could pursue feelings of enjoyment, or focused his Slow System skills on leisure activities.

People who are very high in all four traits are likely to be highly ambitious, but will usually lack the work ethic necessary to achieve their ambitions. They will have very little self-control, living in and enjoying the moment or envisioning the future. Such people are sometimes romantically referred to as Bohemians, but in reality, they are likely to breach group values and are often drawn towards criminal behaviour. Crime may seem a way of satisfying one's desires without committing to long periods of sustained effort, but the resultant lack of commitment to developing a skill base makes a criminal more likely to be apprehended. Criminals who are successful in the longer-term will usually possess the trait of low opportunism, which will incline them to take steps in advance to avoid detection.

A person with four low traits is likely to be very conservative. He may possess a work ethic, but his intense focus on matters of detail and his controlling nature are likely to result in him moving forward very slowly. In other words, people who are low in all four traits are likely to lack any ambition to achieve when judged by normal standards. They are likely to focus on satisfying their basic needs and maintaining the support structures around them. As a result, they are often found in very stable and protective environments; for example, in closed communities or in positions that have a high degree of job security. We need people to re-enforce the stability of groups, so people with low traits often perform valuable roles within society. However, their lack of ambition means that they tend to get left behind, especially in fast-moving, individualistic societies.

For an ambition to be crafted into a realisable proposition and achieved, some degree of focused effort is usually necessary, so people who achieve their ambitions often possess a strong work ethic. Such people will therefore usually have a mixture of high and low traits. Achievement of an ambition is often linked to characteristics associated with the trait of low opportunism by experts in personality. This is because climbing a career ladder is easier if you can operate within structured environments. However, all low traits can assist the realisation of ambitions. For example, the trait of low openness will help a person to develop a coherent set of objectives. Few ambitions can be achieved without the support of other people. People are most likely to be successful and feel secure if their ambitions are aligned with the objectives of their group, and they work together in teams to achieve them.

Whether a person with middling traits is ambitious or displays a work ethic will depend to a significant degree on the culture of his group. If it has an individualistic culture, he is likely to be encouraged to express high trait behaviours and pursue personal ambitions. If it has a collectivist culture, he is likely to be encouraged to exhibit low trait behaviours and develop a work ethic. In the case of groups with establishment or progressive cultures, the group's values will encourage him to develop certain ambitions and/or work hard in particular fields. An establishment culture will encourage people to compete for resources while maintaining structure and coherency within the group. A progressive culture will encourage people to innovate while working hard to maintain a caring and fair society.

The fast pace of life and accessibility of stimulating experiences in modern, individualistic society encourage citizens to be very ambitious, live in the moment and neglect longer-term concerns. People who make money opportunistically or creatively are championed, while those who perform roles that require the use of Slow System skills; for example, in engineering or public service, are valued lowly. As a result, many Millennials have not developed a strong work ethic, and it has become hard for businesses to recruit reliable employees. Skills have not been passed down from one generation to the next either because they have been made redundant by technical advances, or because companies have not been prepared to commit the resources needed to develop expertise or because individuals are not prepared to devote the time required to complete the learning process. People are also less prepared to care for relatives. The UK, in particular, has become economically and socially fragile and reliant on immigrants for skills and labour. In contrast, countries with collectivist cultures like France value people who perform roles that strengthen economic and social infrastructure, and invest in skill development. However, they tend to lose talent as individuals with high traits relocate to countries where their ambitions are more likely to be realised. Also, the lack of innovation in collectivist cultures results in people becoming set in their ways. The work ethic of their populations is undermined by a reluctance to engage with new ideas and processes, making it difficult to increase productivity and maintain competitiveness.

A sense of purpose

When you exercise your talents and skills in pursuit of an objective that is important to you, you will experience a strong **sense of purpose**. A sense of purpose is a powerful force that helps you to maintain direction in life. If you are high trait orientated, your objectives are likely to revolve around personal enjoyment. If you are low trait orientated, they are likely to be related to improving your security. As you will need help from other people to achieve complex objectives, you are most likely to experience a sense of purpose when your personal objectives are aligned with those of a group to which you belong.

Your position in the primal group structure sets you up to perform particular tasks and roles for the benefit of your group. If you take on these responsibilities, other group members assist you and your group's values align with your own, you are likely to experience a strong sense of purpose. If you lack a sense of purpose, it is likely that you are incorrectly positioned within a group, lack support or protection from others or do not subscribe to the current value system or objectives of your group.

Most people have middling traits and balance enjoyable activities with ones that increase their sense of security. They are usually surrounded by people with similar characteristics and beliefs, and will naturally adopt behaviours that advance the interests of, and strengthen their bonds with, this group. They may not immediately be able to state their purpose in life, but it will be apparent from their job roles and contributions to their families. Such people are likely to experience positive feelings most of the time and are unlikely to feel a lack of purpose. Their averageness helps to stabilise groups. If every group member had strong personal motivations, a state of anarchy or decay would result.

When they are harnessed and channelled effectively, high and low trait behaviours can bring benefits to a group including protection, innovation, the acquisition of resources, increased coherence and structure, fairer distribution of resources and a harmonious environment. A person with uniformly high traits is unlikely ever to feel a very strong sense of purpose when performing tasks on behalf of a group because of his self-interested nature, but he is likely to experience positive feelings if he is rewarded for his achievements with praise, respect or some other extrinsic reward. A group can therefore channel the energies of people with high traits by setting goals for them to achieve and rewarding them for achieving them. A person with uniformly low traits is likely to experience a very strong sense of purpose if he uses his Slow System skills for the benefit of his group, but he will need other group members to create a safe environment for him to do so. If people with high or low traits are not able to find roles where they can use their talents and skills for the benefit of their groups, they are likely to engage in selfish behaviour, with the former pursuing enjoyable leisure activities and the latter using their Slow System skills to increase their personal sense of security.

If you are to develop a strong sense of purpose, you will need to assess your talents and skills and find ways to use them to support the achievement of a group's objectives. This presupposes that you identify sufficiently with a group to generate a sense of belonging and responsibility. One way of finding a sense of purpose is to create your own family. People who are low in indifference (mostly women) tend to find a sense of purpose in establishing and caring for a family. Men with establishment traits tend to feel a sense of purpose when they are responsible for protecting and providing for a family. Men with progressive traits and women who are high in indifference are less suited to these traditional family roles. To experience a sense of purpose, such a person may need to find a partner who allows the gender roles to be reversed or use his skills and talents for the benefit of his community or wider society.

In modern, individualistic society, many people no longer have strong ties to families and communities and have instead developed loose networks of friends and acquaintances. This makes it easier for them to engage in avoidance tactics, ignoring potential threats to their security, so that they can pursue self-interested objectives. They are encouraged to acquire money for the purposes of consumption and leisure. As a consequence, people tend to view work as a means of funding their lifestyles away from work. A person who thinks this way is likely to lack a strong sense of purpose as his objectives are likely to be short term and change frequently. The weakness of value systems and conformance and compliance dynamics in groups with individualistic cultures means that people are not encouraged to align their personal objectives with those of groups. A person will therefore often not embark on a journey to find a sense of purpose until he experiences personal hardship that exposes the weakness of his group. At such point, he may realise his purpose lies in creating a harmonious family environment or re-enforcing the values of an organisation. He will, though, be at a disadvantage because it becomes harder to create or develop strong attachments to groups as you age as your energy levels drop and your prospects of reproducing decline. It is particularly difficult for people who are low in openness as they define they only feel comfortable in well-defined, tight-knit groups.

In summary, your level of motivation will be influenced by the cultures, objectives and strength of the groups to which you belong. If your personality traits align with a group's culture and objectives, you are likely to feel motivated. Your ambitions will be more achievable, you will be able to find space to develop a work ethic and you are likely to feel a strong sense of purpose. However, if your personality traits conflict with the group's culture and objectives, or you lack support or protection, you are likely to feel unguided or demotivated, and to experience stress and low moods.

Dealing with life's realities

Objective setting and the path of least resistance

Your emotional system will naturally take the easiest route to its destination – the experience of positive feelings – as this approach avoids wasting time and energy. As a result, if you are unclear about your objectives, you will tend to resort to the most immediate method of restoring or increasing positive feelings - the **path of least resistance**. This may lead you to consume unhealthy mood enhancers. The primeval programming of the human emotional system encourages us to take advantage of opportunities to eat, have sex and participate in other enjoyable experiences. When you are in an environment that encourages you to use your Fast System, you will find these opportunities difficult to resist. If, however, you have clearly defined objectives that would deliver a greater and more consistent level of positive feelings to you in the future if achieved, your mind is likely to focus your attention on achieving these objectives and you will be less likely to be distracted by activities that offer shorter-term benefits. If you wish to be successful, you must therefore devote time to setting and clarifying objectives. If you experience a strong sense of purpose, this is an indication that consciously or subconsciously you have achieved a high level of clarity.

It can be difficult to fix long-term objectives because your environment is constantly changing and new information causes you to review decisions and approaches. Speaking your objectives out aloud or writing them down gives them more permanence. Such **affirmations** are generally considered to be more effective if they are specific and made in the first person with positive feeling. Using the pronoun "I" connects a statement more firmly with you and positivity increases your level of confidence. Affirmations are, though, likely to be less useful and sometimes unhelpful if they are made to reinforce objectives, values or beliefs that are not in tune with your personality traits, as they may cause you to continue in an inappropriate direction or become overconfident.

You will be better placed to set appropriate objectives if you expand your consciousness. The more you understand your environment in both a broad and detailed sense, the easier it is for you to see how you can best use your talents and skills for the benefit of your group. If you have a narrow consciousness, you may become trapped within an unsuitable environment. Your personal development will also be inhibited because you will be less able to recognise opportunities or anticipate threats in the longer term.

An expanded consciousness is a key element in the development of drive and self-control, which is sometimes referred to as **willpower**. You show willpower when your mind reasons that it is worth forgoing immediate reward or putting up with negative feelings to secure a more substantial reward in the longer term. Your emotional system then directs your energies towards achieving the long-term objective. Willpower and drive both involve the envisioning of a better future, but willpower is associated with use of the Slow System, whereas drive is a Fast System motivational state. They go hand in hand. When you are making good progress by deploying schemas, you will be showing drive. When you are solving problems or resisting temptation, you will display willpower. The positive feelings you experience when you are driven and showing willpower override negative feelings generated in response to your immediate environment. However, the negative feelings such as self-doubt are likely to break through at times when your drive and willpower weaken in which case you will need to show resilience if your are to continue towards your objective. People who are working hard to improve their circumstances are therefore likely to experience mixed feelings and frequent mood swings.

A person who is very driven and has strong willpower may become so focused on his objective that he fails to recognise other opportunities or deal with emerging threats. Negative feelings that he is masking may be caused by changed circumstances. As a consequence, if he ultimately achieves his objective, he may find that it is less useful or rewarding than he expected, or that he has left himself vulnerable to harm or hardship. This is most likely to happen if a person disconnects himself from a group or fails to listen to helpful advice from other group members. However, many important discoveries and breakthroughs have been facilitated by drive, willpower and a preparedness to break with current thinking and practice. Breaking new ground is inherently risky.

Some people who are located in unfavourable environments can envisage a positive future so clearly and vividly that they are able to put up with extreme physical and emotional hardship to achieve it. They may appear to have superhuman qualities as they endure extreme levels of discomfort and abuse in order to further their causes. Their drive, willpower and resilience can present a serious threat to the status quo, especially where they seek political power. As a consequence, establishments seek to identify, monitor and restrain such people before they can influence the wider population. This occurs brutally in countries like China and Saudi Arabia, which have very high numbers of executions and political prisoners. However, it also happens more subtly in Western democracies, where such people are excluded from influential circles and undermined publicly by lies and misrepresentation.

Most people will take a pragmatic approach, setting objectives but compromising or adapting them in the light of changed circumstances. It is advantageous to plan ahead, but there may be several routes to your objective and circumstances may require you to change your objectives or take different paths to them. Modern life is fast moving and we are exposed to many new circumstances. We are also bombarded by interesting new information and opportunities for short-term rewards that may distract us from the pursuit of our objectives. It is therefore important to find time and space to reflect on your objectives, and adapt, clarify and prioritise them as appropriate.

Objectives are difficult to achieve without assistance from others. The more individualistic and personal your objectives, then the harder they will be to achieve because the less likely it will be that other people will be interested in helping you. It is therefore preferable to align your objectives with those of a group. If your personality traits match the culture of a group, this is likely to be relatively easy to achieve. If they conflict, it will be unlikely to happen.

If a group is to remain effective, group objectives should reflect the opportunities and challenges in its environment. This alignment is most likely to be achieved if a range of people with different personalities is involved in the objective-setting process. People with high traits can envisage a future reality, but those with low traits add detail to it and develop strategies to achieve it. People with high traits can intervene where they see that people with low traits are getting lost in detail and are failing to see the big picture or recognise when key environmental factors have changed. People with low traits restrain those with high traits where their impulsivity is in danger of jeopardising the achievement of an objective.

In the UK, there is a tendency for governments, head teachers and parents to focus children on achieving high marks in examinations rather than developing their talents and skills. Most teachers lack experience of the wider working world and therefore are unsuited to giving careers advice, but schools still put pressure on students to make decisions that will influence their choice of careers before they are ready. Many young people therefore enter the working world without a good understanding of their talents and skills and embark on further education courses or careers that they later abandon. Children are much more likely to work hard, become self-directing and be successful in later life if they have been helped to understand how the world works and their position within it. Some children with high and/or low traits will show particular attributes at an early age that set them on a particular course in life. If they are encouraged to set long-term objectives, they may progress at a faster pace. However, children with middling traits will be suited to a wide range of careers. There is no need for them to be forced into making early career decisions. Instead, they should be encouraged to expand their consciousness and discover and develop their natural talents and skills.

Information handling and task management

The secret to maintaining operation within your optimal ranges, remaining motivated and being effective is to manage information levels within your environment to suit your personality traits. You need the support and protection of a group to be able to do this. If this is lacking, you are likely to experience stress or low moods or engage in avoidance. In modern, individualistic society, groups tend to be weak and people have loose connections with them so many people either avoid taking responsibility or are forced to handle information and perform tasks that others should ideally be dealing with. **Procrastination** is evidence of a deficient team or an inappropriate allocation of responsibilities. You delay performing tasks because you know that performance of them will cause you to experience negative feelings.

You can perform related actions simultaneously if they have been embedded in a schema. However, your Slow System cannot perform multiple tasks at the same time. It will instead prioritise tasks and switch between them as environmental factors cause the current order of priority to be adjusted. Where you have too many tasks to complete in the time available, you are likely to experience anxiety or chronic stress, which will inhibit Slow System functioning. If you are forced to spend long periods in the stress zone, you will store up issues that need resolving. Therefore, unless you possess relevant high traits that enable you to respond instinctively or you are performing routine tasks, multi-tasking will reduce your efficiency and productivity levels.

There is a current trend in business to increase agility. Companies attribute more value to individuals whose abilities enable organisations to respond rapidly to changes in their environments without losing effectiveness or direction than in previous generations. People who are high in opportunism are naturally flexible and tend to thrive when confronted with unexpected, urgent deadlines. Their ability to deploy appropriate schemas enables them to quickly adapt to new circumstances. They are likely to procrastinate until a task becomes urgent and requires a spontaneous rather than an organised response for its completion. Most people will, however, need to engage their Slow Systems to deal with stress events and will suffer a drop in performance and anxiety or chronic stress if they are not given sufficient time and space to carry out necessary processing.

Recent technological developments have resulted in massive increases in the amount of information in our work and social environments and have raised stress levels within society. At work, many people are overloaded with e-mails and other data, but much of the information we encounter has been designed to stimulate our Fast Systems and provide us with enjoyment. Advertisers, corporate retailers, television broadcasters, mobile phone companies and social media platforms compete and work together to attract our attention away from useful tasks that we need to get done to improve our security. We therefore find it difficult to prioritise tasks and often resort to fire fighting mode, dealing with urgent tasks and devoting little time to long-term objectives.

It is important to focus on tasks that will help you to achieve your goals. Actions that lay the foundations of future success usually take time to complete, but you will not focus sufficient attention on them if you are constantly dealing with urgent tasks. Although some people enjoy fast-paced environments and it can sometimes be beneficial to act instinctively, urgency is often a sign of inefficiency. It is evidence of a lack of anticipation and preparation. Ideally, you should perform tasks to which you are suited at an appropriate speed and in good time. This should be possible most of the time if you are part of a rounded, well-functioning group.

U.S. President Dwight D. Eisenhower pointed out in a speech in 1954 that, to be effective, you must spend your time on tasks that are important and that urgency alone is not a good enough reason for giving a task high priority. If you take time to determine which activities are important and which are urgent, you can avoid becoming distracted by urgent tasks of low importance and release time for the completion of tasks that will enable you to make progress in the longer term.

Tasks can be divided into four categories:

1.   **Important and urgent**: these tasks demand attention because there are likely to be serious consequences if they are not carried out. Some people feel strongly motivated when faced with such tasks because they are suited to using their Fast Systems to complete them. Most people should, though, try to prevent tasks falling into this category to avoid the possibility of them not being completed on time and to minimise the potential for stress. Sometimes, events cause items to appear in this category suddenly, but we tend to allow items to slip into it through procrastination or poor time management.

2.   **Important but not urgent**: these tasks usually relate to your personal development or your long-term security and will often help to strengthen your group. They are likely to involve the use of Slow System skills for sustained periods. You tend to neglect them when you have opportunities to enjoy yourself or are under pressure. This neglect is likely to make you feel less secure in the longer term.

3.   **Urgent but not important**: these tasks are normally labelled as urgent by another person. They seem unimportant to you because either you do not share that person's objectives or you are not suited to performing the tasks. We tend to consider tasks that we are suited to performing to be more important than those that we are not because the latter should be the responsibility of somebody located in a different part of the primal group structure. The fact that you are addressing these tasks at all suggests that you are following the agenda of a person or faction that has power or influence over you,

or that your group is weak and lacks appropriate people to carry them out. When you take on these tasks, you reduce the amount of time you can spend performing important tasks (category 1 and category 2 tasks), undermining your personal development and security and exposing you to the risk of anxiety or chronic stress.

4.   **Neither urgent nor important**: these tasks have the lowest priority and may not be worth addressing at all. Completion of them may, though, provide you with positive feelings, help sustain relationships or build up goodwill. For example, you may do something that is helpful to an acquaintance, and this may cause him to return the favour in the future. However, if you are poor at prioritising tasks, they may add to your workload, causing you to neglect more important tasks or experience a high level of stress.

If you are prone to anxiety or chronic stress, your objective should be to prevent items entering category 1 (Important and urgent), increase the percentage of your workload in category 2 (Important but not urgent), and spend less time performing tasks in category 3 (Urgent but not important) and category 4 (Neither important nor urgent). The more time a person spends carrying out category 3 and category 4 tasks, the less time he will have to devote to important tasks. His decision-making and performance level will therefore decline where it really matters. If you are experiencing suppression or a low mood, you will need to increase the amount of information in your environment and take more risks. In the case of suppression, it is likely that somebody or the prevailing culture is obliging you to perform category 3 tasks. If you are bored, you are probably carrying out too many category 4 tasks. In both cases, you need to reposition yourself in a way that allows you to take on more tasks in categories 1 and 2.

It is now very easy to find yourself performing an excessive amount of category 4 tasks. Technology companies are battling for our attention. Mobile phones, TV and the Internet are constantly bombarding us with data. Social media is particularly invasive because it encourages us to spend large amounts of time communicating with other people. Keeping up with what other group members are doing and showing an interest in their activity helps to keep you informed, maintain your status and sustain relationships. However, the loose nature of modern groups means that many people we waste time engaging with people who have little relevance to or long-term security. Psychologically, you may upgrade these category 4 tasks to category 3 or higher. For example, you may feel an urgency to input your opinion on a social media thread. You may also feel that it is important to maintain membership of online groups. However, unless your online activity is accompanied by physical group strengthening activities and the development of shared objectives, the resultant relationships are unlikely to be capable of protecting or supporting you when you are in real need.

Where a person is not operating within his optimal ranges in his work environment, he will experience stress or low moods and is more likely to go searching for opportunities to experience positive feelings away from work. He may feel entitled to a social life and pursue leisure activities at the expense of tasks that would strengthen his family or his local community. He is also likely to resort to emotion regulation, using social media, betting and similar activities to control his arousal level. Many of these activities will be category 4 tasks. Solitary leisure activities are particularly damaging category 4 tasks as they deter a person from looking for pleasure in the company of others and therefore weaken his group. It is therefore important to limit the number of category 4 tasks and actions that you perform.

The implications of ageing

When young people feel protected, they tend to be exploratory and to seek out enjoyable experiences that give them immediate pleasure. They also have more freedom to take risks than older people because they have the energy and time to recover from setbacks. As people age, they accept long-term obligations such as mortgages and childcare that impact on their ability to adapt their environment. Their energy levels drop and they have less time left in their lives to recover from losses.

The sooner you locate yourself in an environment that is suited to your personality, the sooner you are able to maximise your effectiveness and the more likely you are to be successful in life. A well-functioning society will allow young people opportunities to experiment, but will also channel them towards useful roles to which they are suited. If a person is located within a favourable environment early in life and given appropriate guidance, he will learn quickly and develop skills to a high level. Evidence suggests that people who become world-class experts in their fields do so primarily because they have applied concentrated effort for much longer periods of time than most other people. It has been estimated that 10,000 hours of application is necessary to achieve mastery in a subject area. To put the scale of this task in context, there are 8,760 hours in a year. However, most people struggle to match their talents to their environment over a sustained period in a way that allows them to excel. They get nowhere near achieving the number of hours of practice required to achieve mastery before they become distracted by work, relationships, family life and other competing activities.

You are only likely to put in the time and effort that is needed to be successful if you feel rewarded by doing so. It is therefore critical that you attempt to learn skills that are suited to your personality traits. If you try to develop a skill that requires you to operate outside your optimal ranges, you will experience negative feelings. These feelings will slow you down and may cause you to give up. Many people fall into the trap of applying too much effort to developing skills to which they are unsuited. Sustained operation outside your optimal range will lead to a loss of effectiveness and unhappiness. Even if you do force yourself to develop such skills, you are unlikely to be able to exercise them at a high level in the long term. Without a natural incentive to maintain and refine them, it is likely they will degrade over time.

People who extend the experimentation phase further into adulthood may end up acquiring an unusually broad set of skills, which they may combine profitably later in life. However, in general, people who take a long time to find an appropriate role in life will struggle to keep pace financially with their peers and be susceptible to poor mental health. It is inefficient for people to acquire skills that they do not go on to use or to abandon roles that they have been trained to perform. Making a major career change in later life can be risky because it is likely to involve expending great amounts of time, effort and money acquiring new skills without any guarantee of greater reward. High trait orientated people are generalists by nature and can make positive contributions without needing to spend a lot of time developing skills. Once they find their path, they may be able to regain ground quickly because they will be inclined to take greater risks than an average person. People with low traits will, however, find it more difficult to catch up as the development of Slow System skills takes place over many years and because they tend to be risk averse. Groups with individualistic and progressive cultures give people the freedom to experiment whereas collectivist and establishment cultures tend to tie people to specific roles early on.

At some point, your physical and mental capabilities will start to decline, and you will find it harder to make progress. You may build up a knowledge bank or reserves of wealth that give you an advantage over younger, more energetic colleagues and competitors, but eventually you will need to cede ground to the next generation. You will be forced to accept that some of your ambitions will never be realised, or that mistakes or losses will never be rectified or recovered. Women are more aware of this reality than men because their fertility is time limited. If they wish to establish a traditional family unit, they need to secure a husband, establish a home and give birth to healthy children before their body clocks call time. They are also aware that their attractiveness to men declines with age and makes it harder to achieve this objective. Some women find it difficult to accept declining attractiveness and fertility, resorting to plastic surgery and dressing in clothes suited to younger women. Individualistic cultures encourage such decisions because they promote liberal, outgoing behaviours and the pursuit of enjoyment. The menopause naturally directs women to perform useful roles within the female collective, although in modern, individualistic society many women avoid making such contributions and pursue careers or leisure activities instead. Some men experience a mid-life crisis when their attractiveness to women declines and younger men start to outcompete them. They will usually either attempt to hold back the tide by committing to fitness regimes or buying sports cars or other items that they perceive will increase their status in the eyes of women. In general, however, men lose their fertility slowly, so they tend not to account for it in their plans or to have to make sudden accommodations in relation to its loss.

Men are likely to be more aware of their declining competitiveness in the working arena. Because the culture of the typical male group is competitive, many men start to feel vulnerable when their skills become out-dated or their physical ability reduces. If a man continues to compete while his capabilities are declining, he will experience increased levels of stress. He may become frustrated by his reduced capability and influence, worry about the potential consequences of such loss or experience chronic stress as a result of increased insecurity or declining income. Men, therefore, tend to become increasingly conservative as they age. They focus on protecting their positions and restraining the progress of younger males rather than increasing their resources and influence. They tend to group together to support each other in achieving this objective, especially if they are low in openness and opportunism. Male-dominated organisations, therefore, tend to stagnate until a crisis occurs or a powerful, younger challenger emerges. Women tend to be less fearful of losing resources or influence because they expect to receive support from the female collective and have less need for resources and protection once their children have grown up. They are also more likely than men to look forward with hope to the future because they wish their children to be successful rather than seeing them as threats or liabilities. A woman is, though, likely to experience stress if she finds herself in a vulnerable position. Of course, these are tendencies only, and some people will behave differently due to their personality traits, previous experiences, current environment or prospects. Some people feel insecure when they are young but succeed in building a protective unit around them that allows them to enjoy themselves later in life. Also, men with progressive traits and women with establishment traits are more likely to adopt behaviours associated with the other gender sub-group.

As people see their powers weakening, they tend to focus on creating a legacy. A **legacy** is a benefit that transfers to the next generation. It commonly takes the form of material assets but may be an invention, artwork, institution or family. A legacy allows a person to sustain feelings of usefulness and therefore happiness beyond the point of its creation. In other words, it can enable a person to live out his later years without feelings of regret, disappointment or guilt, or a loss of self-esteem.

Some people are fortunate enough to reach the end of their working lives in good health with enough achievements, interests, resources, friends, relatives and memories to allow them to experience positive feelings and to ensure that they are cared for until death. In developed countries, older generations are benefitting from high property values and generous pensions as a result of population growth and the benign economic conditions in the 30 years prior to the financial crisis. Many companies now recognise the value of older workers and large numbers of people now continue to work beyond their retirement age. Others perform useful roles within the voluntary sector, communities or their own families. However, many people face significant challenges as they age. They may suffer from chronic health conditions, have low incomes or become isolated. Retirement separates a person from work colleagues and longer life expectancy means that some partners remain widowed for many years before they too pass away. Retirement, serious illness or the loss of a partner often results in a loss of purpose and depression. There is little opportunity to engage in loss transference in old age, so people need to come to terms with their mortality and make accommodations. However, some older people struggle to make a steady and rewarding transition to old age, either refusing to accept the reality of their declining abilities and experiencing frustration and anger as a result, or feelings of inadequacy and loneliness.

Most people who survive into their 80s and those who experience a serious, irreversible deterioration in their health will need more support and protection from society than they can give back, either in the present time or the future. They will become dependent on the goodwill of members of their families and communities, and government services, for their continuing survival and wellbeing. The extent to which such support is available will depend to some degree on the culture of their society. In individualistic cultures, people tend to live in the moment and have little interest in the past. Older people tend to be ignored and their contributions to society forgotten. Children are less likely to look after their parents because they do not want to compromise their ability to enjoy themselves and are less likely to have built up enough capital to do so. Also, many people reach old age without having children and so cannot rely on family members for protection and support. Establishment cultures are patriarchal by nature and afford respect to powerful older people, particularly males, but they devote minimal resources to meeting the needs of the elderly in the broader population. Collectivist and progressive cultures are caring by nature with the former being particularly considerate to older people due to their respect for the past.

Figure 21 below illustrates how levels of energy, opportunity, skills and experience change over a person's lifetime. Typically, a person will be at the height of his powers between the ages of 40 and 50, but this point will vary from career to career. A sportsperson will reach his high point much earlier, whereas a politician is likely to do so later.

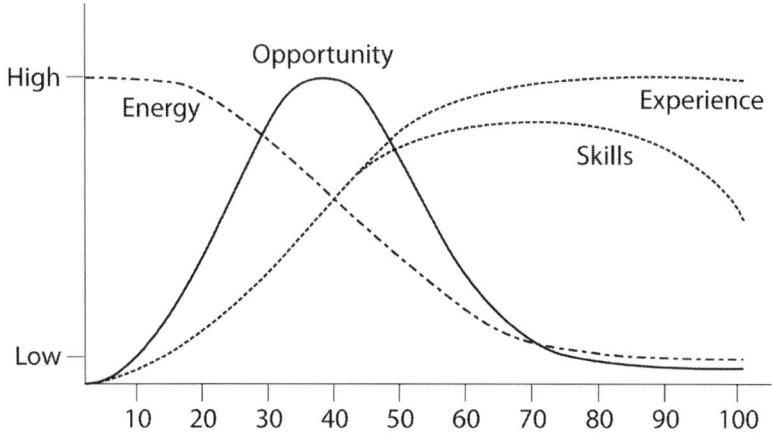

Figure 21. The relationship between energy, opportunity, skills and experience

Teamwork, its limits and the importance of leadership

The value of teamwork

You are only likely to be successful in the long term if you operate within an effective team. Even a person who excels in a very narrowly defined area will need support and protection from others. For example, a concert pianist will be dependent on benefactors, promoters and other people behind the scenes. You will benefit from the help of other people whose personality traits suit them to carrying out tasks that you find difficult. For example, a man who is high in openness and indifference may wish to purchase a new mountain bike. He is likely to feel comfortable negotiating a price as his high level of indifference will allow him to handle interpersonal tension. However, he will be less capable of getting to grips with the technical differences between different models, as his high level of openness will mean he is unlikely to have developed the methodical skills needed to do so. It would make sense for him to seek the advice of a friend who is lower in openness and therefore better suited to the detailed task of comparing specifications.

To set and achieve complex objectives, we need to work within a large team with a wide range of personalities. Most people within such a team will have middling traits that allow them to perform a range of everyday tasks. Teams will, though, usually include people with high and low traits. As well as providing exploratory talents and specialist skills, people with opposing traits will compensate for each other's deficiencies and help to maintain balance within the team.

People who are high in extraversion enjoy exploring the physical environment, participating in group activities and accumulating resources. They need people who are low in extraversion to moderate and compensate for these behaviours. The analytical capabilities and naturally cautious approach of people who are low in extraversion help those who are high in extraversion to avoid making rash decisions that could compromise long-term success and to share out resources more equitably within a group, thereby helping to prevent disadvantaged members experiencing hardship and reducing the potential for internal conflict.

People who are high in openness are energised by new experiences and ideas. By connecting different pieces of information in original ways, they can come up with new ways of doing things. This does not mean that people who are high in openness are good at turning opportunities into successful ventures – quite the reverse. They are not specialists by nature and will struggle to stay interested in an idea or project long enough to develop it for practical use or achieve commercial success. They need support from people who are low in openness, who can focus on detail and eliminate any imperfections in designs and methodology. People who are low in openness also lend stability to organisations by promoting the development of coherent value systems.

People who are high in indifference enjoy competing so they are suited to protecting group members. Because they can tolerate a high degree of inter-personal tension in their environment, they can make hard-nosed decisions that benefit the group. Their competitive behaviour can though promote conflict within a group. A leader will therefore need the support of people who are low in indifference who are able to minimise infighting within the workplace and create a harmonious atmosphere at home suitable for relaxation and the rearing of children.

People who are high in opportunism enjoy being in changing environments. Their natural spontaneity enables them to get to grips quickly with new circumstances and challenges. Their impulsive nature delivers the energy needed to get a project off the ground. Such projects will, however, often lack sustainability unless organised structures are created to perpetuate them. People who are low in opportunism are organised by nature and focus on developing routines that they and other people can follow. As a result, they are suited to sustaining projects and organisations in the longer term.

The spectrum-based nature of personality traits makes it impossible to motivate an entire group using a single motivational technique. Companies that sell motivation services and motivational speakers sometimes give the impression that everybody can become highly motivated, but within a rounded team most people will proceed at a steady pace and there will always be some cultural misfits. Where motivational techniques associated with a particular culture are favoured, the group members whose motivation levels are boosted are likely to be outnumbered by those who experience a drop in motivation, unless environmental circumstances have encouraged a shift towards that culture. A company that operates within a specialist area may recruit people with appropriate personality traits and outsource general business functions in which case it will be easier to motivate the workforce as a whole. However, this approach can be dangerous as it encourages the adoption of an extreme culture that may be at odds with the wider environment and impact on the company's performance.

A group is most likely to maximise motivation levels where it enables group members to perform roles that are suited to their personalities, promotes the development of a culture that is in tune with the group's environment and encourages commitment to shared objectives. The culture of a group will dictate its shared objectives. An establishment culture will promote the acquisition and accumulation of resources and is likely to occur when resources are plentiful, but are being competed for by multiple groups. A collectivist culture will promote cautious behaviours that increase the group's stability and is likely to occur when resources are scarce, but there remains a threat from neighbouring groups. A progressive culture will encourage innovation and promote peace and is likely to occur when resources are scarce and there is no external threat. An individualistic culture will encourage risky, self-interested behaviours and is likely to occur when resources are plentiful and there is no external threat. These different environments and related cultures are illustrated in Figure 22 opposite.

People with establishment traits (i.e. members of the primal hierarchy and a minority of women) are best suited to roles in hierarchical organisations with establishment cultures, such as armies, corporations and governmental authorities, as they are comforted by coherency and structure, will appreciate strong leadership and like clearly defined roles and targets. They tend to be motivated by rewards that cement or raise their position within the organisational structure. Hierarchical organisations become less effective when a progressive culture takes hold. They lose focus on their primary objectives of accumulating resources and defending the group as they are distracted by new ideas, lose their ruthless edge and become concerned with individuals rights and issues of fairness.

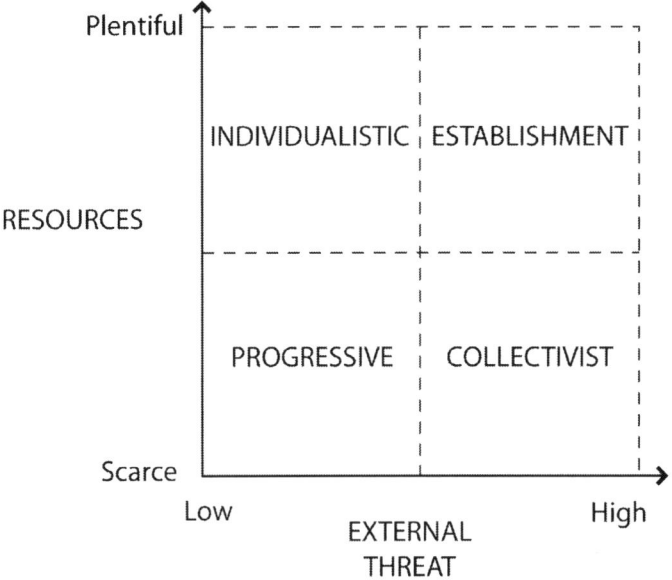

Figure 22. How culture is influenced by resources and external threats

People with progressive traits (i.e. most members of the female collective and progressive males) tend to be suited to roles in loose, networked structures with progressive values, such as hospitals, schools and markets, as they derive intrinsic rewards from independent decision-making, collaborative working and flexible responses. Managers need employees to be responsible and self-motivating as it is harder to implement systems and procedures in networked structures. They also have fewer opportunities to use promotion or individual financial rewards. When such organisations are commercialised and adopt inappropriate corporate approaches, stress levels rise, morale plummets and quality declines. In the UK, the National Health Service and state schooling system are currently suffering crises in employee morale and recruitment due to the government's obsession with targets and the introduction of corporate management techniques.

Some people, particularly those who are high in openness or opportunism, are attracted by self-employment as it enables them to carve out a role suited to their traits. When they begin their new ventures, they are likely to be highly motivated. However, a person who is self-employed will often lack appropriate support from others and struggle to create a viable business. He will be forced to carry out unsuitable tasks and will experience stress and low moods as a consequence. This will reduce his effectiveness and he will have to work harder than employees of a larger business to achieve the same results. Some people set up their own businesses to avoid the complications of working with other people and accommodations needed to fit into an organisation. They may establish "lifestyle" businesses whose focus is on providing pleasure to the business owner, rather than making profit or contributing to the prosperity and wellbeing of a wider group. Such businesses are usually unsustainable because they do not sufficiently address the needs and desires of customers or the threats presented by competitors. Many people who are self-employed are, though, quasi-employees, performing specialist roles for larger businesses rather than generating products and services independently. People with scarce skills or good contacts at senior levels within a company are often able to agree consultancy contracts. Their marketability and connections allow them to secure the benefits of working autonomously while retaining a good income level. In recent years, however, many people have been forced into self-employment by corporations seeking to avoid employment taxes and long-term commitments to employees, such as the payment of pensions.

It makes sense for an individual to build a network of acquaintances through which he can access a range of talents and skills. However, these networks will be incoherent and lack the structure or purpose of a group. You may access the talents and skills of people within your network from time to time, but in most cases, the interaction will take the form of a trade exchange where each party takes some benefit away that promotes his personal objectives, rather than a joint contribution towards a common purpose. Women are more likely to support each other than men because they have a common purpose in looking after children. However, most adults remain dependent on their families, employers and governmental institutions for protection and security. In countries with individualistic cultures, like the UK, a preoccupation with short-term, self-interested objectives has caused families to disintegrate, corporations to neglect their obligations to their workforces and governments to cut funding to public services. As a result, both men and women increasingly struggle to obtain the assistance they need.

Not everybody is suited to having children, or even a long-term partner. However, we all need stimulation, physical and emotional protection, and support from other people. In a well-functioning group of sufficient size, most people will find their natural role. Where a group is too small, group members are forced to multitask, they become less efficient, and they neglect their obligations to wider society. Modern, individualistic society exposes many people to feelings of vulnerability and insecurity because it is characterised by nuclear families, single parent families, childless partnerships and single people.

If you wish to give yourself the best chances of success in life, you need to recognise when your chances of achieving an objective are being compromised by deficiencies in your team. You should be prepared to make an accommodation when you cannot access the talents and skills you need to achieve a desired objective. If you let go of overly optimistic personal objectives and adopt more realistic ones that are shared by others, you are more likely to be successful and to experience positive feelings in the future. Doing so is also likely to make you a more pleasant person for others to spend time with.

The large number and diverse nature of groups in modern society makes it difficult for some people to identify and apply themselves to suitable roles within groups. Many people lack support or protection or have conflicting objectives and split loyalties due to their membership of multiple groups. Also, the individualistic culture that prevailed in countries like the UK in the 30 years before the financial crisis of 2008 encouraged people to pursue enjoyment rather than developing skills. Organisations have therefore become less effective and less competitive. These weaknesses had little effect on citizens of these countries prior to the financial crisis because the economic climate was benign and suited to an individualistic culture. However, since the financial crisis, resources have become scarcer and the competitive threat from developing countries more obvious. Environmental changes are therefore causing a shift towards a more defensive, collectivist culture. However, because of the dynamics of the Circle of Power, such a shift will involve a transition through an establishment or progressive culture.

The corporate world's default setting is establishment culture. During the last 40 years, however, it shifted to adopt individualistic values. The financial crisis and consequent austerity has, however, caused corporations to become more conservative. They have started to sweat their assets rather than invest in new technology. Unemployment has reduced as companies have taken advantage of low cost labour. The natural inclination of corporate boards is to force employees to do more work more quickly for less pay has been strengthened by the need to address reducing competitiveness. As a result, employees are experiencing increasing amounts of stress and their motivation and productivity levels are reducing, further reducing competitiveness. A downward spiral has therefore been created. The way to address this negative dynamic is for corporations to adopt fairer and more compassionate practices. They therefore need to shift further around the Circle of Power and adopt a collectivist culture. However, it will take time for this to occur. Politicians, company directors and shareholders with vested interests resist such adaptions and need to be replaced or constrained before such a shift can take place.

The social character of many countries is moving the other direction around the Circle of Power via progressive culture. Inequality and the abuse of power by alpha males are causing women to become more politically active and strengthen the values of fairness and compassion. However, as the female collective and progressive males do not yet control the global financial system, they are unlikely to be able to maintain a progressive social culture. They need the support of the rank and file to constrain the power of the establishment and, as a result, a more conservative collectivist social culture is likely to emerge.

In this work, I have used the word "progressive" to describe a culture orientated around freedom, tolerance, fairness and harmony because politicians who espouse these values commonly use it for this purpose. You should not, though, fall into the trap of thinking that most people would naturally want to live in a progressive society. Although the word "progressive" sounds positive, people who possess establishment traits will experience strong negative feelings in a progressive culture and lack a sense of purpose and flow because they instinctively resort to exploitation and aggression to achieve their aims. A progressive culture by definition deviates from the place where most group members feel motivated in average circumstances – the centre of the Circle of Power. For this reason, the human race will not inevitably move to a progressive culture marked by peace and sustainability as some people hope. The increasing scarcity of resources is causing a shift away from an individualistic culture, but a progressive culture will only be established in the longer term if members of different groups, and particularly citizens of different nations, feel that they can live peacefully together. Currently, rising fear levels are causing the opposite to occur, resulting in increased discrimination, protectionism and nationalism. If this dynamic is to be reversed and a sustainable global society achieved, people with progressive traits, and particularly women, will need to work together as a team to create a more peaceful and fairer world. People with exceptional leadership qualities will also need to emerge.

The importance of leadership

For a group to be successful, its leader must give group members suitable roles, encourage them to bond, and ensure that the group's objectives correspond with the group's environment. If he achieves this, most group members will be operating within their optimal ranges. The group leader and other senior figures must also help the group to adapt to changing circumstances by promoting shifts in culture.

As most people have middling traits, the optimum cultural position of a group will usually be close to the centre of the Circle of Power. Environmental factors will, however, cause this balancing point to shift at times. Adapting to a new environment can be difficult, as it requires people to change their behaviours. Although most group members will benefit from doing so, some will experience negative feelings and resist change. Leaders are usually most popular when they help group members adapt to changed circumstances. They can achieve this by making group members more aware of potential rewards or by highlighting predicaments. In other words, good leaders help group members to clarify and achieve their objectives. Sometimes a politician can catch the Zeitgeist - the defining spirit or mood of a particular period of history – by expressing the thoughts, feelings, ambitions and fears of the majority in a particularly coherent or inspiring way.

A good leader will help group members to cope better with challenging situations by instilling them with belief. Confidence building has the effect of shifting a person's optimal range up the relevant trait spectrum. This may prevent him from experiencing stress events in situations where he would otherwise do so, enabling him to perform well in difficult circumstances. Alternatively, a leader may focus the attention of group members on the seriousness of a particular threat. By doing so, he will cause group members to experience fear and prompt them to use their Slow System skills to strengthen the group. A manipulative leader can, though, use these techniques to rally group members around objectives that suit his personal interests or frighten them into a submissive state.

As establishments form naturally within groups, group leaders will often possess establishment traits and attempt to introduce establishment cultures. Where environmental circumstances favour one of the other three cultures, a leader will need to take account of the interests of people with progressive traits, otherwise he will risk losing power. Sometimes, a group of outsiders with more progressive values will work together with the objective of securing power and achieving shared objectives. Advancement to senior levels in politics, the media and other fields where organisations have strong establishments is unlikely unless a person has long established bonds of trust with appointers or benefits from favouritism. However, if the outsiders can gain a foothold within the power structure, they can help each other to get promoted. For example, a group of like-minded students may identify a common cause and work together to acquire political power once they leave university. Power corrupts, though, so if a group of outsiders secures the leadership of the group, they are likely to adopt establishment behaviours to some degree as they attempt to protect their positions and project power. Progressive traits promote caution, a lack of coherency, consensus building and disorder, depending on the trait. These behaviours can delay or confuse decision-making and provoke infighting. Therefore, where a group of people who are not members of the establishment gain power, they are unlikely to hold on to it in the long term.

Power imbalances within a group can result in a mismatch between the objectives of leaders and the interests of ordinary group members. A privileged minority within a group is likely to attempt to sustain a culture that is beneficial to them when the group's environment no longer favours such a culture. For example, the objectives of corporations are usually set by, and weighted towards the interests of, directors and shareholders and take insufficient notice of the needs of wider society. This is particularly the case in the UK and USA where regulation is light, and employees and other stakeholders do not have representation on company boards. Consequently, many employees in these countries lack a sense of purpose in their working environment.

Although powerful leaders and establishments will try to cement their privileged positions by acting in an authoritarian way, oppressive actions are only likely to be effective in the medium term because the operational effectiveness of the group will be undermined as a result of the mismatch between the group's culture and environment. It is therefore likely that a challenging force will emerge from within the group or the group will be outcompeted by other higher performing groups. For example, the collectivist culture of the Soviet Union was undermined by the liberal economic culture that prevailed globally, resulting in its disintegration. Groups sometimes establish mechanisms to prevent leaders with extreme traits or powerful sub-groups from imposing an inappropriate culture. Democracy is the form of governance most likely to maintain the culture of the group closest to the centre of the Circle of Power, although countries with first past the post electoral systems often experience shifts between more extreme positions as power shifts between two major parties. However, in terms of human civilisation, democracy is a very recent development. It is currently under threat because the connection between government and voters has been weakened by low voter turnout, the emergence of career politicians and the power of corporations, and because fear of economic decline, immigrants and unemployment is empowering politicians with authoritarian tendencies.

Where a collective consciousness exists, it is more likely that the decisions made by the leadership of the group will reflect the interests of the majority of its members. Ignorance encourages people to accept the status quo and makes them easier to manipulate. Establishment leaders therefore naturally seek to limit the development of individual and collective consciousness. They find it easier to maintain order and pursue their personal objectives if they maintain members of the wider group in a state of ignorance of the wider world. The great challenge of modern times is to expand the consciousness of ordinary people across the world. If this can be achieved, populations will be able to appreciate the exploitative nature of the establishments that seek to control them and the virtues of working collaboratively with other nations to deliver a sustainable global society.

Fitting in

Ambitions, losses and regrets can be powerful motivators. People who are driven can do remarkable things. You are, though, most likely to be effective where you set achievable objectives, taking account of your abilities and environmental constraints, and work together with other people to achieve them. You therefore need to find ways to fit into groups. Life is essentially a journey of discovery and understanding during which you develop your talents and skills and learn how to employ them effectively for the benefit of a group. Sometimes, you will need to adapt your objectives and make accommodations to integrate effectively within a group. This will be more difficult for some people than others. Some people experience poor mental health as a result. If you develop an understanding of the primal group structure and the power dynamics within groups, you will be better able to adapt your behaviour in ways that enable you to fit into groups or build a group around you.

Before humans developed conscious thought processes, life would have been much less complicated. A person would have been directed towards appropriate roles by his emotional system. He would have been born into a single group in a particular geographic location so his environment would have been defined for him to a great degree. Some females would have transferred to other groups, but they would have been constrained by the environment and culture of those groups. Some individuals would have had low status or been marginalised because they had extreme traits, were subject to an unfavourable culture, breached group values or suffered from a disability. However, they would have maintained strong ties with the group because of their need for protection and support from it.

Modern society, however, consists of a multitude of different, overlapping groups. You will belong to a number of these groups at the same time, which is likely to include a family, a workplace, a friendship group and a nation. The structure, objectives and culture of these groups will differ. As a result, your levels of positive and negative feelings will change as you move from one to another. You may feel accepted within some of these groups, but out of place or marginalised in others. You will, though, derive some form of enjoyment, protection or support from each of them.

There are three basic criteria that you need to meet to fit into a group, be effective and experience positive feelings on a sustainable basis. Firstly, you must perform a role that suits your personality traits. Secondly, as you will have deficiencies in certain areas, you will need group members whose roles interact with yours to be similarly well located and competent. Thirdly, you will need the culture and objectives of your group to be favourable to your personality traits.

You will have a natural role within the groups to which you belong (including society), as dictated by the primal group structure, and over time your behaviour will cause you to gravitate towards this position. There are, though, many factors that can prevent you from finding a suitable place, such as your family background and the decisions of influential people within the groups to which you belong. Sometimes we depend on people who exercise control over us to locate us in suitable positions and surround us with helpful colleagues. As children, we are strongly influenced by the choices and directions of parents and teachers. When we are adults, we can decide to change jobs, but we cannot control the recruitment decisions of the companies we work for and have little influence as individuals over their culture.

Because there is a general lack of understanding within society of the influence that personality traits have on a person's ability to function, many managers, parents and teachers do not invest sufficient time in identifying the particular characteristics of their staff, children or students. As a result, many people fail to realise their ambitions or waste energy pursuing lost causes. However, you can use your understanding of personality to identify roles and environments to which you are suited. You can, for example, research the responsibilities associated with a job role, and the values and reputation of the company advertising it, before making an informed decision about whether to enter into an employment contract. If you are self-employed, you can build support networks that integrate well with your personality. The same approach can be applied to other areas of your life.

Where your group is too small to contain the full range of personalities or people around you are performing roles to which they are unsuited, it is likely that you will feel uncomfortable at times. People will have to take on responsibilities to which they are unsuited to compensate for the weaknesses in your group's structure and this will result in personality clashes and other stress responses. You may determine that it is worth putting up with the resultant negative feelings where they are likely to be temporary and may lead to significant future rewards; for example, if you join a start up business. However, such groups are only likely to be successful if the group members show drive, willpower and resilience, and recognise that effective relationships with other members can only be established if they restrain their instinctive behaviours.

You will struggle to fit in if your personality traits conflict with your group's culture. People with middling traits will fit into the different groups that they belong to reasonably well, provided that the culture of those groups is located near the centre of the Circle of Power. They will be able to switch easily between Fast System and Slow System operation, and the characteristics that they display are likely to change as they move from one situation to another. For example, a man may show deference to his boss at work, but adopt the character of dominant male at home. However, there will always be people who possess extreme personality traits that are unsuited to average conditions. They will find it difficult to align their interests with the group's objectives and will be inclined to behave in ways that conflict with the group's values. They are likely to feel stressed or bored in conversations and circumstances that most people find enlivening or relaxing. This seriously limits their ability to establish and nourish relationships, hold down jobs and maintain a good level of mental health. If a person wishes to fit into a group with an unfavourable culture, he will have to adjust his behaviour. He may have to accept that an ambition is unrealistic, or needs modification if he is going to secure help from other group members. He may have to carry out tasks that he considers pointless or which cause him to experience stress if he is to be accepted as part of a team. If he does not make such accommodations, he will risk ending up as an outcast or loner. A person who is isolated is likely to feel insecure, experience stress and low moods and lack self-esteem.

People with extreme traits will usually find it harder to fit into small groups. A large group is more likely to be able to devote time and resources to supporting and protecting such people and it will develop a wider range of roles and sub-cultures. For example, a society may include voluntary groups with collectivist cultures and small technology companies with individualistic cultures. In contrast, a small group will usually be forced to focus on its core objectives if it wishes to survive, and may be destabilised or fall behind competitors if it allows members with extreme traits to take big risks or get lost in details that are not directly related to the achievement of such objectives. Families can be very restrictive both in terms of designating roles and culturally. Close-knit communities can be similarly oppressive, constraining or unsupportive. Some people therefore feel the need to break away from their native groups to develop their talents and skills.

People who suffer from a lack of confidence or who have not recovered fully from traumatic experiences may struggle to locate themselves in appropriate roles within groups. Their behaviour is likely to be unnaturally conservative, as they will not yet have restored their self-belief, enhanced their skills or found an alternative source of protection and support. They will be focused on dealing with the negative feelings that they are experiencing. If they try to perform their natural roles, they are likely to experience anxiety or chronic stress. In modern, individualistic society, people are free to exhibit individualistic behaviours and the groups that have traditionally provided them with protection and support have weakened or disintegrated. As a result of this loss, increasing numbers of people are feeling insecure, experiencing stress and low moods, and adopting confrontational or defensive positions when interacting with people who have different values to their own.

Gaining an understanding of how to fit into group structures and cultures can be a route back to good health. You can make conscious decisions to change your behaviour to fit into groups. You can use your talents and skills more directly for the benefit of a group (or key members of it) to gain more recognition and influence, or you can choose to comply with its values. You may need to make accommodations to do so, but the costs of making them may be outweighed by the support and protection you gain from being accepted within the group, and this may instil in you the drive and willpower to move forward.

A person whose personality is very unsuited to the culture of a group will face a dilemma. He can try to fit in by complying with group values or pursue his natural path regardless. Either way, he will experience negative feelings. If he tries to fit in, he is likely to feel that he is falling short of societal expectations. This is because he will simply be less good at performing average tasks than people with middling traits. If he has a high trait, he is likely to be pulled towards exploratory activities that he finds exhilarating, and if he has a low trait, he is likely to spend too much time attending to detail. He will, therefore, find it difficult to make progress at the same speed as average people. He will experience more stress than the average person due to the efforts he makes to comply and is, therefore, more likely to become fatigued. If he has high traits, he is likely to experience low moods as a result of making accommodations in relation to his ambitions. If he has low traits, he is likely to experience anxiety or chronic stress due to the group's failure to create an environment that gives him a sense of security. He will therefore need to show a great deal of resilience. If he does not comply and instead pursues his own path, he will find it difficult to secure the support and protection that he needs from other group members to realise his objectives and he may be ignored, marginalised or ostracised. He will, therefore, be vulnerable to feelings of isolation and loneliness and the associated states of stress and depression. Such a person may appear lost or seek security in dysfunctional relationships or through membership of groups with extreme or unusual values, such as a monastic community, sect or revolutionary group.

Some people find themselves caught in no man's land. It can be difficult for a person to fully commit to pursuing his natural role in life if it would result in a loss of status or security. He may have built up a good reputation or financial resources as a result of years of compliance or benefitted from an inheritance that he is reluctant to put at risk. Even if he would be prepared to make such a commitment as an individual, he may be prevented from doing so by the lifestyle expectations of a partner or his dependents, the actions of competitors, restrictions on social mobility, gender bias or his own physical or mental deficiencies. A person in this position will feel isolated because his dislocation will prevent him from forming a close bond with his group, and his failure to completely disengage from it will mean that he is unlikely to be accepted by people with like minds who have formed a counter-culture sub-group. For example, members of a group that such a person wishes to join may reject him because his clothing style and behaviour reflect his upbringing, even though the group's culture corresponds with his values and personality.

It is easy for people with average personalities who fit squarely within a group culture to criticise those whose behaviour breaches group values. However, they do not appreciate the intensity of the negative feelings that people with extreme traits experience when they comply. People with ill-fitting personalities often need help to develop resilience, make accommodations and find roles where their natural abilities can be used in a way that furthers their group's objectives. It is much harder to influence such people in adulthood because they will have adopted compensatory behaviours and may have embedded themselves within sub-groups with cultures that are more suited to their personality traits. Unfortunately, such people are often let down by schooling systems and society in general. Citizens generally, and therefore governments, are not usually prepared to spend money on marginalised or low status adults, so people with extreme personality traits often live transient, unhappy lives and are much more likely to find themselves in prison, homeless or destitute than the average person. Some people with very extreme traits will, though, simply be too different to be able to fit into society in a way that allows them to be useful. They will need to be looked after by families, communities, charities or government and/or be restrained to prevent them causing harm to themselves or others.

Some people with high or low traits are not destined to fit in. Their role in life is to act as a balancing mechanism or force for change within groups. They may operate at a distance from the group; for example, as a hermit, philosopher or artist, or agitate to change their group's values as people like Jesus and Gandhi did. Although they are likely to experience hardship and negative feelings as a result of not fitting in, they will experience strong positive feelings and feel a sense of purpose when they pursue their causes. Their efforts can result in an expansion of collective consciousness or prompt a cultural shift.

It is, though, very difficult to change a group's culture by yourself. You will need to work with other group members who share your objectives. However, people who are experiencing poor mental health often find it difficult to do so as they are battling against strong negative feelings and instinctive behaviours. A person who feels insecure may abuse or exert excessive control over others, or adopt other compensatory behaviours that damage relationships with other members of his group. He may distance himself from other group members who share his predicament for fear of being stereotyped or discriminated against. He may even start to discriminate against such people himself in order to increase his identification with and gain acceptance from important members of his group. Disadvantaged people therefore usually find it difficult to work effectively as a team.

10

RELATIONSHIPS

A relationship is a connection between two people who have repeated contact with each other. Your levels of positive feeling and effectiveness will depend to a significant degree on the nature and quality of your relationships. To be successful, you will need to establish good working relationships. If a group is to regenerate itself, its members will need to form sexual relationships. You will also need to develop social relationships to help you relax. Working, sexual and social relationships can occur within a single relationship.

Relationships vary greatly in their nature depending on the balance of personality traits within them. When two people interact with each other independently from other people, they essentially form their own group. The group dynamics discussed in earlier chapters therefore apply to relationships. The two parties will be able to access extremely positive feelings if their objectives and personality traits are complementary. However, the small size of the group means that the parties are more likely to be forced to perform unsuitable tasks. People are therefore more likely to experience stress or low moods in the context of a relationship than within wider group socialisation, especially if they possess extreme traits. Because there are only two people in a relationship, the culture that results may be heavily skewed towards particular personality traits and power may be very unevenly distributed between the two partners.

Working relationships

Working relationships are formed for the purpose of achieving objectives such as developing a business or performing a job role. They extend well beyond the conventional workplace and can be found in families, voluntary organisations, communities and recreational groups, in which case the relationship's objectives could be bringing up a child or winning a doubles match in tennis. People who develop good working relationships are much better placed to be successful in life than those who do not.

Partners in working relationships will often have quite different personality traits and therefore different talents and skills. The primal group structure encourages people with different but complementary talents and skills to work together. If the members of a well-balanced human group are correctly positioned, relationships within it are likely to be relatively easy to establish and maintain, as each person will be suited to his role and surrounded by people with whom he is suited to interacting. Within the primal hierarchy, relationships tend to be built on loyalty and organisation. Orders are given and followed, and there is an emphasis on coherence and simplicity. Within the female collective, relationships are built on empathy, fairness and collaboration, and exist within a networked structure. The positioning of males with progressive traits at the margins of the primal hierarchy enables them to establish relationships with members of the primal hierarchy when their talents and skills are needed without compromising its integrity and purpose.

A good working relationship will usually develop where on balance the experience for both parties is positive. Two people with middling traits are likely to find it relatively easy to get on with each other. They will have the ability to use their learning cycles to filter and process most types of information and are therefore unlikely to become stressed or feel bored in the other person's company. People with extreme traits will find it harder to establish a broad range of working relationships. Their characteristics and behaviours suit them to unusual or specialist roles and make it difficult for them to interact with people with the reverse traits without experiencing strong negative feelings.

Although people naturally gravitate towards their natural positions within the primal group structure, class systems and other impediments create friction within groups, which results in some people being incorrectly located. Also, many groups in modern society are too small to possess the full range of human personality traits or contain an atypical distribution of traits. Consequently, some people are placed in situations where they are required to perform tasks to which they are unsuited and form working relationships with people with conflicting personality traits. This situation is common in politics as elected representatives are required to take on a wide range of responsibilities and have little influence over whom else the electorate votes into office.

If people with opposite traits are required to work together, they are likely to experience negative feelings, stress and low moods as their personalities clash. For example, if an engineer who is low in openness meets with a product designer who is high in openness, he is likely to feel stressed if the designer proposes a radical new approach. His ability to engage in constructive discussions will be compromised, as he will not be able to engage his learning cycle. This is likely to result in the designer becoming frustrated by the lack of progress. He may then express anger or criticism that could damage the relationship between the two.

When two people with opposite traits meet, there will be a narrow window within which they can both experience positive feelings. If both parties are prepared to compromise and actively work to identify and interact in this area, they can learn to work together. I refer to the information environment where people with opposite traits can achieve a common understanding as the **Co-operation Zone**. Figure 23 below illustrates, in relation to a single trait, the range within which a person who is high in a trait can work effectively with a person who is low in the same trait.

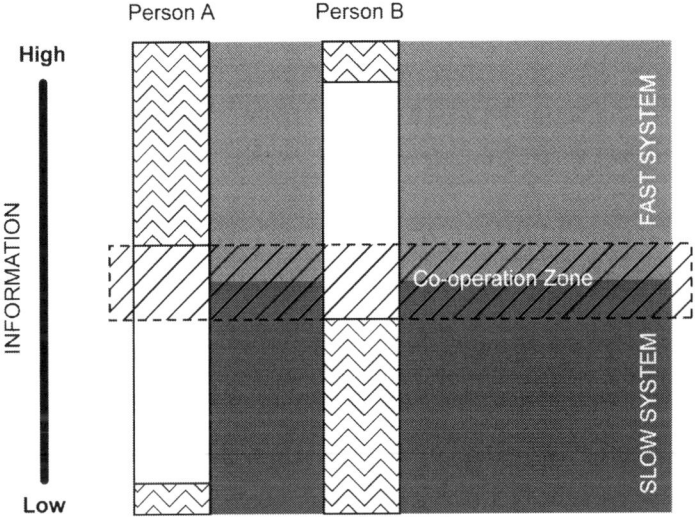

Figure 23. The Co-operation Zone

When people with opposite traits work within the Co-operation Zone, they will both experience positive feelings. Achieving such a working relationship is, however, difficult because of the narrowness of the Co-operation Zone. The person with the high trait will have to restrain his arousal level and be aware that he may cause the other person to experience anxiety or chronic stress if he gets carried away and makes intuitive jumps. The person with the low trait will need to be prepared to allow his arousal level to rise and to be careful not to spend too long talking about details otherwise he will cause the other person to experience suppression or a low mood. At times, one of the parties will stray out of the Co-operation Zone, causing the other to experience negative feelings. The other party will need to show resilience in such situations if a good relationship is to be maintained. He may need to alert the offending party to his lapse otherwise such behaviour is likely to be repeated. Good communication is therefore essential in developing such a relationship. Of course, Figure 23 only relates to one trait spectrum. In reality, two individuals could have opposing traits in more than one spectrum in which case they are likely to find it even more difficult to get on.

People with opposite traits will therefore need to show tolerance and respect to each other if their relationship is to work well. If you demonstrate commitment to a working relationship's objectives through your actions over a period of time, you will build trust and strengthen that relationship. If one party becomes disaffected as a result of the other's inconsiderate or selfish behaviour, or the parties' interests diverge, the relationship is likely to break down and the parties are likely to develop negative attitudes towards each other.

Partners in working relationships will primarily gain pleasure and satisfaction from the performance of their roles and the achievement of the relationship's objectives, not through social interaction. People who get to know each other through group activities therefore often fail to develop strong bilateral social relationships. Many leisure activities revolve around a shared objective, such as the completion of a bike ride. The relationships formed during such activities will often be working ones in terms of character. It is just that the "work" has no broader societal purpose. Therefore, when two riders meet outside the context of a bike ride, they may find that they have little to talk about apart from cycling. Social relationships may, though, develop from working relationships.

As working relationships are based on the achievement of objectives, they are likely to become redundant when the objectives are completed, or a person redefines his objectives; for example, if he changes career. However, many people have roles that require continuing support or anticipate needing to make use of a relationship in the future, so they make efforts to maintain the health of their relationship network. Members of the establishment see relationships as a means of accessing power and wealth in the future. Women tend to see them as a means of securing help and resources for their families, and emotional support for themselves, on an on-going basis.

The uniqueness of our personalities causes each one of us to experience the world differently. Most of us do not take account of this when interacting with other people. Research suggests that we tend to assume others think as we do, or that something is wrong with them if they do not. In modern individualistic society, many people are too pre-occupied with their personal objectives to take account of the needs and desires of other people. When people encounter inappropriate or aggressive behaviour, they tend to attribute it to a failing in the personality of the person displaying such behaviour, ignoring potential environmental causes (including their own contribution). They tend to do the reverse, however, when analysing their own actions, justifying their behaviour by reference to external factors. These tendencies help you to avoid adapting your behaviour, enabling you to pursue your immediate objectives in an uninhibited fashion, but they also limit your ability to build and maintain effective relationships and put at risk the achievement of your longer-term objectives. Individualistic cultures are characterised by avoidance because they encourage people to pursue short-term personal objectives. People within them tend to fail to define or maintain focus on relationship or group objectives. This makes it harder for them to establish and sustain working relationships. The flexibility and looseness of relationships in individualistic cultures does, however, enable groups with such cultures to respond quickly to change and take advantage of opportunities.

Social relationships

Social relationships are not based on the achievement of specific objectives. Unlike working relationships, pleasure is primarily derived from the relationship itself, not the completion of a task. Social relationships help us to relax and regulate our emotions. They also make it easier for us to engage in leisure activities and help us to avoid, or make more bearable, activities that we find difficult, stressful or boring.

As with working relationships, social relationships require the establishment of trust. Liking is a measure of trust and indicates that you feel comfortable in a person's company. Psychologists have determined that the most important factors that promote liking of other people are familiarity, proximity and similarity. A person who is in your presence on a regular basis will become more familiar over time. Familiarity aids trust building as it helps you to overcome any fear you may be experiencing due to lack of knowledge of the other person's character. Proximity enables more frequent contact and therefore promotes familiarity. It also makes establishing relations more worthwhile in terms of a cost/benefit analysis. Finally, people who are evenly matched in their physical appearance, social background and personality, sociability and interests are more likely to like each other because they will be suited to operating within similar environments. They will have similar views and interests, so they are likely to promote positive feelings within each other. Studies have suggested that these latter factors are less important than proximity and familiarity although advances in communications in recent years have enabled people to seek out like minds more easily and therefore may have increased their influence.

Sometimes liking extends to attraction. Liking is a passive state associated with feeling secure and use of the Slow System whereas attraction is an exploratory force associated with use of the Fast System. We are attracted to people who enable us to experience feelings of enjoyment and exhilaration (i.e. people who make it easier for us to spend time in Fast System operation within our optimal ranges). People with high traits introduce stimulating information into their environment and this may enable people around them to experience enjoyment more easily. For example, entertainers are usually high in extraversion. In the context of a performance, behaviours associated with this trait increase the amount of information within the audience's environment, stimulating its members. A person with a high trait will also be able to shield a person with the corresponding low trait from potentially harmful information; for example, where a soldier with a high level of indifference mans a checkpoint at the border of a group's territory. Where such protection is provided, the person with the low trait will be relieved from stress and find it easier to enjoy himself. People who are high in extraversion tend to attract people because their ease with the physical world enables them to be outgoing and take risks that people with lower levels of extraversion would not. Similarly, people who are high in openness, indifference or opportunism can attract people by virtue of their ability to cope with novel situations, competition and changing environments respectively. However, people with high traits also generate a lot of potentially threatening information because they take risks and act instinctively. As a result, people with low traits may find interacting with them stressful. A person's attractiveness will therefore depend on the nature of the information in your environment, whether he is protecting you from the information or directing it at you, and your sensitivity to that information. For example, a stranger who is high in indifference and opportunism may present a threat to you because he is likely to take advantage of opportunities without concern for any harm he may cause you, but a friend with the same traits may give you the protection you need to enjoy yourself in a changing environment.

People with low traits are more likely to blend into the background and proceed cautiously when getting to know new people because they need to establish that strangers do not present a threat to them. People who are low in extraversion look out for physical threats, those who are low in openness check for differences, people who are low in indifference need to guard against potential harm and people who are low in opportunism look out for rule breakers. Therefore, although they may be likeable, people with low traits are, initially at least, less likely to attract other people than people with high traits. However, because people with low traits naturally restrain the behaviour of people with high traits, a person whose high traits tend to get him into trouble may form a relationship with a person with corresponding low traits to benefit from his stabilising influence.

Good-looking, successful people are attractive because they are capable of providing us with protection, resources and entertainment. They serve as focal points for attention, thereby increasing the energy and information in their immediate environment. Associating with such people can heighten your level of self-esteem, enabling you to bask in reflective glory. Studies have shown that physically attractive children receive higher marks from their teachers and are more popular, and that, as adults, they are more successful at work and, unsurprisingly, more sexually experienced. As we tend to feel safer in the company of fellow group members, vulnerable and insecure people may also be attracted to good-looking, successful people. This may explain why babies gaze longer into the eyes of attractive females. Where attention from others instils such a person with confidence, it is likely to further increase his attractiveness and make it easier for him to be even more successful. However, sometimes good looks or success obscures an underlying lack of confidence or ability. In such circumstances, a person may feel uncomfortable taking on the mantle of attractiveness or success. For example, an attractive woman who is low in indifference may feel insecure or stressed when men openly compete for "possession" of her.

High trait orientated people can be very charismatic. **Charisma** is defined as compelling attractiveness or charm that can inspire devotion in others. This is another way of describing a person who is capable of creating the protective bubble described above. Charismatic people, however, usually also possess a low trait that prompts behaviours that make people around him feel comfortable and secure. Men who are high in extraversion and low in indifference, such as Bill Clinton, can be particularly charismatic to women as they are very capable in the physical world, but are naturally caring as well. Men who are high in extraversion and indifference, but low in openness, like Donald Trump, are more likely to be charismatic to members of the rank and file as they offer the prospect of supremacy over other groups, but simplicity in daily life. A person who is low in extraversion will find it difficult to project charisma because he will feel stressed when addressing a group of people. However, if he is high in another trait and is located in an unthreatening physical environment, he may be able to do so. It is highly likely that Jesus was low in extraversion as he preached against the acquisition of wealth and materialism, but he also advocated tolerance so he was probably high in openness The possession of this high trait could have enabled him to project charisma. Attraction creates an imbalance within a relationship, giving one party influence over the other. The person who is attracted may follow the attractor unreservedly in order to sustain the positive feelings that such attraction generates within him. Consequently, charismatic people can be propelled to positions of power by their followers, and military leaders with charisma may persuade their troops to follow them into battles that look like lost causes.

Our ability to establish social relationships where there is mutual liking or attraction is related to our proficiency in certain practical skills, which in turn are related to personality traits. Reciprocal questioning and disclosure are important practices as exchanging personal information about each other helps to build trust. Mirroring body language also tends to make you conversation partner feel more comfortable, provided it does not signal aggressive intent. Behaviours that facilitate reciprocal questioning are associated with use of the Slow System and therefore low traits. A person who is low in extraversion will be inclined to treat the other person fairly, a person who is low in openness will develop a conversation in a methodical way, a person who is low in indifference is likely to have consideration for the other person's interests and a person who is low in opportunism will need to structure a conversation. People who are Fast System orientated will be more selfish by nature and tend to hog the limelight (high extraversion), leap from one subject to another (high openness), dominate the conversation (high indifference) or interrupt impulsively (high opportunism). They may use reciprocation schemas within their conversations or body language, but are less likely to listen or spend time processing information that is released by their partner into the conversation.

People will be reluctant to disclose information that they fear may be used against them. Because high trait orientated people have less to fear, they are likely to disclose information more readily. Such a person is likely to enjoy disclosing information which reveals his status, wealth, intelligence, dominance or flexibility depending on which high traits he possesses. People with high traits are, though, inherently untrustworthy because they will be inclined to act in their personal interests. Their awareness of their own untrustworthiness can make it difficult for them to trust people with the same traits. In contrast, people with low traits are likely to be cautious in disclosing information and to use their Slow Systems to process statements before releasing them into conversation. This is because they are more likely to suffer serious negative consequences when trust is breached. However, people with low traits who have led sheltered lives will be naturally trusting as they will not be aware of the risks that people with the relevant high traits will be prepared to take in pursuit of enjoyment and exhilaration and therefore the dangers such people may present to them. As a consequence, they may disclose information freely. This naivety leaves them open to abuse. Trust building within relationships is therefore a cyclical process. Disclosure increases trust and leads to further disclosure. As most people have a mix of high and low traits and feel secure in some situations but not others, the average person will be inclined to be open with some people and closed with others and willing to disclose certain types of information but reluctant to disclose other types.

The nature of your friendship circle will be influenced by your personality traits. People who are high in extraversion are likely to have a large circle of friends, but will not necessarily know much detail about their lives, as they tend to engage in superficial conversation and not to listen intently to conversation partners. People who are low in extraversion find it harder to initiate new relationships because they are naturally more cautious. They are more inclined to observe and listen than speak, and their tendency to apply analytical skills inclines them to engage in deep and meaningful one to one conversations rather than socialising in groups.

A person who is high in openness is likely to have a wide variety of friends and acquaintances, as this will maximise his chances of encountering novel information. His friends may struggle to get on with each other if he brings them together as the group will lack coherence. As he will be attracted to strangers who he finds interesting, he may turn out to be a fickle friend. In contrast, a person who is low in openness will be comforted by uniformity, so he will tend to establish a cohesive group of friends and re-enforce it through group bonding exercises. His conversation is likely to be focused on establishing common interests, beliefs and experiences.

A person who is high in indifference may find it difficult to develop strong friendships because of his tendency to dominate and exploit other people. Where he does succeed in doing so, his friends are likely either to be equally competitive or grateful for the protection that he can offer them. In contrast, people who are low in indifference are naturally caring and promote harmony. They therefore tend to establish lasting friendships, although their compassionate nature, helpfulness and tendency to be submissive leave them open to exploitation by false friends.

People who are high in opportunism are disorganised and impulsive by nature. They will make new acquaintances spontaneously, but lose touch with people whom they have no immediate reason to contact. In contrast, people who are low in opportunism will have very organised friendship networks and devote a lot of time to maintaining them. They will be cautious when dealing with strangers until they have worked out where they fit in. Their questions are likely to be aimed at finding out who their conversation partners know so they can fix them within their relationship network.

Your four traits will give you a default relationship style. You can use the table below to determine your natural relationship style.

	HIGH	LOW
EXTRAVERSION	Superficial	Meaningful
OPENNESS	Fickle	Loyal
INDIFFERENCE	Competitive	Collaborative
OPPORTUNISM	Unstructured	Organised

The high trait characteristics above are associated with freedom and the low trait ones with control and stability. Low traits therefore provide the foundations for a relationship. As a consequence, collectivist cultures encourage the development of strong, enduring relationships whereas individualistic cultures encourage loose, short-term ones. Members of the establishment build relationships around uniformity and structure, whereas the relationships of people who possess all four progressive traits tend to be founded on collaboration and fairness.

A person with middling traits is likely to have a large circle of friends, as he will experience positive feelings when interacting with most other people. However, a person with extreme traits will have a much smaller and more narrowly defined group, as he will often experience stress or a low mood when conversing or spending time with other people. If he has not learned how to function within the Co-operation Zone or developed a high level of resilience his relationship structure may be very weak. A person who has not yet recovered from a traumatic event is also likely to find it difficult to develop new friendships because he will be focused on strengthening his bonds with his existing group and is likely to feel stressed when he meets strangers.

If a person is trapped in an unfavourable environment or suffering from depression, he may project negativity for a sustained period. Vocalising worries and feelings of unhappiness can become a habit because it helps an individual to feel better. It serves as a release and also aids the clarification process. It can, though, cause other people to experience negative feelings. A person's arousal level will drop if he is forced to consider the misfortunes of another person, and this may cause him to experience suppression or a low mood. In a tight-knit group, other group members are likely to support or at least put up with an unhappy individual. In weaker groups, however, friends and acquaintances may avoid interacting with a person who regularly projects negativity. He may therefore find that his social circle shrinks, increasing the number of issues that he has to complain about and placing more strain on his remaining relationships.

Where a person has a small friendship circle, he may put too much pressure on individuals within it, causing them to distance themselves, thereby resulting in further shrinking of his circle. A small number of friendships will make him susceptible to exploitation and abuse, as the people with whom he does have close relationships will have an unhealthy amount of influence over him. A manipulator or abuser will typically try to maintain his victim in an isolated position because it renders the victim more emotionally vulnerable. Manipulative people usually have a combination of a high trait that drives them to exploit an opportunity and a low trait that gives them the control to take advantage of it. People who are high in indifference and low in opportunism are most likely to be manipulative because they naturally plan ahead and will have little concern for any harm they might cause to their victims.

Sexual relationships

The primary purpose of human groups is to reproduce. This requires individuals to form sexual relationships with members of the opposite sex. Sexual relationships may be very short, lasting not much longer than the act of procreation. As they progress, they may transition to social relationships, or working relationships if the couple have children or are committed to the achievement of a shared objective.

This section considers only heterosexual relationships. Many of the principles I discuss, however, will apply equally to gay and lesbian relationships.

Sexual attraction

Pheromones — a type of scent-bearing chemical secreted in sweat and other bodily fluids – play a key role in promoting sexual attraction. During the fertile period of her menstrual cycle, a woman gives off a pheromone that makes her more attractive to potential male suitors. Chemical changes within a fertile female's body may also affect her appearance and behaviour in ways that make her more attractive to males. A study has suggested that a woman's face appears more attractive to men during the fertile stage of her menstrual cycle. Similarly, it has been found that a woman's voice sounds most seductive at her most fertile point.

As the purpose of sexual intercourse is to produce children, a person's choice of sexual partner is related to his or her ability to produce healthy offspring. People are usually attracted to people with average faces as deviating from the norm presents a risk. Symmetry is particularly important. It is a sign of good health because it implies a lack of mutations. Studies have established that we can assess someone's level of symmetry by smell alone. In an experiment, women who smelt T-shirts belonging to different men preferred those belonging to men with symmetrical features. It has also been suggested that we may be sexually attracted to people with different immune systems in order to improve resistance to disease in the next-generation.

The contraceptive pill appears to interfere with the natural mating process by changing the characteristics that a woman finds attractive in a man. Research has shown that women on the pill display a preference for men with similar genes to their own. This is probably because the hormonal changes involved in pregnancy (which the pill mimics) draw women towards caring men rather than ones capable of providing protection. There is evidence to suggest that within long-term committed relationships, changes in the use of hormonal contraception affect a woman's sexual satisfaction with her male partner. A study has found that women who met their partners while taking the pill and were still currently taking it, or who had never used the pill at any point, reported greater sexual satisfaction than those women who had begun or stopped using the pill during their relationships. Also, use of contraception inclines a woman to wait for a partner who she gets on with well (i.e. one with similar personality traits) and therefore reduces the chances of pregnancies arising from spontaneous sexual liaisons. Therefore, over time, wide use of the pill within a population could reduce diversity within families and communities. It may also divert women away from mates that are better genetic fits and result in more children being born with weak immune systems or other conditions or disabilities than would otherwise be the case.

Sexual attraction is to some extent an extreme form of social attraction. We tend to be attracted to people who enable us to experience feelings of enjoyment and exhilaration through the physicality of intimate contact, exposure to new experiences, competition with rivals or spontaneous interactions. Such exposure increases your arousal level, causing you to spend more time in Fast System operation. You are more likely to act instinctively as a result and take an opportunity to mate when it arises. If you use your Slow System to reason whether or not you should mate with another person, you may not act quickly enough to take advantage. However, pheromones do not improve Fast System functioning. If you lack appropriate schemas, you will experience anxiety or stress when sexually aroused. People with relevant high traits will therefore pursue sexual experiences more freely than people with the corresponding low traits. Those who are high in extraversion are suited to the physical world so they will be inclined to seek physical contact at an early stage. People who possess all four high traits are likely to be very sexually active and unrestrained in their pursuit of sexual gratification.

A person who possesses a low trait may be over-stimulated when faced with a mating opportunity, resulting in a major stress event. He may, therefore, freeze or panic. If he anticipates the possibility of such an event, he may experience anxiety, avoid physical interaction or display frigidity. In modern society, this applies particularly to people who are low in extraversion as there is an expectation of early physical contact. People with other low traits may also experience stress when opportunities for sexual liaisons arise, causing them to proceed with caution, freeze or walk away. A potential partner who wants to try new things may spook a person who is low in openness, the competitive nature of dating may cause a person who is low in indifference to feel tense and a suitor who does not follow standard dating practices may disconcert a person who is low in opportunism. This does not mean that a person with a low trait cannot enjoy sexual contact. It is just that he just will need to feel secure in order to do so. However, because people tend to establish sexual relationships quickly in modern, individualistic society, such a person may not be able to adapt quickly enough to meet the expectations of potential partners.

A person with a low trait is likely to take more risks and experience more positive feelings once he has established an intimate relationship with his partner. Intimacy is an extreme form of familiarity. It promotes trust and enables a person to be more confident and outgoing in front of his partner than he would be with other people. A sexual relationship therefore usually develops through a process of increasingly intimate reciprocal contact and disclosure. A person with a very low trait may, though, never feel confident enough to let go of Slow System operation. If he remains in Slow System operation when having sex, he will not experience feelings of enjoyment or exhilaration at the time. He is, though, likely to make a conscientious lover as he will focus on making the experience feel meaningful, refining his method, pleasing his partner or following instructions. He is also likely to experience a sense of contentment or fulfilment after the event if he feels he has done a good job.

People who possess high traits will often be attractive to people who possess low traits because they are able to protect them from potential threats, allowing them to relax and experience positive feelings. In the typical relationship, the man will be high in indifference and the woman low in indifference. The man is likely to have his level of positive feeling increased by a sexual liaison, as it will evidence his competitive prowess. However, the woman's lower level of indifference will deter her from competing for a mate. Instead, she will look for a man who can offer her protection from competitive forces and potentially harmful situations. If she finds such a man, her stress levels will reduce and she will be able to enjoy herself or focus on tasks that will deliver feelings of contentment and fulfilment. The protective environment that such a man creates for his partner can be witnessed on shared pedestrian and cycling paths. She will often be energised or relaxed and oblivious to the presence of cyclists. The man, however, will usually be aware of cyclists approaching from behind and guide her out of the cyclist's path. Women who have children or who are looking forward to doing so are likely to be attracted to men who are high in extraversion and indifference (i.e. alpha males) as they will be suited to acquiring resources and protecting their families from physical threats.

As people with high traits take greater risks than people with low traits and tend to gravitate towards high information environments, a person with high traits may present a danger to a potential partner with corresponding low traits. A woman with low traits is therefore likely to act defensively when initially dating a man with high traits. He is likely to display outgoing, romantic, dominant or spontaneous behaviour in an effort to win her over. The attraction such behaviours might otherwise engender in her will, though, be muted as she uses her Slow System to assess him and make rational decisions.

Ideal partners

Sexual attraction is not a choice. Although you may spark it by engaging in sexually stimulating behaviour or spending time in close proximity to a potential mate, you do not consciously decide to be attracted to other people. However, many people have ideals by which they measure potential long-term partners. Sexual attraction brings couples together, but partnerships are formed for the achievement of objectives. That objective may be simply the mutual provision of support and protection, but usually there will be an underlying subtext, such as the creation of a family unit, financial gain or social climbing. A person will look for evidence that a potential partner will remain committed to the partnership and the achievement of its objectives.

One study carried out by Fletcher, Simpson, Thomas and Giles at the University of Canterbury in 1999 identified three characteristics that were particularly important in terms of ideal sexual partners – warmth and trustworthiness, attractiveness and vitality, and status and resources. Warmth and trustworthiness were the most important for both sexes, and status and resources the least. The only significant gender difference was that women rated warmth and trustworthiness as slightly less important than men. The researchers also identified two overarching factors that characterised ideal relationships: intimacy and loyalty, and passion.

The phrase **warmth and trustworthiness** was used to describe a range of characteristics identified by participants including "understanding, supportive, considerate, kind, good listener, sensitive, trustworthy, warm, affectionate, reliable, friendly, communicative and honest". The **intimacy and loyalty** factor had a strong correlation with warmth and trustworthiness, and it shares many of the same sub-characteristics, but also included caring, loyalty and respect. These characteristics are almost all associated with use of the Slow System. This is not surprising because a relationship is the basic building block of a group and Slow System skills have evolved to strengthen groups. People who are low in extraversion will look for meaning within a relationship, those who are low in openness will value loyalty, people are low in indifference will work to create a sense of harmony and those who are low in opportunism will try to establish structure and order within the relationship.

The use by the researchers of the words "warmth" and "intimacy" as global terms to describe this range of characteristics was, however, misguided, as they can be easily misinterpreted. True warmth and emotional intimacy emanate from people who seek to deliver harmonious environments and are naturally caring (i.e. those who are low in indifference). However, some people mistake outgoing behaviour for warmth. People who are high in extraversion naturally start conversations with strangers and are expressive and tactile, but this has no relationship to their ability and inclination to care for others or act with integrity.

An alpha male is likely to pretend to be caring when dating in order to secure sexual favours and establish relationships. His high level of extraversion will enable him to do so in very demonstrative ways, for example by professing his love for her publicly or giving her extravagant presents, while his high level of indifference will prevent him from feeling guilty about deceiving his potential partner as to his true motives. Once the relationship is established, he is likely to revert to type and display dominating, self-interested behaviours. In contrast, a person who is low in extraversion and indifference will find dating highly stimulating and often stressful. He is likely to try to maintain Slow System operation, in which case he will adopt a measured approach, which is unlikely to make his potential partner feel special. His analytical behaviour may make him appear cold and he may experience anxiety and worry about behaving inappropriately or hurting the feelings of his object of affection. If he loses control and enters Fast System operation, he is likely to become over-excited, appearing too keen, and to lose access to their caring skills. He will, therefore, struggle to make a good impression. However, if he manages to establish a relationship, his natural warmth is likely to emerge as he becomes more confident with his partner and seeks to establish a meaningful and harmonious relationship.

In the absence of other considerations, physical and emotional intimacy is most likely to result when both partners are high in extraversion and low in indifference. However, this combination is unlikely to occur very often as most men are high in indifference and because the possession of that trait by one partner will help the couple provide for and protect a family. In some relationships, the woman is higher in indifference and takes on the role of protector and provider. Although this role reversal is more common in societies with individualistic or progressive cultures, it is harder to make such a relationship work because it does not conform to traditional practice and because women who attempt to compete in the wider world face barriers erected by incumbent males.

Women have a secret weapon that helps them to moderate male competitive instincts and induce caring behaviours in men. Females that are not in their fertile period, and especially those who are lactating, produce high levels of oxytocin, a hormone that reduces the impact of testosterone, making men less aggressive and self-serving. It is released in larger quantities when a woman is groomed, which explains why men feel relaxed when stroking the hair of a partner (or, indeed, a dog, as dogs release a similar chemical). Babies also give off this chemical in large quantities, thereby encouraging people around them to care for them. Oxytocin enables males to access Slow System caring skills without experiencing frustration or boredom. Consequently, if a man and woman have a row, the best route to a resolution is usually for the woman to behave in a way that prompts supportive physical contact, by, for example, crying. By doing so, she will encourage grooming behaviour and help the male to be more empathetic. If the woman continues to argue, however, the male's arousal level is likely to rise in which case he may become angry and show aggression. Relationships are therefore likely to be more stable if affectionate grooming practices are maintained.

When women gather together, the large amount of oxytocin that is released reduces tension within their environment. In the primeval group, females would have lived and worked together so they would have generated a considerable amount of oxytocin. This would have enabled them to calm down most males within the domestic environment, thereby promoting harmony within the group. However, in monogamous societies, a married woman will be left to counter her husband's aggressive tendencies alone unless she has several daughters living with her.

Men with the warrior gene are, however, unaffected by oxytocin, which means they are likely to display ruthlessness and aggression in circumstances where most men would moderate their behaviour. Oxytocin prompts the production of an enzyme called monoamine oxidase A, which degrades dopamine and other neurotransmitters. People with the warrior gene produce low levels of this enzyme. A woman who is living with a man who possesses the warrior gene will therefore be particularly vulnerable to abuse.

Where a man who lacks empathy displays kindness towards his partner, this may be because he has been influenced by a progressive or collectivist culture, or an important person who subscribes to values associated with one of these cultures, such as his mother. However, it may be because he views his partner as a valuable possession. He may value her because she enhances his status or has ability to deliver sons to him. In this instance, he will "care" for her in the same way he would an expensive car or other object that he values. His kindness will usually be accompanied by a need to "protect" her from the advances of other males and this may cause him to impose restrictions on her freedom. Men with establishment traits often dote on their sons, but this should not be mistaken for caring in the sense that females perform this role. Such behaviour causes them to experience a boost to their confidence and self-esteem because they will be anticipating the increase in power, influence and security that their sons could bring to them in the future.

Males who appear to be caring may simply be low in openness and displaying loyalty. In the case of an alpha male, however, his instinct to be loyal will not usually extend to a commitment to monogamous behaviour, as alpha males have evolved to mate with multiple females. Members of the primal hierarchy will usually require their wives to demonstrate loyalty and obey orders because they possess the controlling traits of low openness and opportunism and wish to ensure the genetic purity of their lineage. Demonstrations of loyalty are likely to put such a man at ease and make him more amenable. Many women appreciate the protection and resources that a member of the establishment can provide and recognise the advantages to be gained from showing loyalty. Women who are high in extraversion will enjoy dressing in stylish clothes and basking in the high status that they derive from their association with an alpha male. Looking after children is easier when you have ready access to resources. Therefore, women who are in relationships with members of the establishment will often be prepared to accept that their partners will not be particularly empathetic or helpful and will look to female friends for emotional support instead. Such women may turn a blind eye to their partners' affairs with other women provided they retain the status of primary partner. The acquisition of equal rights by women in Western society has, though, caused some women to adopt liberal behaviours that their male partners interpret as disloyal or which make them jealous, such as spending time in environments where there are predatory males.

The greater need of women for protection probably explains why researchers found on average that women value warmth and trustworthiness less than men. The ruthlessness that enables a man who is high in indifference to deceive and ensnare females also enables him to outcompete other men, and acquire and accumulate resources. In hostile environments, a woman is likely to prioritise the welfare of her children and accept that she will be manipulated, controlled and cheated on to some degree by her partner in order to secure protection and resources from him. However, in societies with progressive laws that entitle divorced women to state support, alimony or substantial financial settlements, women are less tolerant of infidelity, restraining behaviour and abuse.

The phrase **attractiveness and vitality** was used by the researchers to describe a range of characteristics including "adventurous, nice body, outgoing, sexy, attractive, good lover, active lifestyle, sporty and athletic, confident, independent, interesting, spontaneous and good fun". The **passion** relationship factor had a strong correlation with attractiveness and vitality, and these two factors share many of the same sub-characteristics. These characteristics are mostly associated with use of the Fast System and enjoyment. Some of them are, though, related to good genes and fertility.

As we have seen, women tend to be attracted to men who are able to protect them. A male's physical characteristics give a strong indication of his status and his competitive ability. Alpha males usually possess a large chest, jutting jaw and powerful profile. These characteristics are attention grabbing and are associated with high levels of testosterone. Height and strength in males are usually attractive to females because they also suggest competitive prowess. However, if females were programmed to always seek out the same physical or mental characteristics in a mate, the species would become one-dimensional and less capable of protecting itself or adapting to changing circumstances.

Women are naturally drawn to engage collectively in the process of narrowing down potential partners in order to identify the most suitable male with whom to mate. This makes sense in evolutionary terms as a woman can only have a limited number of children. Women also have no need to establish loyal hierarchies beneath them. Quality is, therefore, more important than quantity to them. The female collective will help its preferred candidate for the position of dominant male to achieve that status. Its primary objective is to produce healthy and capable children so its members will usually favour a male who is a fine physical specimen and suited to the group's environment. The female collective identifies such males through consensus seeking. This may explain why women tend to be attracted to men who are popular with other women. The female collective's tendency to single out a male for advancement within a group can be seen at pop concerts where young, female fans scream adulation at boy bands. In monogamous cultures, this consensus-seeking process is of less relevance, as each woman needs to find her own mate. Some women therefore assemble mental tick lists of required characteristics or features to assist in their selection process.

The male's physical preferences are also affected by perceptions of health and vitality. In the 18th century, large women were considered attractive, as demonstrated by paintings of the time. This was because a fulsome shape implied good health and fertility. Now, being overweight is associated with poor health and men tend to prefer slimmer women, but not to the extent suggested by the media and advertisers. Before the advent of contraception, men would have had an incentive to sleep with a large number of women as by doing so they could have a significant impact on the human gene pool. A man will therefore tend to be less choosy, and more prepared to compromise his ideals, than a female. However, in monogamous cultures, the fact that men are obliged to restrict themselves to one female partner at any one time forces them to be more selective than they would otherwise be. The availability of contraception in modern society has also had an equalising effect as women can now lower their standards in the short-term in the knowledge that pregnancy is unlikely to arise and the resultant delay in women having children means that men who want to have a large family are more likely to achieve this objective if they commit to a partner early on in their lives.

Alpha males are high in extraversion and indifference. These traits promote the pursuit of sexual pleasure and competitive behaviour respectively so alpha males naturally compete to impregnate females. In primeval times, a dominant male would have had access to a large number of potential mates. Younger women would have been a better bet in terms of reproduction so they would have been most sought after. However, high death rates amongst early humans would have made it essential for fertile women of all ages to bear children. This explains why a male reaches his sexual peak at around the age of 18 whereas the female sexual peak is in the region of 35. Young men would have found it difficult to secure mating opportunities because older alpha males would have held power, allocated resources and controlled access to the fertile females. Young males would therefore have needed a lot of energy and perseverance, and would have had to quickly take advantage of the limited mating opportunities that came their way. A high sex drive would have spurred them on. In contrast, young women would have had no problems attracting the attention of males. Older women, however, would have had to work harder. An increased sex drive in their 30s would have motivated them to secure further mating opportunities.

There are also cultural and personality-related reasons why men tend to prefer younger women. In monogamous cultures, an alpha male's ability to father children will be much reduced. As a consequence, it is natural for them to prefer young, fertile women. It has been suggested that in assessing the attractiveness of a female partner men make a sub-conscious calculation as to the number of children she can have in her reproductive lifetime. A man who is high in extraversion will experience positive feelings and a boost to his self-esteem if he shows off a beautiful, young partner in public. Middle-aged men who are high in indifference and extraversion will sometimes compensate for their declining competitiveness by acquiring trophy wives or girlfriends.

Women who are approaching middle age are therefore at a significant disadvantage in the dating arena. The focus that many women place on their careers in modern society reduces their chances of them finding partners with whom to have children. Women are usually very aware of the ageing process and their declining fertility. They use cosmetics, locate themselves in environments with low lighting and undergo plastic surgery to make them appear younger or more attractive. However, in modern individualistic society, the ready availability of enjoyable experiences causes many women to gamble with their fertility by delaying pregnancy.

The researchers found that **status and resources** were significantly less important in terms of ideal characteristics than warmth and trustworthiness, and attractiveness and vitality. This category included the following attributes: "good job, financially secure, nice house, appropriate ethnicity, successful and dresses well". Lesser importance may be attached to this factor because humans have evolved primarily to rely on the strength of their group rather than on inanimate objects. Characteristics associated with warmth and trustworthiness, and attractiveness and vitality, help to create a sustainable family unit, whereas resources may be lost at any moment. In this context, the ability of a partner to provide protection and support through his on-going endeavours is more important than his financial position at the start of the relationship. However, the participants in the study were students so they may not yet have thought seriously about the practicalities of bringing up children. There was no significant difference in the importance attached to status and resources by males and females. The hierarchical structure of male groups encourages men to value status more than women whereas the need of women for protection and resources for their families causes women to be more concerned about securing these assets than men. Therefore, there may be a balancing effect when status and resources are grouped together as a single factor.

In summary, your relationship ideals will be closely related to your personality traits, but your choice of long-term partner will be influenced by your environment, including the structure of the groups to which you belong, and your objectives. As people begin to look forward to the practicalities of bringing up children, they are likely to compromise their ideals. Most young women have few responsibilities and have access to contraception so they are free to enter relationships with men that they find sexually attractive without giving much thought to the future. Once a woman starts to focus on having children she will typically look to form a partnership with a male who is capable of providing her and her future children with support, protection and resources. To some extent, she will look to compensate for her own deficiencies (i.e. she will look to establish a good working relationship). However, her choice will also be influenced by the nature of the threats within her environment. The acquisition of a suitable mate will increase her level of security, reduce her susceptibility to stress and allow her to experience strong positive feelings. Some men also make compromises, choosing to settle down with women who they perceive as likely to be good mothers. Men, though, tend to be more focused on achieving workplace objectives. Their on-average higher level of indifference makes them less aware of the needs of young children and the benefit to them of a harmonious home environment.

A traditional relationship where the man generates income and the woman looks after domestic matters is a reflection of the division of labour between men and women in the primal group. Their higher levels of indifference would have orientated males around hunting and defending the group, whereas the females' lower levels would have focused them on caring responsibilities and creating a harmonious domestic environment. The power dynamics within a relationship, the roles of partners, and the values they are expected to abide by will also be influenced by the partners' environment, including the culture of their wider group.

Where distinct human groups live close together and resources are plentiful, the establishments within these groups compete vigorously with each other and establishment cultures emerge. Members of the establishment are natural protectors and providers within such environments because their high levels of extraversion and indifference enable them to compete effectively for resources and their low levels of openness and opportunism enable them to build hierarchical organisational structures. Women therefore tend to be attracted to members of the establishment in dangerous, competitive environments and will seek the protection of the primal hierarchy. A man with progressive traits is less likely to be able to secure resources and offer protection in such circumstances, but he may make a more suitable partner in other environments. In an individualistic culture, status and wealth are more likely to accrue to men who are novelty seeking and flexible than those who are methodical and organised. In a collectivist culture, the stock of men who naturally promote fairness and harmony will rise. As progressive cultures are rare, men who possess all four progressive traits are likely to be the least attractive to women who are looking to establish a family. Their personalities correspond with the default culture of the female collective so their talents and skills are likely to already be available to women through the collective. However, a woman who feels safe, has a higher level of indifference or has access to resources may opt for such a man, as he is likely to be interesting, honest, caring and prepared to relieve her of some of her childcare responsibilities.

Like minds, soul mates and teammates

The nature of a relationship will be affected by the balance between high and low traits within it, and the distribution of traits between the partners. Although the female is likely to be lower in indifference and more caring than the male, the Slow System skills associated with the other trait spectrums, such as analysis, method and organisation, are not skewed towards one gender. If two people have middling personality traits, interaction between them will in normal circumstances generate feelings of enjoyment and contentment. As both partners will be suited to average environments, they are likely to share responsibilities. If their personality traits differ slightly, they will be able to use each other to regulate their moods. For example, a person who is low in extraversion and who has spent the day focused on analytical processes may be shifted into a state of enjoyment by the return home of his more outgoing partner. Where a person with middling traits establishes a relationship with a like mind, he is therefore likely to establish a strong social relationship without significantly compromising his ability to achieve his objectives.

A person who struggles to fit into society may attempt to find a soul mate – a like mind that shares his ambitions, fears and emotional pain. By forming a close bond, soul mates create a refuge from the negative feelings that they experience when interacting with wider society. Soul mates will usually have very similar personality traits, but they may also be drawn together by common problems or circumstances. A person with a like mind can help a partner who is incorrectly positioned within society discover his true personality and role in life by providing him with opportunities to express his natural behaviours. Partners who share the same extreme traits are, however, likely to face difficulties in navigating the complexities of life together due to their narrow combined skill set. Soul mates may both experience a decline in mental health in the longer term as a result.

Where differences in personality are substantial, a more volatile relationship is likely to result, causing the partners to experience stress and low moods on a regular basis. Such a relationship is likely to be held together by mutual dependency. For example, if a man who is high in extraversion and opportunism marries a woman who is low in extraversion and opportunism, the man is likely to depend on the woman to impose some control on his materialistic and impulsive tendencies whereas the woman is likely to depend on the man to secure resources and cope with changing circumstances. This type of relationship functions best when the partners perform distinct roles to which they are suited and a good working relationship develops based on the achievement of common objectives. In other words, when the partners work together as a team. If the relationship is to achieve its goals, the partners will have to respect the differing attributes of the other person and tolerate negative feelings caused by differences in their arousal levels. In other words, they will have to operate in the Co-operation Zone. If they succeed in doing so, their efforts are likely to result in a strong base on which to build a family due to their wide combined skill set. People are more likely to seek out partners with opposite traits when they are young as their lack of life skills makes a working relationship particularly beneficial for them. Such relationships are, though, likely to break down in the long term if the partners lose focus on their primary objective, which is usually the bringing up of children, or once that objective is achieved.

Relationships should, however, be seen in the context of a wider group. A single, monogamous relationship is too small to operate effectively as a human group. A couple will therefore need access to the resources and skills of other people. In modern society, many of the functions that are needed to support a family are outsourced. Tradesmen are engaged to maintain houses, food is sourced from supermarkets and children are educated in schools. In difficult times, though, you are more likely to be able to depend on people with whom you have a common interest than those you deal with on a purely commercial basis. Therefore, for most of the period in which humans have practised monogamy, couples have lived in extended family groups that have offered support and protection – a halfway house between the primal group and the nuclear family. Where both partners in a relationship are embedded within an extended family and possess a strong network of friends, they put less pressure on their relationship. They will be happier than partners who find themselves isolated either as a couple or individually within a relationship. If both partners have middling traits, the unit they establish is likely to fit within their community and benefit from a broad range of social and working relationships. If one or both of the partners possesses extreme traits, the couple will find it harder to fit in and access such assistance, and one or both partners may be marginalised.

Love

So where does love fit in? Psychologists have broken down love into subcategories such as passionate love, romantic love, infatuation and companionate love. Individuals do not make such distinctions and, if asked, tend to have a rather unclear concept of love.

The reality is that our personality traits, experiences and environment set each of us up to perceive and experience love in a unique and individual way. Our experience of love also alters as we age and gain experience, and as a relationship progresses.

You feel love towards people who enable you to experience positive feelings on a sustainable basis. All forms of love involve a reliance on your partner, relative or friend for stimulation, protection or support. It is the permanence of this connection that distinguishes love from other feelings. When two people love each other, there will be mutual dependency. The nature of this dependency will vary from couple to couple. It may be limited to sexual gratification or the parties' interests may be deeply entangled. If a person has reason to question the other person's commitment to that bargain, or his own dependence ceases, feelings of love will dissipate. In the first instance, these feelings will be replaced by anxiety or other negative feelings. In the second, new objectives, a change to his environment or use of mood enhancers may cause him to transfer his affections to another person who is better able satisfy his needs and wants or decide that he can survive without a relationship.

The nature of the feelings you experience when you are in love will depend on the balance of your needs and wants at that particular time, which will be influenced by your personality traits and your sex drive. Passionate love is associated with high trait, wanting behaviours such as sexual conquest, adventure and experimentation. Companionate love is characterised by a deep commitment to one another and occurs where passion has subsided, but deep affection remains. It is therefore founded on the stabilising, needing behaviours prompted by low traits. In the absence of sexual attraction, you may experience platonic or familial love.

Falling in love can be a rollercoaster of highs and lows. A sexual relationship potentially marks the separation of the participants from their existing groups and the creation of a new group. There is, therefore, a lot at stake, and this pressure raises arousal levels and promotes excitement. The possibility or likelihood of missing out on such an opportunity can generate strong negative feelings, such as anger, frustration, envy and jealousy, resulting in wild mood swings between joy and despair. Extreme mood swings are most often associated with youth when sex hormones are at high levels, group bonds are weak and the experience of love is novel. Surges of dopamine create feelings of elation while heightened testosterone levels and the societal pressure placed on individuals to find and retain a partner promote competition and mistrust.

Partners move in and out of sync as their individual objectives, environments and hormone levels change. In any long-term relationship there will be times when one or both partners are not receiving the stimulation, protection or support from the other that they need to sustain feelings of love. The maintenance of a relationship requires partners to take a pragmatic approach to many issues, but to sustain love it helps to retain a degree of idealism. Putting somebody on a pedestal can prevent you from moving on or leave you open to abuse, but nourishing a sense of wonder and reverence towards your partner can help to sustain a relationship through difficult times. There is some evidence to suggest that our minds help us to do so by causing us to perceive long-term partners visually as more youthful than they actually are. This may be because frequent contact makes it harder for people to notice the subtle process of ageing or because current feelings towards a partner will be coloured by the recollection of memories of positive shared experiences. When a person looks at his partner with affection, he may tap into such memories and superimpose them over the current reality.

As the experience of love is directly related to the receipt of stimulation, protection or support, a person who is correctly located within a group and benefits from a favourable culture will experience a lot of love whereas a person who is and does not is likely to be deprived of it. A person in the former situation will spread his love around whereas a person who is dislocated or marginalised within his group is likely to focus it unhealthily on a single person when he gets an opportunity. People whose groups have disintegrated find it particularly difficult to find love. Modern, individualistic society encourages people to seek passionate love and spread their net wider geographically. Many people waste enormous amounts of time on online dating sites trying to arrange dates with prospective partners who are completely disconnected from them. This reduces the time they have available to interact with people in their local communities and participate in activities that would strengthen their relationship networks and develop platonic love within them. Sexual relationships that are formed online tend to break up after a short period due to the lack of stabilising influences.

Relationship structures

The discussion so far in this chapter has been based on two assumptions: firstly, that we naturally establish long-term monogamous relationships; and secondly, that a female's partner is partly determined by her environment. These two assumptions are, however, inconsistent because the fact that there are roughly equal numbers of males and females in human groups means that in a monogamous culture males who are less well equipped to cope with the current environment will still secure mates. The first assumption is in fact not always true. Other relationship structures have existed within human society at various times, most commonly **polygyny** (where a powerful man has sexual relationships with more than one woman at the same time). So what factors determine the relationship structure that humans adopt?

Species that engage in polygyny are characterised by significant gender differences in size and physiology. In polygynous cultures, males must compete intensely for mates. Over time, sexual selection causes males to increase in size and strength, or to develop features that are attractive to females. For example, male gorillas are much larger than females. However, there tend to be few differences in size or appearance in species that are monogamous. Human males are generally larger than females, but often not greatly so. Also, if one ignores the sexual organs, there is relatively little difference physiologically between the two sexes. Males from polygynous species have larger testicles than those from monogamous ones, as dominant males need to distribute their sperm amongst multiple partners. It is also advantageous for them to produce large amounts of sperm because, where females engage in sexual intercourse with two partners in close succession, sperm from both males will compete to reach the egg. On average, human males have much smaller testicles in relation to their size than gorillas, but larger ones than monogamous apes.

Certain hormones appear to promote pair bonding. Oxytocin prompts romantic behaviour and emotional connection between human partners. It is released during acts of intimate contact such as kissing, cuddling and orgasm, when a woman lactates and by babies, and encourages a male to become attached to a female and to offer protection and support to her and her children during this challenging period. Vasopressin may also play a part in pair bonding by promoting possessive behaviours and feelings such as aggression and jealousy. However, other behaviours prompted by hormonal changes suggest that men and women have not evolved to form long-term monogamous partnerships. Males maintain steady levels of testosterone from day to day and usually remain capable of siring children throughout their lifetime. They are essentially primed to take advantage of a mating opportunity whenever it arises. Their testosterone levels are increased by about four times in the presence of a fertile female. However, fertile females are only capable of conceiving during a six-day window in their monthly menstrual cycle. During this window, a female's hormonal balance will change, causing her to be sexually attracted to men with high testosterone levels. She will be drawn towards males who will compete for the right to mate with her. Her testosterone level will also rise, which will help her withstand this competitive environment and encourage her to be more selfish in pursuit of a mate. During the remainder of her cycle, her hormonal balance will deter her from close association with males and she will be inclined to spend time with the female collective.

It is interesting that following sexual intercourse, males and females often display incompatible behaviours. A male is likely to fall asleep while the female feels the need for hugging and the display of tenderness. On the face of it, this seems illogical. This may, however, be a primeval mechanism that allows a second male access to the female. It would take the dominant male out of the equation and allow another male, perhaps one with more caring and sympathetic tendencies, his opportunity for procreation. This would have helped to maintain diversity within the species.

There is, therefore, little evidence to suggest that we are biologically compelled to establish long-term monogamous relationships. Marriage is considered by many young women to be a key objective in life. However, it was probably first introduced within groups with polygynous relationship structures as a means of controlling women. If a woman is free to have sexual liaisons with multiple men, there will be uncertainty as to the paternity of her children. In such circumstances, leading males will not be able to establish strong bonds with their sons and create powerful dynasties. Traditionally, marriage ceremonies required the wife to be subservient to her husband. Practices like the wearing of the hijab, niqab and burqa, and female genital mutilation, also restrict the freedom of, or reduce the incentive for, women to associate with other men. Marriage remains a key element of the empire building strategies of establishment men although they will often have sexual relationships with other women concurrently and therefore in reality be practising polygyny. Such men usually oppose abortion as it gives women the power to restrict the development of their hierarchies, and deprive their wives, and women generally, of career and learning resources to limit their ability to engage with the wider world.

Members of the establishment become more powerful where human groups compete against each other as other group members look to them to provide protection and secure resources. They exploit this power in the sexual arena and this results in the adoption of polygynous relationship structures. Polygyny is therefore associated with groups that have establishment cultures. Long-term monogamous relationships are associated with collectivist culture because they promote stabilising behaviours associated with the four low traits: conformity, organisation, fairness and collaboration. In groups with a collectivist culture, the male and female are equal partners, but have distinct responsibilities in the working and domestic environments respectively. Men and women are encouraged to marry and establish a family early.

The practice of men and women living together in monogamous marriages for life was promoted by Christianity, but has also existed for millennia in some Eastern cultures, most notably the Chinese. Islam permits a man to have up to four wives, but most

Muslim men have a single wife. Most Western countries have laws that prevent a person from marrying a second person whilst already married. The direction of travel has, therefore, been towards monogamous marriage. It has been suggested that monogamy may have been initially adopted to make it easier for men to go on hunting expeditions. According to this theory, men would have felt more comfortable leaving their partners in the company of other men if they had committed to a pair bond. However, it is more likely that monogamy outcompeted other relationship structures because its practice reduces infighting amongst males and re-directs their energy away from sexual conquest towards other activities that are more beneficial to the group including aiding the development of the group's children.

As polygynous societies transitioned to monogamous ones, the establishment's informal ownership rights over females devolved to individual males. Consequently, when a man married a woman, he would have seen his wife and daughters as his personal property and would have instinctively tried to prevent them from consorting with other males. This instinct lies behind the battle for control and freedom between a father and his daughter in her teenage years. Religion was used to restrict the influence of women, obliging them to submit to the authority of their husbands. Therefore, although monogamy is associated with collectivist culture, for much of recorded history leading males were able to limit the influence of the female collective and maintain an establishment culture.

The adoption of long-term monogamous relationships in Western society forced men and women to make compromises regarding their sexual partners. Although it is commonly perceived that women attempt to tie men down into marriage, it is women in general who make the greater sacrifice materially and genetically. In primeval times, most men would have had limited mating opportunities because they would have been outcompeted by alpha males. However, in monogamous cultures, alpha males are obliged to restrain their instinct to compete for women. They are only allowed to marry one woman and will struggle to maintain relationships with a large number of women at the same time. The typical male, therefore, benefits greatly from monogamy, as he is much more likely to secure a mate.

In contrast, most females lose the protection of an establishment male and access to his resources. Monogamous cultures compel women to compete for the most desirable mates. Those women who do not succeed in marrying a member of the establishment will be forced to form relationships with members of the rank and file who are likely to lack ambition, or men with progressive traits who may struggle to fit into society, if they wish to start a family. These men will be much less likely to accumulate resources than members of the establishment. This leaves a lot of scope for dissatisfaction on the woman's part. From an early age, females are encouraged to look forward to their wedding day. Perhaps this is a mechanism to help a bride overcome her sense of disappointment at having to compromise her ideals. Their on average low level of indifference means that women in general are unsuited to competition and are likely to experience anxiety or chronic stress in competitive environments. Monogamy therefore promotes feelings of fear, jealousy and resentment within the female collective. What is more, when a woman marries a man, he is psychologically elevated to the position of alpha male. This boosts his self-esteem, increases his confidence and encourages him to bask in his enhanced glory rather than perform helpful tasks. Many men complain that they cannot understand the minds of women, but they do not consider that they may be the root cause of what they perceive to be erratic behaviour.

A monogamous culture will, though, free large numbers of women from the grip of members of the establishment. Other males will be less likely to be ruthless or controlling, or more likely to be considerate or caring, than establishment men. They may, therefore, allow their wives to exercise more influence within the relationship. Many women are not naturally suited to partner alpha males. Some will be inclined to behave more liberally or freely than such a male would allow, or have an instinct to explore or dominate. Women who possess establishment traits may take over the role of dominant male in monogamous relationships and exert control over their male partners.

The propensity for males to use force to resolve issues means that many women are exposed to domestic violence within monogamous relationships. While a woman may be able to seek emotional support from other female friends, the lack of physical presence of the female collective means that she can be more easily isolated and abused. Of course, some men are abused within relationships, although this is more likely to take the form of emotional abuse; for example, where a woman undermines a man's self-esteem. Men who are low in indifference are particularly vulnerable as they will struggle to compete against other males and provide resources for their family, and will be inclined to adopt submissive behaviour.

Our familiarity with monogamy has probably deceived us into thinking that humans are naturally inclined to develop long-term monogamous relationships when in fact monogamy is a cultural phenomenon. The range of personality traits within human populations actually allows for four basic relationship structures to emerge depending on environmental conditions and group culture: polygyny, monogamy, polyandry and polyamory. **Polyandry** occurs when a single female has multiple male partners. **Polyamory** occurs when males and females have multiple partners with the knowledge and consent of all partners.

Polyandry promotes the sharing of resources and responsibilities by males. It therefore gives females more freedom. If a female mates with several males before becoming pregnant, she is likely to receive support from more than one male during pregnancy and beyond. Each male will instinctively know that she may be carrying his offspring and will therefore have an interest in the survival of her children. In some primate species, where multiple males have mated with a single female, the potential fathers compete to look after her infant after it is born. In polyandrous cultures, females tend to have fewer children than they would otherwise do, as they are not required to submit to males. This can limit population growth and enhance child survival. Polyandrous practices are associated with progressive cultures because they promote personal freedom, fairness and harmony.

Polyandry equates to a transfer of power from the establishment to the female collective. Members of the establishment are forced to submit to the will of females, resulting in a matriarchal society. Polyandry occurs rarely because it is only possible where male competitive instincts are restrained. The female collective's primary weapon in the battle of the sexes is the use sexual favours. If women engage sexually with men on a frequent basis, they maximise the effect of oxytocin, reducing male aggressiveness and promoting harmony, and gain more influence over them. Such behaviour therefore weakens the bond between the establishment and the rest of the primal hierarchy. If a woman mates with multiple males at the same time, she weakens the connection between her sons and their fathers because her mates will be unable to determine with certainty whether they have fathered her children. If she moves from one partner to another after giving birth, she will reduce the contact time between her sons and their fathers. In both cases, she will in a position to exert more influence over their behaviour and values. Bonobos, who along with chimps are our closest primate cousins, live with a polyandrous culture. Sexual activity is very apparent in bonobo society and is used by females as a means of limiting the power of alpha males and promoting social cohesion.

It is interesting to view prostitution in this light. Prostitution is a polyandrous behaviour because prostitutes benefit from the support of multiple men. However, it also benefits men because it allows them to experience the pleasure of sexual intercourse without expending effort on courtship or incurring continuing obligations. Prostitution therefore weakens the bargaining power of women who are seeking to establish or maintain long-term relationships with such men. Also, because prostitutes operate independently of the female collective, they leave themselves open to exploitation by pimps and market forces; they are not able to engage in collective bargaining. In a truly polyandrous culture, competition is restrained and women work together, using sexual favours and other tools at their disposal to secure resources and assistance from males for common benefit.

Polyandry is most likely to emerge in harsh environments where natural resources are scarce and where there is little threat from other human groups. In such circumstances, competition for resources within a group is likely to result in wasted resources and divert men away from productive labour, threatening the viability of the group. Where women control a group's resources, they are more likely than men to redistribute them to those in need and are less likely to resort to war to improve the group's access to resources. Because resources are scarce in mountainous regions, there is a strong incentive to share and avoid inter-group conflict. It is not therefore surprising that polyandry was practised in Himalayan communities.

Progressive cultures oblige husbands and men generally to adopt behaviours and pursue activities that align with the female collective's primary objective – to promote the security, health and development of children. In societies with progressive cultures, social security systems, divorce settlements and child support legislation enable a woman to retain access to resources after separation from her partner. Therefore, in effect, a woman can benefit from the work of multiple men at the same time. Establishment men find such polyandrous practices distasteful because they only have an interest in supporting women and children for as long as they remain under their control and are supporting the development of a hierarchy beneath them. Therefore, they seek to water down or eliminate such rights. Societal structures that promote monogamy such as Christian marriage limit the power of establishment men, but they also prevent the adoption of a truly polyandrous culture and therefore the full empowerment of the female collective.

Polyamorous relationships are associated with individualistic cultures and high trait sexual behaviours such as competition for mates, intimate physical contact, short-term relationships, experimentation and spontaneous interactions. The phrase polyamorous relationship is, though, an oxymoron as polyamorous behaviours undermine long-term relationships. The absence of stabilising low trait influences promotes orgiastic behaviours orientated around the pursuit of enjoyment, causing individuals to neglect responsibilities to family members and destabilising society as a consequence.

An individualistic culture enables a woman to marry a male without losing her freedom in other aspects of her life, such as the working environment. However, it also undermines relationships by encouraging partners to pursue enjoyable experiences without regard for the likely long-term consequences of their actions. Monogamy is embedded within the culture of countries like the UK so few people have multiple partners at the same time. However, many people move quickly from one relationship to another or are seeking new relationships. According to the UK's most recent census, over 50% of adults are either living together in non-marital partnerships or are single.

Although societies with monogamous cultures have been most successful in terms of numbers of people, of the 1,231 societies listed in the 1980 Ethnographic Atlas, only 186 were found to be monogamous; 453 practised occasional polygyny; 588 practised more frequent polygyny, but only 4 practised polyandry. Polyamory was not considered as a category, probably because it was not viewed as a form of relationship given its fluid nature. It is, though, misleading to attribute a single relationship structure to a society because the real picture will be much more diverse. For human groups to work effectively, they need to maintain a wide range of different skills and personalities within them. A typical early human group would have been quite large, numbering about 150 people, making it impossible for the dominant male to control all females within it. It is therefore likely that a variety of relationship structures would have existed within a group at any one time and that a person would have been drawn towards polygynous, monogamous, polyandrous or polyamorous relationships depending on his personality traits. Evidence for this theory can be found in the groups of chimpanzees. There are several mating patterns in chimp groups, but they do not form long-term monogamous relationships. The dominant male of the group shows possessive behaviour towards fertile females and attempts to prevent other males from mating with them. However, he is not able to mate with all females within the group. The numbers are against him, so other males are able to gain access to them. Females who are inclined to wander out of his sight are free to engage with males who occupy positions on the margins of the group. A popular female may develop a troop of male admirers. In this case, rather than directly competing with each other, these males adopt submissive, adoring behaviour.

Most people's traits do not fit neatly within a particular relationship structure, either because they do not possess all four relevant traits or because they possess middling ones. People with middling traits tend to adopt a structure that is suited to their environment or dictated by their group's culture. However, any group or society that attempts to impose a single relationship structure on its members will inevitably cause people who are not suited to that structure to experience stress or low moods. In cultures that promote long-term monogamous relationships, many people find themselves locked in relationships that cause them to experience negative feelings. Such people may relieve negative feelings by viewing pornography, having affairs, using prostitutes or swinging. Therefore, polygynous, polyandrous or polyamorous relationships and practices still occur within such cultures. They are just pushed into the shadows.

Relationship formation

Alpha males have evolved to be ruthless in their pursuit of mates. As a consequence, they often have multiple sexual partners. As in other situations, people with relevant high traits tend to have an advantage because they can see the big picture. For alpha males, the big picture is impregnation, not the formation of a relationship, although relationships are important to establishment males because they are the means by which they build hierarchies beneath them. A woman may feel hurt or betrayed if her mate ignores her after a one-night stand or has an affair, but these acts are a natural consequence of the alpha male's desire for sexual conquest. Men who are low in extraversion and low indifference will find it harder to secure dates or establish sexual relationships than alpha males. Opportunities are likely to pass them by before their trust building processes have been completed. Their cautious approaches may cause potential partners to lose interest or allow an alpha male to step in. Also, men with these traits will lack the ability to see the big picture in terms of procreation, and instead tend to focus on minor details that are unimportant in the great scheme of things. For example, a man who is low in extraversion may delay physical intimacy because he is unsure how to initiate it or worries about the reaction of the female. Similarly, a man who is low in indifference is not likely to adopt the ruthless behaviour needed to outcompete other males, such as lying about his long-term intentions, and may refrain from expressing his feelings for fear of introducing tension into the environment. Many women see such men as unsuitable mates as they perceive them as losers, which in reality they generally are if you judge a person's success by his ability to secure status and resources. Men with these traits may, therefore, develop a fear of rejection and avoidant behaviour, which deters them from asking women out. They will, though, be helpful by nature and see women as equals rather than sexual objects. As a result, they will often have a wide circle of female friends.

One saying that is often used as evidence of the differences between men and women is that "men need to have sex to feel loved whereas women need to feel loved to have sex". This is, in fact, an expression of our natural instincts. Alpha males are likely to feel fulfilled once they have ejaculated. A woman, however, will be seeking a demonstration that a potential partner is capable of, and willing to, protect her and her child during her pregnancy and thereafter. A woman will, therefore, expect a certain degree of commitment to be demonstrated by a potential partner before she is prepared to give away her valuable fertility. A man who is attentive to his prospective partner's needs and gives her presents will give the impression that he will be kind to his children and an effective provider. If he demonstrates that he understands and is prepared to follow rules and conventions, he is more likely to be able to fit in his wider group and benefit from the protection and support that it offers.

It is in the interests of the female to distinguish between fickle or opportunistic alpha males and members of the establishment. The former are more likely to leave females in the lurch following sexual intercourse whereas the latter are likely to provide their partners with protection and resources on a continuing basis. A man who is high in openness is likely to be interesting due to the variety of his activities, but he will also be less likely to assemble a loyal group of solid friends around him than a man who is low in openness. This means he is less likely to be able to perform the role of protector and provider. The opportunistic behaviour of males who are high in opportunism may provide excitement, but it also makes them unreliable.

A male will therefore usually have to give his prospective partner an opportunity to assess him, if he is to secure her as a mate. Courtship or dating is a skill acquired through the refinement of method and practice. A woman may feel hurt when she finds out that a particular poem or song, which she perceived to be personal to her, was recited or sung to previous girlfriends. However, men who are low in openness will naturally refine techniques that have proved to work in the past and men who are low in opportunism will try to manipulate situations so that they can deploy favoured routines. Members of the establishment are, of course, low in openness and opportunism. As they are also high in extraversion and indifference, they receive more interest from females than other males and therefore get more opportunity to practice. As a result, they will usually be confident on the dating scene. Men who are high in openness or opportunism are likely to be less successful and therefore less confident. The former will constantly be trying out new strategies and will therefore struggle to develop reliable dating techniques. The latter will not be able to follow dating protocols due to their spontaneous and disorganised nature.

The dynamics described in this chapter are very evident in Internet dating. Alpha males tend to play a numbers game, assuming that the more approaches they make, the more likely they will be successful. Females of childbearing age tend to be contacted by large numbers of potential suitors while older women receive fewer approaches. Women tend to be choosier than men, focusing on a much more limited number of potential mates. However, because of their more selective approach, a large number of women will be targeting a smaller number of men. Many women therefore find that men they date quickly move on to new targets. A large number of them remain single, waiting in anticipation, while their fertility declines. The online dating format makes it easier for alpha males to maintain liaisons with multiple women at the same time. Meanwhile, many non-alphas remain single as a result of them failing to meet the selection criteria of potential partners. They are often rejected before being given a chance to exercise dating techniques or release sex hormones in face-to-face meetings. The wide geographic coverage of online dating sites encourages people to ignore potential partners in their immediate physical environment who at first instance may be less attractive, but may present a better bet in the longer term. Therefore, although the Internet allows a person to make contact with a large number of potential partners, many subscribers to dating sites do not secure partners through them, and the relationships that are formed tend to be short-term and sexually orientated.

Other dynamics within modern, individualistic society also make it harder to form long-term relationships. People are busier and have diverse and geographically widespread friendship networks so they have less time to invest in relationship building. Women have greater access to well-paid and rewarding careers so they are inclined to delay marrying and starting a family. Such a woman may not realise until it is too late that ageing is making her less attractive to potential mates. Financially successful women who are attracted to alpha males find it particularly difficult to find mates because they tend to rule out men who earn less than them. The increased sexual freedom available to women has also made it more difficult for those women wishing to settle down to find a partner. This is because the more women who are available on the dating scene, the more dates and short-term relationships will be available to single men. One of the factors that encourage a man to commit to a woman is the fear that his options may be narrowing and that he may be left alone or be marginalised within friendship circles that are becoming dominated by couples.

Although a monogamous culture gives the average person a much greater likelihood of establishing a long-term relationship than other forms of relationship structure, some people will not do so. This may be because their personality traits are not suited to such relationships or because circumstances have prevented them from forming them. A long-term relationship is usually founded on the common understanding that children are likely to result from it. Most women grow up believing that they will have children one day. Some, though, are sure that they do not want children, or are ambivalent towards that decision. For example, a high trait orientated woman may want to retain her freedom and enjoy moving from one short-term relationship to another. Others experience anxiety as a result of their inability to decide whether they want children or not. Such indecision indicates that the pros and cons are finely balanced, or that there are unknowns that cannot be factored into the decision-making process. In life, where you are forced to make a big, irreversible decision with equally balanced but uncertain outcomes that cannot be clarified by further investigation, the best course of action is to make a decision and move on. Delaying a decision and worrying about potential outcomes will not improve your situation unless some random factor intervenes to your benefit. If it turns out that you made the wrong decision in hindsight, you must reach an accommodation with yourself and make the most of your current situation.

Most males are not members of the establishment so they are not naturally inclined to take on the responsibility of protecting and providing for a family. They will, therefore, be less likely than women to regret not having children. They are more likely to focus on potential sexual liaisons that have failed to materialise. Opportunities to establish sexual relationships are often fleeting and the circumstances of life mean that they rarely come around again with the same person. A person may feel regret after making an error which resulted in rejection or a missed opportunity, but regret is simply a prompt for him to learn from his mistake. Once he has learned the lesson, he is more likely to be successful when a new opportunity arises.

In modern society, people waste enormous amounts of time on dating sites when they could be doing something more useful, which might as a by-product introduce them to potential partners. Relationship management and childcare are also time-consuming activities and can prevent people from performing other important tasks. Most people have middling personality traits that suit them to bringing up a family. People with more extreme traits are, however, likely to have more unusual talents or be suited to performing specialist skills. The demands of a family can prevent them from maximising their potential. There is a famous saying that "behind every great man is a great woman", but perhaps more accurately it should read: "behind every great man is a strong, miserable woman". Some of the greatest men in history, like Charles Darwin, only achieved what they did because they neglected their wives and left them to deal with family responsibilities alone. As humans have evolved to promote the success of groups, not individuals, there is no need for every person, and particularly every man, to participate in the reproductive process. Being single need not condemn a person to isolation and unhappiness. The flexibility of human personality and the wide variety of roles that need to be performed within modern society give individuals many opportunities to use their talents and skills in ways that can move human civilisation forward. Many people are motivated to use dating sites by their need to relieve feelings of insecurity and loneliness. If society functioned in a more balanced way, people would be able focus on performing their natural roles with the confidence that their wider family group, community or national government would meet their future need for support and protection.

Lost love and relationship breakdown

A very strong emotional connection may be established within a long-term relationship. Each partner may become the other's supreme source of energy and comfort, regulating his levels of arousal and maintaining his positive state. In other words, partners may become emotionally dependent on each other. Where a person is suddenly deprived of such a partner, he will feel very vulnerable and experience a great sense of loss. As a result, people who are separated, divorced or widowed are often forced into spontaneous and piecemeal actions of regulation (for example, taking drugs and alcohol).

A person can feel intense feelings of loss when a relationship breaks down in its initial stages, or even when he experiences unrequited love. A relationship may fail to develop for a number of reasons including a lack of mutual attraction, a breakdown of communication between the partners, a mismatch in their status or confidence, differences in the partners' objectives, poor timing, the presence of incumbent partners, the intervention of competitors, or interference by friends or relatives. However, individuals can very quickly become dependent on the positive feelings that another person generates within them. Our ability to look ahead enables us to mentally bank positive feelings that we envisage in future scenarios. Consequently, a person may be deeply affected by the failure of a relationship to progress beyond its initial stages. The subject of his affection may have no idea of the personal investment that he has made in the relationship, or the feelings of love he is experiencing. This is most likely to be the case when the person experiencing restrains the expression of his feelings due to insecurity or lack of confidence.

The feelings of sadness that you experience when you suffer a loss encourage you to repair the damage to your group. In the context of the breakdown of a relationship, the natural reaction is to seek a replacement partner. Some people stay single for a while, using that time to process information relating to the break up and rebuild their friendship and family groups. These recovery steps help them to overcome feelings of hurt and increase their security, enabling them to move on and take further risks in the dating arena. Others rebound, jumping into a new relationship without giving their Slow Systems time to learn from the experience. Their new relationships are less likely to be successful because such a person is likely to seek out a partner with similar characteristics to his previous partner. There will be a strong chance of him either going through the same experience again with the new partner or resolving the cause of the breakdown of the previous relationship at some point and recognising the unsuitability of his new partner as a result.

Rejection and relationship break ups in early life may cause a person to become more skilled or realistic in identifying potential partners. Such accommodations are necessary as people age because their energy levels and attractiveness usually reduce, making it harder for them to satisfy their ideals. Many people hold candles for people in their pasts, but establish rewarding relationships with new partners subsequently. However, if you dream of ideal mates and perfect family environments, but cannot reconcile those dreams with the reality of your current relationship, you are likely to become bitter or resentful.

Some people are prevented from moving on by the fear of experiencing further hurt or disappointment at the hands of a new partner, or embarrassment or ridicule in relation to their wider group. Their inability to escape the trauma of a rejection or break up may cause them to avoid situations that could result in the formation of a new relationship or inhibit their ability to develop strong feelings of attachment in relation to new partners. Other people struggle to find a partner who can generate the same level of positive feeling within them as their former lovers. If a relationship is severed at the peak of enjoyment and satisfaction, it can be particularly difficult to move on. Those positive feelings become a marker by which potential partners are measured.

As people age and become more experienced, the process of entering a relationship becomes more familiar and the levels of sex hormones circulating in their bodies drop. Their emotional responses will be less volatile as a result. This enables them to establish sexual relationships in a more balanced way, and improves their chances of establishing a stable relationship. As pure sexual attraction diminishes, the balance of personality traits within a relationship becomes more relevant. When people have complex objectives to achieve, such as child rearing, they will tend to look for partners with whom they can establish good working relationships. In later life, they have more freedom to develop social relationships. People who lack confidence or skills in dating are, though, likely to find it even harder to establish relationships once they enter middle age. There will be fewer opportunities for them to build confidence, as potential partners are likely to be less tolerant of breaches of dating protocols, and the skill gap will be harder to bridge, when sexual desire is burning less brightly.

A person who is suited to his environment will be better placed to secure a replacement mate, as he is more likely to be surrounded by people with whom he gets on. People with middling traits tend to find it easier to move on, as they are more likely to meet people with whom they are compatible. People who are dislocated or possess extreme traits find it much more difficult to establish new relationships because there will be fewer people around them who can satisfy their demands for exhilaration or need for security. Other people will be restricted in their ability to establish relationships by mental or physical characteristics or deficiencies, a lack of material assets, unfavourable environmental circumstances or the ageing process.

Some people cannot cope with the negative feelings they experience when they are alone. This explains why women who are abused by their partners often return to them or form a new relationship with another man with similar characteristics. Such a woman is likely to have at least one extreme personality trait that makes her susceptible to sustained stress, anxiety or suppression in normal circumstances, but less so in the presence of her partner. She may be able to overcome the blow to her self-esteem of revealing the abuse to others, and the fear of her partner seeking retribution, but in the absence of a group that is capable of providing the protection and support she needs, she returns to the arms of a person who she knows can make her feel good at least for some of the time.

Humans have developed the capacity to relieve feelings of loss associated with lost love and broken relationships by applying their skills and talents to alternative projects and objectives. A sense of loss can imbue a person with a sense of purpose and drive him on to achieve great things. By engaging in such loss transference, he can rebuild his self-esteem and justify the breakdown. A famous example occurred in 1791 when the Earl of Longford refused Arthur Wellesley permission to marry his sister, Kitty Pakenham, because he considered him to lack prospects. Arthur was devastated by the rebuttal. He enjoyed making music, but he burnt his violins and resolved to pursue a military career in earnest. He became possibly Britain's greatest ever general, defeating Napoleon at Waterloo in 1815 and was given the title of Duke of Wellington.

We have seen that humans have not evolved to live together in long-term, monogamous relationships. Where partners are like minds or soul mates, their relationship may endure. In many cases, however, and particularly when partners possess opposing traits, a relationship will have a natural, finite term. Once the woman feels that she can survive without the support and protection of her partner, the dynamics of the relationship change and the partners will be set on a course towards separation. The bargain on which the relationship was founded – the submission of a female to a male in exchange for protection and the provision of resources for the purpose of creating the next generation – no longer has any relevance.

Infidelity is to some degree a reaction against the imposition of long-term monogamous relationships on people who are unsuited to them. Although it may relieve pressures that have built up in a relationship, it undermines the innocent party's bargaining position by reducing his partner's dependence on him. Also, if it is discovered, the innocent party will lose trust in his partner, making the relationship less robust and reducing its effectiveness. In the modern world, infidelity by a husband is more likely to result in relationship break up than in previous times, as divorce is now more socially acceptable.

In primeval times, partners would probably have separated at the point a child was weaned. In modern society, many women do not feel secure enough to instigate divorce proceedings until their children have left home. They are likely to be more concerned about the potential damage that divorce can cause to family life and the mental health of their children than their male partners, due to their lower levels of indifference. However, women are more inclined to sever dysfunctional relationships in societies that support single mothers financially and enable them to secure equitable divorce settlements (i.e. ones with progressive cultures). In countries with individualistic cultures like the UK, the bonds that partners establish with each other are weaker. Marriage is less common and individuals more selfish, so relationships are easier to terminate. Marriages tend to be stronger in collectivist and establishment cultures, but infidelity is more common as a consequence. In establishment cultures, women are likely to be punished severely if then engage in adultery, but in collectivist cultures the more equal balance of power means that it is often acceptable for both men and women to take lovers, as was historically common in France.

Quitting a relationship may allow you to access feelings of excitement or relief in the short term, but this does not mean that you will be better off in the long term because you may not be able to find a replacement partner and may find yourself lacking in support and protection in later life. One reason why it is generally harder to establish strong relationships as you age is because your prospective partner is more likely to be firmly embedded within his own group. When people are younger they have more freedom to forge a new path, but in later life they tend to balance their commitment to a new relationship with their obligations to their existing groups. This is why it is so refreshing to meet up with friends you made when you were young. Those relationships were formed at a time when you were building your social group and system of support and protection around you. You were not required to make compromises and this gives these relationships a particular purity and energy.

Long-term relationships tend to weaken as the partners enter middle and old age. In humans, pure sexual attraction is masked to a significant degree by other factors related to our personality traits that encourage us to seek the company of the opposite sex. These include the pleasure of physical contact, the excitement of meeting someone new, the thrill of romance, the desire to build a family and the need for security. As they age, however, females become less sexually attractive to males and naturally spend more time associating with other females. Some middle-aged men have affairs with younger women. However, most find that their libidos decline or recognise that their ability to compete for fertile women is much reduced. They tend to spend more time bonding with other men or pursuing solitary activities. Both partners in the relationship will still need some protection and support, but once the children have left home, it becomes easier to obtain help from other sources. Of course, this does not mean that men and women in middle or later age cannot establish or maintain loving relationships. Such relationships are, however, likely to be founded upon social compatibility.

The acceptability of divorce within modern, individualistic society has resulted in a large increase in the number of single-parent families and older single people. Both men and women are at risk of becoming isolated when long-term relationships end in mid or later life. Women, however, generally find it easier to rebuild friendship circles because of the inclusive nature of the female collective. When a couple splits up, it is usually the woman that takes primary responsibility for looking after any children. Although she may receive financial support from her former partner, she is likely to face additional pressures as she takes on responsibilities that her partner used to perform. She is, though, likely to receive support from other women, as women tend to share their resources. Men find it more difficult than women to rebuild supportive structures because bonds within male groups are built up over many years. They tend to be distrustful of other men who they do not know well. Underlying this lack of a trust is a fear that their interests will be compromised. As men age, they become increasingly aware of the threat to their position in society presented by younger males. As a consequence, they become protective of their resources. A man will feel even more insecure if his wife divorces him and takes their children and a large proportion of the marital assets with her.

Most people will be deprived of further opportunities to reproduce at some point by younger, more attractive competitors, or as a result of declining fertility or the breakdown of relationships. Coming to terms with this reality can be challenging as there is no stronger purpose within humans than reproduction, and the feelings of exhilaration and fulfilment involved in the process are difficult to replace. High trait orientated people can find it difficult to accept the compromises forced upon them by their declining sexual attraction and reduced marketability. A low trait orientated person will struggle to cope with the loss of security he experiences when he is unable to replace a mate. At this point, feeling a sense of belonging to a group and having a broader group of people to love, and who love you, in a platonic or familial sense becomes much more important.

Maintaining healthy relationships

A relationship is likely to be sustainable if it is established between two people with similar personality traits or who have shared objectives, and those partners are embedded within a broader group that gives them support and protection. Some people establish dysfunctional relationships because they have failed to recover from loss, lack confidence, are dislocated from their natural position within the primal group structure, belong to an unbalanced or undersized group, or have been forced to comply with societal rules.

A couple is too small a group to survive independently of other people. In the absence of assistance from others, the partners will be exposed to negative feelings as they attempt tasks to which they are unsuited or are exposed to situations that make them fearful or cause them harm. The culture of society will also affect the feelings of partners and effectiveness of a relationship. If a person feels obliged to adopt a particular relationship structure that does not suit his personality traits, he will experience negative feelings. The dynamics within a relationship are affected by changes in the partners' individual circumstances and the environment in which the relationship exists. Such changes alter the balance of needs and wants within the relationship, potentially destabilising it. Sexual relationships are particularly complex and expose partners to a great deal of change, especially if they stay together in the long-term. If partners are forced to remain within a dysfunctional relationship by societal expectations, legal commitments or a lack of better alternatives, the partners are likely to experience stress and low moods.

The Duke of Wellington's love life makes a useful example. He did eventually marry Kitty in 1806, once he had achieved higher status, but the marriage was not a happy one. Kitty had lost much of her good looks and vitality by the time they married and Arthur took advantage of the opportunities for sexual liaisons that presented themselves to a man of his standing during their marriage. Arthur was not, however, an alpha male. Although he acquired the nickname "The Iron Duke", his behaviour suggests that he possessed all four progressive traits. He was awkward in his youth and felt lonely at Eton College, which indicates he was treated as an outsider. His mother considered him to be idle and he liked gambling, suggesting he was high in opportunism. He found associating with other officers uncomfortable, preferring to spend time with regular troops, indicating that he disliked status-seeking individuals.

He was also very analytical and adopted a conservative approach on the battlefield. He dressed conservatively in black, hated attention and was embarrassed by public displays of appreciation. His plainness of speech was often mistaken for arrogance and he never addressed his troops en masse, considering such behaviour to be the "stuff of players". These are characteristics of low extraversion. He hated violence and avoided unnecessary bloodshed. As a junior officer, he often failed to punish the men who thieved and pillaged on his watch and he cried when he read the list of dead after the Battle of Waterloo. This suggests he was low in indifference. His willingness to adopt new ideas on the battlefield was a sign of high openness.

Arthur would therefore have spent much of his early life trying to fit in to an establishment culture to which he would have been completely unsuited. His relationship style would have been meaningful, fickle, collaborative and unstructured – the complete opposite of what would have been expected of him by a female who was embedded in an establishment culture. It is likely that his attraction to Kitty was born largely of sexual desire, although her higher status may also have contributed to her attractiveness. Their personalities were not well matched so once Arthur had achieved success in his own right and Kitty's looks had faded, she had little to offer him. She did bear him two children, but Arthur's personality traits would not have caused him to place a particularly high value on establishing a lineage. His success enabled him to give free rein to his amusing, easy-going character in later life and he was renowned for throwing parties for his friends. Although he had many illicit relationships, they had polyandrous qualities. Correspondence has revealed his kindness to his lovers. However, his behaviour caused him and Kitty to live apart and Kitty to feel rejected and dishonoured. Arthur regretted that his relationship with Kitty had not worked out better and felt very sad when she died. On her death he said that after "half a lifetime together, they had come to understand each other at the end".

The relationship between Arthur and Kitty demonstrates the dangers of establishing a relationship with a person whose personality is not suited to his environment and how changes to your or your partner's circumstances can affect a relationship. It also shows the fragility of relationships that lack purpose. It is important for partners to recognise each other's value and to develop and maintain a shared vision of their future if they are to develop a rewarding long-term relationship. Where a partner becomes focused on his personal objectives or regulating his emotional state, the relationship is likely to deteriorate. If one partner is no longer pulling his weight, the other partner is likely to become stressed due to his additional workload or loss of protection, or experience low moods. This may lead to resentment, vindictive responses or vengeful actions. Where selfish behaviours continue, such responses can become habitual, further undermining the relationship's strength. A person may seek to limit the potential for his partner to behave in ways that would cause him to experience stress by exerting control over him or the couple's environment. This may cause his partner to experience boredom, restlessness or suppression, and exhibit frustration or other impulsive behaviours that may be perceived by the other partner as disrespectful, provocative or acts of bullying.

Making a success of a long-term relationship requires commitment and hard work. When one or both partners experience stress or a low mood, their characters will be tested. Qualities such as honesty, self-control, mutual respect and a commitment to doing "the right thing", will help to maintain the strength and durability of the relationship. The culture of the partners' wider group will influence their reactions in such situations. Collectivist and establishment cultures promote strong family units, communities and organisations. They give people less personal freedom, encouraging them to settle down earlier and may force people into arranged marriages. Although this may cause resentment and other negative behaviours, an early marriage allows the partners to devote more time to their careers and family than would otherwise be the case. Collectivist and establishment cultures also introduce laws and conventions that deter couples from breaking up. Progressive cultures promote looser, networked structures, but women in such cultures need to sustain relationships with men in order to benefit from their assistance and restrain their competitive behaviour. Individualistic cultures promote the disintegration of groups and relationships. A woman who wishes to encourage her boyfriend to settle down will typically try to develop a shared vision of their future together as a family, but the freedom available to people who live in individualistic societies makes it difficult for partners to sustain such a vision over a long period.

Some people who believe they are bad at relationships are actually better at them than they think. It is just that the type of relationship style and structure that they are suited to does not match up with the current culture of their group. For example, an alpha male may be made to feel ashamed for having a mistress, or a woman may be considered to have loose morals if she changes sexual partners frequently. In reality, such people are likely to be following their natural instincts and establishing relationships that suit their personalities.

Relationship commitments limit a person's ability to use his talents and skills for his wider group. Also, in individualistic society, the disintegration of family and community groups makes it more difficult for people to help others. A person who is naturally inclined to be helpful and supportive may seek out a partner who needs a lot of assistance or who shirks responsibility to give him more opportunity to exercise his talents and skills. In the latter case, he will be giving his partner undue attention or assistance. The helping partner may end up treating the benefitting partner in an overprotective way, rescuing him from self-imposed predicaments, accepting the burden created by his actions or encouraging his irresponsible behaviours. A relationship of this nature (sometimes referred to as a co-dependent relationship) places great pressure on the helping partner because the physical, emotional, or financial resources that he puts in are not replenished by reciprocal actions by the benefitting partner. If he does not receive assistance from friends, family or the state, he is likely to experience exhaustion, physical hardship and poor mental health.

The challenges associated with managing and adapting to change during the course of a relationship mean that at times one or both partners will experience negative feelings. In the absence of any commitment to a wider group, it is easy for one partner to walk away. If partners help each other to overcome their challenges, they will usually find a way through a difficult period. However, some relationships are destined to be of short or medium length. Remaining in a relationship that has served its purpose prevents the reallocation of the partners' talents and skills to more appropriate tasks of benefit to the wider group.

Managing differing levels of indifference

Men who are high in indifference do not usually feel insecure when they are in confrontational environments and are inclined to use aggression to solve problems. If they do feel insecure, it is likely to be because they have a physical or mental weakness, lack support or possess a low trait in one of the other three personality spectrums. If they possess one of these low traits they are likely to promote fairness, coherence or structure within their groups, but not show compassion or sympathy.

Females who are not in the fertile stage tend to focus on building relationships with other women based on common interest whereas they become more concerned with interacting with the opposite sex when they are in the fertile stage. Before humans adopted monogamy, females would have used their infertile stage to strengthen bonds within the female collective and help each other with domestic responsibilities. In monogamous societies, however, women tend to have looser connections with fellow females. As a result, they often look to their male partners to be caring and supportive. Unfortunately, as alpha males are unlikely to possess these characteristics, this can cause their partners to become upset or disenchanted. If a woman is feeling unloved and, as a result, seeks consolation from her friends, she will be behaving perfectly naturally as the typical female's lower level of indifference naturally causes her to offer help and support to other women. It is just that the practice of monogamy has created unrealistic expectations of male-female relationships.

The fact that females find themselves attracted to men who are high in testosterone in one phase of their menstrual cycle and repelled by them in another means that women who enter long-term relationships with such men are likely to have somewhat of a rollercoaster ride. Tension can be generated when a husband and wife with typical levels of indifference for their genders attempt to perform a task together. The wife will be operating at a higher level of arousal than her husband because of her greater sensitivity to harmful information. She may interpret her husband's more relaxed state as a lack of commitment to the task or as reckless or irresponsible behaviour. He may struggle to understand why she is becoming stressed because he is oblivious to the stressor that she is reacting to or considers it inconsequential. If so, he may become frustrated or angry. This may cause the wife's arousal level to increase further, causing her to issue an angry or fearful response. If the task is a domestic one, the lack of competitive information in the environment may cause the husband to experience boredom or suppression. He is likely to consider the task as unimportant or not his responsibility in which case he may display irritation or grumpiness. Arguments and resentment are therefore likely to result unless both parties can learn to operate in the Co-operation Zone. Therefore, although the modern man is expected to share household duties, doing so may not be the most productive or relationship-enhancing course of action where the partners have contrasting levels of indifference.

Contrasting levels of indifference partly explain why men and women tend to laugh at different jokes. Comedians often specialise in exploiting other people's misfortune. There will always be a boundary between what the bulk of the audience will consider acceptable and what is out of order. Because most comedians are male, they tend to set the bar high. Some women in the audience will, as a result, become stressed. Similarly, many men will not find a comedienne funny if she is targeting a female audience because they will not be able to pick up on the subtlety of the humour – the bar will be set too low for them.

Women tend to be more concerned about the health of sexual relationships than men. This is partly because the loss of a protector and provider is likely to make a woman's life more difficult unless she lives in a group with a progressive culture. It is also because her lower level of indifference will make her more sensitive to harmful information within the couple's environment including information generated by the two partners. Although the male may value the relationship highly, he may fail to appreciate where damage is being caused to it by his actions because of his lower level of sensitivity to harmful information.

11

SELF-EMPOWERMENT

The pursuit of happiness

In an ideal environment, where the information levels within it allow you to operate consistently with your optimal ranges, you will be switching frequently between Fast System and Slow System operation, learning effectively and experiencing a sense of flow. You will be experiencing only positive feelings. In other words, you will feel happy. Your personality traits, talents and skills and interpretation of your abilities will dictate the nature of your ideal environment and the happy feelings that you experience within it.

People who are centrally located in all four personality spectrums are most likely to feel happy as they will be suited to average environments. In such environments, they will be able to switch between Fast System and Slow System operation easily while only experiencing minor stress events. They will primarily experience happiness in the form of enjoyment and contentment, although they will be able to access feelings of exhilaration and fulfilment occasionally. The higher up a trait spectrum that a person is positioned, the more capable he will be of experiencing feelings of enjoyment and exhilaration. A person who is high in all four traits will seek out environments with high levels of information so that he can access such feelings. His ability to function well in such environments will mean that he will be unconcerned about threats that other group members consider to be serious. He will, therefore, appear carefree, fun loving, reckless or hedonistic to them. He will, though, find it very difficult to experience feelings of contentment and fulfilment because he will spend most of his time in Fast System operation. In contrast, the lower down a trait spectrum that a person is positioned, the more capable he will be of experiencing feelings of contentment and fulfilment. These feelings are generated by actions and behaviours that make you feel more secure. A person with low traits will need to work harder than an average person to find or create an environment in which he feels secure enough to give his Fast System free rein. People with low traits may, therefore, be perceived as too serious or uptight by friends and associates, and may become workaholics. A person who possesses all four low traits is likely to find it very difficult to experience enjoyment and exhilaration because he will be susceptible to major stress events in most environments. If your environment is favourable or you are very confident, you will be able to access feelings of happiness more often than would otherwise be the case. If your wider environment is unfavourable, but you engage in avoidance tactics, you will be able to sustain feelings of happiness, at least in the short term.

If a person has both high and low traits, he will be able to experience the full range of positive feelings. If he is correctly positioned within a group with a favourable culture, he will alternate between exploratory behaviours that deliver enjoyment and exhilaration and controlling behaviours that deliver feelings of contentment and fulfilment. However, the range of environments in which he can experience such feelings will be quite narrow so his grip on happiness may be quite tenuous. If his environment changes only slightly, he is likely to experience stress, low moods and negative feelings. For example, a person who is high in extraversion and low in opportunism would, other things being equal, be suited to being a tour guide because he will enjoy being the centre of attention and will be suited to organising. However, once a tour has finished and he finds himself alone, he is likely to feel bored due to a lack of stimulation or stressed as he waits to see if and when enough people will turn up to enable him to take another tour.

When your experience negative feelings, you may feel unhappy. You are likely to experience general feelings of unhappiness when your emotional system is prevented from relocating you to a more favourable environment or is struggling to come to terms with a loss that you have suffered. Unhappiness is experienced at a low arousal level and is therefore a Slow System state. When you are experiencing anxiety or chronic stress you will not feel unhappy because your arousal level will be higher and you will be preoccupied with the related stressors. In other words, you will be under too much pressure to enter a reflective state. However, in quieter moments feelings of unhappiness may surface if your Slow System is unable to resolve the problems and insecurity caused by the stressors. Unhappiness is likely to be accompanied by feelings of helplessness, listless behaviour and tiredness.

It is difficult to locate yourself in an ideal environment. Restrictions on social mobility, obligations to family members, educational deficiencies, or physical or mental limitations may prevent you from relocating yourself to your natural position within the primal group structure. Even if you manage to secure your ideal job role, you may experience negative feelings as a result of a lack of support or protection from work colleagues, family and friends, or an unfavourable group culture. People with one or more high or low traits will in general experience more unhappiness and stress than people with middling traits This is because they will be suited to operating within extreme or niche environments that are difficult to find or maintain. The very particular circumstances that are likely to deliver feelings of happiness to people with multiple high and/or low traits may occur rarely, or not at all, in their lifetimes. For example, a person whose traits suit him to be a warrior is likely to be happy in times of armed conflict when most other people are scared, but he will struggle to adapt to civilian life. Also, as such people will be relatively few in numbers, they are unlikely to be able to shift group culture towards their ideal culture unless they achieve positions of high status and power or exceptional circumstances occur that increase the value of their talents and skills. These environments and circumstances will often be short-lived, as the actions of the majority with middling traits will cause the group to return to a state of averageness. People with extreme traits may, therefore, find it difficult to maintain a happy state. Even where such a person finds a niche in the working world that suits his traits, he is still likely to have to deal with other worldly issues that are liable to cause him to experience stress or low moods, such as carrying out family responsibilities or other everyday tasks.

Humans have, though, evolved primarily to contribute to the success of their groups. An individual's feelings must therefore be seen in the context of wider group dynamics. Groups generate a wide variety of personalities so that they can maximise their chances of success in the long term. Different combinations of personality traits give rise to different talents and skills, which collectively enable a group to cope with most situations that it is likely to encounter. At any point in time, some people will possess personalities that are suited to their group's environment, culture and objectives. They are likely to be valued by other group members and experience feelings of happiness. Others will find that their talents and skills are not needed or valued lowly, or that their behaviour is constrained due to cultural mismatches. They will experience negative feelings.

Individualistic culture encourages people to pursue activities that deliver enjoyment and exhilaration, and happiness within such a culture tends to be associated with the experience of such feelings. Such a culture suits high trait orientated people, but people with low traits find it hard to locate themselves within safe spaces, so they become more susceptible to anxiety and chronic stress and are more likely to engage in avoidance. In a collectivist culture, as exists in France, happiness is associated with contentment and fulfilment. Low trait orientated people are likely to be happy in such a culture while those with high traits will tend to feel unhappy and to experience boredom, frustration and suppression. Establishment and progressive cultures are characterised by a mixture of high and low traits. Whether such a culture predisposes a person to feel happy or unhappy will depend on the particular high and low traits he possesses. For example, a person with establishment traits is likely to experience the full range of positive feelings within an establishment culture, as exists in the rural mid-west of the USA, but find it difficult to maintain a happy state in a progressive culture, as exists within Sweden, and vice versa.

As most people have middling traits, a group or society will, other things being equal, be at its optimum point of happiness when its culture is located at the centre of the Circle of Power. This balancing point can shift due to environmental factors or where confidence levels within a group increase or decrease. Where a leader or ruling clique imposes a culture, which is unsuited to the environment of the wider group, a greater number of people will feel unhappy. Disadvantaged group members will naturally seek to eliminate negative feelings caused by an unfavourable group culture. They may do so by engaging in emotional regulation or taking action to prompt a cultural shift. Most people will take the first option, but some will become campaigners or activists and serve as a counteracting force. For example, a person who is high in openness and low in extraversion will be tolerant and fair by nature. If he lives in an establishment culture, he is likely to experience frequent bouts of frustration and suppression as a result of its intolerant and inequitable nature. He may, therefore, join a social democratic political party that seeks to counter the illiberal and materialistic tendencies of the establishment. If the actions of a group's leader cause a cultural shift away from the centre of the Circle of Power, activists and campaigners will attract support from moderate group members, increasing their influence within the group. This is likely to cause the leader to change or moderate his approach. Human groups, therefore, possess a natural self-righting mechanism that helps them to maintain levels of happiness amongst their members.

It is in the interests of leaders, and particularly those who depend on re-election for the maintenance of power, to recognise when group members in general are becoming unhappy. Their focus is primarily on economic issues, as people are particularly sensitive to factors that affect their financial security. However, politicians are increasingly taking notice of happiness indicators, and happiness is becoming a mainstream policy objective of national governments. In 2011, the United Nations General Assembly invited members to measure the happiness of their people and to use this to guide their public policies. The United Nations and other organisations now produce annual league tables recording the happiness levels around the world.

The World Happiness Report 2018 ranks 156 countries by their happiness levels. On a scale of zero to 10, Finland was ranked top, scoring 7.632, and Burundi was ranked bottom, scoring 2.905. Unsurprisingly countries where citizens' survival is threatened by war, disease or famine have the lowest levels of happiness. Most developed, democratic countries score over 6. Electorates within these countries tend to elect governments whose policies reflect the interests and objectives of the majority of citizens. As a result, they will usually have higher levels of happiness than people who live in countries that are subject to authoritarian rule or that have high levels of political corruption.

The report's findings show that environmental conditions, including standards of governance, greatly affect levels of happiness. The report does not, however, consider the impact of personality on happiness and, therefore, does not recognise the fact that there will always be some people whose personality traits are at odds with the values and structure of society. Even prosperous, democratic countries with diverse economies that provide opportunities for people with high and low traits to find their niches do not score above 8 points. It is difficult for any of these countries to increase their score above 8, as they will already be close to achieving optimal environmental circumstances (which might be equated to the utilitarian principle of the greatest happiness of the greatest number). There will always be people whose personality traits do not suit the culture of their society, who are struggling to come to terms with loss or who are experiencing feelings of unhappiness due to illness or disability or some other disadvantage that government cannot easily compensate for.

As people who are unhappy play an important role in rebalancing groups, powerful figures and organisations that wish to maintain the status quo will be tempted to resort to quick fixes to happiness levels. If a government enables people to relieve feelings of unhappiness by allowing them to access stimulants, depressants and other regulatory substances and activities, the rebalancing dynamic will be undermined and an extreme culture may become embedded within society. The mass medication of individuals who have been diagnosed with stress or depression in modern society has prevented many of them from taking action to change their wider environment for the better. This has sustained individualistic behaviours, deterred people from strengthening their families, communities and society and contributed significantly to increased levels of inequality and hardship.

Most people who are not living in war-torn environments or impoverished circumstances will describe themselves as reasonably happy. If asked what their primary objective in life is, many people who are experiencing negative feelings will say: "to be happy". Our emotional systems compel us to strive for happiness. We elect politicians to manage society in a way that enables us to feel happy. However, we are not entitled to be happy and, for some people, happiness will remain out of reach. This reality was recognised within the USA's Declaration of Independence, adopted on 4th July 1776. The Declaration stated: "We hold these truths to be self-evident, that all men are created equal, that they are endowed by their Creator with certain unalienable Rights, that among these are Life, Liberty and the pursuit of Happiness." Most of us need to adapt our environment or manage our emotional states from time to time if we are to sustain feelings of happiness. Once you understand the principles of personality and the dynamics of groups, you will be able to exert a greater influence over events and your environment and be better placed to access feelings of happiness on a sustainable basis.

Identity

To be effective in life, you need to pursue your goals with a strong sense of purpose, well-founded confidence in your capabilities, and the support and protection of groups. It is therefore useful for you to develop an appreciation of who you are as an individual and an understanding of how your connections to groups affect your behaviour. In other words, you will benefit from exploring your identity.

As your personality traits will predispose you to develop certain talents, skills, values, interests, ambitions, limitations and fears, they will form the basis of your **individual identity**. The groups you belong to will have their distinct values and culture, which essentially form a **group identity**. Both individual and group identities are influenced by environmental factors, including knowledge gained from past experiences. Therefore, unlike your personality traits, which are fixed, individual and group identities morph over time.

We develop allegiances to groups and define ourselves by reference to their general characteristics, which may, for example, be familial, ethnic, religious or geographical. This is particularly the case when we feel insecure and need more protection. In such circumstances, we feel safer in the company of people who share our values, characteristics and background. We are also influenced by the expectations of groups and important people within them. Groups impose obligations upon us, encourage us to accept responsibility and set behavioural parameters. As a result, you undertake tasks to which you are unsuited and restrain yourself from behaving in ways that might be considered inappropriate. In other words, groups mask your individuality to some degree.

Most people lack a clear understanding of their identity. This is because it develops sub-consciously as a consequence of your background, the activities you undertake and your interactions with other people. In our daily lives, we are not challenged to explain how our qualities, beliefs and associations connect us to or distinguish us from other people. Also, you do not display all the skills and behaviours associated with your identity at the same time. You will select the ones that are appropriate for current circumstances and push the others into the background. Your outward facing persona will, therefore, vary as you move between different tasks, groups and environments.

Modern human groups vary greatly in size and composition. They include families, schools, workplaces, social circles, special interest groups and society itself. You will belong to many different groups and adopt different personas at different times depending on the particular expectations of the group with which you are engaging and your level of desire or need to fit in. In some groups, you will fit in well and be able to behave naturally. In others, you will adapt your behaviour to gain acceptance or improve your status, or you will react against the prevailing culture.

To varying degrees, we are all engaged in a battle to free ourselves from the constraints of parental expectations, schooling and cultural norms that conflict with our personality traits. At the same time, we establish and re-enforce bonds with other people that offer us protection and provide us with a sense of belonging. In other words, we are constantly trying to re-reposition ourselves within groups so we can operate within our optimal ranges. In most cases, the acts of defiance and adaptions that we make will be subtle, but sometimes, especially in teenage years, they can be very apparent. For example, a teenage daughter may display aggressive behaviour when her father imposes constraints on her ability to socialise with young men. Similarly, a young man may feel compelled to take more risks than his personality would dictate to gain acceptance by a gang that he wishes to join. The persona he presents to gang members will, therefore, be different to the one his parents are used to.

A person may never have cause to define or question his identity if he has the good fortune to find himself in a job role and position within society that allows him to use his talents and skills effectively, and if other citizens value his contribution. People who are less fortunate may struggle to find their place in society in terms of role or status. They will experience stress and low moods, and perform beneath their potential as a result. Such a person is likely to feel out of place or unappreciated, but he may not be able to identify why. This uncertainty is likely to further reduce his effectiveness and increase his level of negative feeling.

If you have a good understanding of your individual identity, you can adapt your behaviour temporarily to suit specific circumstances or achieve short-term objectives without losing a sense of direction. You will find it easier to realise when you are being exposed to unfavourable environments and cultures, and to resist being negatively influenced by powerful people and group dynamics. Achieving such an understanding will help you to maintain good mental health. You cannot escape entirely from your group identity, though. To some extent, it will be represented physically in the colour of your skin and your bone structure. Your background and early life experiences will have embedded schemas in your mind that you will find difficult to delete or adapt. You will also need to find a way to fit into groups to secure support and protection from them and this will require you to identify as a group member to some degree.

Some people have a weak connection to group identity. If a person is marginalised by a group or feels out of place within it, he is likely to go searching for like minds and rewarding experiences at its edges or beyond its bounds. The knowledge he acquires and relationships he develops are likely to reflect and bolster his individual identity. For example, people who struggle to bond with their peer group often develop friendships with younger or older people who share their particular interests or values.

It has been established that we are selective in the information that we use to define our individual identities. We strongly identify with certain characteristics that are important to us, but filter out characteristics that we consider less important. Making an accurate assessment of your individual identity requires hard work, as your emotional system will discourage you from engaging with or believing information that could damage your self-esteem. Experiments have shown that although we naturally take steps to understand and verify information about our personalities, we tend to focus on positive rather than negative aspects.

It is likely that there will be a strong correlation between your assessment of your individual identity and your natural attributes derived from your personality traits. We can, though, be misled by false assumptions or environmental factors. You will form opinions about your personality and abilities based on other people's reactions to your behaviour. However, you probably have little idea of what people truly think of you, even your closest friends, because people very rarely ask that question. To do so would be too great a risk to their levels of self-esteem. Negative feedback may cause the sense of identity that you have carefully nurtured to crumble. You now know that there is a good chance that your self-image differs significantly from how your friends see you. Are you going to check this out? Will you ask them? The chances are you will not – an inner force will be saying "no". Some people whose traits are not suited to their environment and who have not had the opportunity to experience a favourable one may be misled into thinking that their behaviour is representative of their personalities, rather than a result of compliance, in which case they will be displaying imposter traits. Such a person may be so entrenched in a particular group or culture that he cannot dissociate himself from it, even though he will be experiencing stress and displaying aggressive, unpleasant or listless behaviours as a consequence.

If you work hard at developing your emotional literacy skills, a more accurate understanding of your individual identity and your groups' identities will start to crystallise within your mind. You will be better able to manipulate your behaviour to make a good impression on other people and empowered to stick to your principles when the agenda of a group conflicts with your objectives or values.

Developing emotional literacy skills

If you are to be effective and achieve your objectives, you will need to position yourself so that you can operate within your optimal ranges. At times, though, you will need to stretch yourself, risking episodes of anxiety or sustained stress, or force yourself to undertake tasks that cause you to experience suppression. You will need to put up with negative feelings if you are to show reliability, build successful relationships and develop a reputation for integrity. However, if you occupy environments that cause you to experience negative feelings on a sustained basis, you are likely to suffer from poor mental health.

Our early life experiences are very important. The degree to which parents and teachers show empathy, give encouragement and impose discipline greatly influences a person's emotional development. The cultures within which children grow up can have long-lasting effects on their confidence levels, embedding limiting or enabling beliefs within their minds. It can be difficult to adapt your behaviour once you reach adulthood because you will have taken on board more schemas by then and will have greater access to regulatory substances and activities. You can, though, increase your emotional stability, effectiveness, and levels of motivation, confidence and happiness, by consciously developing emotional literacy skills. Most people would benefit from improving their ability to monitor and control their emotional responses and decision-making. Gaining an understanding of your personality and emotional system can enable you to better direct your energies, limit the effect of potentially damaging instincts and build stronger relationships. It can also help you to get back on track when you experience setbacks or losses. Increasing numbers of people are experiencing serious, long-term mental health issues in modern society. Many of them could significantly improve their health and wellbeing if they enhanced their emotional literacy skills.

The Personality Revolution's Model of Personality sets out eight steps in the development of strong emotional literacy skills:

1. Developing your self-awareness capabilities;

2. Understanding your personality traits and how they interact with your environment to trigger emotional responses;

3. Identifying your position within the primal group structure and assessing your compatibility with the groups to which you belong;

4. Identifying your strengths and weaknesses;

5. Identifying where you have suffered losses that have not been recouped;

6. Broadening consciousness and identifying areas where you are engaging in avoidance;

7. Setting clear objectives that are allied to a sense of purpose; and

8. Exercising control over the learning cycle and embracing resilience.

These steps tie together the information presented in previous chapters into a process. Each time you go through the process you will gain a deeper understanding of your individual identity, your relationship with your group and your purpose.

1.   Developing your self-awareness capabilities

The fundamental skill that underpins emotional literacy is self-awareness. Self-awareness enables you to recognise and interpret your feelings, thoughts and behaviours. If you develop your ability to monitor, assess and manage these responses in real time, you can become self-directing. If you reflect on emotional responses after the event, you will gain a broader perspective on life, which can help you make better decisions in the future. Improved self-awareness will therefore help you to achieve your objectives and maintain a good level of mental health.

Self-awareness is a Slow System function. You can improve your self-awareness capabilities by creating triggers that jolt you out of Fast System operation and into a state of self-awareness. If you consciously identify particular environments, behaviours or feelings as potential threats to your wellbeing, your emotional system will initiate the fight or flight mechanism when it experiences them, prompting activation of your Slow System and an adjustment to your behaviour. For example, if a person has a tendency to dominate conversations and annoy his conversation partners as a consequence. If he is aware of this risk, his emotional system is likely to intervene and stop him getting carried away. When it does so, it will give his Slow System the opportunity to assess the situation to see if his conversation partner is being stressed by his behaviour. When you use your self-awareness skills in this way, you refine your understanding of the threats within your environment and define more accurately the circumstances where you can use your Fast System safely. You will also gain a clearer understanding of the value systems of the groups to which you belong and this will help you to fit in and function within such groups.

You will find it difficult to engage your self-awareness capabilities when you are in an environment that keeps you in a state of high arousal. This makes sense from an evolutionary perspective, as in most cases quick thinking or even no thinking (i.e. an instinctive reaction) is most likely to give the best chance of survival where there are serious threats in your immediate environment. For example, if you sense real danger to your life, your instinct to run will probably serve you well. It is difficult to think clearly in such situations because your arousal level will be raised. If you have access to your Slow System at all, it will be preoccupied with identifying immediate threats. You should therefore try to avoid highly stressful situations.

People with low traits spend more time than those with high traits in Slow System operation so they are more likely to develop a high level of self-awareness. People who are low in extraversion, in particular, engage deep analytical thought processes when given the space to do so and naturally establish assessment and monitoring loops within their minds. It is more difficult for people who are high trait orientated to access and maintain a state of self-awareness because they prefer to use their Fast Systems. They risk experiencing suppression if they try to do so, so they tend to avoid reflecting on their actions, feelings and behaviour. People with high traits therefore need to work harder to develop self-awareness skills. Having said that, in environments with high levels of information, people who are high trait orientated find it easier to maintain access to their Slow Systems than people with low traits. They are therefore more likely to be able to use their self-awareness skills in real time. In such situations, they will be able to momentarily assess their actions and behaviours to ensure that they are aligned to their desired objectives.

2.   Understanding your personality traits and how they interact with your environment to trigger emotional responses

The nature of your emotional responses will be greatly affected by your sensitivity to information. It is therefore essential for anybody wishing to develop a high level of emotional literacy to develop an understanding of his tolerances to particular types of information. The more time you devote to understanding the circumstances that cause you to experience stress or low moods, the better placed you will be to avoid or deal with them in the future. Personality models like The Personality Revolution's Model of Personality provide a framework for the development of such an understanding by grouping types of information into spectrums.

If you consistently operate within a suitable environment, you are likely to experience a state of flow, and appear confident and emotionally stable. The more that you operate in an unsuitable environment, the more you will experience stress, low moods and negative feelings. If you possess one or more extreme traits, it is more likely that you will be at odds with your environment, operating outside your optimal ranges and experiencing stress or low moods, and negative feelings. If you possess both high and low traits, you will be even more susceptible, and may experience a high level of emotional instability.

3.   Identifying your position within the primal group structure and assessing your compatibility with the groups to which you belong

Your personality traits will dictate your position within the primal group structure and may also suit you to a particular group culture. Inappropriate positioning, a lack of support or protection or an unfavourable culture can result in negative feelings, isolation, a reduction in confidence, the development of limiting beliefs or low self-esteem. Once you understand where you fit into the primal group structure and how different cultures emerge, you will be able to see how the dynamics of groups affect you. You will see the role that you should play within such groups, as dictated by your personality traits, and be able to compare it with your actual role. You will also be able to appreciate the benefits that people with other personality traits bring to your group, and where its members lack the ability or inclination to offer you support or protection.

Once you know your natural position and favoured culture, you will be better placed to determine the cause of negative feelings that you may experience, such as envy, jealousy, isolation or low self-esteem. You will find it easier to identify people within your group who are incorrectly positioned or are promoting an unfavourable culture and whose behaviour may cause you to experience stress or a low mood. You may not be able to expel such a person from your environment, but the knowledge that it is that person, not yourself, who is at fault can be liberating and empower you to relocate yourself or work with others to reduce his influence. You may realise that you are being held back by other factors such as your intelligence level, background or life experiences. You will be able to address some of these factors while others will present lifelong limitations, but in both cases clarifying their nature will help you to increase your effectiveness.

4. Identifying your strengths and weaknesses

Once you understand the basic principles of personality and group dynamics, you will be able to identify your strengths and weaknesses more accurately. You can use your self-awareness skills to identify situations where you perform at a high level and others where you struggle. You can use this knowledge to re-orientate yourself towards activities that are likely to deliver positive feelings and greater effectiveness, such as a more suitable career. You will also be better able to determine when you need help from other people. Where you are located in a well-balanced team, you will be a stronger contributor if you perform appropriate tasks and recruit or trust other people to carry out those to which you are unsuited.

5. Identifying where you have suffered losses that have not been recouped

From time to time, you will experience negative feelings that are associated with loss, such as anger, sadness, regret and guilt. If you experience serious loss and you do not recoup or replace the lost person, asset or opportunity, you will be liable to experience stress and depression. These feelings can have debilitating effects, and their associated behaviours can destabilise relationships. It is therefore important for you to determine whether you are still being affected by past losses, and if so, how it has deprived you of stimulation, protection or support. Some losses cannot easily be recouped or compensated for. However, if you gain a clearer understanding of the damage caused by a loss, it becomes easier to focus on the tasks that need to be completed to recover from it, or to alleviate the associated negative feelings by making accommodations.

6. Broadening consciousness and identifying areas where you are engaging in avoidance

Your personality traits locate you within a particular position within the primal group structure. If you perform tasks that are appropriate to this position and receive support and protection from other people who are similarly well located, you are likely to experience positive feelings on a regular basis. However, you will essentially be a cog in a machine. If the machine begins to malfunction or is abused by the people controlling it, you are likely to find life difficult.

If you feel good, you will not need to question whether other parts of the machine are performing well, so you will be living in a bubble. If you start to experience negative feelings, you will naturally take the path of least resistance and implement quick fixes to restore the integrity of your bubble. In other words, you will engage in avoidance. You may resort to unhealthy regulatory techniques to maintain positive feelings or even exert control or bully those nearest to you to maintain the integrity of his bubble. If your bubble bursts, you will suddenly be faced with the threats that you have been avoiding. They are likely to require hard work and time to counter, and you may need assistance from others to do so. If you lack appropriate support and protection, you may become trapped in a negative state and experience chronic stress and depression.

The more that you look beyond your immediate circumstances and improve your understanding of the power dynamics within your groups, the better placed you will be to identify threats to your security. Once you have identified the threats within your wider environment (including factors that are impacting on efficiency and productivity of the machine in which you are operating), you will be able to assess your behaviour to see where you are engaging in avoidance tactics. You will also be able to take action to prevent these threats from damaging the group structure on which you depend for support and protection. Broadening your consciousness is a challenge, as you will need to expose yourself to knowledge and circumstances that you find stressful or boring. It therefore requires courage and commitment. In the longer term, however, your ability to understand the motivations of other people and interpret their behaviour will improve, and you will be able to function more effectively within groups as a consequence.

7.   Setting clear objectives that are allied to a sense of purpose

If you lack a sense of purpose, you are probably not using your talents and skills to achieve an appropriate objective or have not defined that objective sufficiently clearly. You may fail to set appropriate objectives because you lack an understanding of your strengths and weaknesses, are incorrectly positioned within your group or society, or are being influenced by an unfavourable culture. You may lack clarity because you have not spent enough time using your Fast System to explore your environment or your Slow System skills to identify risks and develop strategy, or because you are not working within an effective team. You will find it harder to set appropriate objectives if you have a low level of consciousness.

You are likely to lack a sense of purpose when you are operating as an individual or within an unbalanced group rather than as part of an effective team. We have evolved to work together in groups and we feel motivated when we pursue group objectives. People with high traits will be more inclined to pursue personal agendas, but they will still feel rewarded and experience a sense of purpose if they find a way to use their talents for the benefit of their groups.

Young people who grow up within supportive environments and adults who are healthy and financially well off tend not to appreciate the security that a strong group can offer. Neither do people who live in societies with individualistic societies because they are encouraged to live in the moment and pursue experiences that deliver enjoyment rather than consider the potential for hardship in the future. Such people are likely to feel entitled to the benefits that they are receiving and are less likely to feel an obligation to contribute to their groups or wider society. They will therefore be inclined to jump from one short-term objective to another, or drift around aimlessly, without a sense of purpose.

If you understand your personality traits and natural role within the primal group structure, you will be well placed to set appropriate objectives. If you find a way to use your natural talents and skills for the benefit of a group with a culture that is aligned to your personality traits, you are likely to experience a strong sense of purpose. If other members of the group appreciate that contribution, your self-esteem will be boosted. The sooner in your life that you identify with and commit to a group, the greater the benefit you can deliver to that group, and the happier you are likely to be. Sometimes, though, your ideal group may not exist or be accessible to you, or your group's culture may cause it to set objectives that are contrary to your personal values. In such instances, you can develop a sense of purpose by working with like minds to form a new group or secure a shift in the culture of the existing one.

8.   Exercising control over the learning cycle and embracing resilience

To be happy and effective you need to maintain your arousal level within your optimal range and balance the use of your Fast System and Slow System. In other words, you need to keep your learning cycle functioning. The achievement of long-term objectives usually requires the deployment of a wide range of skills. Ideally, you will utilise the skills of other people or engage technology to carry out tasks to which you are unsuited, but sometimes you will have to deal with such situations and deal with the associated stress or low moods.

If you do not understand how your learning cycle works, you are more likely to find yourself in circumstances that cause you to experience negative feelings and will find it more difficult to escape from them. Once you understand the principles of personality, you can more easily identify the stressors that are preventing your learning cycle from operating effectively. Sometimes, it is possible to implement immediate solutions. However, in many cases, you will be prevented from doing so by obligations to others or factors over which you have no control. You will need to engage in acts of emotional regulation and show resilience if you are to return to and maintain a positive mood. Each of us has our own regulatory toolset that helps us to manage our emotions and keep the learning cycle working.

In the context of emotional literacy and personality, resilience relates to the capacity of a person to confront and cope with life's challenges and to maintain wellbeing in the face of adversity. Resilience underpins other emotional literacy skills because it enables you to function effectively in difficult circumstances. There is no easy way to develop resilience. A person only becomes resilient by being exposed to negative feelings for a sustained period. This may be through his choice or at the instigation of others. Unless a person has a clearly defined long-term objective that allows him to display drive and willpower, it is unlikely that he will force himself into such situations. As a consequence, resilience tends to be formed at an early age under duress at school, in the family home or in the early stages of a career. Although it is hard won, people who develop high levels of resilience tend to be happier in the long term than those who do not as they are better able to recover from setbacks and are less likely to break down in times of adversity.

We have unprecedented access to substances and activities that can help us to regulate our moods. Managing your emotions in this way may make it easier to hold down a job or cope with the stresses of family life, but short-term remedies can reduce your incentive to find longer-term solutions and may damage your health. They can also deprive you of learning experiences where they artificially maintain you in one stage of the learning cycle. At a societal level, they perpetuate the status quo by reducing the incentive for people to campaign for change. People with high levels of emotional literacy can prevent unwanted increases or drops in their arousal levels by employing healthy regulatory techniques. You can, for example, use breathing techniques, engage in exercise, recall positive memories, visualise the future, or mentally reframe your environment and the challenges you face.

Related approaches to mental health

A wide range of psychological theories, treatments and practices has been developed to help people who are experiencing stress or low moods, many of which overlap. The emphasis has shifted in recent years from specific clinically led treatments to therapies and actions that can be progressed independently by individuals or which promote general wellbeing. **Wellbeing** has been described by the World Health Organization as a state in which an individual "is able to realise his or her own abilities, and cope with the normal stresses of life, can work productively and fruitfully, and is able to make a contribution to his or her community". Wellbeing can be summed up by two phrases: "feeling good" and "functioning well".

Cognitive behavioural therapy (CBT), which is focused on developing strategies and skills to help address dysfunctional emotions, behaviours and cognitive processes, is now widely recognised by doctors in general practice as a valuable tool in treating poor mental health. Therapists use CBT techniques to "help individuals challenge their unhelpful beliefs and behaviours by replacing "errors" in thinking such as over-generalising, magnifying negatives, and minimising positives, with more realistic and effective thoughts, or to help patients take a more open, mindful and aware posture towards such thoughts and behaviour so as to diminish their impact". CBT helps people to reduce emotional distress and tackle self-defeating behaviours. It is therefore closely related to the model set out in this book.

Therapies that focus on adjusting specific behaviours can, though, leave a person without a holistic understanding of the nature of his condition. This can result in him becoming trapped within his environment, managing his symptoms rather than addressing the root causes of his condition. He may, therefore, fail to strike out in a new direction that could have improved his state of mind, productivity and levels of happiness on a more permanent basis. In such circumstances, he is more likely to experience recurring episodes of poor mental health and may become dependent on counselling or psychiatric care, or become addicted to using unhealthy, short-term regulatory fixes. The Personality Revolution's approach encourages you to link your emotional responses to your environment and to view your circumstances in the broader context of group dynamics. This enables you to make adjustments to your lifestyle and behaviours that will give you a greater chance of experiencing feelings of happiness in the longer term.

The New Economics Foundation has set out five ways to wellbeing:

- Connecting with the people around you;

- Being active;

- Taking notice;

- Learning; and

- Giving.

"Connecting with people around you" is central to achieving a sense of wellbeing. The most significant difference between people with mental health problems and those without them is social participation. People with fewer than three close relatives or friends are much more likely to experience mental health problems than those with three or more close relationships. This makes having good social networks as important as not smoking, moderate alcohol intake and regular exercise in terms of good health. Connecting is not just about seeking stimulating company. The disintegration of families and communities means that increasing numbers of people are looking for a sense of belonging, and the support and protection that a group can offer.

As regards "being active", physical activity is associated with lower rates of anxiety and depression, better brain function and improved wellbeing across all age groups. It is also the most important modifiable health behaviour in terms of addressing potentially chronic disease. Outdoor activity has been found to be particularly beneficial for people's wellbeing. The World Health Organisation estimates physical inactivity causes 1.9 million deaths a year worldwide, including 10% to 16% of breast cancer, colon disease and diabetes cases, and about 22% of coronary heart disease cases. The NHS recommends that adults exercise at moderate intensity for at least two and a half hours a week. Most adults, however, do not take sufficient exercise. One study using data from 1 million people in England found that 80% failed to meet the government target of taking moderate exercise at least 12 times in a four-week period. It found that 8% of adults who were physically able to walk had not walked even for five minutes continuously during such period, 88% had not been swimming, and 90% had not used a gym.

"Taking notice" of your environment, appreciating novelty, beauty, detail and change, also helps to improve mental states. It is proven to help with stress, anxiety, depression and addictive behaviours, and can have a positive effect on physical problems like hypertension, heart disease and chronic pain. Taking notice is simply a means of exploring or providing more detail for the purpose of processing. In other words, it prompts activation of the learning cycle. When directed in the right way, taking notice enables you to create an environment that is suited to your personality traits. You could, of course, take notice of potential threats, increasing your arousal level and the likelihood of anxiety or chronic stress. Taking notice in the sense used by The New Economics Foundation is therefore essentially equivalent to a leisure activity and amounts to an act of avoidance.

Mindfulness, which is a form of taking notice, is the state of being attentive to and aware of what is taking place in the present, has been shown to enhance wellbeing and relieve mental distress. It can be experienced by taking walks in the countryside or even by performing mundane, repetitive tasks like washing up. When you are in a state of mindfulness, you will not be stressed because your arousal level low and you will be using your Slow System without fear of interruption. People who are low in extraversion need time to observe and analyse, people who are low in openness benefit from focusing on methodical processes, those who are low in indifference feel more content when they care for others or undertake tasks that make their environment more harmonious, and people who are low in opportunism increase their level of comfort by imposing control and organisation within their environments. You must, however, select activities that are associated with your low traits otherwise you are likely to experience suppression. For example, a man who is high in indifference but low in openness will experience suppression if he participates in a group focused on creating harmony and offering mutual support, but is likely to find tinkering with a car in his garage rewarding because it allows him to engage in a methodical process.

As we have seen, the human mind has a refined ability to "learn". We learn when we meet new people, encounter new ideas and experiences, challenge ourselves to compete or put ourselves in changeable situations, and then process the new information that we have been exposed to. We have seen that people have different learning styles depending on their personality traits and will learn effectively in some environments and experience stress or low moods in others. Where you learn effectively, you will experience positive feelings that will contribute significantly to your wellbeing.

Finally, "giving" and active participation in community life are important predictors of life satisfaction. Volunteering, in particular, has been found to increase people's sense of purpose, improve self-worth and wellbeing, and reduce anxiety. Studies have shown that it results in a longer lifespan, greater happiness, better pain management and lower blood pressure. People tend to report that feeling useful greatly contributes to their sense of wellbeing. This is not surprising as we are genetically programmed to work together in groups for the benefit of the group. We have seen, though, that this instinct varies in intensity depending on a person's personality traits.

When you make useful contributions, and these contributions are recognised as valuable, you are likely to experience a sense of contentment or fulfilment and a boost to your self-esteem. This encourages you to continue with your good deeds. Consequently, once a person gets over the initial hurdle of volunteering, he will usually find it relatively easy to sustain. However, it is important for managers to match volunteers to suitable tasks otherwise they will become stressed or bored. Unfortunately, most voluntary groups lack the resources and knowledge to do this. Also, it is important for the success of a group that recognition is tied to performance. Some high trait-orientated people accept positions of responsibility to further their interests and boost their self-esteem while seeking to minimise the effort that they have to expend. They may delight in offering opinions and giving orders, but avoid the hard work that is needed to fulfil the organisation's objectives.

Your personal journey

When you are correctly positioned within a well-functioning group that has a favourable culture, you will be operating within your optimal range and experiencing a sense of flow. You will adopt behaviours and perform roles that correspond to your personality traits. Opportunities will abound, serendipitous events will seem to occur frequently and you will feel happy. This is where we would all like to be.

Some self-help books and religious faiths encourage people to believe that each person has a natural path in life that will deliver feelings of happiness to him if he follows it. Such a belief can be comforting and motivating because it relieves uncertainty and can imbue a person with a sense of purpose. The concept of a natural path suggests that there is a route that is available to you that will ultimately deliver positive feelings on a sustainable basis. This is not the case, however, because of the nature of group dynamics. Human personalities vary greatly and there will always be some people who will be unsuited to their current environment, and have low status and lack influence within their groups as a consequence. They will be denied the opportunity to experience happiness because it is not in the interests of their group or powerful people within it to allow them to adopt the behaviours that would generate such feelings. The concept of a natural path therefore ignores the fact that we have evolved to work within groups for common interest, not the interests of individuals.

Your scope to dictate your own future is limited. When you make a decision, your mind either carries out a calculating process or acts instinctively, deploying schemas that have previously been created by such a calculating process. You will take the course of action that your emotional system determines is most likely to locate you within a favourable environment. It is likely that you have no free will and are at the mercy of events and circumstances. Your ambitions, fears and behaviour will be dictated by your personality traits, which are fixed, your mental and physical capabilities, which are genetically influenced and developed in the context of your environment, and your previous experiences. If you adopt this fatalistic view, you will have only one path in life over which you have no influence.

People who are low in opportunism will feel comfortable when they are embedded in a system, but most of us like to think that we have some influence over the course of our lives. People who are unhappy need to believe that they can find happiness, which is why we cling on to hope in difficult circumstances. Even if your life is predestined, the fact we live in a complex system makes it impossible for you to predict your future circumstances with any certainty. Your choices in life may be determined by your personality traits and environment, but your self-awareness capability allows you to experience decision-making as an act of self-determination. The human mind has therefore evolved the flexibility to allow individuals to construct their own belief systems and motivational frameworks.

I prefer to see life as a journey of discovery and understanding during which you develop your natural abilities and find ways to use them effectively for the benefit of society. If you commit to this journey, you will identify your weaknesses and learn where you need support or protection from others. You will also broaden your consciousness. This will help you to understand the dynamics of groups, set appropriate objectives and recognise circumstances that place limits on your ability to achieve. You are likely to experience good and bad times on your journey, but your effectiveness is likely to increase as you develop your emotional literacy skills. As you become more proficient, you will set more achievable objectives and find it easier to make accommodations where they are necessary. You will also become more confident and develop a clearer understanding of your identity.

Your journey will be entwined with the journeys of the people with whom you interact. If you are to function effectively, you will need to invest time in relationship building. Your ultimate destination is a location within a group that can offer you the support and protection you need on a sustainable basis. If there is one lesson to learn from this book above any other, it is that you need to be part of an effective group to experience feelings of happiness consistently. However, interacting within a group can cause you to experience a wide range of negative feelings and require you to put up with stress and low moods. The challenge you face is, therefore, to locate yourself in a position within a group that enables you to use your talents and skills in a way that brings you feelings of happiness. People who succeed in locating themselves in such a position early in life may achieve great things. They will be better placed to take advantage of opportunities and devote time to skill development than their peers, and this will propel them forward in their chosen field. They are likely to feel happy as a result. In contrast, a person who has not positioned himself appropriately within a well-functioning group will find life unrewarding or difficult. He is likely to either drift without direction or purpose, occasionally striking out impulsively, or to adopt defensive, controlling behaviours that hold back his development.

People with high or low traits often find it difficult to locate themselves in environments that can deliver sustainable feelings of happiness, as they will be suited to very specific job roles and extreme or unusual cultures. They will usually need to comply with group values if they are to receive assistance from other group members. The compromises they make will cause them to experience stress or low moods. The more extreme a person's traits are, the harder it will be for him to comply, the more resilience he will need to show and the greater the accommodations he will have to make. People with extreme traits are therefore caught between the devil and the deep blue sea. They are likely to display unpleasant or anti-social behaviours at times and to resort to drugs and other damaging mood enhancers to relieve their discomfort. If they are not prepared or are unable to make the compromises needed to fit in, or cannot find socially acceptable ways of relieving negative feelings, they are likely to find themselves living beyond the boundaries of normal society as troublemakers, radicals, criminals, eccentrics or loners.

Even when a person with extreme traits finds an ideal role within a group with a favourable culture, his behaviours and objectives will set him apart from most other group members. His happiness will depend on the maintenance of a very particular set of environmental conditions. Even if he receives support and protection from other people, he is quite likely to be unsuccessful in his endeavours as the tasks that people with extreme traits have evolved to undertake push the boundaries of the group's experience, requiring a high level of risk-taking or great skill. People with extreme traits therefore often encounter obstacles that they cannot overcome, or go down blind alleys, spending time developing and applying skills in ways that deliver no real benefit. Because a person with high traits will be suited to releasing high amounts of energy over a short period, the period during which he is in his element will often be relatively short. For example, a pop star whose traits drive him to create music and seek the adulation of a crowd is likely to find that his attractiveness declines as he ages and that his creative ability is inhibited as his comfortable lifestyle deprives him of the experiences that informed his early song writing. In contrast, people with low traits are suited to the long haul. They advance slowly and cautiously to ensure that they do not make mistakes. As a consequence, a low trait orientated person may need to find his path early in life and follow it for many years before being able to make an impact, for example by making a scientific breakthrough. Of course, a person may possess both high and low traits and be primed to develop a skillset that can only be exercised productively in a very limited range of circumstances.

The challenges that people with extreme traits face may cause them to look enviously into the lives of people who occupy the middle ground because of the apparent ease with which they seem to transact their lives and access feelings of happiness. People with middling traits are suited to average environments and can adapt relatively easily to the changes that typically occur within them. Such a person is likely to establish a stable social circle, and cope well with family life. He is unlikely to stand out from the crowd by achieving great things, but he will be able to hold down a job and will be suited to a family environment. Where societal culture is close to the centre of the Circle of Power, people with middling traits are unlikely to feel the need or have the motivation to make major changes to their lives because they will be relatively comfortable in their current positions. Any negative feelings that they do experience are likely to be low-level, temporary, and capable of relief through regulatory means. However, people with middling traits will be vulnerable to more serious mental health problems where they find themselves inappropriately located due to class structures, parental expectations, educational deficiencies or weak groups, or subject to an extreme group or societal culture, or where they have failed to recover from traumatic experiences. Modern society is extremely individualistic and characterised by small, dysfunctional groups, so a significant number of people with middling traits are experiencing stress and low moods due to a lack of support and protection.

You may experience a sudden improvement in your mental health if you make a change to your life that repositions you in a more suitable environment. However, once you realise that you need to change the nature of your environment, it will usually take time to achieve such a transition, as you will need to develop relevant skills and build useful relationships. On your journey, events will occur that throw you off course and you may find yourself stuck within an unsuitable culture or environment. You are likely to lack support or protection at times and experience stress or low moods as a consequence. Battling through difficult circumstances will cause you to develop a high level of resilience. However, you can use other emotional literacy skills to reboot yourself and avoid becoming trapped in a negative state. It is particularly important to spend time visualising a better future and designing and clarifying a route to it. By doing so, you can avoid taking the path of least resistance and sustain the drive and willpower needed to achieve your objectives. There may be multiple ways of arriving at your destination and you will encounter obstacles along the way. However, provided your emotional system can envisage your objectives clearly enough, it will continue to work towards their achievement. When it encounters a brick wall, it will recalibrate like a sat nav. If you work hard to acquire emotional literacy skills, you will also gain a broader perspective on life and a deeper insight into the troubles of others than most other people.

It is important not be too hard on yourself. Your objectives may not be immediately achievable. Group dynamics cannot usually be altered by the actions of a single person. It takes time and the right environmental circumstances to build an effective team, and for its actions to yield results. You should therefore be prepared to make accommodations, and take time to relax in order to recharge your batteries. You should not consider yourself a failure if you experience setbacks or relapse. Life is more challenging for some people than others. Returning briefly to unhealthy acts of emotional regulation can sometimes release a build-up of pressure, and enable you to collect your thoughts and restore the energy that you need to embark on the next stage of your journey. You should draw comfort from the fact that every step forward is either taking you towards a better place, or building up your level of resilience and giving you the opportunity to develop other useful emotional literacy skills. Although unfavourable circumstances may deprive you of opportunities to experience happiness early in life, the emotional literacy skills that you gain along the way may ultimately enable you to be more successful and happier than many people who started off in better situations.

12

THE PERSONALITY REVOLUTION

The disintegration of modern, individualistic society

In primeval times, humans would have belonged to a single extended family group. Expulsion would have had potentially life-threatening consequences so individuals would have had a strong incentive to abide by group values. The fact that early humans would have had no concept of property beyond rights of precedence to food and mating would have limited the scope for internal conflict. Also, their low level of consciousness and knowledge would have limited their ability to develop challenging ideas. Since then, technological developments have had an enormous impact on the structure and culture of human groups. They have enabled groups to increase from their natural size of about 150 people to hundreds of millions in the case of the largest countries that exist today, and enabled us to belong to multiple groups at the same time. We are now able to store and share vast amounts of knowledge and to use it creatively.

Men tend to be more interested in technology and machinery and less interested in people than women because their higher levels of indifference mean they are less concerned about maintaining harmony within a group or caring for others. Members of the establishment fear innovation as it threatens the status quo, but they will usually engage inventors to develop weapons and other machines that can help them to exert dominance and accumulate wealth. Technological breakthroughs have therefore tended to promote conflict between different human groups and tipped the balance of power within groups towards the primal hierarchy, disadvantaging the female collective. As a result, establishment cultures became the norm within human societies.

In the 19th century, technology began to have a positive effect on the lives of ordinary people. The Industrial Revolution released labourers from feudal ties and gave them the freedom to market their services in towns and cities. Although most workers were exploited in their workplaces, enduring dreadful conditions, middle classes began to emerge and businesses began to produce consumer products on a large scale. As democracies became established in Western countries in the early 20th century and workers created and joined unions, resources started to be spread more evenly across society. Pensions and other social security benefits were introduced. Later in that century, the introduction of universal systems of healthcare encouraged investment in medical research and the development of pharmaceutical products, which benefited whole populations. By the late 1970s, democratisation and the pursuit of social justice had resulted in most nations in the developed world adopting collectivist cultures. However, the control exerted by unions, state-controlled industries and government bodies suppressed creative forces and entrepreneurial spirit.

In the early 1980s, the governments of Ronald Reagan in the USA and Margaret Thatcher in the UK introduced policies that shifted the economies of those nations away from collectivist state control towards free market liberalism. Traditional industries were allowed to decline as manufacturing was outsourced to developing countries, and large numbers of people moved into employment in the service sector or became self-employed. There was a massive expansion in higher education and the size of the middle classes increased relative to the working class. The developed world experienced high levels of economic growth, and the benefits of such growth were spread broadly across their populations. As the disposable income of citizens increased, so did the variety of leisure options available to them. Technological advances, such as electronic share trading, allowed many people beyond the establishment to pursue the acquisition of wealth. People at all levels of society found it easy to access finance. As a result, they consumed at high levels and travelled extensively. In other words, there was a shift towards an individualistic culture within these countries.

Liberal economic policies contributed to rapid advances in computing and information technology. Increased connectivity and cross-border trading enmeshed the economies of nation states together into a global economic system and enabled multi-national companies to become extremely powerful. Many people benefited from the increased flexibility, access to knowledge and ability to communicate that smartphones and other computerised products delivered. However, the forces of globalisation weakened the authority of national governments and traditional values around the world. A global culture of individualism and liberal values began to emerge, which undermined the foundations of countries with strongly collectivist cultures like France. Large numbers of high trait orientated citizens moved to countries like the USA and UK to access opportunities for personal gain and enjoyment. Consequently, these collectivist countries struggled to remain competitive and unemployment rose amongst the rank and file and young people.

When we go about our lives, we do some things to satisfy our personal desires and other things that help to strengthen society or support loved ones, but we feel less inclined to do the latter if we feel secure. Favourable environments therefore promote individualistic behaviours. People start believing that they can be self-sufficient and tend to make hay in the present rather than looking out for danger in the future. They become reluctant to sacrifice their time for the benefit of others and pursue enjoyable, self-interested activities instead. The peace and prosperity that developed countries experienced in the second half of the 20th century raised levels of security. The existence of government safety nets also encouraged people to take risks. People therefore devoted less time to their families and communities and diverted money away from long-term investments in their future wellbeing. These choices were reflected in government policy, so tax rates were reduced, investment in public infrastructure and services were cut, and people were forced increasingly to rely on the free market to meet their needs. Group structures within society, including families and communities, became less coherent and connections within them become looser and in many cases completely disintegrated.

Technology greatly contributed to this disintegration. It has allowed people to operate independently from each other, or at least at a distance from each other, to a much greater extent than ever before. Individuals now have the freedom to operate out of sight and earshot of colleagues, neighbours and family members. Cars and improved transport links have enabled people to build social networks over large geographic areas and social media has resulted in the creation of huge numbers of groups whose members are connected through common interest rather than location.

The relationships that people establish in individualistic cultures tend to lack sustainability. Partners pursue individualistic behaviours rather than developing skills and exhibiting behaviours that could hold their relationships together. Therefore, even couples that appear to be settled and functioning well are vulnerable to relationship breakdown when they encounter difficulties. In modern, individualistic society, divorce and birth outside marriage have become socially acceptable. Separating partners have equal rights to marital assets on divorce and single parents benefit from state support. The basic unit on which human civilisation was founded – the long-term monogamous relationship – has therefore been greatly undermined.

The coherency of society is undermined by liberal social policies that prioritise the rights of individuals over groups. For example, currently, there is a strong movement in the UK and USA advocating transgender rights. A liberal-minded person will recognise the benefit to an individual of allowing him to self-identify and will see no broader harm in doing so. However, they neglect to factor in the high level of stress than the resultant incoherency generates in some people who are low in openness. The more that people deviate from group norms, the more that people with this trait will experience discomfort. Such discomfort reflects an actual weakening of the group so, in respect of the example above, uncertainty as to a person's gender is likely to prevent a person who is low in openness from bonding with him.

The more individualistic a society becomes, the more that formal codes of behaviour and laws are needed to compensate for the reduced effectiveness of group values. People are less aware of social conventions so, although violent and other serious crime reduced in the UK in the decades prior to the financial crisis of 2008, thoughtless and selfish behaviour increased. The freedom that people have to create new social networks in modern, individualistic society makes it much less likely that they will know their neighbours or respect their interests. A person will, for example, feel under less of an obligation to keep his front garden tidy or to refrain from noisy activity.

People with low traits usually feel insecure in individualistic cultures. They are exposed to greater risk and lack protection. The complexity of modern job roles presents a barrier to entry for many members of the rank and file, whose low levels of openness suit them to simple, methodical tasks. Insecure employment and flexible working presents challenges to people who are low in opportunism who find it difficult to adapt to change. People who are low in indifference tend to be out-competed and are deprived of harmonious environments. Those who are low in extraversion find it difficult to operate physically in groups or take risks with money or other resources. For most people, however, the disintegration of group structures mattered little in the short-term. The majority of people have middling traits that enable them to function effectively when the environment is suited to an individualistic culture. However, we cannot survive in the longer term without support from groups so eventually this decay starts to impact on the lives of citizens.

Countries with individualistic cultures are initially very productive as they promote innovative, flexible, materialistic and competitive behaviours. People and companies operate at a fast pace and take advantage of opportunities. Businesses focus on satisfying the desires of consumers and produce a wide range of new products as a result. However, if self-interested behaviours are not controlled, they start to negatively affect a group's performance. Excessive competition causes harm to vulnerable individuals, and greed depletes resources and distributes wealth unfairly. Personal freedom encourages people to act spontaneously, so they neglect to plan and are more inclined to break rules. Diversity reduces coherency and makes it harder for the group to maintain consistency and quality in terms of its output. Insufficient funding is directed towards long-term investment as short-term profits and objectives are prioritised.

As people prioritise enjoyment in individualistic cultures, they tend to have fewer children. Improvements in healthcare have also extended lifespans so many developed countries have ageing populations. The proportion of people of working age has fallen as a result, and this problem has been exacerbated by a lack of investment in skill development. Many people have failed to acquire basic skills that are needed in the building trade and light industry. People are also reluctant to accept basic labouring, agricultural and caring jobs because they consider them to be boring, hard work or beneath their status. Governments have therefore been forced to rely on migrant workers.

Many groups within modern, individualistic society are too small, incoherent and fluid to function effectively. Resources are used inefficiently as people and organisations buy their own tools and machinery rather than sharing them. People enjoy the freedom that cars and living alone gives them, but their carbon footprint increases substantially when they do so. They also use their time inefficiently by, for example, participating in leisure activities or establishing marginal, lifestyle businesses.

In the workplace, companies focus on short-term profit and the remuneration of their directors at the expense of long-term investment and stability. Resources, including employees, are ruthlessly exploited or wasted in producing consumer products with no societal benefit. Employees lack motivation as companies fail to engender a sense of purpose or belonging. Efficiency and productivity levels therefore decline. People, therefore, find themselves working harder than they would otherwise need to and their incomes fall in real terms as other nations with better functioning economies and societies prove to be more competitive in the longer term.

The disintegration of families and communities and the exploitative behaviours of powerful individuals and companies have contributed to an epidemic of unhappiness amongst middle-aged and older people. Large numbers are living alone or feeling insecure and experiencing poor physical and mental health as a consequence. Young people are, however, not immune. They are bearing the burden of the mistakes of their parents and grandparents. While the older generation has benefitted from increases in property prices and a wide range of free public services during their lifetimes, young people are finding that services and benefits are being cut at a time when they are struggling to secure decent jobs, salaries and housing.

Lack of investment in public services is a feature of countries with individualistic cultures. Its effects begin to show as society becomes more unequal and its inefficiencies push large numbers of people into difficult financial circumstances. People with high levels of opportunism and indifference will be tempted to make money by using illegal short cuts so robberies, swindling and other theft-based crimes increase. As they become aware of the inability of overstretched police forces to respond effectively, such people become emboldened and are joined by people who are low in opportunism. Organised crime therefore becomes embedded with society.

As individualistic cultures encourage people to prioritise immediate enjoyment over longer-term security, most people living within them fail to take sufficient responsibility for their health. People are more susceptible to anxiety and chronic stress in high information environments so the use of depressants, such as alcohol, increases. The fast pace of life and high levels of stress in such cultures also induces tiredness, so more people resort to stimulants to keep them alert. Consequently, there has been a massive increase in the number of coffee shops in UK high streets in recent years. Alcohol, caffeine and other stimulants and depressants are associated with serious health conditions, such as cirrhosis of the liver, heart disease and high blood pressure. Also, because people tend not to develop Slow System skills in individualistic cultures, they are less likely to adopt a reasoned and measured approach when they fall ill and more likely to rush to a doctor. This imposes extra strain on health services.

We need the support of groups when we experience serious loss, fall ill, suffer an injury or disability or reach old age. However, in individualistic cultures, people avoid taking responsibility for the welfare of vulnerable people. In the absence of tight family groups and strong communities, individuals tend to use their talents and skills to accumulate wealth and then retire early to pursue leisure activities. Some people contribute their time in a voluntary capacity, but many are not prepared to sacrifice leisure time or moneymaking opportunities to do so. As people tend not to consider or plan for future ill health or retirement, they think less about, and devote fewer resources towards, meeting the challenges faced by older people. As caring is a Slow System skill, people are also less likely to care for others. Sharp rises in asset prices over the last 40 years have benefitted the older generation so older people tend not to be materially disadvantaged, but many of them are living alone as a result of the fragmentation of their families and are experiencing poor mental health as a result.

Young people are also neglected in large numbers in countries with individualistic cultures as they lack protection and support from families, communities and government. Children are also more likely to be exposed to stress than in previous generations, as their parents and schools are unable or unwilling to carve out safe spaces in which they can develop and exercise their Slow System skills. As a result, the mental health of young people in the UK has deteriorated rapidly. Individualistic societies give people who are inclined to abuse or bully others (typically those who are high in indifference) more opportunity to do so, as they are subject to less regulation and have more opportunities to prey on victims out of sight of people who might intervene to stop them. The lack of protective and supportive groups leaves many young people feeling isolated and vulnerable. Increasingly, young men feel the need to join gangs or carry knives for protection. High levels of stress and a culture that promotes spontaneous, competitive responses is a lethal combination and has resulted in a steep rise in fatal stabbings in London over the last few years.

Individuals, families and communities are unable to provide advanced medical support. People, therefore, depend increasingly on governmental bodies to provide them with care and other support. Advances in medicine and reducing taxation receipts are, however, placing great strain on health services and social security systems. People delivering these services are over-worked and under-resourced and are experiencing poor mental health and exhaustion as a consequence. Large numbers are off work with long-term sickness or leaving their professions, and this is increasing the pressure on those who remain in the workplace. Flexible employment practices have also reduced efficiency as they interrupt the continuity of care and make mistakes more likely. The fact that people are less inclined to care for others means that health and care services can only be sustained by employing immigrant labour. Countries like the UK are facing a time bomb as subsequent generations will have fewer resources in retirement and future governments are likely to struggle to recruit sufficient workers to care for elderly people. In the UK, Brexit has exacerbated this problem by dissuading workers from EU countries from working for the NHS.

Although people living within societies with individualistic cultures become more reliant on companies and public bodies for the resources and services they need, they devote little time to maintaining the health of, or promoting positive cultures within, these organisations. As a result, self-interested individuals tend to rise to positions of authority within them and use their power and resources for personal gain. Their actions undermine the societal purpose of these organisations so they cease to look after the interests of their employees and other stakeholders. Within individualistic cultures, people also tend to vote in governments that are committed to opening up public services to market forces. Consequently, subsidies are reduced and sharp practices are introduced to maximise profit. People with limited financial resources find it harder to access such services and those with limited intelligence or education are exploited.

Individualistic behaviours are also driving climate change and environmental destruction. Air travel, car ownership and materialistic consumption result in the burning of huge amounts of fossil fuels. The fast pace of modern life and people's prioritisation of enjoyment causes people to choose convenience over responsibility. Technological innovations make it easier for companies to exploit natural resources and competitive forces encourage them to release new products on to the market before any long-term disadvantages are discovered. People are too busy seeking enjoyment to consider properly the effects that their actions are having on the environment. Multinational corporations and opportunistic business people are therefore able to destroy forests and other precious natural environments, and replace them with monocultures or leave them desolated.

Extreme cultures usually emerge in response to unusual environmental conditions. They will be sustainable as long as those conditions persist. However, the group's environment will revert to a more balanced position at some point or alter in favour of a different culture. It will do so when people with middling traits start to experience persistent negative feelings. They will join with people with more extreme traits who have been more seriously disadvantaged by the prevailing culture and together they will promote a cultural shift. However, it is difficult to change the behaviour of people who are enjoying themselves because feelings of enjoyment are addictive. They tend to lack the awareness and motivation to recognise and address negative dynamics within society before they become dangerous. They are also inclined to resort to avoidance tactics to maintain their positive states. The ready availability of mood enhancers and regulatory activities in modern society has allowed people to ignore threats for longer than they would otherwise do. A vicious circle has been created whereby people have avoided taking responsibility, which has allowed threats within their environment to become more potent, which has led to increased avoidance. Governments of countries with individualistic cultures like the UK and USA have been complicit, as they have avoided taking the steps necessary to rebalance society. This has delayed a cultural shift away from individualism and caused more people with low traits to experience chronic stress than would otherwise have been the case.

There comes a point, though, when avoidance is no longer possible and people are forced to deal with the threats within their environment. The bubbles within which they live become smaller and smaller and eventually burst. This can happen gradually, but sometimes an event occurs that jolts large numbers of people out of their avoidant states. The financial crisis of 2008 could have been such an event, but national governments prevented a major shock by bailing out the banks. However, the underlying causes of the crisis were not remedied and we have been left with widespread economic stagnation. Wealth is still concentrating in the hands of the wealthy elite so the disposable income of ordinary citizens continues to reduce. Meanwhile, developing countries continue to achieve high levels of economic growth and are presenting a more obvious competitive challenge to developed nations. This has prompted a backlash by people who are low in openness whose insecurity has been heightened by the lack of coherency and traditional values in modern society and the loss of working class jobs due to technology and free trade. Opposition to immigration has become more vocal and widespread, as personal finances have tightened. Many people in developed countries now feel vulnerable and are experiencing physical hardship or poor mental health. Increasing numbers of people are living from hand to mouth and are only one or two steps away from homelessness. Consequently, people with middling traits are adopting more defensive behaviours and this is prompting a shift away from individualistic culture.

There is a section of society (those with uniformly high traits) that is suited to operating within an individualistic culture. There is a larger group whose members have some high traits and are avoiding threats related to their low traits. The former continue to prosper within a degenerating individualistic culture long after people with lower traits have started to experience hardship. The latter believe they are continuing to benefit. Both groups will attempt to hold on to their freedoms, rights and privileges as societal culture begins to shift. They are also likely to show a sense of entitlement as their environment becomes less favourable to them. Such people tend to mass in liberal cities so they can be found in large numbers in New York and London. In the UK, they are likely to be vehement Remainers (people who oppose Brexit) as the UK's departure from the UK is seen in their circles as an infringement on their freedom to travel and experience different cultures.

A society with an individualistic culture is likely to disintegrate at a relatively fast rate once the favourable circumstances that prompted the development of that culture disappear. It takes time, however, for people, organisations and nations to adapt to changed conditions. Behaviours become ingrained and remedial actions do not have immediate effects. Families in particular take generations to rebuild. The weakness of families and communities, the underfunding of public services and the shirking of responsibility by corporations means that the death of a close relative, the loss of a job, or a divorce can be enough to cause a person to experience a breakdown, become impoverished or lose his home. As a result, a person can transition from a state of happiness to a state of distress very quickly, in which case he is unlikely to be able to take remedial action before he is overwhelmed. Extreme and prolonged avoidance makes a shift to a more appropriate culture harder to achieve. As a result, the UK and USA are facing very serious economic and social challenges. Countries with collectivist cultures are, however, also experiencing challenging circumstances. Although we are experiencing a shift towards a more collectivist culture, the global culture of individualism has weakened their economies and promoted immigration, prompting the emergence of reactionary politics and potentially civil unrest.

Globalisation and the re-emergence of establishment forces

Individualistic cultures give people the freedom to compete for resources so people who are high in extraversion and indifference tend to accumulate wealth. For example, security and currency trading markets are more easily accessible to individuals than ever before and allow many people to trade from home in their spare time. However, to become very wealthy, a person needs systems to store money and harvest resources. As members of the establishment possess the traits of low openness and low opportunism, they have the ability to create coherent and organised systems and structures, such as companies. People who value processes and structure are attracted to organisations. Many employees of large organisations therefore possess the traits of low openness and low opportunism. Their skills enable these organisations to engage effectively with other systems. Consequently multinational companies have been able to manipulate complex regulatory systems (particularly those governing international trade) to their advantage. As they have grown in size, they have also benefitted from economies of scale, and been able to exploit their market power, influence politicians and emasculate national governments. Their directors, shareholders and financiers have created a global trading system that has delivered wealth and power to a new global elite. The resultant unequal distribution of wealth has reduced disposable incomes within the wider global population and reduced tax revenues, holding back economic growth and forcing cuts to public services.

The elite that has benefitted from this dynamic has dislocated itself from nation states. Wealthy individuals from different nations increasingly associate with each other, invest together and look after each other's interests. They spend their time socialising with each other on yachts and estates away from public view so they have no incentive to invest in local communities or even nations. They are unrestrained by the values of wider society and the global nature of their interests means that they can evade regulation at a national level. Meanwhile, citizens of democratic countries have been losing influence on world events as their governments' power and authority have been undermined. Looking at the big picture, the forces of globalisation have weakened the world order of nation states, which has existed for centuries, and are consolidating the human race into a single global super group under the control of a global establishment. This new group is undemocratic, and its establishment is not accountable to group members.

The inability or unwillingness of national establishments to protect their citizens from the negative effects of globalisation has created unrest. Members of the rank and file (i.e. men who are low in openness) feel that they have not been protected from the threats presented by immigrants and technological change. Those of them who also possess the trait of high opportunism (typically libertarians and opportunistic businessmen) also see their national establishments as too controlling in an organisational sense. They seek to abolish laws that restrict their ability to compete or exert dominance over others. The dynamic of globalisation has therefore caused fearful, frustrated and disillusioned men to transfer their allegiance to populist, reactionary politicians who they believe they can trust to stand up for their interests.

Donald Trump, who is high in opportunism and low in openness. He was elected on a promise to "drain the swamp" in Washington. Although, this has been much more difficult than he anticipated, since his election, he has followed through with many of his election promises, adopting protectionist policies and prioritising national self-interest. He has also repealed employment and environmental laws, which have helped to increase the competitiveness of US industry and created jobs for members of the working class, at least temporarily. He has also adopted a more conservative approach on social issues. He was therefore able to retain the support of his core vote in the 2018 mid-term elections. In the UK, people who were low in openness and high in opportunism were attracted to the UK Independence Party (UKIP). Although this party never achieved electoral success at a national level, it did help to establish a dynamic that resulted in voters rejecting the European Union establishment by opting to leave that organisation. As European countries tend to have more collectivist cultures than the UK, the rank and file is more prominent within the continental populist movement. Political parties with anti-immigration policies have gained support, including the Front National in France and the Alternative für Deutschland (AfD) in Germany. The populist dynamic extends beyond Europe and the USA, however. Populist leaders with authoritarian leadership styles have risen to power in countries that previously were moving towards liberal democracy, such as Turkey and the Philippines.

Liberal-minded people (those who are characterised by the trait of high openness) have reacted in horror to this populist dynamic. They are typically highly educated, well travelled and open-minded. The shift away from traditional industries and the growth of the knowledge economy benefitted them greatly, and they have used their relatively high incomes to expand their horizons geographically and culturally. In normal circumstances, the establishment marginalises liberal-minded people, but the ability of such people to create wealth in modern society caused members of the establishment to embrace them temporarily. Liberals have now joined the global establishment in trying to protect the status quo as they fear being deprived of the resources and freedoms that enable them to enjoy life – diverse cultures, the ability to travel and access to education. People who are high in openness tend to welcome immigration because of the increased diversity it offers. Cheap labour also helps them to sustain the enjoyable lifestyles that they have become used to. This defensive alliance was evident in the Brexit referendum and the subsequent exit negotiation period when liberal-minded people and directors of multinational companies campaigned to remain with the EU. Liberals associate the EU with diversity and culture, and perceive that the maintenance of their comfortable lifestyles depends on membership of it. The UK's national establishment has been weakened significantly by the fact that many of its members have transitioned to the new global establishment, or have ambitions to do so. The financial interests of many of these people are now closely tied to trade with other EU countries. Although David Cameron, the leader of the Conservative Party in the UK at the time, initiated the referendum process because he dis so for domestic political reasons and was certain that he would secure a decision to remain within the EU.

The alliance between liberals and the establishment is an unnatural one. The long-term interests of the establishment lie in stifling creativity and innovation, and promoting conformity. In contrast, liberal-minded people constantly seek out new experiences and they find homogeneous environments oppressive. The terms of trade in this alliance are moving in favour of the establishment, and this is creating tensions. Liberal-minded people, particularly young adults and their parents, are slowly realising that governments, corporations and the global economic system are conspiring to reduce choice and prevent middle class people from sharing the benefits of growth. Governments are reducing investment in cultural assets, products and services are becoming more uniform, and young people are being deprived of opportunities to use their creative abilities in the workplace. A shift towards an establishment culture is therefore taking place. Whether under establishment or populist control, citizens are in danger of becoming trapped within exploitative and oppressive systems that will deprive them of time, freedom and resources.

Since the financial crisis, the voices of people who are low in extraversion and indifference have been drowned out by the angry and fearful reactions of populist politicians and their supporters. People with these progressive traits (most of whom are female) try to resolve problems by working collaboratively. They seek to deliver a more compassionate and fairer society, but are disempowered where people, groups and nations compete intensely for resources. The insecurity created by the financial crisis and subsequent economic malaise have encouraged people to focus on their own narrow interests and made them susceptible to populist influences. As a consequence, mainstream politicians and parties have failed to reflect the views of people with low levels of extraversion and indifference in the Brexit debate and 2016 US Presidential Election. Many of them therefore felt disenfranchised. Low extraversion and low indifference are the core traits of the socialist movement. Socialist parties have, though, been unable to develop a cohesive response to the populist dynamic because of internal divisions. Supporters of the hard left are attracted to the conformist, nationalist approach of populists whereas many social democrats are still closely attached to the fading liberal world order. This is beginning to change though as politicians whose priorities are fairness and compassion, such as Jeremy Corbyn, are gaining influence.

The interests of people who are low in extraversion and indifference are also underrepresented because many of them, particularly women, are still living in bubbles. The female collective naturally focuses on creating an environment suitable for children. Its members instinctively depend on the primal hierarchy to protect them and provide them with food and other resources. If a woman secures this assistance, she can focus on her domestic priorities and ignore dynamics in the wider world. Therefore, although women often manage household budgets, many of them do not take an interest in issues affecting wider society. When they do, they tend to pursue social or environmental objectives rather than economic or financial ones. As males tend to be higher in indifference and usually obliged to operate in the wider world, they tend to be more aware of dynamics that impact on their competitiveness and ability to secure resources. It is in the interests of the establishment to keep women in such bubbles because they are less likely to notice that members of this establishment are accumulating wealth and causing harm to others in such circumstances.

In the last 40 years, people with progressive traits have made advances in terms of civil rights, schooling, healthcare and environmental protection. However, these gains were made within a bubble. Outside that bubble, establishment behaviours were weakening the structures that delivered and maintained these gains. In particular, the new global establishment's control of the global economic and financial system allowed members of the establishment to extract wealth from national economies, depriving governments of the taxation receipts they needed to sustain public services and institutions. The dominance of capitalist ideology in modern economic policy has driven out compassion and fairness from decision-making processes so when budgets are tight, austerity measures are introduced that hurt the poorest and most vulnerable.

Initially, the liberalisation and computerisation of financial markets in the 1980s promoted a redistribution of wealth. Many ordinary people were enticed into trading shares and fortunes were made and lost very quickly. However, it did not take long for bankers, international investors and multinational companies to find ways to accumulate, store and hide much of this newly generated wealth by, for example, creating complex financial instruments, moving capital across international boundaries and manipulating laws governing international trade. Their control over the global economic and financial system and dislocation from nations enabled members of the new global establishment to increase their power and wealth and avoid sharing their gains with other members of society. As a result, wealth has concentrated within a very small percentage of the world's population.

Economics is often portrayed as a complicated subject, but the basics are simple. To maintain a strong economy, money must circulate widely within a population. The more that it becomes concentrated in a small sub-group, the fewer transactions happen, the weaker the economy becomes and the less tax is collected. People who are not concerned about fairness or equality naturally accumulate resources because that is their primary focus. Progressive taxation is therefore needed to compensate for their selfishness, redistribute wealth and maintain balance within an economy. The lack of restraints on the new global establishment has resulted in increased inequality and tax avoidance, weakened the economies of developed countries and undermined social security systems, healthcare and public services. Before the financial crisis, this dynamic was hidden by the availability of cheap money, but it became obvious thereafter. The crisis consolidated wealth in the hands of the establishment as its members closed ranks to protect the financial system that generates and stores their wealth. Since then, quantitative easing has inflated the price of assets, which are, of course, mostly held by the rich, and enabled people who are credit-worthy (the same people) to borrow money at very low interest rates. Meanwhile, ordinary citizens have faced rising rents, declining disposable incomes and reductions in social security benefits and public services. Many developed countries are limping along economically. Economic stagnation suits an establishment whose members possess the bulk of the resources within its environment. Its members' priorities switch from accumulating wealth to cementing control over their assets. Potential challengers are therefore denied opportunities to develop skills and build successful rival businesses.

Democracy has a fundamental weakness. It encourages short-term thinking, as politicians tend to focus on re-election. When in financial difficulty, democratic governments tend to borrow money. In so doing, they push the burden of repayment on to future generations. Most countries attempted to reinvigorate their economies after the financial crisis by borrowing money and investing it in infrastructure projects. Exceptionally, the Conservative government in the UK imposed austerity measures, cutting public spending severely. Both approaches resulted in large increases in national debt. In the first instance, due to the additional borrowing, and in the second, because the UK economy predictably shrunk, resulting in falling tax revenues. The UK's ratio of debt to GDP increased from 42% in 2007 to 85% in 2017, France's from 64% to 98% and the USA's from 67% to 105%. A government cannot continue to increase its level of borrowing indefinitely as at some point lenders will question its ability to repay, prompt the flight of capital and render the country insolvent. A prudent government therefore trims its expenditure and builds up a surplus when times are good. Some countries, including Germany, have maintained more balanced, sustainable economies, although Germany has been greatly helped by the fact its use of the Euro keeps its exchange rate artificially low. However, even Germany has a national debt amounting to 65% of its Gross Domestic Product (GDP). The lenders on whom governments depend to fund the national debt are predominantly members of the establishment. Therefore, although democracy is a progressive practice, countries that become reliant on commercial loans to fund national debt repayments and budget deficits become trapped within, and end up sustaining, the establishment's financial system.

Neither Vladimir Putin nor Donald Trump is a member of the establishment by virtue of his personality traits as Putin is low in extraversion and Trump high in opportunism. They are therefore both outsiders trying to fit in. Putin appears on TV stripped to the waist in the wild and performing martial arts to try to appear more physically capable than he is, while Trump's decision to run for the White House was perhaps an attempt to overcome a lack of self-esteem that he feels due to his inability to adopt the organised behaviours needed to gain acceptance within the American establishment. However, they both possess the traits of low openness and high indifference, which partly explains why they have some affinity with each other. Their low levels of openness cause them to fear people who are different and to promote conformity as a consequence. Where authoritarian or populist leaders gain influence or power, they undermine the interests of women and men with progressive traits. They seek to consolidate their power by constraining innovative forces, placing controls on news organisations, publishing fake news, reducing expenditure on education, health and social care, and strengthening military capability. Leaders like Putin and Trump, therefore, present a serious threat to democracy and other civil rights and freedoms that were carved out during the twentieth century.

People who are low in openness will be inclined to view people who are high in openness as dangerous and unreliable. When people are high in openness and also possess the establishment traits of high extraversion, high indifference and low opportunism, they are likely to operate as a liberal establishment. This is most likely to happen when the rank and file has little influence or purpose; for example, where its members' roles have been made redundant by technology. Donald Trump has effectively channelled the anger and frustration of the rank and file against these liberal elites, which have established themselves in established social democratic political parties and certain business sectors, particularly the media industry. It seems Hilary Clinton possesses three of the four personality traits that characterise the liberal elite (high openness, high indifference and low opportunism) and she sourced much of the funding for her presidential campaign from its members.

The real leaders of the new global establishment are, though, super-rich financiers, investors and business owners. However, as the global super-group is still forming, its establishment has not yet knitted together. It currently has an oligarchic structure with its members possessing power bases in different countries or industries; for example, through ownership of national utilities. An oligarchy develops when a group lacks a dominant male capable of enforcing his will over other alpha males. This is most likely to occur when a new group is forming as establishment members bring with them resources and supporters from existing groups. Oligarchs have conflicting interests. On the one hand, an oligarch will be attracted by the power and security that membership of the group can give him and the possibility that he could ultimately secure leadership of the group. On the other hand, he will be protective of his own power base and be aware that his position could be undermined if somebody else secures leadership of the group.

Putin and Trump have taken advantage of the global economic and financial system and their international networks to make money and store their personal wealth. They have also used the power that leadership of superpowers has given them to position themselves as oligarchs within the new global super group. If they are to maintain these positions, however, they need to retain the support of their populations. Therefore, both of them have committed themselves to restore the fortunes of their states. One of the reasons that Putin, Trump and other populist and authoritarian leaders get on is that they recognise that their interests lie in maintaining control over their fiefdoms and supporting each other in their efforts to do so. Most people, including members of their national establishments, have not recognised the existence of this oligarchic dynamic and are therefore confused by Trump's close relationship with Putin. Relationships between oligarchs can easily break down, though, because they will be seeking to extend their personal influence within the oligarchy at the expense of other oligarchs. Consequently, Putin and Trump have an interest in ensuring that the Russian and American governmental machines remain alert to economic, military and political threats posed by the other.

Sometimes the interests of a national establishment and the new global establishment coincide. For example, Putin's attempts to promote divisions between European nations are reducing their ability to stand up against Russia militarily, economically and ethically. They are also weakening the ability of those countries to work together to limit the excesses of multinational companies and introduce effective international taxation regimes. Similarly Trump has used his powers to reduce taxation on wealthy individuals and corporations. In general, though, the forces of globalisation and the power of the new global establishment are undermining nation states and therefore national establishments. The economies of most developed countries are fundamentally unsustainable in their current form because of the concentration of wealth within the new global establishment. So are the lifestyles of their citizens, which have been funded by personal, corporate and government loans from, and which are founded upon the exploitation of finite natural resources by, this establishment. Most of these countries have ageing populations that are imposing great pressure on health services, but these populations are also becoming increasingly opposed to immigration, which offers a short-term solution to an age imbalance. Meanwhile, developing countries like China and India have been growing at a fast rate and in many areas are more productive and efficient than developed countries. Developed countries still have an advantage in technically advanced or knowledge-based industries due to their more educated workforces, but low-skilled and manual workers in these countries have seen their job roles become obsolete or transferred to developing countries over the last 40 years. Technology and increasing educational and skill levels in developing countries are now similarly affecting middle-class roles. These pressures are increasing levels of stress within populations and may eventually result in widespread disorder, the disintegration of nation states within, conflict between states or the emergence of authoritarian rulers.

The lack of stability that we are currently seeing in national politics and international relations is therefore largely a result of the emergence of the new global establishment. National establishments are reacting against this dynamic and so too are citizens who feel constrained or left unprotected by this new establishment. There are two significant differences between national establishments and the new global establishment. Firstly, the racial and cultural differences between members of the rank and file around the world make it unlikely that the new global establishment will ever be able to depend on their support as a coherent body. Secondly, the global super group by definition has no external competitor, bar invasion from aliens, and therefore will not be able to control people by promoting fear of conquest by such a force. These differences mean that, if the new global establishment is to establish complete control, it will need to compartmentalise the world's population into manageable units and prevent the emergence of threats to its position from within that population. An oligarchic structure may be the best way of achieving these objectives so the new global establishment may never become fully fledged. However, the natural dynamics of groups dictate that one person will outcompete his rivals and secure the position of dominant male. If a supreme leader does emerge, he will naturally try to prevent people from working together to unseat him. He will also need to establish and maintain a global command chain. Both these objectives are now achievable as technological developments are already enabling companies to segregate customers and manage global operations, and governments to monitor the behaviour of potential agitators.

You may be thinking that my presumption of the existence of a shadowy but highly influential establishment sounds a bit like a conspiracy theory. However, the behaviours and dynamics that I describe are inevitable consequences of the interaction of people within groups. Whether or not members of the establishment consciously appreciate what is happening, the dynamics of groups will cause them to behave in ways that will promote the development of an establishment culture. Similarly, if environmental conditions favour people with progressive traits, establishment dynamics will be constrained, and a progressive culture will emerge. The emergence of the new global establishment presents a very real threat to the freedoms that many of us take for granted and we need to take action now if we are to maintain them.

Come the Personality Revolution!

When an establishment becomes too dominant and abusive, it is in the interests of other group members to restrain it. The new global establishment has become extremely powerful and is shifting the global super group towards an establishment culture. People with progressive traits are being marginalised or suppressed as society becomes more systemised and uncaring. Authoritarian and populist leaders are undermining democracy while corporations are destroying our natural environment, and reducing choice and access to reliable information. Unlike traditional establishment cultures, though, the one that is emerging now is neglecting the rank and file. Many working class jobs have been supplanted by technology and members of the rank and file have been left to atrophy or take on insecure, low paid work. There is, therefore, a basis for disaffected sub-groups to work together to reverse this establishment dynamic.

To date, opposition to establishment forces has largely come from populist politicians and their supporters, who possess the traits of low openness, high indifference and high opportunism. Liberals and non-establishment members who have benefitted financially during the last 40 years have sided with this new establishment to protect their current privileges and interests. Other people are living in bubbles or too preoccupied with day-to-day affairs to develop strong opinions. These different sub-groups need to recognise that they have a common interest in restraining this establishment, that they need access to each other's talents and skills in order to achieve this objective and that effective collaboration can only be achieved if they are prepared to compromise.

The female collective is, though, the natural counterweight to the establishment, as its interests lie in promoting fairness, equality, freedom and diversity. As women are more collaborative by nature and less fearful of foreigners (or at least foreign women) than men, they are better placed to create a global movement capable of restraining the new global establishment. However, although the female collective has the ability to bring people together to work in the common interest, its members are not yet sufficiently aware of the danger that the current establishment dynamic presents to them. Many women have taken advantage of the freedoms they have gained in modern individualistic society to consume excessively, pursue enjoyable activities and develop careers. They have been avoiding the increasing evidence of inequality and social and environmental harm, and have not therefore been acting in the interests of the female collective, which lie in shifting society back towards a more progressive culture. Now that the damage this neglect has caused to society and the natural environment is becoming more obvious, this is beginning to change. Women are starting to come together to exert a counteracting force. Evidence of this emergent force can be seen in the "me too" movement, a collaborative effort by women posting on social media to demonstrate the widespread prevalence of sexual assault and harassment, especially in the workplace, and the campaign for equal pay in respect of gender in the UK.

However, the female collective cannot succeed in restraining the new global establishment unless it secures help from men. The typical female lacks access to and knowledge about the global economic and financial system. She will also be unsuited to operating within hostile environments and will naturally focus on performing family, domestic and caring tasks rather than taking an interest in political and economic issues. These tasks are important. If progressive values are to be adopted more widely within society, the next generation must be educated appropriately and cared for. Their skills are also needed to help the large number of adults who are experiencing poor mental health, low levels of education or poverty as a result of lack of protection within modern individualistic society. Many of these people could be active participants within a global anti-establishment movement if they were restored to good health and received appropriate training. The female collective therefore needs the support of men with progressive traits and members of the command chain and rank and file if it is to assemble the weight of numbers to achieve its objectives. Men can also exert influence on members of the establishment in different ways to women as they have access to all-male environments and are physically more imposing, and because their on-average higher levels of indifference make it easier for them to cope with hostile environments and the threatening behaviour of establishment members. Men who possess all four progressive traits are most likely to gain the trust of women because their personalities are aligned with the values of the female collective, and therefore may rise to positions of authority within progressive movements. In normal times, such men are likely to be marginalised or ridiculed by members of the primal hierarchy, but their honest and incorruptible nature, and commitment to fairness, can result in them attracting broad-based support where the establishment is abusing members of the primal hierarchy.

Men who are high in opportunism have an interest in securing such reform because the control over national economies exerted by multinationals and other large companies severely limits their ability to use their entrepreneurial talents. Their impulsive actions and desire from freedom of action can promote change. They are useful because they disrupt and break up the systems that the establishment uses to maintain power. They are, though, naturally disruptive, and instinctively destabilise groups and promote change. As a result, they find it very difficult to work together in groups. They tend to fall out with each other and may disengage and attempt to create their own micro-fiefdoms. To restrain the establishment in the long-term, the female collective will need to work with men who are more organised (i.e. those who are low in opportunism). Such men naturally form part of the command chain and have historically been valued by corporations. However, the roles that they have previously performed are increasingly being made obsolete through the introduction of technology so increasing numbers of men with this trait are feeling isolated. They can help anti-establishment forces to become more organised and develop structures capable of holding the establishment to account. The support of the rank and file is needed because it brings weight of numbers and coherency to a cause. Its members naturally support establishment leaders, but they depend on the establishment to shield them from new information and provide them with work. Where the establishment neglects this responsibility, anti-establishment forces have an opportunity to provide members of the rank and file with support and protection, and exert influence over them. Men who are low in extraversion and/ or indifference tend to be natural allies of the female collective because these traits promote fairness and collaboration respectively. They will benefit from the protection of the establishment in conflict scenarios, but otherwise they are likely to be exploited and abused by its members. Therefore, although populist politicians have courted disaffected males, the female collective has the potential to embrace them and engage their services within a broader anti-establishment movement.

The female collective operates a loose, networked structure. However, this structure has not evolved to incorporate men. Some form of organised structure is needed to bring together people who share a common interest within a mixed gender group. Some people see modern technology companies as bulwarks of freedom, resisting establishment forces and the authoritarian tendencies of government and providing opportunities for people to connect and exchange information. In their infancy this is usually the case as freethinking, creative entities promote networking and sharing. However, as these companies grow larger, establishment forces in the form of accountants, financiers and shareholders gain control of them. As a consequence, they adopt monopolistic behaviours and seek favourable treatment from establishment politicians. They segment their customers using algorithms and restrict their access to information generated beyond their platforms. They do this primarily to market their products more effectively, but by doing so they limit their customers' ability to develop relationships, exchange information and discuss ideas with people who are different to them. The sale of advertising space to politically motivated organisations tends to favour establishment parties as they usually have greater financial resources.

Liberal democracy remains the structure best suited to limiting establishment power and securing a government that reflects the ambitions and concerns of its population. The lack of uniformity within, and the huge size of, the global super group makes it unlikely that a single global democracy will ever be established. Therefore, the new global establishment can only be restrained if democratic nations work together to do so. Unfortunately, the weakness of nation states and the emergence of career politicians have devalued democracy in the eyes of ordinary citizens. Also, during the last 40 years, the world has lacked inspirational and effective progressive politicians capable of convincing populations of the need to restrain establishment forces and reconfigure the global economic and financial system. Barack Obama offered great hope and Angela Merkel has stood firm against the populist dynamic, but both possess some establishment traits, which deterred them from adopting more progressive policies. Macron, the new hope of France, is similarly compromised. Too often, liberal or socialist politicians and bureaucrats have succumbed to greed and allowed themselves to be corrupted by multinationals, or have failed to challenge practices and principles that protect or promote the interests of the establishment.

The European Union started as a community of democratic, nation states and, prior to the era of individualism, pursued a broadly progressive policy agenda. Its policies are still environmentally and socially more responsible than those of the UK's Conservative government, and it currently seems prepared to stand up against Donald Trump's bullying behaviour. Tragically, however, establishment forces have corrupted the EU's original organisational model. The EU's senior bureaucrats have promoted closer integration and increased conformity with the aim of establishing a European super state with its own army. They have therefore acted like a national establishment. As they are unelected, their connection to citizens is weak. As a consequence, the new global establishment has been able to gain a hold over them to some degree, as demonstrated the manipulation of EU product tests to suit the interests of multinationals, most notably in relation to diesel emissions for vehicles. The EU's ability and inclination to restrain establishment forces and promote progressive values and sustainable practices within the EU and around the world has declined significantly in recent years. This dynamic is unlikely to be reversed without major reform of the EU, but once an organisation develops an unaccountable establishment, reform is very difficult to achieve. It may only be possible if multiple countries leave or threaten to leave the union, rendering it unviable in its current form. Many Remainers describe those who voted to leave in the Brexit campaign as stupid, but British culture is characterised by a high level of opportunism, so the decision of many Leavers would have been influenced by their recognition of, or instinctively prompted by their sub-conscious reaction against, this establishment dynamic. However, Europe, as a community of democratic nation states, still has the potential to be a force for good, and going it alone leaves a country exposed to the bullying behaviours of more powerful nations. It is not therefore surprising that many voters in the UK's Brexit referendum found it difficult to decide which way to vote.

The lack of an effective progressive political movement has presented politicians with establishment traits with the opportunity to undermine liberal democracy and promote establishment values around the world, which they are duly taking. Despite his high level of opportunism, Trump showed very little regard for the democratic process in his election campaign and there are strong suspicions that he was assisted by fake news distributed on the Internet by the Russian government. Poland and Austria are moving strongly in authoritarian, nationalist directions. The Conservative government in the UK is currently taking the country backwards, promoting the exploitation of fossil fuels, backsliding on its commitments to tackle global warming and undermining civil and democratic rights that have been hard won over centuries.

The establishment is a small sub-group so when the remaining group members are united in their demands, it must adhere to their wishes or risk a revolt. It is therefore in the interests of the establishment to pursue a policy of divide and rule. The dynamics of modern individualistic society have made it easy for it to do so. Individualistic behaviours have reduced the coherency of society, creating divisions and misunderstandings between individuals. The looseness of group structures has allowed members to develop personal value sets and given them the freedom to object to or dismiss opinions held by other people. The fast pace of life gives people less opportunity for reasoned debate and inclines them to compete rather than collaborate. Families and geographic communities have disintegrated as people who have the money and flexibility to do so have sought more freedom and moved to areas that suit their lifestyles and personality traits. The resultant social separation has made it easier for people to adopt black and white approaches and extreme viewpoints. Members of these sub-groups have less cause to consider the interests of members of other sub-groups. Some of these sub-groups have found themselves pitched against each other as opinions have become polarised. Such a division has opened up at a national level in the USA between liberal, metropolitan voters living on the seaboards, who vote Democrat, and traditional, rural voters living in the Mid West, who vote Republican. Similar divisions are emerging within other developed countries including the UK. Social media is exacerbating these divisions because it enables people to find like minds very easily. As a result, people increasingly communicate in feedback loops that confirm their own opinions and ignore or abuse people with different views. In other words, they are more likely to be subject to confirmation bias. Establishment forces are using social media it to promote discord between different sub-groups within society or portray progressive politicians as dangerous and unreliable.

There are signs, however, that progressive forces are beginning to fight back. Individualistic nature of modern society has enabled more women to pursue careers in politics, and a significant number of countries now have female leaders. These women tend to be higher in indifference than the average female because of the hostile nature of the political arena so it should not be assumed that any female politician is more progressive in her views than her male colleagues by virtue of her gender. If she makes progressive soundings, she may just be engaging in virtue signalling – the conspicuous expression of moral values with the intent of enhancing her standing. Even so female politicians will usually hold some allegiance to the female collective. Their freedom of action will be constrained to some degree by the fact that most political parties are male-dominated, but they will be quietly advancing the interests of women to some degree. As more women are empowered, leading female politicians will be strengthened in their positions, but they will also feel under greater pressure to implement progressive policies. For example, Theresa May, the UK's current Prime Minister and leader of the Conservative Party, proposed the removal of provisions that recognised that animals were sentient beings from the draft Brexit legislation transferring EU law into English law. There is some dispute as to whether this was a deliberate attempt to weaken animal rights legislation for the benefit of farmers and landowners, but it seems certain that this was the preferred outcome of Conservative MPs given their establishment personalities. The outcry that followed, generated primarily by women, caused her to adopt, at least outwardly, a more animal-friendly position.

As the effects of inequality and environmental mismanagement become increasingly obvious, progressive politicians are beginning to emerge from the shadows and build broad-based support for anti-establishment policies. Bernie Sanders, who possesses all four progressive traits, took the lead when he ran Hillary Clinton very close in the race for the Democratic candidacy in the 2016 US presidential election. He secured the support of large numbers of young female voters and would probably have won that nomination if the establishment within the Democratic Party had not undermined him. The US mid-term elections in 2018 saw the election of an unprecedented number of female politicians. On the European mainland, new parties such as Podemos in Spain are marshalling this progressive force. These parties are seeking to hold the establishment to account, and aspire to a democratised Europe that puts people before profit. These new parties have emerged because traditional socialist parties have not yet had the inclination or courage to campaign openly for reform of the EU or the loosening of their countries' relationships with it.

Prior to the UK's preoccupation with Brexit, Jeremy Corbyn had been steadily building support for his progressive policy agenda. He served as a focal point for those seeking a fairer and more compassionate society, and this was reflected in the party's improved performance in the UK's 2017 general election. He was assisted in that election by the decision of other progressive parties, particularly the Green Party, not to stand candidates in constituencies where the Conservative and Labour candidates were in a tight race. The one establishment trait that Corbyn does possess – low openness - is, however, preventing him from reaching out to other progressive parties in a substantial way. This trait causes him to feel a sense of solidarity with socialist movements in other countries and is the basis for his reluctance to criticise authoritarian socialist leaders who draw their support from the working class. It also explains why he appears reluctant to promote females to senior positions, and indeed, why he likes collecting pictures of drain and manhole covers. His low openness inclines him to reward loyalty to the Labour Party and to see politics in terms of a class struggle, and this makes it difficult to for him to contemplate a broader coalition. However, he probably needs the cooperation of other progressive parties if he is to secure a parliamentary majority that is willing to pass the more radical elements of his policy agenda into law.

The stage is, therefore, set for a grand battle between establishment and progressive forces. The advanced nature of facial recognition software and other surveillance technologies now mean that it would be very difficult for ordinary citizens to remove or restrain an authoritarian global establishment. Therefore, if the new global establishment wins the battle, it is likely that democracy would be extinguished, most people would be exploited, abused or impoverished, and the natural environment would be irreparably damaged. This apocalyptic vision has been portrayed in the Terminator and Bladerunner films. If progressive forces gain the upper hand, however, inequality will be reduced, a compassionate culture will emerge, and there will be a drive to create a sustainable environment and society. The best current example of a country with a progressive culture is probably Sweden, although it too is experiencing a reactionary backlash due to a high level of immigration. In terms of movies, the Star Trek franchise envisages a future where a united human race explores the universe with a mission to spread progressive values.

We can only transition to a sustainable world that delivers feelings of happiness to as many people as possible if the global establishment is brought under control. It is in the interests of most people to restrain the exploitative instincts of this establishment, but if we are to succeed in doing so, we need to recognise our shared interest and work effectively as a team. Our collective consciousness needs to be expanded so we can understand how we are being exploited and appreciate the benefits of working collaboratively to achieve progress. We need to realise that our interests now lie in establishing a balanced global culture with values that allow people to explore, create and learn, but which also encourages them to take on responsibilities within a societal, community and family context. In short, we all need to commit to delivering a sustainable global society. If people are to work together to achieve this end, they will need to improve their emotional literacy skills significantly. If this can be achieved, the ground will have been prepared for The Personality Revolution, which is the title of Volume 2 of this work (scheduled to be published in 2020). This volume will explain the societal dynamics that we are experiencing in more detail and use the principles of personality and group dynamics to set out a pathway towards an economically, socially and environmentally sustainable global society.

Taking responsibility

This book has explained how your personality traits orientate you towards particular information environments, and how your emotional system causes you to gravitate towards them. However, you do not exist within a static environment. Life is a dynamic process, so you will encounter challenging circumstances from time to time. You, therefore, need to be pro-active in managing your environment and regulating your mood if you are to operate effectively and experience positive feelings on a regular basis.

If you understand your strengths and weaknesses as dictated by your personality traits, you will be able to make better use of your attributes and appreciate more readily when you need support from others. If you know the circumstances that are likely to cause you to experience stress or a low mood, you can adapt your lifestyle to avoid them, or at least be better prepared for them and escape from them more quickly than you would otherwise have done. A good understanding of your personality will, therefore, equip you to shape your environment favourably, improve your performance, and help you to set career and personal goals that are likely to be achievable and rewarding.

Learning is critical to this shaping process. If you wish to develop your natural abilities, it is important for you to operate within suitable learning environments. If you understand your natural learning style, you can make changes to your social and working environment that will help you learn more effectively. Also, if you wish to make good progress and avoid setbacks, it is helpful to understand your risk profile. If you adopt a suitable learning style and risk profile, you are likely to develop confidence and have a positive outlook on life. If you take excessive risk or are too risk-averse, or put yourself in unsuitable learning environments, you will experience negative feelings and your development will be inhibited. However, it is helpful to understand your wider environment and particularly the systems and structures in which you are embedded so that you can appreciate when you are being abused, exploited or manipulated. This will involve expanding your consciousness and require you to display resilience.

During the late 20th century, most people living in developed countries found themselves within benign environments that allowed them to seek out enjoyable experiences. However, since the financial crisis, fears of economic decline have become widespread. Social media has exposed us to people with values and opinions that conflict with our own, with whom we would previously never had cause to interact or at least engage in political or values-based conversation. However, the Internet and related advances in communications have also increased people's awareness of the abuse and exploitation of vulnerable members of society, the harmful consequences of war and the damage we are causing to the natural environment. Your consciousness is therefore being expanded, whether you like it or not, and it is becoming increasingly difficult for people who are engaging in avoidance tactics to maintain the integrity of their protective bubbles.

If you cannot avoid threats, you must neutralise them if you are to restore feelings of happiness. However, the individualistic nature of modern society has distracted us. We are too busy to consider the longer-term consequences of our actions. In most cases, you need to be part of an effective team to improve your environment, but self-interested behaviours have weakened group structures, so large numbers of people lack the support and protection that they need to be effective. They are experiencing feelings of anger, frustration, stress, helplessness and lowness as a result of potential threats, actual losses and missed opportunities.

We are currently hurtling towards disaster as a species. If you are to play your part in delivering a sustainable global society, you need to get off the train and look around. You must carve out time in your life to redefine your objectives and develop your natural talents and skills. When you are following other people's agendas, you will need to either challenge the culture of your group, or join or establish a new one that aligns with your values. You have the ability to write your own story, but to make a real difference and feel truly fulfilled; you need to work with others for the benefit of a group.

There will be people experiencing abuse, exploitation, hardship or insecurity within your own family, community or workplace. We must recognise the weaknesses within our groups, and commit to playing our parts in strengthening them. There will be groups that would benefit from your help in your neighbourhood, including your family, community and voluntary organisations, but there are also many other groups within wider society that perform valuable functions which you could assist. Your personality traits, physical and mental ability, and previous experiences will dictate your natural role.

When you make your final accommodation and depart from this world, you would like to do so with feelings of happiness. Most of the regrets that people who are close to death describe are associated with a failure to position themselves correctly within their supportive groups, or with weaknesses in such groups. Many people feel that they have failed to make the most of their abilities because they have spent too much time furthering other people's agendas or using their time ineffectively. Others wish they had been encouraged to express their feelings and not been restrained from doing so by fear of possible negative consequences. The wide geographic spread of groups within modern society means that many people are separated from friends or family as they near death, so people tend to regret not maintaining stronger bonds. You may have had many enjoyable experiences during your life, but ultimately, when you are on your deathbed, you are most likely to be comforted by a sense of belonging and feelings of fulfilment, or in other words, by the knowledge that you have been useful to a group of people and the realisation that its members respect you for your contribution.

Taking responsibility can deliver positive feelings if you perform roles and tasks to which you are naturally suited. However, it is also likely to trigger some negative feelings, as it will cause you to miss out on opportunities to enjoy yourself and involve some tasks that you find difficult. You will therefore need to show resilience and look after your own mental and physical health. You will therefore benefit from developing your emotional literacy skills, especially if you are starting from a point where you are experiencing emotional distress or lack support or protection. Once you have done so, you will be better able to look beyond your immediate circumstances and exert a positive effect on society.

To be continued in volume 2 - **The Personality Revolution**

The Personality Revolution, is scheduled to be published in 2020. If you would like to be notified of the publication date, you can sign up to our e-mail list at
thepersonalityrevolution.com

You can also find us on Facebook and Twitter – search for
The Personality Revolution

BIBLIOGRAPHY

Cain, C. (2012). *Quiet: The power of introverts in a world that can't stop talking.* London: Penguin Group.

Florida, R. (2002). *The rise of the creative class ... and how it's transforming work, leisure, community and everyday life.* New York: Basic Books.

Fox, E. (2008). *Emotion science.* Basingstoke: Palgrave Macmillan.

Gladwell, M. (2005). *Blink: The power of thinking without thinking.* London: Penguin Group

Gladwell, M. (2008). *Outliers: The story of success.* London: Penguin Group

Goleman, D. (1996). *Emotional intelligence: Why it can matter more than IQ.* London: Bloomsbury Publishing Plc.

Hogg, M. & Vaughan, M. (2011). *Social Psychology (6th Edn.).* Harlow: Pearson Education Ltd.

Laney, M. (2002). The Introvert Advantage: How to thrive in an extrovert world. New York: Workman Publishing Company, Inc.

Merzel, D. (2003). *The Path of the Human Being: Zen Teachings on the Bodhisattva Way.* Boston: Shambhala Publications, Inc.

Morris, D. (1967). *The Naked Ape.* London: Vintage

Nettle, D. (2007). *Personality: What makes you the way you are.* New York: Oxford University Press Inc.

Pink, D. (2009) Drive: *The surprising truth about what motivates us.* New York: Riverhead Books.

Winston, R. (2003). *Human instinct: How our primeval impulses shape our modern lives.* London: Transworld Publishers.

Printed in Poland
by Amazon Fulfillment
Poland Sp. z o.o., Wrocław